Next Generation
Java™ Testing

Next Generation Java™ Testing

TestNG and Advanced Concepts

Cédric Beust
Hani Suleiman

✦✦Addison-Wesley

Upper Saddle River, NJ • Boston • Indianapolis • San Francisco
New York • Toronto • Montreal • London • Munich • Paris • Madrid
Capetown • Sydney • Tokyo • Singapore • Mexico City

Many of the designations used by manufacturers and sellers to distinguish their products are claimed as trademarks. Where those designations appear in this book, and the publisher was aware of a trademark claim, the designations have been printed with initial capital letters or in all capitals.

The authors and publisher have taken care in the preparation of this book, but make no expressed or implied warranty of any kind and assume no responsibility for errors or omissions. No liability is assumed for incidental or consequential damages in connection with or arising out of the use of the information or programs contained herein.

The publisher offers excellent discounts on this book when ordered in quantity for bulk purchases or special sales, which may include electronic versions and/or custom covers and content particular to your business, training goals, marketing focus, and branding interests. For more information, please contact:

U.S. Corporate and Government Sales
(800) 382-3419
corpsales@pearsontechgroup.com

For sales outside the United States please contact:

International Sales
international@pearsoned.com

 **This Book Is Safari Enabled**

The Safari® Enabled icon on the cover of your favorite technology book means the book is available through Safari Bookshelf. When you buy this book, you get free access to the online edition for 45 days.

Safari Bookshelf is an electronic reference library that lets you easily search thousands of technical books, find code samples, download chapters, and access technical information whenever and wherever you need it.

To gain 45-day Safari Enabled access to this book:

- Go to http://www.awprofessional.com/safarienabled
- Complete the brief registration form
- Enter the coupon code ALQC-DBMP-FMAU-A9PP-24WU

If you have difficulty registering on Safari Bookshelf or accessing the online edition, please e-mail customer-service@safaribooksonline.com.

Visit us on the Web: www.awprofessional.com

Library of Congress Cataloging-in-Publication Data
Beust, Cédric.
    Next generation Java testing : TestNG and advanced concepts / Cédric Beust, Hani Suleiman.
        p. cm.
    Includes bibliographical references and index.
    ISBN 0-321-50310-4 (pbk. : alk. paper)
  1. Java (Computer program language) 2. Computer software—Testing. I. Suleiman, Hani. II. Title.
    QA76.73.J3B49 2007
    005.13'3—dc22   2007031939

ISBN-13: 978-0-321-50310-7
ISBN-10:   0-321-50310-4
Text printed in the United States on recycled paper at Courier in Stoughton, Massachusetts.
First printing, October 2007

Contents

Foreword

Doing the right thing is rarely easy. Most of us should probably eat better, exercise more, and spend more time with our families. But each day, when confronted with the choice of being good or doing the easy thing, we often choose the easy thing because, well, it's easier.

It is the same way with software testing. We all know that we *should* spend more effort on testing, that more testing will make our code more reliable and maintainable, that our users will thank us if we do, that it will help us better understand our own programs, but each day when we sit down to the computer and choose between writing more tests and writing more application code, it is very tempting to reach for the easy choice.

Today, it is largely accepted that unit testing is the responsibility of developers, not QA, but this is a relatively recent development, one for which we can largely thank the JUnit testing framework. It is notable that JUnit had such an impact because there's not really very much to it—it's a simple framework, with not a lot of code. What enabled JUnit to change developer behavior where years of lecturing and guilt could not was that, for the first time, the pain of writing unit tests was reduced to a bearable level, making it practical for the merely responsible to include unit testing in our daily coding. Rather than make testing more desirable, which is not such an easy sell (eat those vegetables, they're good for you!), JUnit simply made it easier to do the right thing.

With all the righteousness of the newly converted, many developers proclaimed their zeal for testing, proudly calling themselves "test-infected." This is all well and good—few could argue that software developers were doing *too much* testing, so more is probably an improvement—but it is only the first step. There's more to testing than unit tests, and if we expect developers to take this next step we must provide testing tools that reduce the pain of creating them—and demand testability as a fundamental design requirement. If software engineering is ever to become a true engineering discipline, testing will form one of the critical pillars on which it will be built. (Perhaps one day, writing code without tests will be considered as professionally irresponsible as constructing a bridge without performing a structural analysis.)

This book is dedicated to the notion that we've only just begun our relationship with responsible testing. The TestNG project aims to help developers take the next step—the NG stands for "next generation"—enabling broader and deeper test coverage that encompasses not only unit tests but also acceptance, functional, and integration tests. Among other useful features, it provides a rich mechanism for specifying and parameterizing test suites, encompassing concurrent testing and a flexible mechanism for decoupling test code from its data source. (And, as proof that TestNG is succeeding, a number of its features have been adopted in more recent versions of JUnit.)

One challenge to more effective developer testing, no matter what tools are provided, is that writing effective tests requires different skills than writing effective code. But, like most skills, testing can be learned, and one of the best ways to learn is to watch how more experienced hands might do it. Throughout this book, Hani and Cédric share with you their favorite techniques for effectively testing Java applications and for designing applications and components for testability. (This last skill—designing for testability—is probably one of the most valuable lessons from this book. Designing code for testability forces you to think about the interactions and dependencies between components earlier, thereby encouraging you to build cleaner, more loosely coupled code.) Of course, the TestNG framework is used to illustrate these techniques, but even if you are not a TestNG user (and not interested in becoming one), the practical techniques presented here will help you to be a better tester and, in turn, a better engineer.

Brian Goetz
Senior Staff Engineer, Sun Microsystems

Preface

We're all in the business of software development. Code is written and then deployed. Once we've deployed the code, our customers will express pleasure or, depressingly often, displeasure.

For the last few decades, much has been written about how to minimize this displeasure. We have countless languages, methodologies, tools, management techniques, and plain old-fashioned mythology to help address this issue.

Some of these approaches are more effective than others. There has certainly been a renewed emphasis and focus on testing lately, along with the pleasures said testing would bring to developers and users alike.

Much has been written extolling the virtues of testing. It can make your code better, faster, and lighter. It can add some sorely needed spice to the drudgery of coding. It's exciting and new (and therefore worth trying), not to mention the feeling of responsibility and accountability it imparts; there's something mysteriously satisfying about adding a feature and having a test to prove you did it right.

Unfortunately, religion has also crept into the science of testing. You won't have to look far to find holy commandments or Persons of Authority handing down instructions either applauding or scolding certain testing behavior.

This book attempts to distill some of the wisdom that has emerged over the last few years in the realm of Java testing. Neither of us has ever had a job where we're paid to sell testing, nor has testing been forced on us. Neither of us works at a place where one methodology has been proclaimed the "winner" and must be followed religiously.

Instead, we're pragmatic testers. Testing to us is simply another valuable tool that helps us as part of the software development cycle. We're not particularly "test infected," the term coined by JUnit early on that's gained so much adoption. We write tests when and where it makes sense; testing is a choice and not an infectious disease for us.

As a result of this approach, we've noticed a rather large hole in our testing arsenal: Very few tools seem to be practical and to lend themselves to the sort of tests we'd like to write. The dominant force in Java testing is JUnit, and in many cases, it's easy and intuitive to think of a test we'd like to run. The main obstacle, however, ends up being the tooling and its inability to capture concepts that are second nature to us in the code we'd like to test—concepts such as encapsulation, state sharing, scopes, and ordering.

JUnit, for all its flaws, really brought the concept of testing to the forefront. No longer was it an ad hoc approach. Instead, tests now had a framework and a measure of standardization applied. JUnit-based tests could be easily automated and replayed in a variety of environments using any number of visualization tools. This ease of use encouraged its massive adoption and the increased awareness of Java testing in general.

Its success has also spilled over to a number of other languages, with ports to other languages all based on the same underlying concepts.

As with any successful tool, however, the success came at a price. A subtle shift took place where instead of testing being the concern, and JUnit a tool to help achieve that, JUnit became the main focus, with testing that didn't fit in its narrow confines resulting in doubts about the test, rather than the tool.

Many will proclaim that a test that cannot be easily expressed in a simple "unit" is a flawed test. It's not a unit test since it has requirements beyond the simplistic ones that JUnit provides for. It's a functional test that happens later, after having built the unit building blocks. We find this argument perplexing, to say the least. Ultimately there is no one right way to do testing. It would be equally ridiculous to proclaim that development must start from implementing small units to completion first, before thinking of higher-level concerns. There are cases where that makes the most sense, just as there are many where it doesn't. Testing is a means to an end, and the end is better software. It's crucial to keep this in mind at all times.

Why Another Book about Testing?

This is a book about Java testing. Every chapter and section you will read in the following pages will discuss testing in some way or another. Regardless of what testing framework you use or whether you use tools that we don't cover, our goal is to show you some practices that have worked for us in some way. We also tried to draw general conclusions from our own experiences and use these to make recommendations for future scenarios that might arise.

Even though we use TestNG in this book to illustrate our ideas, we firmly believe that you will find some of it useful, whether or not you use JUnit—even if you're not programming on the Java platform. There are plenty of TestNG/JUnit-like frameworks for other languages (C# and C++ come to mind), and the ideas used in a testing framework are usually universal enough to transcend the implementation details that you will encounter here and there.

This book is about pragmatic testing. You will not find absolute statements, unfounded religious proclamations, and golden rules that guarantee robust code in this book. Instead, we always try to present pros and cons for every situation because ultimately you, the developer, are the one with the experience and the knowledge of the system you are working with. We can't help you with the specifics, but we can definitely show you various options for solving common problems and let you decide which one fits you best.

With that in mind, let's address the question asked above: Why another book about testing?

There are plenty of books (some very good) about Java testing, but when we tried to look more closely, we came to the conclusion that hardly any books covered a broad topic that we found very important to our day-to-day job: modern Java testing.

Yes, using the adjective *modern* in a book is dangerous because, by nature, books don't remain modern very long. We don't think this book will be the exception to this rule, but it is clear to us that current books on Java testing do not properly address the challenges that we, Java developers, face these days. As you can see in the table of contents, we cover a very broad range of frameworks, most of which have come into existence only in the last three years.

In our research on prior art, we also realized that most books on Java testing use JUnit, which, despite its qualities, is a testing framework that has barely evolved since its inception in 2001.[1] It's not just JUnit's age that we found limiting in certain ways but also its very design goal: JUnit is a unit testing framework. If you are trying to do more than unit testing with JUnit (e.g., testing the deployment of a real servlet in an application server), you are probably using the wrong tool for the job.

Finally, we also cover a few frameworks that are quite recent and are just beginning to be adopted (e.g., Guice) but that we believe have such a

---

1. JUnit 4, which came out in 2006, was the first update in five years that JUnit received, but at the time of writing, its adoption is still quite marginal, as most Java projects are still using JUnit 3.

potential and open so many doors when used with a modern testing framework such as TestNG that we just couldn't resist writing about them. Hopefully, our coverage of these bleeding-edge frameworks will convince you to give them a try as well.

Throughout the book, we have tried hard to demonstrate a pragmatic application of testing. Many patterns are captured in these pages. It's not an explicit list that we expect to be recited; rather, it's more of a group of examples to ensure you develop the right approach and way of thinking when it comes to testing code.

We achieve this through two separate approaches, the first of which is TestNG usage specifics. We discuss most of its features, explaining how and why they arose, as well as practical real-world examples of where they might be applicable. Through this discussion, we'll see how testing patterns can be captured by the framework and what goes into a robust maintainable test suite (and more importantly, what doesn't!).

The second aspect is showing how TestNG integrates with your existing code and the larger ecosystem of Java frameworks and libraries. Few of us are lucky enough to work on projects that are started completely from scratch. There are always components to reuse or integrate, legacy subsystems to invoke, or backward compatibility concerns to address. It would be equally foolish to demand redesigns and rewrites just to enable testing. Instead, we try to show how it's possible to work with existing code and how small incremental changes can make code more testable and more robust over time. Again, through this approach, a number of patterns emerge, along with more practices on how to write tests and approach testing in general.

We hope you enjoy reading this book as much as we enjoyed writing it. We feel very strongly about testing, but we feel equally strongly that it isn't a golden hammer in a world of nails. Despite what many would like to believe, there are no solutions or approaches that absolve you from the need to think and the need to understand your goals and ensure that your testing journey is a rational and well-considered one, where both the downsides and upsides have received equal consideration.

Audience

So, what is this book and who is it for? In short, it's for any Java developer who is interested in testing.

We are also targeting developers who have been testing their code for quite a while (with JUnit or any other framework) but still find themselves sometimes intimidated by the apparent complexity of their code and, by extension, by the amount of effort needed to test it. With the help of the TestNG community over these years, we have made a lot of progress in understanding some of the best practices in testing all kinds of Java code, and we hope that this book will capture enough of them that nobody will ever be stuck when confronted with a testing problem.

This book uses TestNG for its code samples, but don't let that intimidate you if you're not a TestNG user: A lot of these principles are very easy to adapt (or port) to the latest version of JUnit.

Whether you use TestNG or not, we hope that once you close this book, you will have learned new techniques for testing your Java code that you will be able to apply right away.

Acknowledgments

Many people helped us throughout the writing of this book, and we'd like to take some time to thank them.

First of all, our gratitude goes to Alexandru Popescu for his tireless work on TestNG since the very early days and his absolute dedication to users. Without him, TestNG wouldn't be what it is today.

A few people helped us proofread early versions of this book, and they caught a lot of errors and inaccuracies that we would have missed otherwise. In alphabetical order, we'd like to give our special "QA thanks" to Tom Adams, Mike Aizatsky, Kevin Bourrillion, Brian Goetz, Erik Koerber, Tim McNerney, Bill Michell, Brian Slesinsky, James Strachan, and Joe Walnes.

We'd like to extend special thanks to Bob Lee and Patrick Linskey for the random discussions we had with them over these past years on a lot of different topics, which eventually impacted TestNG (and this book) in some way.

None of this would have been possible without the wonderful people on the TestNG mailing lists. Over the years, they have provided encouragement, insight, patches, and use cases, as well as enough constructive criticism to help us refine our ideas and thoughts in the realm of testing in ways we didn't expect.

Hani would like to thank his parents and siblings (Sara, Ghalib, Khalid, and May), wife (Terry), and the *Lost* Gang—all of whom tried very hard to not laugh and point out how unlikely he was to actually finish writing this book.

Cédric would like to thank his wife, Anne Marie, for her patience and support throughout the writing of this book.

Finally, a special mention in the "No thanks" category to Blizzard, the creators of World of Warcraft, without which this book would have been much easier to write.

Cédric (70 Rogue) and Hani (70 Warlock)

About the Authors

Cédric Beust is a software engineer at Google. His fascination with computers started at a very young age and is not giving any signs of fading anytime soon. His interests cover all aspects of software engineering, ranging from object-oriented programming to testing and optimizing techniques, including other topics such as programming languages, user interfaces, and any practices that can help him make his code easier to use. When Cédric is not posting on his blog at http://beust.com/weblog, he can usually be found playing tennis, squash, golf, or volleyball or going scuba diving.

Hani Suleiman is the CTO of Formicary, a company specializing in investment banking and integration solutions. Hani is a member of the Java Community Process (JCP) Executive Committee and is active on a number of enterprise Java Specification Requests (JSRs). When he gets angry or irate, he expresses himself at great length on the lively and fairly controversial BileBlog at www.bileblog.org.

CHAPTER 1

Getting Started

Here is a short anecdote from one of the authors that we will use in the rest of this chapter to introduce some of the concepts we will develop in this book.

A few years ago, I faced what appeared to be a simple problem: One of the tests of the product I was working on at the time had failed earlier that day, and I had already spent hours trying to locate the problem. I had gone through most of the code base that was being exercised by this test. I had placed numerous breakpoints in various places in my code, but the variables always contained the correct values, and the flow of the code followed the exact path it was supposed to.

I was running out of ideas, and I was slowly coming to the conclusion that if the problem was not in our code, it might be in the tools.

When faced with a software problem, I have learned to resist the urge to blame tools or other layers that don't belong to me, especially when these have been working flawlessly for such a long time. But I couldn't think of any other way to explain the mysterious failure I was seeing.

Therefore, I pointed my debugger to JUnit and started yet another breakpoint session.

And I made a startling discovery.

I don't remember the exact code that caused this behavior, but I know that it basically boiled down to the code in Listing 1–1.

Listing 1–1 Basic JUnit test

```
public class MyTest extends TestCase {
  private int count = 0;

  public void test1() {
    count++;
    assertEquals(1, count);
  }
```

```
public void test2() {
  count++;
  assertEquals(1, count);
  }
}
```

Take a quick look at this test case and imagine running it with JUnit. What do you think will happen? Pass or fail?

The answer: It passes.

I remember shaking my head in disbelief when I saw this result. I truly couldn't believe my eyes, and I was certain that I had been working too much and that I wasn't thinking straight. But debugging into the JUnit code confirmed this observation: JUnit reinstantiates the test class before each test method, thereby explaining why the count field is reset to zero each time.

Of course, my next question was to wonder whether this was a bug in JUnit or an intended behavior. Deep inside, I felt that it couldn't be a bug because JUnit is a framework used by countless Java projects, and such behavior would undoubtedly have been reported if it were not intended.

So I did some research and exchanged a few emails with Kent Beck and Erich Gamma. They confirmed that this was the intended behavior and said that the reason behind this idea is to make sure that each test starts with state that has been reset, in order to make sure that tests don't depend on each other or, worse, have side effects on each other.

A part of me could definitely see some value in this idea. After all, the more independent your tests are, the easier it is to run them in isolation. But I couldn't get over the fact that I had been completely taken by surprise by this behavior and that, if one could argue that the JUnit implementation was justified, it was hard to dispute that it was also extremely counterintuitive. I would certainly not be happy if Java or C++ adopted the same semantics.

This innocuous incident in my work was just the beginning of a long path that led me to step back from my testing habits and completely revisit all these testing practices that I had been using blindly for years without really thinking about them. JUnit is undoubtedly the de facto standard for testing in the Java world, but I slowly started to realize that this widespread use had also come at a price and that my testing habits had become a lot more automatic than the results of reflections.

In this short chapter, we will give you an overview of what awaits you in this book and the motivation behind its purpose.

Beyond JUnit 3

Like most Java developers, we have a long history with JUnit,[1] and we certainly give it credit for making our tests more reliable and more robust. But over the years, we have also encountered what we perceived as limitations in this framework. We'd like to emphasize the verb we just used: *perceived*. Many of the behaviors we complained about were actually implemented by design by JUnit's authors.

We will start by showing a few examples, and then we'll conclude this section by explaining how we propose to work around this limitation and help you, the reader, make a jump into the next generation of testing.

Stateful Classes

Let's go back to the problem discussed at the start of this chapter. The bug happened because we were trying to maintain state between two test methods: We were setting a field to a certain value in a test method, and we expected this value to be present in another test method.

JUnit seems to be saying that we should not do such a thing, and in order to enforce this practice, it reinitializes the class between each method invocation.

Should we feel bad for attempting to maintain state in a test class?

If you have read about testing practices in books or articles, you know that such a practice is indeed very much frowned upon, but despite this, we found ourselves repeatedly having this need in our testing activities. So why is JUnit getting in the way?

It turns out that there is a workaround in JUnit, and it's recommended as a design pattern: Use a static variable to store the value, and this way it won't be reinitialized every time.

Fine. But static variables come at a price.

- They are not same-JVM friendly. Run your tests several times in the same JVM (such as using the `<java>` `ant` task without specifying `fork="yes"`) and your static variable will bleed from one run to the other.

- Static variables also introduce several thread safety pitfalls and are usually better avoided, if at all possible.

---

1. Unless specified otherwise, the term *JUnit* used throughout this book refers to JUnit 3.

But most of all, we felt that JUnit was being intrusive: It was forcing us to modify code that we wrote initially in order to work around limitations of the framework.

We discuss state in tests in more detail in Chapters 2 and 7.

Parameters

Test methods with JUnit have the following constraints.

- Their names need to start with `test`.
- They can't return any values.
- They can't have any parameters.

This last restriction is something that has often bothered us. Why can't we pass parameters to our test methods? After all, passing parameters to methods and functions is an idea that has been present in programming languages for decades, and we can't think of a programmer who wouldn't be familiar with the idea.

Passing parameters to test methods seems to be very natural and, sometimes, extremely practical. Again, we found that you can't do this in JUnit, and the only way you can approximate the result is by using a convoluted design pattern, which is described in more detail in the section about Data Providers in Chapter 2.

Base Classes

Another requirement for a Java class to be considered a JUnit test class is that it needs to extend `TestCase`.

This class serves several purposes: It makes available a set of assert methods, and it enables the `setUp`/`tearDown` lifecycle methods that are crucial to the correct execution of your tests.

Still, being forced to extend a base class can be considered intrusive, especially since features that appeared in JDK 1.4 (asserts) and Java 5 (static imports) make this constraint unnecessary.

Exceptions Are Not That Exceptional

Any developer who is serious about testing will spend a great deal of time making sure that his or her code handles exceptions gracefully. It is important to make sure that your program supplies the expected functionalities, but it is equally important to verify that expected error cases are either handled or presented to the user in a friendly manner.

JUnit has no support for what we call exception testing, and you will find yourself writing convoluted code whenever you are faced with this situation. Listing 1–2 shows an example.

Listing 1–2 Handling expected exceptions in JUnit-based tests

```
public void testShouldThrowIfPlaneIsFull() {
  plane plane = createPlane();
  plane.bookAllSeats();
  try {
    plane.bookPlane(createValidItinerary(), null);
    fail("The reservation should have failed");
  }
  catch(ReservationException ex) {
    // success, do nothing: the test will pass
  }
}
```

Do you find this code easy to read? If you do, you definitely need to read the section dedicated to this topic in Chapter 2.

Running Tests

The standard JUnit distribution does little to help you run tests. For example, a common usage when writing or debugging tests is to run only one test method or a subset of your entire test suite. For the longest time, we used to achieve this goal by renaming our test methods (e.g., `testAccount` would become `_testAccount`). Because of the underscore character, JUnit would no longer run this test method, and we could concentrate on the one we were trying to debug.

Needless to say, this practice doesn't scale very well (imagine renaming 19 methods out of 20 in a test class), and it also forces you to recompile your tests before you can rerun them, another thing that struck us as unnecessary.

IDEs now allow us to pinpoint methods that we want to run, but this still doesn't solve the more general problem of being able to run very specific subsets of your tests (e.g., only tests that exercise the database).

The Test Groups section in Chapter 2 gives more details on how we solve this problem.

Real-World Testing

In our daily testing activities, we find ourselves repeatedly needing support for concepts such as:

- Concurrency and testing for thread safety
- Load testing
- Data-Driven Testing (in which the test code is the same, but it needs to be run with different parameters supplied by an external source, such as a text file, a spreadsheet, or a database)

Over the years, a formidable ecosystem has emerged around JUnit, and there is no doubt that an add-on exists for each of these scenarios. Tracking these add-ons and making sure they are still supported is a different matter, though, and in our experience, it's very often a frustrating endeavor.

Configuration Methods

JUnit lets you specify a pair of methods called `setUp` and `tearDown` that are invoked around your test methods. This idiom is very powerful and very flexible, but have you ever needed to perform a similar operation at the class level? In other words, you want a certain method to be invoked before any test method on a specific class is invoked. You also want another method to be invoked once all the test methods on this class have run.

And come to think of it, we have certainly often felt the need to have similar methods that would wrap an entire suite (e.g., such a method would start an application server or create a set of JDBC connections).

There is no support in JUnit for such configuration methods, and the only way to work around this limitation is to implement your own decorator (a technique that suffers from significant drawbacks, such as not being integrated in IDEs).

This chapter gives you an extensive explanation of the various types of configuration methods that TestNG offers and shows how more flexible an approach using Java annotations really is compared with the inheritance approach that JUnit uses.

Dependencies

If your test code base is significant, there is a good chance that you already have tests that depend on each other. JUnit makes sure that you can't easily implement this situation, but again, the reality is that in some conditions, if a test fails, there is simply no point in even trying to run the following five hundred tests.

Not only would you like these tests to be skipped by the testing framework, you would also like them to be reported as such, not as failures.

TestNG supports dependency tests, and as you will learn in Chapter 2, they can be used in conjunction with test groups to form a powerful combination.

Epiphanies

We'd like to make two points clear at this stage of the book.

1. All the previous observations made us realize that over the years, we hadn't been writing tests—we had been writing JUnit tests. After all, maybe we didn't *have* to face these various pains, and maybe we could look at testing in a different light and design a testing framework that approaches testing from a different angle: Ask developers what they are trying to test, and give them the tools to achieve their goals with minimal resistance.

2. Don't take the criticism we voiced as a condemnation of JUnit. We don't really believe that JUnit is deeply flawed, but we do think that it has outlived its usefulness. As its name implies, JUnit is a unit testing framework. If you are trying to do more than just unit testing (such as testing your system as a whole), it should not come as a surprise that JUnit is no longer the best tool for this job.

JUnit 4

A couple of years after TestNG came out, work on JUnit was resumed and culminated a few months later with the release of JUnit 4.0, which was the first major release the project had seen in almost four years.

JUnit 4 borrowed a lot of concepts from TestNG—something that we take great pride in—among which are expected exceptions, annotations, a few more configuration methods, and timeouts. If you are currently using JUnit 3 and you are considering upgrading to a better framework, we hope that this book will help you make your decision.

Designing for Testability

Not all code is testable, and not all testable code is necessarily good code. Writing good production code that can also be easily tested is a constant challenge that today's developers need to keep in mind at all times. As we will see in this section, designing for testability requires making compromises and, sometimes, letting go of principles that we have taken for granted for a long time.

Object-Oriented Programming and Encapsulation

There is no question that object-oriented programming (OOP) is now considered the mainstream technique for producing quality code. Simula, the programming language usually acknowledged as being the first to introduce object-oriented concepts, was conceived in the 1960s, which makes OOP more than forty years old.

OOP didn't catch on right away, and for a long period of time, Fortran and C remained the undisputed leaders in mindshare. But the OOP principles put forth by Simula eventually made it into Smalltalk, C++, and, in 1995, Java, ushering the computer world into the era of object-oriented programming.

Whether you studied them in school or learned in the workplace, you have undoubtedly been exposed to the principal tenets of OOP in some way and have adopted them to a large extent in your programming habits. The purpose of this section is not to give a definition or an overview of what these principles are but to focus on a particular one called encapsulation.

The idea behind encapsulation is that we should do our best to hide the private state of classes and make sure it is accessible to other objects and classes only through a specific interface that we control. This principle led to several rules of thumb, such as the following, that programmers around the world have been using with great success.

- Don't expose fields directly; use accessors and mutators (get/set).[2]
- Restrict the visibility of your methods and classes as much as possible. In Java, this translates into doing your best to use the following

---

2. Certain programming languages such as C# or Eiffel offer mechanisms that make this observation irrelevant. Unfortunately, Java doesn't have any similar feature, and we are therefore forced to follow this suggestion, which has a tendency to make Java classes much more verbose than they could be.

visibilities for your methods, in order of decreasing preference: `private`, `package protected`, `protected`, and `public`.[3]

By now, forty years after its first appearance in a programming language, encapsulation and certain other OOP concepts such as polymorphism and delegation are deeply ingrained in every developer's mind. For the most part, this has resulted in an indisputable increase in software quality.

Unfortunately, the downside of this extreme popularity is that not only has testability (and more to the point, automated testability) been largely overlooked until the early 2000s, but it also appears that some of these OOP principles that we hold so dear are sometimes directly at odds with testing.

But before we get into details about these, we need to digress again and mention another very important landmark in software engineering history.

The Design Patterns Revolution

In 1995, Addison-Wesley published an innocuous-looking book under the obscure title *Design Patterns: Elements of Reusable Object-Oriented Software*. Written by four authors who immediately became known as the Gang of Four (Erich Gamma, Richard Helm, Ralph Johnson, and John Vlissides), this book had a puzzling premise and content that could make you wonder about its usefulness, since it didn't contain any radically novel or innovative ideas.

Instead, this book proposed a categorization of software design patterns. According to the authors, a design pattern is not isolated code but a general description of how certain portions of software can cooperate with each other to achieve a certain goal. The book captured the commonality in various implementations of these ideas and tried to come up with general guidelines describing canonical ways to assemble these patterns.

Design Patterns struck a chord because suddenly ideas that programmers had been using and reusing for years not only were clearly described in plain terms but also received a name, making it very easy for everyone to exchange ideas without having to spend too much time on the details. Even better: The book offered a canonical way to implement these ideas, so that we no longer needed to reinvent the wheel whenever they were needed.

---

3. Even this simple rule of thumb can be argued in many ways. For example, many programmers tend to stay away from protected methods completely; others are much more liberal with public methods, following the idea that they trust users of their classes. Let's keep the debate simple at this point since the goal of this section is not to debate this particular point.

The significance of the book is that we didn't need to know the details of each of these patterns by heart. All that we needed to remember was the existence of a certain design pattern and its name, and we could turn to the book to find the most optimal way to implement it.

The book made certain design patterns immediately popular: Factory, Singleton, Façade, Proxy, and so on. These names were so convenient that soon they were used in many mailing lists, newsgroups, meetings, articles, and books. And the beauty of it is that we never needed to explain anything more: As soon as we used one of these names, everybody knew right away what we meant, allowing us to focus exclusively on the point we were trying to make.

The impact that *Design Patterns* had on the modern software industry cannot be understated, and we place it at the very same level of contribution as object-oriented programming.

Having said this, the book was not perfect, and it contributed to propagating a few practices and ideas that are now being questioned. Here are some of the omissions that are relevant to our current topic of discussion.

- The book made the Singleton design pattern popular. While the need for a unique instance throughout an application arises quite frequently, there are better ways to address it than with a static instance, which is the approach that the book recommends (see the next point).
- The book didn't say anything about mock objects or Dependency Injection. To be clear, these concepts started becoming popular only in recent years, so their omission in the book is quite understandable. However, if the authors had known about these ideas, they would probably have revisited some of their design patterns.

In hindsight, we wish the book had used more caution in its recommendation of static methods and static fields since, as we will see in the next section, they represent an obstacle to testing.

Identifying the Enemy

Throughout this book, we will show various ways in which we can make code more testable, both with general recommendations and specific examples. In general, we have found that the software technologies we use today to write our Java applications lend themselves very well to extensive automated testing, but a few practices make testing more problematic:

- Mutable static fields, which are dangerous because they can leak state from one invocation to the next (a problem that immutable static fields do not have)
- Static methods that use mutable static fields, for similar reasons (although static methods that do not alter any static state do not have this problem)
- Extreme encapsulation
- Passing of concrete classes to methods, which causes more problems than passing interfaces to methods does
- Liberal use of `new` instead of relying on factories, injections, or Aspect-Oriented Programming (AOP)

Let's take a look at a few concrete examples.

The Problem with Static Methods and Fields

Consider an application that displays a graphical window unless it's invoked with the `-nogui` parameter as in Listing 1–3, in which case it will run in interactive mode in the terminal.

Listing 1–3 Example class with a command line configuration

```
public class Foo {
  private static boolean noGui = false;

  public static void main(String[] argv) {
    if (/* argv contains -nogui */) {
      noGui = true;
    }

    // run the program
  }
}
```

Now imagine that we invoke the program twice in the same build file. Listing 1–4 is an excerpt of an `ant` build file that does that. (Keep in mind that by default, the `<java>` task runs successive main classes in the same process.)

Listing 1–4 `ant build.xml` to run with a different configuration

```
<java classname="Foo" line="-nogui"/>
<!-- ... and somewhere else -->
<java classname="Foo" />
```

You will probably be surprised to see the second invocation run in `-nogui` mode as well.

Listing 1–5 also highlights the problem when we try to test this parameter switch.

Listing 1–5 Tests for different configurations

```
@Test
public void verifyWithGui() {
  Foo.main(new String[0]);
  // make sure the window is up
}

@Test
public void verifyWithNoGui() {
  Foo.main(new String[] { "-nogui" });
  // make sure that no window was created
}
```

Depending on the order in which these two test methods are invoked (which is not predictable), we will have either one test for each mode (which is what we want) or two tests launched with the `-nogui` parameter (which is not).

Listing 1–6 shows one way to get rid of the static method, by passing the arguments in parameters to an instance.

Listing 1–6 A better way to parameterize a configuration

```
public static void main(String[] argv) {
  new Foo(argv).run();
}

public Foo(String[] argv) {
  // parse the parameters, store them in nonstatic fields
}
```

```
public void run() {
  // run the application
}
```

This version of the code might look very similar to the one we started with, but the removal of the static field has two very beneficial effects.

1. Now that the application runs from an instance, consecutive runs with different command line parameters will not have surprising effects because each instance will use its own set of parameters.

2. By passing the command line arguments in parameters (i.e., injecting them) in an instance, we can test our application more easily since each instance will be isolated from the others.

Listing 1–7 is the test for the new version.

Listing 1–7 Updated test for the refactored class

```
@Test
public void verifyWithGui() {
  new Foo(new String[0]).run();
  // verify that the window is up
}

@Test
public void verifyWithNoGui() {
  new Foo(new String[] { "-nogui" }).run();
  // make sure that no window was created
}
```

No matter in which order these test methods are invoked, the tests will run as expected.

This approach is usually referred to as *Dependency Injection* because we are now injecting the resources we depend on directly into the object.[4]

---

4. For this reason, this technique is also known as *Inversion of Control*, although this name has since fallen out of favor.

The configuration is now performed externally rather than being done by the object itself reaching out for its dependencies.

With this technique, it is possible to replace any use of static fields or methods, including singletons, which has the benefit of making code more testable. Of course, this technique has a few drawbacks, one of them being that methods are now receiving more parameters than they used to. While this is fairly easy to achieve even with a simple editor, it can become quite tedious when we have to pass this parameter into the deeper layers of our code.

For this reason, several Dependency Injection frameworks have emerged over the past years (the most popular one being the Spring framework), which we encourage you to look into if you decide to use this technique extensively.

The Problem with Extreme Encapsulation

Consider Listing 1–8, which needs to perform some expensive initialization when the class gets loaded.

Listing 1–8 Example class with expensive static initialization

```
final public class HeavyClass {
  static {
    expensiveInitialization();
  }

  private static void expensiveInitialization() { ... }
}
```

When it's time to test this class, we can test it without needing anything from the expensive initialization that is performed at load time (maybe because we are using mock objects), so we try to devise ways to create instances of this class without it.

A common trick to neutralize undesirable behavior, shown in Listing 1–9, is to override the offending method with an empty one.

Listing 1–9 Stubbing out expensive initialization

```
public class TestHeavyClass extends HeavyClass {
  protected void expensiveInitialization() { /* do nothing */
}
```

Obviously, this is not possible for several reasons.

- The method we want to override is static, so it can't be overridden.
- The class is final, so it can't be extended.

To make the class more testable (and also more extensible), we can rewrite it as shown in Listing 1–10.

Listing 1–10 Refactored class to improve testability

```
public class HeavyClass {
  public HeavyClass() {
    onInitialize();
  }

  private static boolean initialized = false;

  protected void onInitialize() {
    if (! initialized) {
      expensiveInitialization();
      initialized = true;
    }
  }
}

public TestHeavyClass extends HeavyClass {
  public void onInitialize() {
    // do nothing
  }
}
```

In this refactored version, not only have we limited the use of statics to a strict minimum (just a Boolean field now), we have also removed a few `final` keywords, promoted a private method to protected status (so it can be overridden in subclasses), and finally, introduced a special method called `onInitialize()`, which is traditionally referred to as a *hook* (we are allowing subclasses to hook into your logic through these methods).

With this practice, we have created a new class aimed specifically at testing, but we have also improved our design by making our class easier to invoke and removing undesirable side effects.

We can solve this problem in a different way. If you don't feel comfortable overriding a method from a parent class with an empty method, you could consider passing an initializer object, as in Listing 1–11, that can either perform the heavy initialization shown earlier or do nothing (or use mocks) if you are testing.

Listing 1–11 Refactored class to parameterize the initialization strategy

```
public class HeavyClass {
  public HeavyClass(InitializationStrategy
  initializationStrategy) {
    initializationStrategy.initialize();
  }
}

public class InitializationStrategy {
  public void initialize() {
    expensiveInitialization();
  }
}
```

There are other incarnations of extreme encapsulation, such as classes with an abundance of private methods. When you come across such cases, make sure that you have tests, and then feel free to refactor the class to make it more testable, like we just did.

Recommendations

In these sections, we have illustrated how the keywords `static` and `final` can be an obstacle to testability, and we have shown a few examples on how you can refactor code to avoid them.

We have only scratched the surface of this complex problem, so if you are interested in learning more techniques to improve your code and make it more testable, we recommend you read Michael Feathers' book *Working Effectively with Legacy Code* (Prentice Hall, 2005), which covers this topic extensively.

TestNG

We will be using the TestNG framework throughout this book, so before proceeding any further, let's spend a bit of time describing the main ideas behind this testing framework.

Annotations

The traditional way to indicate test methods in JUnit 3 is by prefixing their name with `test`. This is a very effective method for tagging certain methods in a class as having a special meaning, but the naming doesn't scale very well (what if we want to add more tags for different frameworks?) and is rather inflexible (what if we want to pass additional parameters to the testing framework?).

Annotations were formally added to the Java language in JDK 5, and TestNG made the choice to use annotations to annotate test classes.[5] Listing 1–12 shows a basic example.

Listing 1–12 Basic TestNG test

```
public class FirstTest {
  @BeforeMethod
  public void init() {
  }

  @Test(groups = { "unit", "functional" })
  public void aTest() {
  }
}
```

There are a few obvious benefits in this code.

■ Method names are not restricted to any pattern or format since TestNG will identify the methods it is interested in by looking up annotations and not method names.

---

5. Note that TestNG can also run with JDK 1.4 by using Javadocs comments as annotations. More details on this later.

- We can pass additional parameters to annotations.
- Annotations are strongly typed, so the compiler will flag any mistakes right away.
- Test classes no longer need to extend anything (such as `TestCase`, for JUnit 3).
- Here is the list of annotations that TestNG supports:
  - `@BeforeSuite`, `@BeforeTest`, `@BeforeClass`, `@BeforeMethod`, `@BeforeGroups`
  - `@AfterSuite`, `@AfterTest`, `@AfterClass`, `@AfterMethod`, `@AfterGroups`
  - `@DataProvider`
  - `@ExpectedExceptions`
  - `@Factory`
  - `@Test`
  - `@Parameters`

We won't spend any more time explaining what these annotations do since we will be explaining their usage in detail in the next chapters, but you can also refer to the Javadocs in Appendix B for a quick overview at this point.

For now, let's turn our attention to another important component of the TestNG framework.

Tests, Suites, and Configuration Annotations

TestNG defines a very specific terminology to describe tests, which is illustrated in Listing 1–13.

Listing 1–13 Sample `testng.xml`

```
<!DOCTYPE suite SYSTEM "http://testng.org/testng-1.0.dtd" >⁶

<suite name="TestNG JDK 1.5">
  <test name="Regression1" >
    <classes>
```

---

6. By default, TestNG is configured to looks for its DTD in the distribution, so it should never fetch it from the http://testng.org Web site. However, this can sometimes happen when you are using an IDE, in which case we recommend making a copy of the DTD file (which you can find inside the distribution) and put it in a classpath directory that your IDE knows.

```
      <class name="com.example.ParameterSample" />
      <class name="com.example.ParameterTest" >
        <methods>
          <include name="database.*" />
          <exclude name="inProgress" />
        </methods>
      </class>
    </classes>
  </test>
</suite>
```

This file tells TestNG to run all the methods found in the class `ParameterSample` and all the methods in the class `ParameterTest` that start with `database` and to exclude the method called `inProgress`.[7]

Listing 1–14 also shows how packages can be specified.

Listing 1–14 Specifying packages in `testng.xml`

```
<suite name="Package suite">
  <test name="Parameters" />
    <packages>
      <package name="test.parameters.Parameter*" />
    </packages>
  </test>
</suite>
```

The `testng.xml` file captures a very simple terminology.

- A *suite* is made of one or more tests.
- A *test* is made of one or more classes.
- A *class* is made or one or more methods.

This terminology is important because it is intimately connected to configuration annotations.

---

7. Note that all these methods and classes are being given to TestNG only for consideration. Once TestNG has gathered the entire set of candidate methods, additional conditions, such as their belonging to certain groups and attributes to their `@Test` annotations, will eventually decide whether they should be run or excluded.

Configuration annotations are all the annotations that start with `@Before` or `@After`. Each of these methods defines events in the TestNG lifecycle. As we saw in the previous section, TestNG defines five different configuration annotations. Every time a method is annotated with one of these annotations, it will be run at the following time:

- `@BeforeSuite` / `@AfterSuite`—before a suite starts / after all the test methods in a certain suite have been run
- `@BeforeTest` / `@AfterTest`—before a test starts / after all the test methods in a certain test have been run (remember that a test is made of one or more classes)
- `@BeforeClass` / `@AfterClass`—before a test class starts / after all the test methods in a certain class have been run[8]
- `@BeforeMethod` / `@AfterMethod`—before a test method is run / after a test method has been run
- `@BeforeGroups` / `@AfterGroups`—before any test method in a given group is run / after all the test methods in a given group have been run

As we will see in the following chapters, configuration annotations offer a very flexible and granular way to initialize and clean up your tests.

Groups

Another feature that sets TestNG apart is the ability to put test methods in groups. The names and number of these groups are entirely up to you (we suggest a few ideas for names in Chapter 2) and are specified using the `@Test` annotation to specify groups, as in Listing 1–15.

Listing 1–15 Specifying groups in a test

```
@Test(groups = { "fast", "unit", "database" })
public void rowShouldBeInserted() {
}
```

---

8. To be more specific, `@BeforeClass` and `@AfterClass` wrap instances, not classes. Therefore, if you happen to create two instances of the test class `MyTest` in your suite definition, the corresponding `@BeforeClass` and `@AfterClass` will be run twice.

Once you have defined your groups in the annotations, you can run tests and include or exclude these groups from the run, as shown in Listing 1–16.

Listing 1–16 Specifying groups on the command line

```
java org.testng.TestNG —groups fast com.example.MyTest
```

We cover test groups in more details in Chapter 2.

testng.xml

testng.xml is a file that captures your entire testing in XML. This file makes it easy to describe all your test suites and their parameters in one file, which you can check in your code repository or email to coworkers. It also makes it easy to extract subsets of your tests or split several runtime configurations (e.g., testng-database.xml would run only tests that exercise your database).

Since this file is not mandatory for running TestNG tests, we are deferring its description to Appendix C, although you will encounter simple versions of it in the next chapters.

Conclusion

In this short chapter, we examined the current state of testing as well as some of the issues surrounding JUnit, along with some of the bad patterns that are easy to fall into when developing tests.

We took some time to introduce some basic concepts about testing, and we gave a short overview of TestNG. We hope this has whetted your appetite for more; the real work starts in the next chapter, where we will dive deep into testing design patterns. We will also expand our knowledge of TestNG in the process.

CHAPTER 2

Testing Design Patterns

While we are all very familiar with general object-oriented design patterns, testing design patterns are not nearly as well understood or prevalent because the mechanics of writing tests is easy, and almost any testing framework we use is likely to be fairly simple and easy to understand.

More interesting than just writing tests, however, is writing tests that will stand the test of time, tests that will handle future requirements and changes, ones that can be easily maintained by any new developers who might join the team or take over the code base.

In this chapter, we'll examine a number of patterns and common problems that have emerged through practical applications of testing. Starting with failure testing, we will also explore Data-Driven Testing, concurrency testing, the role of mocks and stubs in the testing world, techniques for effective test grouping, and ways to use code coverage as a testing aid.

Since there is so much ground to cover, this chapter is unusually long and contains a very wide range of testing design patterns. You don't have to read it sequentially, and you are welcome to use the table of contents to jump directly to the section you find the most relevant to you at the moment. We hope that by the time you've finished reading this content, you will have a clear idea of the various ways to tackle testing problems.

Testing for Failures

One of the goals of testing is to make sure that your code works the way it is expected to. This testing should be done either at the user level ("If I press this button, a new account gets created") or at the programming level ("This function returns the square root of its argument"). Each of these two categories is tested by functional tests and unit tests, respectively.

Very often, these specifications also define how the program should behave when a legitimate error occurs. For example, on a Web email system, someone might want to create an email address that already exists. The

Web site should respond by letting the user know he or she can't use that particular account name and should pick another account name. This is not a crash, and this behavior should be clearly defined in the documentation.

The same observation applies at the language level: What should happen if a square root method is passed a negative integer? Mathematics clearly states that such an argument is not legal (well, the result is an imaginary number, which is not legal for our purposes), so the method should report this error to the user, and reporting this error should be part of the method's specification.

In this section, we'll examine how to test for failures.

Reporting Errors

The first question we need to answer is this: How do we report errors in our programs?

In the early days, the traditional way to report errors in programs was to use return codes. For example, if your method was expected to return a positive integer, you would use a special negative value such as –1 to indicate that something went wrong.

There are several problems with this approach.

- When the caller of your method receives the value, it needs to perform a test to know whether the call was successful or not, and this results in contrived code of nested `if/else` statements.

- You need to define a singular value that is clearly different from the usual values returned by this method. It's easy in certain cases, such as the example above, but what error code do you return when all integers (zero, positive, and negative) are legal?

- What if several error cases can arise and each of them must be dealt with separately? How do you encode these cases in the singular value so they can be differentiated? What if more than one value needs to be returned to represent the error accurately, such as the time and the geographic location describing what went wrong?

- There is no consistent way to indicate an error condition and therefore no consistent way to check for an error.

- There is not always a reasonable value that can be returned to indicate an error.

For all these reasons, the software community quickly realized that something better than return codes needed to be invented in order to represent failures in an effective and maintainable manner.

The next step in error reporting was to use parameters instead of return values to signal errors. For example, the method that created an account would receive the name of the account to be created and also an additional parameter that, when the method returned, would contain the error description if anything went wrong.

While more expressive than returning error codes, this approach is also fraught with severe restrictions.

- It doesn't provide any easy way to distinguish the regular parameters from those that contain the error.
- It makes the signatures of your methods harder to read.
- Not all programming languages support out parameters (parameters that can be modified by the function they are passed to) natively, making the code harder to read and to interpret.

About fifteen years ago, C++ popularized a very powerful idea to express errors: exceptions. This approach has become the de facto standard in most programming languages these days, and it presents the following advantages.

- The signature of the method cleanly separates the parameters from the errors that can possibly happen.
- These errors can be handled where it makes most sense, as opposed to being handled by the caller of the method, which doesn't necessarily know how to react to an error.
- Being objects themselves, exceptions can carry arbitrarily complex payloads, which makes it possible to describe any imaginable error.

Explaining how exceptions work in Java and how to use them correctly is beyond the scope of this book, but before we start exploring how to test our exceptions, we'd like to cover a very important aspect of exceptions that is often misunderstood.

Runtime and Checked Exceptions

Java offers two different types of exceptions: runtime exceptions, which extend the class `java.lang.RuntimeException`, and checked exceptions, which extend the class `java.lang.Exception`.

The only difference between them is that the compiler will force you to handle a checked exception, either by catching it and acting on it or by declaring it in your `throws` clause and thereby requiring your caller to deal with this exception. On the other hand, runtime exceptions can be completely ignored by your code, and they can even never be mentioned in the code that throws them at all.

As you write your code, you might discover that one of your methods needs to throw an exception. At this point, you have to decide whether you want to throw a runtime exception or a checked exception, and this choice can have a very big impact on the maintainability and readability of your code.

There is no absolute answer to this question. You should be very skeptical of anyone who tells you that you should never use checked exceptions or that you should always use them. Still, exceptions appear to be a very emotional topic among Java programmers, and we hear a lot of unreasonable arguments from each side to defend their point of view, so we'll just dispel some of those ideas to help you make the right decision.

Myth: Checked Exceptions Pollute Your Code

This is a consequence of the fact that checked exceptions are enforced by the compiler, so that if you invoke a method that throws a checked exception, you need to alter your code to deal with it. What opponents of checked exceptions often forget to mention is that it's still easy for you to not handle this exception if you don't think you can: Declare it in the `throws` clause of your method.

Myth: Runtime Exceptions Represent the Best of Both Worlds

No, they don't. Since the programmer is not forced to document what runtime exceptions the methods throw, you never really know in what way the invocation can fail, which makes it very hard for you to test your own code. It is theoretically possible to ship code that will throw an exception that you never heard of. Wouldn't you have preferred to be aware of such a possibility?

The thing to remember is that checked exceptions come at a price that is their added value: They force you to think about the consequences of throwing or catching that exception.

With that in mind, here is a rule of thumb for deciding whether you should throw a checked exception: Can the caller do something about this exception? If the answer is yes, you should probably use a checked exception; otherwise, a runtime exception is a better choice.

For example, `java.io.FileNotFoundException` is a checked exception because most of the time, the caller might be able to do something to address the problem, such as prompt the user for a different file. On the other hand, `java.lang.NullPointerException` and `java.lang.OutOfMemoryError` are unchecked runtime exceptions, not only because they are usually fatal but also because they can potentially happen at any moment in your program.

Testing Whether Your Code Handles Failures Gracefully

Now that we have taken a quick tour of why testing for errors is important, let's take a look at a concrete example. In this section, we'll use the method shown in Listing 2–1, which, as you can see, allows you to book a plane ticket based on an itinerary and a seat request. The Javadocs comments give you more details about what this method does and in what ways it's expected to fail.

Listing 2–1 Method to test for failure

```
/**
 * @param itinerary The desired itinerary
 * @param seat The seat request. If null, an available
 * seat will be returned.
 * @return The Confirmation object if the reservation
 * was successfully made.
 * @throws ReservationException If the reservation could
 * not be made. This object will contain more details
 * on why the reservation failed.
 */
public Confirmation bookPlane(ItineraryRequest itinerary,
                              SeatRequest seat)
    throws ReservationException;
```

Listing 2–2 shows a first attempt at making sure that an exception is thrown if we try to make a reservation on a plane that is full.

Listing 2–2 First attempt to check for a failed reservation

```
@Test
public void shouldThrowIfPlaneIsFull() {
```

```
Plane plane = createPlane();
plane.bookAllSeats();
try {
  plane.bookPlane(createValidItinerary(), null);
  fail("The reservation should have failed");
}
catch(ReservationException ex) {
  // success, do nothing: the test will pass
}
}
```

This is a traditional testing design pattern that has been made popular by JUnit 3, and while it works, its reverse logic ("pass if an exception is thrown, fail when all goes well") makes the code a bit harder to read than it should be.

We are purposely not giving much detail on the first three lines of the test method (`createPlane()`, `bookAllSeats()`, and `bookPlane()`) since we will cover the important topic of test setup later in this chapter, but for now, suffice it to say that you could either create real objects or use mocks to achieve that effect.

Since testing for failure is such a common task, TestNG supports it natively in its `@Test` annotation, as shown in Listing 2–3.

Listing 2–3 Improved test for a failed reservation

```
@Test(expectedExceptions = ReservationException.class)
public void shouldThrowIfPlaneIsFull() {
  plane plane = createPlane();
  plane.bookAllSeats();
  plane.bookPlane(createValidItinerary(), null);
}
```

The attribute `expectedExceptions` is an array of classes that contains the list of exception classes expected to be thrown in this test method. If either (1) no exceptions or (2) an exception that is not listed in the attribute is thrown, TestNG will mark the test method as a failure. On the other hand, if this method throws an exception listed in this attribute, TestNG will mark this test as passed.

Supporting exceptions in the `@Test` annotation has two benefits.

- It makes the intent very clear: You read the `@Test` annotation and you know immediately what is supposed to happen, which is not exactly the case when you read the first version of the test method.
- It removes all the noise in the code created by the try/catch/fail/ empty statement (always a code smell, hence the explicit comment), thereby allowing the test method to focus purely on the business logic.

Now, we have a confession to make: The example we used is not very well designed. As you might guess from making a plane reservation, several things can go wrong, so the generic `ReservationException` is not really sufficient to supply enough details to the caller.

Let's fix this by changing the `throws` clause of our test method, as shown in Listing 2–4.

Listing 2–4 Adding another exception to the method

```
public Confirmation bookPlane(ItineraryRequest itinerary,
                              SeatRequest seat)
  throws PlaneFullException, FlightCanceledException;
```

The caller now has the option to act if something goes wrong by, for example, displaying a more specific message to the user.

Of course, we must now make sure that under the right conditions, our method will throw the correct exception. A first approach is to use the fact that `@Test` lets you specify more than one exception in its `expectedExceptions` attribute, as follows in Listing 2–5.

Listing 2–5 Updated test for a new exception

```
@Test(expectedExceptions = {
  PlaneFullException.class, FlightCanceledException.class })
public void shouldThrowIfSomehingGoesWrong() { ... }
```

However, this didn't buy us much because we're still not quite sure what exception was thrown and in what circumstances. So we need to break the tests into two distinct parts, as shown in Listing 2–6.

Listing 2–6 Refactored test to check for one exception at a time

```
@Test(expectedExceptions = PlaneFullException.class)
public void shouldThrowIfPlaneIsFull() {
  Plane plane = createPlane();
  plane.bookAllSeats();
  plane.bookPlane(createValidItinerary(), null);
}

@Test(expectedExceptions = FlightCanceledException.class)
public void shouldThrowIfFlightIsCanceled() {
  Plane plane = createPlane();
  cancelFlight(/* ... */);
  plane.bookPlane(createValidItinerary(), null);
}
```

We now have two distinct tests that accurately represent the expected functionality, and if one of these test methods fails, we will know right away what exception is not being thrown.

In the spirit of polishing this example, we'll finally note that we're violating a very important principle in software engineering in this short example, called the DRY principle (Don't Repeat Yourself). While these two tests exercise different portions of the code, they share a common initialization in the way they create a `Plane` object, so we should therefore isolate this isolation in an `@BeforeMethod` (since we want this object to be recreated from scratch before each invocation).

Our final test class looks like Listing 2–7.

Listing 2–7 Updated test class

```
public class BookingTest {
  private Plane plane;

  @BeforeMethod
  public void init() {
    plane = createPlane();
  }

  @Test(expectedExceptions = PlaneFullException.class)
  public void shouldThrowIfPlaneIsFull() {
    plane.bookAllSeats();
    plane.bookPlane(createValidItinerary(), null);
  }
```

```
@Test(expectedExceptions = FlightCanceledException.class)
public void shouldThrowIfFlightIsCanceled() {
  cancelFlight(/* ... */);
  plane.bookPlane(createValidItinerary(), null);
}
}
```

Notice how each method in the test class is focused on a very specialized task (thereby enforcing another important software engineering principle known as the Single Responsibility principle) and that the various nouns and verbs used in the code make the intent of each code fragment very clear.

When Not to Use expectedExceptions

While the attribute expectedExceptions will likely cover your needs for exception testing most of the time, when the only thing you are interested in is to make sure that a certain exception is thrown, sometimes your tests will be more demanding.

For example, consider a situation where the message inside the exception object (which you obtain by calling getMessage()) needs to contain certain words (or conversely, should not contain certain words, such as sensitive information or passwords). This can sometimes happen when this message ends up being logged in a file or even shown to the user.[1]

Another example is when you have created your own exception class in order to be able to put extra information inside. The fact that this exception gets thrown under the right circumstances is not enough to assert that your code is correct. You also need to make sure the object that is being thrown contains the right values.

In either of these cases, you are probably better off reverting to the old way of testing for exceptions, as illustrated at the beginning of this section. Surround the code with try/catch, fail the test if the code inside the try gets invoked, and use the catch statement to perform the additional tests.

Finally, one last word of caution against testing the content of getMessage(): Think about internationalization.

---

1. Showing exception messages to the user is not a recommended practice (let alone showing entire stack traces). You usually want to have a layer between something as low-level as exceptions and something that is user-facing that will perform the appropriate translation between a system message and a well-phrased message (that should most likely be internationalized).

Is the content of this message to be read by users or only logged and destined for developers? If the former, you should probably use a more specific exception that will contain enough information for the code to be able to look up the string in the appropriate locale. Make sure you test against that localized string and not the one contained in the message.

`testng-failed.xml`

There are many reasons why a developer might be debugging a test, but the most common one is to investigate a failure. It is a fairly common scenario. You come to work in the morning, check the test reports from last night, write down the new failures, and then investigate them one by one.

It has always been striking that such a common activity has never been supported natively by existing test frameworks. For example, the typical way to achieve this goal with JUnit is to write down the name of the method that failed and then rerun it by itself. If you are using the command line, running an individual test method with JUnit can be very challenging. (This author used to rename all the other test methods in his class with a leading underscore until only the method that failed was left, and then he would rerun the entire class.) If you are using an IDE, things are a little easier since you can usually select an individual test method to run, but you still need to load the class that contains the failed test in your IDE and then run it manually.

This shortcoming has always been puzzling since test frameworks have full knowledge of which methods passed and which ones failed, and it's a pity that they share this information with the user only in the form of a report that a human must read and then act on.

As it turns out, TestNG already possesses a very convenient way to store test configurations: `testng.xml`. Leveraging this file makes it trivial to rerun failed tests.

The idea is very simple. Whenever you run a suite that contains errors, TestNG will automatically generate a file called `testng-failed.xml` in your output directory (by default, `test-output/`). This XML file contains a subset of the original `testng.xml` with only the methods that failed.

Consider the test in Listing 2–8, which contains two methods that fail.

Listing 2–8 Example of failing tests

```
public class FailedTest {
  @Test
  public void depend() {
  }
```

```
@Test(dependsOnMethods = "depend")
public void f() {
  throw new RuntimeException();
}

@Test
public void failed() {
  throw new RuntimeException();
}
}
```

When we run this test, we get the output shown in Listing 2–9.

Listing 2–9 Test output

```
PASSED: depend
FAILED: f
java.lang.RuntimeException
... Removed 22 stack frames
FAILED: failed
java.lang.RuntimeException
... Removed 22 stack frames


===============================================
    T2
    Tests run: 3, Failures: 2, Skips: 0
===============================================
```

Now let's take a look at `test-output/testng-failed.xml`, shown in Listing 2–10.

Listing 2–10 Generated `testng-failed.xml`

```
<!DOCTYPE suite SYSTEM "http://testng.org/testng-1.0.dtd">
<suite thread-count="5" verbose="2"
       name="Failed suite [Main suite]" parallel="none"
       annotations="JDK">
  <test name="T2(failed)" junit="false" parallel="none"
        annotations="JDK">
```

```
      <classes>
        <class name="org.testngbook.FailedTest">
          <methods>
            <include name="f"/>
            <include name="depend"/>
            <include name="failed"/>
          </methods>
        </class>
      </classes>
    </test>
</suite>
```

As you can see, TestNG picked all the methods that failed and created a `testng-failed.xml` file that contains only these methods. You will also notice that TestNG included the method called `depend()`, even though it didn't fail. This is because the method `f()` depends on it, and since `f()` failed, not only does it need to be included, so do all the methods that it depends on.

With the existence of this file, a typical TestNG session therefore looks like Listing 2–11.

Listing 2–11 Rerunning the failed tests

```
$ java org.testng.TestNG testng.xml
$ java org.testng.TestNG test-output/testng-failed.xml
```

With `testng-failed.xml`, TestNG makes it very easy for you to debug your failed tests without wasting time isolating the methods that failed.

Factories

As we learned in the previous sections, whenever you pass test classes to TestNG, through the command line, `ant`, or `testng.xml`, TestNG instantiates these classes for you by invoking their no-argument constructor and then proceeds to run all the test methods that can be found on each class.

In this section, we'll explore how TestNG allows you to create your own instances with the `@Factory` annotation.

@Factory

Consider the following testing scenario: Your application is using a lot of images, some of which are statically put in a directory and others of which are generated. In order to make sure that you are not shipping your code with corrupted images, you have created a test infrastructure that, given the name of a picture file, will return various expected attributes in this file: width, height, depth, certain colors or patterns of bytes, and so on. The logic of your test must therefore find the file, look up its expected attributes, and then match them to those found in the file picture.

Ideally, you would like your test class to look like Listing 2–12.

Listing 2–12 Ideal parameterized test

```
public class PictureTest {
  private Image image;
  private int width;
  private int height;
  private String path;

  public PictureTest(String path, int width, int height,
      int depth)
    throws IOException
  {
    File f = new File(path);
    this.path = path;
    this.image = ImageIO.read(f);
    this.width = width;
    this.height = height;
  }

  @Test
  public void testWidth() {}

  @Test
  public void testHeight() {}
}
```

This is just an abbreviated example; a more thorough image-testing class would also verify that certain bytes can be found at predetermined offsets, have tests on the color palette, and so on.

If you declare this class in your `testng.xml` as is, TestNG will issue an error because it will not be able to instantiate it (this class doesn't have a no-argument constructor). And even if you did add such a constructor, the test would still fail because the various fields would not be initialized properly.

In order to address this scenario, TestNG gives you the option to instantiate test classes yourself. This is done with the `@Factory` annotation, which must be put on top of a method that returns an array of objects. Each of these objects should be an instance of a class that contains TestNG annotations. These objects will also be inspected by TestNG to find out whether they have `@Factory` annotations as well, in which case the cycle starts again, until TestNG is left with either instances that have no `@Factory` annotations on them or instances that have `@Factory` methods that have already been invoked.

Note that you can safely have both `@Factory` and `@Test` annotations on the same class since TestNG guarantees that your `@Factory` method will be invoked exactly once.

Since `@Factory` methods can add new test classes to your testing world, they are always invoked first, before any `@Test` and configuration methods are invoked. Only when all the `@Factory` methods have been invoked does TestNG start running your configuration and test methods.

For the purposes of this example, let's assume the existence of a helper function that, given the path of a picture file, will return its expected attributes. This is shown in Listing 2–13.

Listing 2–13 Encapsulated attributes in a class

```
public class ExpectedAttributes {
  public int width;
  public int height;
  public int depth;
}

/**
 * @return the expected attributes for the picture file passed
 * in parameters.
 */
private static ExpectedAttributes findExpectedAttributes(String
  path) {
  // ...
}
```

Then we have another help function that will give us an array of strings containing the paths of all the images that we are testing, as shown in Listing 2–14.

Listing 2–14 Helper method to get all image file names

```
private static String[] findImageFileNames() {
  // ...
}
```

Listing 2–15 shows our new constructor and factory method.

Listing 2–15 Test with a custom factory

```
public PictureTest(String path, int width, int height,
    int depth)
  throws IOException
{
  File f = new File(path);
  this.path = path;
  this.image = ImageIO.read(f);
  this.width = width;
  this.height = height;
}

@Factory
public static Object[] create() throws IOException {
  List result = new ArrayList();

  // Inspect directory, find all image file names
  String[] paths = findImageFileNames();
  // Retrieve the expected attributes for each picture
  // and create a test case with them
  for (String path : paths) {
    ExpectedAttributes ea = findAttributes(path);
    result.add(new PictureTest(path, ea.width,
      ea.height, ea.depth));
  }

  return result.toArray();
}
```

This code will now create one instance of `PictureTest` per picture found. When running this code, TestNG will test that the various attributes contain the expected values. If we run it with two files, we obtain the result shown in Listing 2–16.

Listing 2–16 Test output

```
PASSED: testWidth
PASSED: testWidth
PASSED: testHeight
PASSED: testHeight


==================================================
    PictureTest
    Tests run: 4, Failures: 0, Skips: 0
==================================================
```

The advantage of being able to express factories with Java code is that there is virtually no limit to the way you can create your tests. In this example, as time goes by and you add new pictures to that directory, the test will keep working just fine as long as you remember to update the data that returns the `ExpectedAttributes` for each file. Because it's easy to forget to update that data, you should probably make sure that `findExpectedAttributes()` throws a clear exception whenever it is asked to provide attributes for a file name that it knows nothing about. This will guarantee that no new picture will be added without being covered by a test.

org.testng.ITest

You might find that the output shown in Listing 2–16 is not very helpful: We had only two test classes in this example, and already we're not quite sure what objects the tests are running on. Consider the situation where you have hundreds of objects created by your factory. When one of these tests fail, you will need some additional information in order to figure out what's going on.

The easiest way to do this is to have your test class implement the interface `org.testng.ITest`, as shown in Listing 2–17.

Listing 2–17 *ITest* interface

```
public interface ITest {
  public String getTestName();
}
```

Whenever TestNG encounters a test class that implements this interface, it will include the information returned by `getTestName()` in the various reports that it generates (both text and HTML).

Let's implement this interface in our test class to display the file name of the current picture, as shown in Listing 2–18.

Listing 2–18 Updated test to include the file name

```
public class PictureTest implements ITest {
  public String getTestName() {
    return "[Picture: " + name + "]";
  }
```

Listing 2–19 shows our output.

Listing 2–19 Output with custom test names

```
PASSED: testWidth ([Picture: a.png])
PASSED: testWidth ([Picture: b.png])
PASSED: testHeight ([Picture: a.png])
PASSED: testHeight ([Picture: b.png])


===============================================
    PictureTest
    Tests run: 4, Failures: 0, Skips: 0
===============================================
```

Data-Driven Testing

Let's start this section with a simple example. The application you are writing is a servlet that will receive requests from mobile devices. Its goal is to look up the user agent of the browser being used and to return the correct HTTP response code, depending on whether you support that browser or not, such as 200 (OK), 301 (Moved Permanently), 404 (Not Found), or a special value, –1, to indicate that the browser is not currently supported.

Initially, only very few browsers are supported, but you know that the list will expand as developers and QA staff validate the application on more browsers.

Listing 2–20 shows our initial test.

Listing 2–20 Test using multiple data values inline

```
@Test
public void verifyUserAgentSupport() {
  assertEquals(200, getReturnCodeFor("MSIE"));
  assertEquals(200, getReturnCodeFor("WAP"));
  assertEquals(301, getReturnCodeFor("OpenWave");
  assertEquals(-1, getReturnCodeFor("Firefox"));
}
```

Not long after your initial test implementation, a coworker tells you she added support for the WebKit browser, so you dutifully update your test by adding the line shown in Listing 2–21.

Listing 2–21 Adding a new data point to the test

```
assertEquals(200, getReturnCodeFor ("WebKit"));
```

You recompile your code, run it, and commit it.

As more and more browsers get supported by various teams throughout the organization, you begin to realize that this process doesn't scale very well, especially considering all the user agent strings and their variations reported by mobile browsers across the world. Not only are developers from different countries adding this support, but they also don't really have access to your integration tests (although, hopefully, they have their own unit tests).

It occurs to you that you could make your life a bit easier by externalizing the data you are testing. Therefore, you create a text file that contains a list of user agent strings and the expected return value, and instead of hardcoding these values in your code, you parse the file. A properties file seems to be the easiest way at the moment.

Listing 2–22 shows the properties file, called `user-agents.properties`.

Listing 2–22 Externalized user agents (`user-agent.properties`)

```
MSIE = 200
WAP = 200
OpenWave = 301
FireFox = -1
```

Listing 2–23 shows the new test.

Listing 2–23 Using the externalized data in our test

```
@Test
public void verifyUserAgentSupport() {
  Properties p = new Properties();
  p.load(new FileInputStream(new File
  ("user-agents.properties")));
  for (Enumeration e = p.propertyNames(); e.hasNext(); ) {
    String userAgent = (String) e.next();
    String returnCode = p.getProperty(userAgent);
    assertEquals(Integer.parseInt(returnCode),
      getReturnCodeFor(userAgent));
  }
}
```

You have made some progress: When a new user agent is supported, you no longer need to recompile your code. All you need to do is update the properties file and the new string will automatically be tested next time you run your tests.

However, the bug report system quickly gets filled with requests from developers to add more and more of these strings, and soon, you realize that this process is not going to scale much further unless you can give the developers an easy way to update the properties file themselves.

Let's pause for a moment and try to understand what is going on here.

While this example is obviously very specific to a particular domain, the testing challenge it represents is actually very common. Here are the main characteristics of this problem.

- The test needs to run through a lot of data that is similarly structured (our example uses simple key/value pairs, but in other situations the data could be any number of values of any types, such as integers, floats, or entire Java objects created from a database).
- The actual testing logic is the same; it's just the data that changes.
- The data can be modified by a number of different people.

This kind of testing problem is usually nicely solved by a practice known as Data-Driven Testing because, as opposed to what we have seen so far, the important part of what is being tested is not the Java logic but the data on which this code operates.

TestNG supports Data-Driven Testing natively, and this is what we will be looking at in this section. But before we go further, let's make a quick detour to discuss test method parameters.

Parameters and Test Methods

Traditional Java testing frameworks are fairly stringent in the way they define a test method.

- It needs to be public.
- It needs to be void.
- It can't have any parameters.

While we understand the first two requirements, the latter is something that has always deeply puzzled us. Passing parameters to methods is extremely natural and has been around pretty much ever since programming languages were invented, and we very often find ourselves needing to pass parameters to tests methods.

Since JUnit 3 does not support passing parameters, for example, various design patterns have emerged to work around this limitation, the most common one being the Parameterized Test Case.

In order to simulate parameter passing with JUnit 3, your test class needs to have a constructor that takes the same parameters as your test method. Then the Parameterized Test Case pattern does the following.

- The constructor stores these parameters in various fields.
- When the test method is invoked, it uses the values in those fields as parameters.

Another added complexity to this approach is that since you need to invoke a specific constructor with the right values, you need to create the test class yourself, as opposed to letting JUnit instantiate it for you.

Listing 2–24 shows a JUnit 3 version of our data-driven test that users the Parameterized Test Case pattern.

Listing 2–24 JUnit 3 data-driven test

```
public class UserAgentTest extends TestCase {
  private int responseCode;
  private String userAgent;

  public UserAgentTest(String userAgent, int responseCode) {
    super("testUserAgent");
    this.userAgent = userAgent;
    this.responseCode = responseCode;
  }

  public static Test suite() {
    TestSuite result = new TestSuite();
    result.addTest(new UserAgentTest("MSIE", 200));
    result.addTest(new UserAgentTest("WAP", 200));
    return result;
  }

  public void testUserAgent() {
    assertEquals(responseCode, getReturnCodeFor(userAgent));
  }
}
```

There are a few problems with this approach.

- Its intent is not clear. The example is fairly convoluted, it uses a lot of JUnit-specific syntactic sugar, and it's not exactly easy to extract from this listing the fact that this is actually a test case driven by some external data.

- You need to create one instance of your test class per set of parameters. This can very quickly become prohibitive, especially when you need to combine the parameters in various ways: Test three parameters that can each receive four values, and you suddenly find yourself with twelve instances of the test.

- This example won't scale to large numbers of parameter combinations. Since all the instances are created before the test starts, it's possible to run out of memory before you even begin.

- There is no logical isolation between tests. Since each test has access to all the fields of your class, it's not obvious which methods will use which values.[2] The advantage of method parameters is that they are very clearly scoped to the current method and to that method only.

- Your class will become very messy if various test methods need to use different parameters. Imagine a test class with ten methods, each of which accepts two parameters that are different from the other methods. This leads to a class containing twenty fields, a constructor that receives that many parameters, and, again, no clear understanding of which field is being used in which method.

Ideally, you want your testing framework to support the simplest way to pass parameters to your test methods, and that's exactly what TestNG does.

TestNG lets you pass parameters directly to your test methods in two different ways:

- With `testng.xml`
- With Data Providers

The next sections explore these two approaches and then discuss their respective pros and cons.

Passing Parameters with `testng.xml`

This technique lets us define simple parameters in the `testng.xml` file and then reference those parameters in source files.

First, we define one or more parameters by providing their names and values, as shown in Listing 2–25.

---

2. Note that JUnit enforces physical isolation by reinstantiating your test class for each invocation, but the point here is to underline the lack of logical isolation: When you read the code, you just can't tell right away which fields are being used in which test method.

Listing 2–25 Defining suite-level parameters

```
<suite name="Parameters" >
<parameter name="xml-file" value="accounts.xml" />
<parameter name="hostname" value="arkonis.example.com" />
```

Note that we can also declare parameters at the `<test>` level, as shown in Listing 2–26.

Listing 2–26 Defining test-level parameters

```
<test name="ParameterTest" >
  <parameter name="hostname" value="terra.example.com" />
  ...
</test>
```

The regular scoping rules apply, meaning that if we merge the two snippets from these listings into one file, the two parameters named `xml-file` and `hostname` are declared at the suite level, but `hostname` is overridden in the `<test>` named `ParameterTest`, which means that any class inside this tag will see the value `terra.example.com`, while the classes in the rest of the `testng.xml` file will see `arkonis.example.com`.

We can now reference these parameters in our test, as shown in Listing 2–27.

Listing 2–27 Specifying parameters in the test method

```
@Test(parameters = { "xml-file"})
public void validateFile(String xmlFile) {
  // xmlFile has the value "accounts.xml"
}
```

TestNG will try to find a parameter named `xml-file` first in the `<test>` tag that contains the current class, and then, if it can't find it, in the `<suite>` tag that encloses it.

Of course, we can use as many parameters as needed, as shown in Listing 2–28.

Listing 2–28 Multiple parameters in a test method

```
@Test
@Parameters({ "hostname", "xml-file"})
public void fileShouldExistOnFtpServer(String hostName,
 String xmlFile)
{
  // xmlFile has the value "xml-file" and
  // hostname is "terra.example.com"
}
```

TestNG will automatically try to convert the value specified in `testng.xml` to the type of your parameter. Here are the types supported:

- `String`
- `int`/`Integer`
- `boolean`/`Boolean`
- `byte`/`Byte`
- `char`/`Character`
- `double`/`Double`
- `float`/`Float`
- `long`/`Long`
- `short`/`Short`

TestNG will throw an exception if we make one of the following mistakes:

- Specifying a parameter value in `testng.xml` that cannot be converted to the type of the corresponding method parameter (e.g., making the `xmlFile` parameter an `Integer`)
- Declaring an `@Parameters` annotation referencing a parameter name that is not declared in `testng.xml`

While this approach has the merit of being simple and explicit (the values are clearly shown in the `testng.xml` file), it also suffers from a few limitations, which we discuss below. If we need to pass parameters to test methods that are not basic Java types or if the values we need can be created only at runtime, we should instead consider using the `@DataProvider` annotation.

Passing Parameters with `@DataProvider`

A Data Provider is a method annotated with `@DataProvider`. This annotation has only one string attribute: its name. If the name is not supplied, the Data Provider's name automatically defaults to the method's name.

A Data Provider returns Java objects that will be passed as parameters to an `@Test` method. The name of the Data Provider to receive parameters from is specified in the `dataProvider` attribute of the `@Test` annotation.

Fundamentally, a Data Provider serves two simultaneous purposes:

1. To pass an arbitrary number of parameters (of any Java type) to a test method
2. To allow its test method to be invoked as many times as it needs with different sets of parameters

Let's consider a simple example to clarify these ideas. Suppose we are trying to test the following method, as shown in Listing 2–29.

Listing 2–29 Example method for Data-Driven Testing

```
/**
 * @return true if n is greater than or equal to lower and less
 * than or equal to upper.
 */
  public boolean isBetween(int n, int lower, int upper)
```

We can quickly come up with a few test cases that will test the basic functionality of this method: when n is less than both `lower` and `upper`, when it's between `lower` and `upper`, and when it's greater than both `upper` and `lower`. Let's throw in a couple of extra cases to make sure we cover the entire contract described in the Javadocs by also testing cases where n is exactly equal to `lower` and then `upper`.

As you can see, in order to test this contract thoroughly, we have to introduce two dimensions: one in the number of tests (we have five so far) and one in the number of parameters passed to the method at each attempt (our method takes three parameters).

With this in mind, a Data Provider returns a double array of objects, which represent exactly these two dimensions.

Listing 2–30 shows a Data Provider test of this method.

Listing 2–30 Data-driven test with a Data Provider

```
@Test(dataProvider = "range-provider")
public void testIsBetween(int n, int lower,
   int upper, boolean expected)
{
   println("Received " + n + " " + lower + "-"
         + upper + " expected: " + expected);
   Assert.assertEquals(expected, isBetween(n, lower, upper));
}

@DataProvider(name = "range-provider")
public Object[][] rangeData() {
   int lower = 5;
   int upper = 10;
   return new Object[][] {
       { lower-1, lower, upper, false },
       { lower,   lower, upper, true },
       { lower+1, lower, upper, true },
       { upper,   lower, upper, true},
       { upper+1, lower, upper, false },
   };
}
```

The first thing to notice is that our @Test annotation is now using the attribute dataProvider, which it assigns to the Data Provider name range-provider. Our test function expects the three parameters it will pass to the method under test and a fourth parameter, the Boolean expected in return.

The Data Provider is called range-provider and it returns a double array of objects. The formatting of this source code should help us understand how these values will be used: Each line corresponds to exactly one invocation of the test method with the parameters as they are enumerated: n, lower, upper, and the expected Boolean result.

The logic of each of these lines respects exactly the use cases described earlier. The first and last set of parameters exercise the case where n is outside the range (hence the expected Boolean result of false), while the three middle sets of parameters cover the case where n is equal to the lower bound, is between the lower and upper bounds, and is equal to the upper bound.

Listing 2–31 shows the output of this run.

Listing 2–31 Data-driven test output

```
Received 4 5-10 expected: false
Received 5 5-10 expected: true
Received 6 5-10 expected: true
Received 10 5-10 expected: true
Received 11 5-10 expected: false
=================================================
Parameter Suite
Total tests run: 5, Failures: 0, Skips: 0
=================================================
```

Here are two observations about this example.

- The `name` attribute of `@DataProvider` is optional. If you don't specify it, the name of the method will be used. In general, we discourage using this facility because our tests might break if we rename the Data Provider method, since its name is also referenced in the `@Test` annotation that, unless we have special TestNG support, will not be modified by the refactoring.

- The test method relies only on the two constants `lower` and `upper`, declared at the beginning of the code. Of course, it would have been possible to use the constants inline, but it would be poor practice. Not only would we be repeating the same values over and over, but the logical intention of the test wouldn't be as obvious. By expressing all the use cases in terms of `lower` and `upper`, we convey our intention better ("in the first line, n is equal to `lower-1`, which guarantees that it will be outside the range").

Now that we've covered the basics of how Data Providers work, let's take a closer look at the consequences for our tests.

First of all, since the Data Provider is a method in our test class, it can belong to a superclass and therefore be reused by several test methods. We can also have several Data Providers (with different names), as long as they are defined either on the test class or on one of its subclasses. This can come in very handy when we want to capture the data source in one convenient place and reuse it in several test methods.

More importantly, we can now specify the parameters of our methods with Java code, and this opens up a lot of possibilities.

Of course, our example in this section is not a clear improvement over the `testng.xml` approach, but that's because we hardcoded the values in our code. It doesn't have to be so. For example, we could modify our Data Provider to retrieve its data from a text file, a Microsoft Excel spreadsheet, or even a database. The following section examines these various possibilities with their pros and cons, so we'll just focus here on the important benefit of Data Providers: They abstract your test code from the data that drives them. Once you have externalized your test data appropriately, this data can be modified without any change to your Java code (as long as the test methods don't need to change, of course).

The example that started this section is actually a good example of a situation where the test logic can be fairly simple or very unlikely to change, while the data that is fed to it is guaranteed to grow a lot over time.

Parameters for Data Providers

Data Providers themselves can receive two types of parameters: `Method` and `ITestContext`.

TestNG sets these two parameters before invoking your Data Provider, and they allow you to have some context in your code before deciding what to do. We can specify any combination of these parameters depending on what we need. Therefore, any of the four signatures shown in Listing 2–32 are valid.

Listing 2–32 Data Provider method parameters

```
@DataProvider
public void create() { ... }
@DataProvider
public void create(Method method) { ... }
@DataProvider
public void create(ITestContext context) { ... }
@DataProvider
public void create(Method method, ITestContext context) { ... }
```

We'll examine these parameters in the next two sections.

The `Method` Parameter

If the first parameter in a Data Provider is a `java.lang.reflect.Method`, TestNG will pass the test method that is about to be invoked. This is particularly useful if the data that you want to return from your Data Provider needs to be different depending on the test method that you are about to feed.

Listing 2–33 shows an example.

Listing 2–33 Example of a method-specific Data Provider

```
@DataProvider
public Object[][] provideNumbers(Method method) {
  Object[][] result = null;

  if (method.getName().equals("two")) {
    result = new Object[][] { new Object[] { 2 }};
  }
  else if (method.getName().equals("three")) {
    result = new Object[][] { new Object[] { 3 }};
  }

  return result;
}

@Test(dataProvider = "provideNumbers")
public void two(int param) {
  System.out.println("Two received: "  + param);
}

@Test(dataProvider = "provideNumbers")
public void three(int param) {
  System.out.println("Three received: "  + param);
}
```

This Data Provider will return the integer 2 if the method about to be invoked is called `two` and it will return 3 for `three`. Therefore, we get the output shown in Listing 2–34.

Listing 2–34 Test output for the method-specific Data Provider

```
Two received: 2
Three received: 3
PASSED: two(2)
PASSED: three(3)
```

Note that the output in the console shows the value of the parameters passed to each method. The HTML reports also contain these values, which makes it very easy to find out what went wrong in case test methods with parameters fail. (Reports are covered later in this chapter.)

Obviously, this particular example would probably be easier to read if instead of using the same Data Provider these two methods used a different one that doesn't need to use the reflection API to do its job. However, there are certain cases where using the same Data Provider is useful.

- The code that the Data Providers would use is fairly complex and should be kept in one convenient place. (We can also consider extracting this complex code in a separate method, but since we are talking about returning arrays of arrays of objects, this refactoring sometimes leads to the creation of extra objects.)
- The test methods we are passing data to take a lot of parameters, and only very few of these parameters differ.
- We are introducing a special case for a particular method. For example, this particular test method might be broken at the moment or too slow (we'd like to pass smaller values to it), or it doesn't implement all its functionalities yet.

Keep this functionality in mind in case you ever find yourself in need of providing different data depending on which test method will receive it.

The `ITestContext` Parameter

If a Data Provider declares a parameter of type `ITestContext` in its signature, TestNG will set it to the test context that is currently active, which makes it possible to know what runtime parameters the current test run was invoked with.

For example, Listing 2–35 shows a Data Provider that returns an array of two random integers if the group being run is `unit-test` and ten if it's `functional-test`.

Listing 2–35 *ITestContext*-aware Data Provider

```
@DataProvider
public Object[][] randomIntegers(ITestContext context) {
  String[] groups = context.getIncludedGroups();
  // If we are including the group "functional-test",
```

```
    // set the size to 10, otherwise, 2
    int size = 2;   // default
    for (String group : groups) {
      if (group.equals("functional-test")) {
        size = 10;
        break;
      }
    }

    // Return an array of "size" random integers
    Object[][] result = new Object[size][];
    Random r = new Random();
    for (int i = 0; i < size; i++) {
      result[i] = new Object[] { new Integer(r.nextInt()) };
    }

    return result;
}

@Test(dataProvider = "randomIntegers",
      groups = {"unit-test", "functional-test" })
public void random(Integer n) {
  // will be invoked twice if we include the group
  // "unit-test" and ten times if we include the
  // group "functional-test"
}
```

Listing 2–36 contains the output when we run the group unit-test.

Listing 2–36 Output for the *unit-test* group of the *ITestContext*-aware Data Provider

```
PASSED: random(1292625632)
PASSED: random(2013205310)


================================================
Main suite
Total tests run: 2, Failures: 0, Skips: 0
================================================
```

Listing 2–37 shows the output of running the group functional-test.

Listing 2–37 Output for the *functional-test* group of the *ITestContext*-aware Data Provider

```
PASSED:  random(806744230)
PASSED:  random(-200527178)
PASSED:  random(898848896)
PASSED:  random(-1653971163)
PASSED:  random(-830139397)
PASSED:  random(1900153938)
PASSED:  random(-662821003)
PASSED:  random(94678969)
PASSED:  random(803437657)
PASSED:  random(882366204)


===================================================
Main suite
Total tests run: 10, Failures: 0, Skips: 0
===================================================
```

Notice that the console displays the parameter used for each invocation (the HTML reports will also show them). Also, keep in mind that the data returned by the ITestContext object is the runtime information, not the static one: The test method we are running belongs to both groups unit-test and functional-test (this is the static information), but at runtime, we decided to include only functional-test, which is the value that gets returned by ITestContext#getIncludedGroups.

Lazy Data Providers

Consider the following scenario. We need to run a test on all the customer accounts handled by each employee of the company. We start by writing a Data Provider that looks like Listing 2–38.

Listing 2–38 Data Provider for all the accounts handled by all the employees

```java
@DataProvider(name = "generate-accounts")
public Object[][] generateAccounts() {
  List<Account> allAccounts = new ArrayList<Account>();
  for (Employee e : getAllEmployees()) {
    for (Account a : e.getAccounts()) {
      allAccounts.add(a);
    }
  }
```

```
Object[][] result = new Object[allAccounts.size()][];
for (int i = 0; i < result.length; i++) {
  result[i] = new Object[] { allAccounts.get(i) };
}
return result;
}


@Test(dataProvider = "generate-accounts")
public void testAccount(Account a) {
  out.println("Testing account " + a);
}
```

This code enumerates all the employees and then retrieves all the accounts handled by each employee. Finally, the list of accounts is turned into a double array of objects, so that the test method will be passed each account, one by one.

We run the test and, surprise: TestNG fails with an `OutOfMemoryException`.

We take a quick look at the tables in the database and realize that there are more than 100,000 employees in our company and that each employee manages anywhere between 10 and 100 customer accounts. Therefore, the list of all accounts contains about 10 million objects, each of these several bytes in size. In short, our Data Provider is taking up about 100MB of memory, and that's before we even invoke the first test method. No wonder it ran out of memory!

Obviously, this situation is not optimal, but there's a simple way to solve it: As soon as we create an `Account` object, we run the test method on it and then discard the object before testing the next one.

This principle is called lazy initialization, and it's used in many areas in software engineering.[3] The idea is simply that you should create an object only right before you really need, and not sooner.

In order to make that possible, TestNG allows us to return an `Iterator` from the Data Provider instead of an array of arrays of objects.

`Iterator` is an interface from the package `java.util` that has the signature shown in Listing 2–39.

---

3. Here are two examples: (1) object-relational frameworks such as EJB3 or Hibernate (Java objects that represent rows in the database are initially empty and go to the database only when one of the values they contain is actually used) and (2) sophisticated user interfaces such as Eclipse (the plug-ins and graphic objects get created only once the user clicks on them in order to minimize start-up time).

Listing 2–39 *java.util.Iterator* interface

```
public interface Iterator {
  public boolean hasNext();
  public Object next();
  public void remove();
}
```

The difference with the array is that whenever TestNG needs to get the next set of parameters from the Data Provider, it will invoke the `next()` method of the `Iterator`, thereby giving us a chance to instantiate the correct object at the last minute, just before the test method gets invoked with the parameters returned.

Here is how we can rewrite (and slightly modify, for clarification purposes) our example. In the code shown in Listing 2–40, we implement two Data Providers (a regular one and a lazy one). We also implement an `Iterator` that will return four `Account` objects with different IDs.

Listing 2–40 Test with a lazy-init Data Provider

```
@DataProvider(name = "generate-accounts")
public Object[][] generateAccounts() {
  int n = 0;
  return new Object[][] {
    new Object[] { new Account(n++) },
    new Object[] { new Account(n++) },
    new Object[] { new Account(n++) },
    new Object[] { new Account(n++) },
  };
}

@DataProvider(name="generate-accounts-lazy")
public Iterator generateAccountsLazy() {
  return new AccountIterator();
}

@Test(dataProvider = "generate-accounts-lazy")
public void testAccount(Account a) {
  out.println("Testing account " + a);
}
```

```
class AccountIterator implements Iterator {
  static private final int MAX = 4;
  private int index = 0;

  public boolean hasNext() {
    return index < MAX;
  }

  public Object next() {
    return new Object[] { new Account(index++)};
  }

  public void remove() {
    throw new UnsupportedOperationException();// N/A
  }
}
```

Finally, we added a trace in the constructor of `Account` and in the test method in order to keep track of who gets called and when. Let's look at the output of two runs of this test, first with the regular Data Provider (Listing 2–41):

Listing 2–41 Output with upfront initialization of accounts

```
Creating account
Creating account
Creating account
Creating account
Testing account [Account:0]
Testing account [Account:1]
Testing account [Account:2]
Testing account [Account:3]
```

and then with the lazy Data Provider (Listing 2–42):

Listing 2–42 Output with lazy account creation

```
Creating account
Testing account [Account:0]
Creating account
```

```
Testing account [Account:1]
Creating account
Testing account [Account:2]
Creating account
Testing account [Account:3]
```

As you can see, the iterator-based Data Provider allows us to create the objects only when they are needed, which will solve the memory problem we encountered.

When using lazy Data Providers, the main challenge we will encounter will most likely be to write an iterator class that fits our purpose. Our example here is not very realistic, so before we move on to the next section, let's write an iterator that will provide a lazy initialization solution to the `Account` creation problem.

In order to get a list of all the `Account` objects needed for the test, the code needs to enumerate all the employees first and then retrieve all the accounts that each employee manages. Therefore, we need our iterator to keep track of the current employee being scanned along with the next account that we need to return. The iterator can look like Listing 2–43.

Listing 2–43 Example of a lazy-load account iterator

```java
public class AccountIterator2 implements Iterator {
  private int m_employeeIndex = 0;
  private int m_accountIndex = 0;

  public boolean hasNext() {
    boolean result = false;
    List<Employee> employees = Employees.getEmployees();
    if (m_employeeIndex < employees.size()) {
      Employee e = employees.get(m_employeeIndex);
      if (m_accountIndex < e.getAccounts().size()) {
        result = true;
      }
    }

    return result;
  }

  public Object next() {
    List<Account> accounts =
      Employees.getEmployees().get(m_employeeIndex).getAccounts();
```

```
    Account result = accounts.get(m_accountIndex);
    m_accountIndex++;
    if (m_accountIndex >= accounts.size()) {
      m_employeeIndex++;
      m_accountIndex = 0;
    }

    return result;
  }

  public void remove() {
    throw new UnsupportedOperationException();// N/A
  }
}
```

The `hasNext()` function returns `true` unless we are currently on the last account of the last employee.

The `next()` method returns the account that corresponds to the current employee and index account and then increments the account index. If we are past the number of accounts of the current employee, then we reset the account number and move on to the next employee.

Notice how lightweight this iterator is: It maintains only two integers and nothing more. Of course, this saving comes at some speed expense, since we find ourselves having to do repeated lookups into the list of employees and accounts. The first version of the example we showed at the beginning of this section was very fast and used a lot of memory, and the iterator version lies at the other end of the spectrum: It uses very little memory but will run slower. Eventually, you will want to measure how your tests perform and possibly find a middle ground (e.g., the `Iterator` could store the current employee being scanned, which costs only a few more bytes and will reduce the number of lookups needed).

We've covered a lot of techniques to implement Data-Driven Testing in this section, so now it's time to step back and compare all these approaches, so that when confronted with this kind of problem, it is easy (easier, at any rate!) to make the right choice and implement it correctly.

Pros and Cons of Both Approaches

We just covered TestNG's ability to pass parameters with two different techniques. In order to help you decide which one you should choose, Table 2–1 gives a list of pros and cons for each approach.

Table 2–1 Comparison between the two approaches to pass parameters to your methods

	Pros	Cons
`testng.xml`	Values are specified in `testng.xml`, which is easy to modify and doesn't require any recompilation. The values are passed to test methods automatically by TestNG (no need to marshal them).	You need a `testng.xml` file. The values cannot be computed dynamically. Values in `testng.xml` can represent only basic types (strings, integers, floats, etc.) and not complex Java objects.
Data Provider	Any valid Java type can be passed to test methods. This approach is extremely flexible: The values can be computed dynamically and fetched from any kind of storage accessible by Java code.	This approach requires implementing some logic to return the correct objects.

In summary, the `testng.xml` approach is good enough when the parameters we are passing are simple and constant, such as a string, a host name, or a JDBC driver name. As soon as we need more flexibility and know that the number of parameters and values will increase with time, we should probably opt for `@DataProvider` instead.

Supplying the Data

There are several different ways a Data Provider can supply data to test methods. Table 2–2 shows some ideas, along with their pros and cons.

Note that storing data on a network is not mutually exclusive from the other storage means. For the test writer, the data is coming through one unified location represented by a network endpoint. After that, it's very easy for the originators of the test data to implement whatever storage strategy seems fit: They could start with a simple text file and then, as the data sample grows, move to a database without any impact for the data consumers. Of course, this could also become a liability since changes in the feed could then be performed by remote users, which could lead to test results that vary for reasons that might not be easy to pinpoint.

Table 2–2 Various ways to fetch data to pass to your tests

Location of the data	Pros	Cons
Hardcoded in the Java source	Is easy for the developer to update and parse.	Forces a recompilation for each data change. Is hard for anyone else besides the developer (or even, sometimes, developers outside the team) to modify these values.
In a text file (e.g., comma-separated values)	Is relatively easy for the developer to parse, although it depends on the format used. Doesn't require a recompilation. (All the following items have this nice property, which we will therefore not repeat.)	Is error prone. Since the text file can be modified with any text editor, someone entering new values could easily break the format by accident. Requires the file to be shared among its users. (All the subsequent items except for the database location suffer from this limitation, which we will therefore not repeat.) Several techniques can be used to achieve this goal (e.g., using a shared network file system, or submitting the file to your source control system), but in general, sharing a file among several users presents several risks that can lead to loss of data.
In a properties file	Is easy to turn the data into a `Properties` object for the developer.	Is limited in its structure: You can only represent key/value pairs. Does not use ordering.
In a Microsoft Excel spreadsheet	Is easy for developers to parse (although they will need to use an external library). Is easier for nondevelopers to manipulate. Is easier to make sure the data entered is correct (it can be validated by Excel with macros or similar functionalities).	Requires the presence of Excel on the computer to be readable since this is a proprietary binary format. (You can alleviate this problem by saving a companion `.csv` file, at the cost of losing some Excel-specific metadata.)

(continued)

Table 2–2 Various ways to fetch data to pass to your tests *(continued)*

Location of the data	Pros	Cons
In a database	Is highly structured and flexible. Any kind of data can be stored and retrieved with complex SQL queries. SQL and JDBC are natively supported in the JDK and extremely well documented everywhere. Allows the database to be made accessible anywhere on the network.	Requires more complex parsing logic on the developer side (a burden that can be alleviated by using one of the many database-binding Java frameworks available, such as Hibernate). Requires a front end (such as a Web page) when entering new data in the database, especially if nondevelopers will enter the data. Needs extra overhead for tests, requiring a database populated with data in order to run.
On the network	Abstracts how the data is really stored (it could come from a machine next door or from a data center halfway across the country). Can use a wide range of network protocols (straight TCP/IP, JMS, Web services, etc.).	Requires more complex programming logic, as well as extra setup and configuration.

Data Provider or Factory?

In the previous sections, we studied factories, which are methods that return instances of test classes. You might have noticed some similarity between Data Providers and factories: Data Providers let you pass parameters to test methods, while factories allow you to pass parameters to constructors.

Obviously, whenever a Data Provider can be used, a factory can be used just as well, and vice versa, so when should you choose one over the other?

If you're not sure which one to pick, it is worth looking at the parameters used in the test methods. Do several test methods need to receive the same parameters? If so, you're probably better off saving these parameters in a field and then reusing that field in your methods, which means a factory is probably a better choice. On the other hand, if all the test methods need to get passed different parameters, a Data Provider is the better option.

Of course, nothing stops you from using both in a class, and it's really up to you to decide when it's acceptable to put a parameter in a class field and when you'd rather store no state at all in your test class and pass the same parameters repeatedly to test methods. Ultimately, while there are some guidelines, the final answer is far more dependent on the specific case or test than on an arbitrary set of rules.

Tying It All Together

Let's conclude this section with a full example. This code was shared on the TestNG user mailing list by Jacob Robertson. It's a Data Provider that returns data provided in files containing comma-separated values (whose file names end in `.csv`). The interesting thing about this example is that each test method receives its own file, based on its name.

For example, the test method `com.example#db(String v1, String v2)` will receive its values from the file `com/example/db.csv`, which contains a series of lines, each made of two string values separated by a comma. This format is very flexible since each method can have its own signature as long as its corresponding `.csv` file contains the correct number of parameters (and these parameters can be converted to the correct Java type).

Table 2–3 shows how methods get mapped to their respective `.csv` files (assuming that all the methods are in the package `com.example`).

We start with two static factory methods that create the `Iterator` object that TestNG expects, as shown in Listing 2–44.

Table 2–3 Examples of how a method maps to a `.csv` file

Test method	Name of the file	Content
`name(String s1, String s2)`	`com/example/db.csv`	Cedric,Beust Hani,Suleiman
`extract(String s, int n1, int n2)`	`com/example/extract.csv`	A string, 2, 4 Another string, 3, 5

Listing 2–44 Test-specific lazy-load Data Providers

```
/**
 * The main TestNG Data Provider.
 * @param method the method TestNG passes to you
 */
@DataProvider(name = "CsvDataProvider")
public static Iterator getDataProvider(Method method)
  throws IOException
{
  return getDataProvider(method.getDeclaringClass(),
    method);
}


/**
 * Call this directly when necessary, to avoid issues
 * with the method's declaring class not being the test class.
 * @param cls The actual test class - matters for
 * the CsvFileName and the class loader
 */
public static Iterator getDataProvider(Class cls, Method method)
    throws IOException
{
  String className = cls.getName();
  String dirPlusPrefix = className.replace('.', '/');
  String fileName = method.getName() + ".csv";
  String filePath = dirPlusPrefix + "." + fileName;

  return new CsvDataProviderIterator(cls, method, filePath);
}
```

These methods use the test `Method` object to access the test class, and from there, calculate the path where the `.csv` file will be found.

Next is the constructor of the `Iterator`, which effectively parses the `.csv` file and sets up type converters in order to convert the values found in the file into the correct Java type. We show this constructor in Listing 2–45.

Listing 2–45 Implementation of the lazy-load `.csv` file loader iterator

```
/**
 * Basic constructor that will provide the data from
 * the given file for the given method
```

```
   * @throws IOException when file io fails
   */
public CsvDataProviderIterator(Class cls, Method method,
  String csvFilePath)
    throws IOException
{
  InputStream is = cls.getClassLoader().
    getResourceAsStream(csvFilePath);
  InputStreamReader isr = new InputStreamReader(is);
  reader = new CSVReader(isr);
  parameterTypes = method.getParameterTypes();
  int len = parameterTypes.length;
  parameterConverters = new Converter[len];
  for (int i = 0; i < len; i++) {
    parameterConverters[i] =
  ConvertUtils.lookup(parameterTypes[i]);
  }
}
```

Finally, we implement the `Iterator` interface and add a few helper methods for clarity in Listing 2–46.

Listing 2–46 Implementation of the rest of the `Iterator` interface

```
// The latest row we returned
private String[] last;

public boolean hasNext() {
  last = reader.readNext();
  return last != null;
}

/**
 * Get the next line, or the current line if it's already there.
 * @return the line.
 */
private String[] getNextLine() {
  if (last == null) {
    try {
      last = reader.readNext();
    }
    catch (IOException ioe) {
      throw new RuntimeException(ioe);
```

```
      }
    }
    return last;
  }

  /**
   * @return the Object[] representation of the next line
   */
  public Object next() {
    String[] next;
    if (last != null) {
      next = last;
    }
    else {
      next = getNextLine();
    }
    last = null;
    Object[] args = parseLine(next);
    return args;
  }

  /**
   * @return the correctly parsed and wrapped values
   * @todo need a standard third-party CSV parser plugged in here
   */
  private Object[] parseLine(String[] svals) {
    int len = svals.length;
    Object[] result = new Object[len];
    for (int i = 0; i < len; i++) {
      result[i] =
    parameterConverters[i].convert(parameterTypes[i], svals[i]);
    }
    return result;
  }
```

The next() method reads the next line from the file, converts each value into the correct Java type, and returns an array of the values calculated. Note that we omitted a few details from this code (such as the remove() method, which does nothing, and the classes CvsReader and ConvertUtils, which can be easily inferred).

This Iterator is a great example of how we can combine the features offered by TestNG's support for Data-Driven Testing. We demonstrated these features:

- The `@DataProvider` annotation
- A Data Provider returning an `Iterator` for lazy-loading purposes
- The use of a `Method` parameter to return different values based on the test method that's about to be invoked

Asynchronous Testing

In this section, we are reviewing an aspect of networked applications that has typically been harder to test: asynchronous code.

Asynchronous code is usually found in the following areas.

- A message-based framework (such as JMS), where senders and receivers are decoupled (they don't know about each other) and in which you post messages to a central hub that is in charge of dispatching them to the correct recipients.
- Asynchronous facilities offered by `java.util.concurrent` (such as `FutureTask`).
- A graphical user interface developed with a toolkit such as SWT or Swing, where the code runs in a different thread from the main graphical one. In order to achieve this, you need to post your request to a particular thread (e.g., `invokeLater()` in Swing). There are no guarantees that the request will be executed immediately; all you know is that it has been scheduled for execution.

What makes asynchronous code more problematic to test than synchronous code can be boiled down to two characteristics.

1. It is impossible to determine when an asynchronous call will be executed.
2. It is impossible to determine whether an asynchronous call will complete.

This is clearly different from what we are used to. In Java (and most programming languages), when a method is invoked, we know it will be invoked right away, and we are pretty much guaranteed that it will either return right away or throw an exception. Therefore, testing for the correct or incorrect completion of this call is trivial. When the call is asynchronous, there are three possible outcomes.

1. The call completed and succeeded.
2. The call completed and failed.
3. The call didn't complete.

On top of that, we will have to make these verifications at some time in the future, not when the call is made.

Essentially, asynchronous coding follows a very simple pattern: A request is issued specifying an object or a function (callback) that will be invoked by the system once the response has been received, and that's about it. Once the request has executed and the result is received, the callback object will receive its notification, and we can retrieve the result to continue our work.

Since asynchronous coding is so consistent in the way it's performed, it's not surprising to see that testing synchronous code is similarly very simple and follows this pattern.

- Issue the asynchronous call, which will return right away. If possible, specify a callback method.
- If you have a callback method:
  - Wait for the answer and set a Boolean when it arrives to reflect whether the response is what you expected.
  - In the test method, watch the Boolean variable and exit when its value is set or when a certain amount of time has elapsed (whichever comes first).
- If you don't have a callback method:
  - In the test method, regularly check for the expected value (avoid doing busy waiting, which we'll discuss soon) and abort with a failure if that value hasn't arrived after a certain time.

The availability of a callback method typically depends on how modern your code is. With JDK 1.4 and older, the support for asynchronous tests was rudimentary (or required the assistance of external libraries), so the typical idiom was to spawn a thread. The introduction of `java.util.concurrent` in JDK 5.0 allowed for more powerful asynchronous patterns that allow us to specify return values (also called "futures"), therefore making it easier for us to retrieve the results of asynchronous calls.

We'll examine these two approaches in the following snippets of code, starting with the simpler case where we can't specify a callback (we omitted a few `throws/catch` clauses to make the code clearer). The first approach is shown in Listing 2–47.

Listing 2–47 Test for asynchronous code

```
private volatile boolean success = false;

@BeforeClass
public void sendMessage() {
// send the message
// Successful completion should eventually set success to true
}

@Test(timeOut = 10000)
public void waitForAnswer() {
  while (! success) {
    Thread.sleep(1000);
  }
}
```

In this test, the message is sent as part of the initialization of the test with `@BeforeClass`, guaranteeing that this code will be executed before the test methods are invoked (and only once, since this is an `@BeforeClass` annotation).

After the initialization, TestNG will invoke the `waitForAnswer()` test method, which will be doing some partially busy waiting. (This is just for clarity: Messaging systems typically provide better ways to wait for the reception of a message.) The loop will exit as soon as the callback has received the right message, but in order not to block TestNG forever, we specify a timeout in the `@Test` annotation.

In a real-world example, we would probably not need the `sleep()` call, and if we did, we could replace it with a `wait()`/`notify()` pair (or a `CountdownLatch` if we were using JDK 5), which would at least give us a chance of returning before the first second had elapsed.

This code is not very different if the asynchronous system we are using lets us specify a callback (and ideally, a return value). Still, if we don't have an explicit return value, we can check for whatever condition would mean that the call succeeded and, similarly to what was suggested above, signal the blocked test for success or failure.

This code can be adapted to more sophisticated needs. For example, if the send of the message can also fail and we want to test that as well, we should turn `sendMessage()` into an `@Test` method, and in order to guarantee that it will be called before `waitForAnswer()`, simply have `waitForAnswer()` depend on `sendMessage()`. This is shown in Listing 2–48.

Listing 2–48 Revised test to handle timeouts

```
@Test(groups = "send")
public void sendMessage() {
  // send the message
}

@Test(timeOut = 10000, dependsOnGroups = { "send" })
public void waitForAnswer() {
  while (! success) {
    Thread.sleep(1000);
  }
}
```

The difference with this code is that now that `sendMessage()` is an `@Test` method, it will be included in the final report. Also, if sending the message fails, TestNG will skip the `waitForAnswer()` test method and will flag it as a SKIP, which is useful data when you check the reports of your tests.

It is not uncommon for messaging systems to be unreliable (or more precisely, "as reliable as the underlying medium"), so our business logic should take into account the potential loss of packets. To achieve this, we can use the partial failure feature of TestNG, as shown in Listing 2–49.

Listing 2–49 Specifying partial failure

```
@Test(timeOut = 10000, invocationCount = 1000,
  successPercentage = 98)
public void waitForAnswer() {
  while (! success) {
    Thread.sleep(1000);
  }
}
```

This annotation attribute instructs TestNG to invoke this method a thousand times, but to consider the overall test passed even if only 98% of the invocations succeed (of course, in order for this test to work, we should invoke `sendMessage()` a thousand times as well).

Finally, one last piece of advice: Run asynchronous tests in multiple threads. From the samples in this section, you know that you should be using a timeout in test methods since it's the only way you can tell whether an asynchronous call is not returning. Because of this, an asynchronous test method can potentially take seconds before it completes, and running a lot of tests this way in a single thread can make tests take a very long time. If TestNG is configured to run tests in several threads, we are guaranteed to speed up test times significantly. Multithreaded testing is covered in the next section.

Testing Multithreaded Code

> "By 2009, game developers will face CPUs with 20+ cores, 80+ hardware threads, greater than 1 TFLOP of computing power and GPUs with general computing capabilities."
>
> —Tim Sweeney, in a 2005 keynote speech
> about the future of video game engines[4]

Tim Sweeney is not the only one predicting a vertiginous rise in parallel processing in the next few years. For the past thirty years, Moore's Law has correctly predicted that the number of transistors on an integrated circuit would double every 18 months, and as a consequence, we have been able to enjoy predictable and free upgrades on a regular basis. We didn't need to worry about speed too much since, soon enough, computers would become fast enough to hide the performance flaws of the code we wrote.

The problem is that we have recently started to see the predictive power of Moore's Law slow down, and while we are still far from its theoretical physical limit, the economic factor is causing chip manufacturers to start exploring different approaches in order to offer the doubling in speed that computer users expect. Whether this approach is called multiprocessor or multicore, the undeniable fact is that for the past couple of years already, regular desktops have started sporting more than one processor, and more recently, even laptops are beginning to follow suit.

Concurrent programming has therefore become a necessity, and in this section, we'll examine TestNG's concurrency support.

TestNG has built-in support for concurrency, which translates into two distinct features.

---

4. From "The Next Mainstream Programming Language: A Game Developer's Perspective," p. 61. Accessed on August 1, 2007, from www.st.cs.uni-sb.de/edu/seminare/2005/advanced-fp/docs/sweeny.pdf.

1. *Concurrent testing*: With this feature, you can quickly create tests that will run your code in a heavily multithreaded environment, thereby allowing you to get a good sense on how thread safe it is.

2. *Concurrent running of tests*: At runtime, TestNG can be configured to run tests in parallel mode, which will tell TestNG to run all tests in separate threads for maximum speed. This mode can be extensively configured and can result in spectacular gains in test execution times.

We'll discuss these features in this section.

Concurrent Testing

How do we verify that our code is thread safe?

There is no easy answer to this question. Actually, there is no definitive answer to this question, either. Past a certain size, it's impossible to prove with 100% certainty that a given portion of code will behave as expected if several threads access it simultaneously.

Consider the example shown in Listing 2–50.

Listing 2–50 Common Singleton pattern implementation

```
public class Singleton {
  private static Singleton instance = null;

  public static Singleton getInstance() {
    if (instance == null) {
      instance = new Singleton();
    }

    return instance;
  }
}
```

This is the familiar Singleton design pattern: It guarantees that the class `Singleton` will be instantiated only once and that all the calls to `getInstance()` will return only that instance. (Note that this class should also contain a private constructor.)

There is no simpler code to implement a lazily instantiated singleton, and yet, this simple class has a subtle bug that makes it not thread safe.

In order to identify this bug, let's write a simple TestNG test, as shown in Listing 2–51.

Listing 2–51 Singleton test

```
private Singleton singleton;

@BeforeClass
public void init() {
  singleton = new Singleton();
}

@Test(invocationCount = 100, threadPoolSize = 10)
public void testSingleton() {
  Thread.yield();
  Singleton p = singleton.getInstance();
}
```

In order to actually test something (the code in Listing 2–51 only retrieves an instance and doesn't do anything with it), let's alter our `getInstance()` method as shown in Listing 2–52 (the two lines in bold are new).

Listing 2–52 Modified Singleton code

```
public static Singleton getInstance() {
    if (instance == null) {
      Thread.yield();
      Assert.assertNull(instance);
      instance = new Singleton();
    }

    return instance;
  }
```

Here are a couple of comments about these two code listings before we actually run the new code.

■ Notice that the `@Test` annotation now has two new attributes called `invocationCount` and `threadPoolSize`. We'll get back to them in more detail soon, but for now, suffice it to say that they will cause TestNG to invoke the test method 100 times and from 10 different threads (the total number of invocations is still 100), regardless of the number of threads.

■ We are asserting that the instance is null before assigning it to a new `Singleton` object. This might seem very odd, since we only enter this part of the court if `instance == null`, so how could this assertion possibly fail?

We'll explain the reason for `Thread.yield()` shortly.

For now, let's just run the code. Listing 2–53 shows the output.

Listing 2–53 Singleton test output

```
===============================================
Concurrent testing
Total tests run: 100, Failures: 5, Skips: 0
===============================================
```

This doesn't come as a complete surprise, does it?

Let's run it a couple more times, as shown in Listing 2–54.

Listing 2–54 More Singleton test output

```
===============================================
Concurrent testing
Total tests run: 100, Failures: 2, Skips: 0
===============================================


===============================================
Concurrent testing
Total tests run: 100, Failures: 0, Skips: 0
===============================================
```

These results seem to be completely erratic to the point that sometimes the tests actually all pass. But most of the time, several of them fail on the `assert` we inserted above.

We are clearly dealing with code that is not thread safe, and since the listing is very simple in this case, it's easy to see why: Assume that thread T1 enters the `if` block and then gets preempted by thread T2 before it gets a chance to create a new instance. T2 enters the `if` block, goes all the way (thereby creating an instance of the `Singleton`). Later, T1 resumes and creates a second version of `Singleton`, overriding the one that T2 had just initialized.

Moral of the story: We created more than one instance of our `Singleton`, possibly breaking our entire application. Now, some of our callers refer to the first instance, while others refer to the second instance, and it's probably not necessary to explain how hard such a problem can be to debug.

Before we look in closer detail at what exactly happened here, we promised you an explanation for `Thread.yield()`, so here it is, and along with it, a confession: Without `Thread.yield()`, this demonstration wouldn't work.

The problem is that this example is too short, and because the `getInstance()` method is so small, the JVM will typically never bother preempting it. Therefore, it will always be run as one synchronized block, even though it's not synchronized.

Does this mean that this code is thread safe? No, definitely not. And you can bet that in time, as our hardware progresses and as more and more desktop computers are shipped with more cores and more CPUs, the bug will show. Consider that `Thread.yield()` is a placeholder for more complex code, which your application most certainly has. The more complicated the code is, the more likely the JVM is to preempt it when you run this code with multiple threads. In fact, it's fairly common for these singletons to be fairly heavy in that they incur a relatively significant start-up cost, so in a real-world singleton example, the yield is not necessary and the existing initialization is sufficient overhead to highlight the lack of thread safety.

threadPoolSize, invocationCount, and timeOut

In this example, we used two new attributes of the `@Test` annotation: `threadPoolSize` and `invocationCount`.

`invocationCount` is fairly straightforward and can be used outside of any concurrent consideration: It determines how many times TestNG should invoke a test method. As expected, it also increases the number of tests run, so that if one `@Test` method is discovered, but this method specifies `invocationCount = 5`, the total number of tests run will be 5.

Another example where `invocationCount` can be useful is for stress testing (also called load testing). Suppose that we are trying to see how well a Web server responds when it receives a lot of simultaneous requests. Listing 2–55 shows an example of invocation in this situation.

Listing 2–55 Invoking a test multiple times

```
@Test(invocationCount = 1000)
public void getShouldWork() {
    performGetOnWebServer("http://example.com");
}
```

Of course, we could also consider doing more than just reading a URL, such as performing a POST that would, in turn, cause a database to be updated in the back end. However, we're still limited in this example because, by default, TestNG will run these 1,000 requests serially, so while this simple test might reveal limitations in the way our Web server scales under load, we are not likely to see many failures in terms of data consistency.

What we really want to do is simulate a lot of concurrent accesses that will compete for the database and, possibly, the same rows on this database. And at the end of the test, we will make sure that the data entered in the database is consistent.

We'll review testing databases in Chapter 4, so instead of getting into details here, we'll just cover one last attribute that is also very useful when using TestNG's concurrency support features: timeOut.

Just like invocationCount, timeOut is an attribute that can be used by itself, regardless of any concurrent considerations. Listing 2–56 shows a simple test that specifies a timeout of 3,000 milliseconds (3 seconds) and its behavior when the test method returns before that amount of time (success) and when it returns in more than 3 seconds (failure).

Listing 2–56 Tests with a timeout

```
@Test(timeOut = 3000)
public void shouldSucceed() throws InterruptedException {
    Thread.sleep(1000);
}

@Test(timeOut = 3000)
public void shouldFail() throws InterruptedException {
    Thread.sleep(5000);
}
```

The output appears as shown in Listing 2–57.

Listing 2–57 Output of the tests with a timeout

```
PASSED: shouldSucceed
FAILED: shouldFail
```

The `timeout` attribute should probably be used whenever you are testing something that can potentially take a long time to return, such as network access. If a test fails to return within the allotted time, TestNG will forcefully abort it and mark it as failed.

But a more interesting use of the `timeout` attribute is when it is combined with `threadPoolSize`.

As its name implies, `threadPoolSize` asks TestNG to allocate a certain number of threads and to use these threads to invoke the test methods. As soon as one test completes, the thread that was used to run it is returned to the pool, where it can be reused for the next invocation.

The allocation of threads and test methods is absolutely nondeterministic, so you should not make any assumption in that regard. If the size of the thread pool is bigger than the number of test invocations, you are pretty much guaranteed than all the invocations will start right away, but if you don't have enough threads to cover all the invocations, some of these will have to wait until a thread becomes available.

To illustrate these principles, let's use the simple test shown in Listing 2–58.

Listing 2–58 Test with multiple threads

```
@Test(invocationCount = 5, threadPoolSize = 10)
public void bigThreadPool() {
  System.out.println("[Big] Thread#: " +
      Thread.currentThread().getId());
}
```

In this example, the method will be invoked five times from a pool of ten threads. Listing 2–59 shows the output.

Listing 2–59 Output of the test with multiple threads

```
[Big] Thread#: 11
[Big] Thread#: 12
[Big] Thread#: 10
[Big] Thread#: 9
[Big] Thread#: 8
```

As we can see, each invocation received its own new thread, and we also allocated five extra threads that were never used.

Contrast this with the test shown in Listing 2–60, which specifies five invocations but only three threads.

Listing 2–60 Test with multiple threads and a smaller pool

```
@Test(invocationCount = 5, threadPoolSize = 3)
public void smallThreadPool() {
   System.out.println("[Small] Thread#: " +
         Thread.currentThread().getId());
}
```

Listing 2–61 shows the output for this test.

Listing 2–61 Output of the test with multiple threads and a smaller pool

```
[Small] Thread#: 14
[Small] Thread#: 13
[Small] Thread#: 15
[Small] Thread#: 14
[Small] Thread#: 13
```

Here, only three threads (13, 14, and 15) were allocated, as expected. After the first three invocations on each of these threads, no threads were ~~ıle~~ from the pool, so TestNG waited for at least one of these threads ~~ırn~~. When this happened, the thread was reclaimed (in this case, it ~~ıread~~ 14) and used for the next invocation (the fourth one). After that, ~~ı~~ 13 became free and was therefore reused to invoke the test method a ~~:ime~~.

Concurrent Running

Since using multiple threads to run an application can yield so much bene-fit, why wouldn't we leverage this feature to run our tests faster? Instead of using threads to verify that our code is multithread safe, how about using threads to make our own tests run faster?

As mentioned earlier, more and more personal computers these days (even laptops) ship with dual CPUs or dual cores, which means that they can in effect run more than one process physically in parallel. If we have one hundred test methods to run, doesn't this mean that running these methods on two different threads should approximately divide the running time by two?

To TestNG, a test suite is a simple set of test methods that need to be arranged in a certain order before they get executed. With this in mind, we can allocate a thread pool of a given size and use these threads to execute our test methods, exactly like the `threadPoolSize` does for our test methods. Of course, if we have only two CPUs but we allocate a pool of ten threads, it will be approximately equivalent to allocating a pool of two threads, but there is no reason to limit ourselves since setting this size to a higher number that we can run on one machine means that our tests will go faster if they ever get run on a machine that contains more than two processors.[5]

Like most configurations in TestNG, this is achieved in the `testng.xml` file. Listing 2–62 shows an example.

Listing 2–62 Specifying the thread pool size in the configuration file

```
<suite name="TestNG JDK 1.5" verbose="1"
       parallel="methods" thread-count="2">
...
</suite>
```

The attribute `thread-count` determines the number of threads that TestNG will use to run all the test methods found in this suite, and the attribute `parallel` is what tells TestNG the kind of parallel mode you are requesting for your tests. We can specify two values for this attribute.

---

5. Actually, current operating systems are still capable of running several processes in parallel even when only one CPU is available (e.g., I/O operations), so as a rule of thumb, don't be afraid to specify a high number in your thread pool size and do some measurements.

1. `parallel="methods"`: In this mode, each test method will be run in its own thread.

2. `parallel="tests"`: In this mode, all the test methods found in a given `<test>` tag will be run in their own thread.

Before explaining the rationale behind these two modes, let's quickly illustrate how they work. Let's create the class shown in Listing 2–63.

Listing 2–63 Threading behavior sample test

```java
public class A {
  @Test
  public void a1() {
    System.out.println("[A] " + Thread.currentThread().getId()
      + " a1()");
  }

  @Test
  public void a2() {
    System.out.println("[A] " + Thread.currentThread().getId()
      + " a2()");
  }
}
```

And we create similar classes named B and C containing, respectively, the test methods `b1()`, `b2()`, `c1()`, and `c2()`.

In our first attempt, we run these tests in single-threaded mode, as shown in Listing 2–64.

Listing 2–64 Test configuration for running tests serially

```xml
<suite name="Concurrent Suite" >
  <test name="Test1">
    <classes>
      <class name="org.testngbook.A" />
      <class name="org.testngbook.B" />
    </classes>
  </test>

  <test name="Test2">
```

```
      <classes>
        <class name="org.testngbook.C" />
      </classes>
    </test>
  </suite>
```

Not surprisingly, all six methods indicate they are being run in the same (and unique) thread created by TestNG, as shown in Listing 2–65.

Listing 2–65 Output of running tests serially

```
[A] 1 a2()
[A] 1 a1()
[B] 1 b1()
[B] 1 b2()
[C] 1 c1()
[C] 1 c2()
```

We are now creating two threads and using the `methods` parallel mode, as shown in Listing 2–66.

Listing 2–66 Test configuration for running methods in parallel

```
<suite name="Concurrent Suite" parallel="methods"
       thread-count="2" verbose="1" >
```

And we now get the output shown in Listing 2–67.

Listing 2–67 Output of running methods in parallel

```
[A] 8 a1()
[A] 7 a2()
[B] 7 b2()
[B] 8 b1()
[C] 7 c2()
[C] 8 c1()
```

This time, the six methods are competing for two threads, regardless of which <test> they belong to.

Let's switch to the `tests` parallel mode (Listing 2–68):

Listing 2–68 Test configuration for running tests in parallel

```
<suite name="Concurrent Suite" parallel="tests"
       thread-count="2" verbose="1" >
```

Listing 2–69 shows the resulting output.

Listing 2–69 Output of running tests in parallel

```
[A] 7 a2()
[C] 8 c1()
[A] 7 a1()
[C] 8 c2()
[B] 7 b1()
[B] 7 b2()
```

This time, each <test> runs in its own thread, which means that `a1()`, `a2()`, `b1()`, and `b2()` run in thread 7, and `c1()` and `c2()` run in thread 8.

These last two runs look very similar, but they differ in a very important way: in `tests` mode, TestNG guarantees that each <test> will run in its own thread. This is very important if you want to test code that you know is not multithread safe. In `methods` mode, all bets are off as you have no way to predict which methods will run in the same thread and which will run in different threads.

This distinction will become clearer in the following section.

Turning on the Parallel Bit

With all these options at your disposal, how do you move from a single-threaded test configuration to leveraging the parallel mode?

The first thing you need to be aware of is that switching to parallel testing comes at a cost: While it can significantly speed up the running time, it can also lead to false negatives, that is, tests that appear to be failing but really are not. Why? Because you might accidentally be running test methods in different threads that are testing business code that is not thread safe.

Keep in mind that this is not necessarily a bug! Very often, there is no need to make your code thread safe, and it's perfectly acceptable for your application to expect that it is running in one unique thread. Faced with this problem, you have two options:

1. Change the business code to make it thread safe.
2. Avoid using parallel mode to test that business code.

While we are usually fairly open to the idea of modifying code to make it more testable, we believe that making code thread safe just for the sake of a test goes a little bit too far because it can have a very significant impact on the performance and complexity of the application. Therefore, it's preferable to make an exception in the testing code and to indicate that there are portions that should not be tested in a parallel environment.

Let's assume that we have a working test configuration made of hundreds of test methods, and we decide to leverage TestNG's `parallel="tests"` mode. Several things can happen.

- All tests still pass. It's the best-case scenario: The business code is already thread safe, and we have nothing else to do.
- Some of the tests fail. If we can isolate the classes that fail and confirm that they pass if we revert to the single-threaded mode, the best course of action is to put these failing classes in the same `<test>` tag and to use the `parallel="tests"` mode.
- Most of the tests fail. At this point, we can either revert to single-threaded mode or, if we want to investigate, switch to `parallel="tests"`, put all classes in one single `<test>`, verify that the tests pass (right now, we are back to running all the tests in one thread), and then pick the test classes one by one and put them in their separate `<test>` stanzas. The idea behind this approach is to identify which classes can safely be run in separate threads and which ones need to be invoked from a single thread.

Performance Testing

In this section, we'll discuss an area that is often overlooked in testing efforts: performance testing. But before we start looking at some code, let's take a step back and try to formalize what we mean exactly by performance testing in order to clarify our goals.

Algorithm Complexity

A common way to measure the complexity and speed of an algorithm is to use what is referred to as *big O notation*. Even if you've never used it, you have probably come across this notation in books or articles, and it looks like this: O(n), O(n^2), O(log n), and so on.

The concepts behind this notation are much simpler than they appear, and you certainly don't need a computer science degree to understand them, so we'll explain briefly what this notation means. Let's start with a simple example.

Assume that you're trying to evaluate how well a function scales. In order to do that, you call it with data sets of increasing size, and you measure the time it takes to run. Table 2–4 shows some sample measures. What can you conclude from these numbers?

What's striking is that the response time seems to be growing very fast, much faster than the size of the input data. Whenever we multiply the input set by 10, the response time gets multiplied by more than 100. If the input set is multiplied by 100, the response time is multiplied by more than 10,000.

In other words, the response time appears to grow as the square of the size of the input set, and this is expressed by the following statement: This function's complexity is O(n^2).

There are formal ways to prove this statement, but they are not always trivial, and these calculations can become quite involved as soon as the code becomes a bit complex, so empiric measurements are just as valid.

Let's take a look at another example: sorting.

Java offers a set of sorting functions in the classes `java.util.Arrays` and `java.util.Collections`. Let's see if we can get a sense of the com-

Table 2–4 Comparing data size and response time growths

Data size	Response time (ms)
100	1
1,000	110
10,000	12,000
100,000	1,140,000

Table 2–5 Comparing data size and response time growths for `sort()`

Data size	Response time (ms)
100	13
1,000	128
10,000	1,588
100,000	19,882

plexity of `Arrays.sort(int[])` by making a few measurements, shown in Table 2–5.

What we can see from this quick survey is that whenever we multiply the size of the input set by n, the response time seems to grow by n times something. We can't really say for sure what this something is, but it definitely looks like it's less than n; otherwise, we would be seeing numbers that look like the $O(n^2)$ case we looked at earlier.[6]

Note how these results seem to be both consistent (the rate at which the response rates increase seems to follow a certain law) and inconsistent (the measurements vary, and if you run these tests several times in a row, you will never get the same measurements twice). However, it is very likely[7] that the overall proportion in which they compare to each other will look the same.

If there is one thing you need to remember about big O notation, it's that it's a measure of *scalability*, and not a measure of *performance* as is commonly believed: It gives us a predictable way to measure how well our code will behave if the data set that it works on grows by orders of magnitude.

With that in mind, we now have a better idea of what we might want to test for in terms of performance. First of all, we need to measure our current algorithm, either empirically (as we did) or more formally (looking at the code and calculating the complexity by measuring the number of loops

6. The curious reader can refer to the Javadocs of the `Arrays.sort()` method at http://java.sun.com/j2se/1.5.0/docs/api/java/util/Arrays.html#sort(int[],%20int,%20int) to find out what that number is: "This algorithm offers n*log(n) performance." If you are not mathematically inclined, all you need to know is that log(n) is indeed a number that's less than n.

7. The only time where even the ratios might vary wildly is if the machine you are using to run these tests suddenly suffers from a spike in its load. The only way to eliminate these occasional incorrect readings is to run the tests many times.

and statements it contains). Once we have an idea of its O complexity, we write a test that guarantees this complexity in order to make sure that future modifications of the code won't cause any drastic regression in performance.

Before we get to this, let's address a simple case: Why not simply run the function once, measure its execution time, and then write a test that compares the running time against this value (say, 1,000 elements and 128 ms, from Table 2–5)?

Indeed, this is a valid way to address performance testing and probably one that we'd recommend most of the time. The only thing to keep in mind is that time measurements can vary greatly from one run to the other. For example, the machine we are running on might be under heavy load (maybe it's running other tests simultaneously or serving requests for a different application). Therefore, the risk is seeing tests fail sporadically.

Tests that fail randomly should be avoided as much as possible because they can generate a lot of churn and panic and cause the team to waste a lot of time chasing a failure that doesn't really exist (and that, most likely, they won't even be able to reproduce consistently).

So if we can live with this limitation and keep in mind that "it's okay if these tests fail once in a while, it's expected," then testing performance in the absolute is a quick and easy way to get started with performance testing.

However, once this is in place and these sporadic failures start popping up, we strongly suggest moving to the more sophisticated relative way of measuring performance.

The approach boils down to the following.

- *Absolute performance testing*: Run the tests on n elements, and make sure the running time is less than t.
- *Relative performance testing*: Run the tests on n1 elements, and measure t1. Run the tests on n1 * 10 elements, and measure t2. Make sure that the relation between t1 and t2 is what you expect (e.g., t2 ~= t1, or t2 ~= 100 * t1, or t2 ~= 10 * t1, and so on).

Although the relative approach will be more robust, it is still possible for it to fail because assessing the complexity of an algorithm is not an exact science. For example, an algorithm can be linear, $O(n)$, while showing running times that vary from n * 1 to n * 2. Therefore, the safest way to approach relative performance testing is not to assert the complexity exactly but to make sure that the measurements we are seeing are within the range expected. In order to do this, we need to rank the various complexities. Here is a quick chart:

```
O(1) < O(log(n)) < O(n) < O(n * log(n)) < O(n²) < O(n³) < O(kⁿ)
```

We're showing only the most common complexities since there is obviously an infinity of combinations, such as $O(n^2 * \log(n))$, but figuring out their place in this ranking order should be trivial. The only one that might be puzzling to you is $O(1)$, which simply means constant time: Regardless of the value of n, an algorithm in constant time will always return in the same amount of time (a rare and often sought-after quality that very few algorithms achieve, the most famous one being the retrieval of an element from a hash table).

Note also that by convention, constants are always ignored when measuring complexities: $O(2 * \log(n))$ and $O(5 * \log(n))$ are both considered equivalent to $O(\log(n))$.

Testing Complexity

Let's assume we have measured our code to be $O(\log(n))$. How do we assert that in a test?

We can proceed in two ways.

1. *Ignore the complexity aspect*: Measure the running time (ideally by running our code several times and taking the average) and assert this in the test.

2. *Measure against the next bigger complexity in the ranking order*: In other words, if we expect our code to run in $O(\log(n))$, we make sure that the code never becomes $O(n)$ (the complexity just after $O(\log(n))$).

Listing 2–70a shows how this could be accomplished.

Listing 2–70a Testing complexity

```
@DataProvider(name = "timingsAbsolute")
public Object[][] getAbsoluteTimings() {
  return new Object[][] {
    // 1st parameter = size, 2nd = timing
    new Object[] { 10000, 12 },
    new Object[] { 100000, 80 },
  };
}

@Test(dataProvider = "timingsAbsolute")
```

```
public void verifyPerformanceAbsolute(int dataSize, int timing)
  {
  int actualTime = measureAlgorithm(dataSize);
  double tenPercent = timing * .1;
  double lowerBound = timing - tenPercent;
  double upperBound = timing + tenPercent;

  Assert.assertTrue(actualTime > lowerBound &&
      actualTime < upperBound);
  }
```

In this example, our test method takes two parameters: the size of the data to pass to our algorithm and the expected response time. We allow for a 10% variation in this response time (which is probably too strict and is likely to generate false failures), and in the end, we make sure the code ran within this margin.

As mentioned earlier, this approach is very fragile and is likely to fail if the computer on which the test is being run is suddenly under heavy load or, more likely, if this test is run on a faster or slower computer.

Contrast this with the second approach shown in Listing 2–70b, which uses relative measurements instead.

Listing 2–70b Using relative measurements

```
@DataProvider(name = "timingsRelative")
public Object[][] getRelativeTimings() {
  return new Object[][] {
    new Object[] { 10000 },
    new Object[] { 100000 },
  };
}

@Test(dataProvider = "timingsRelative")
public void verifyPerformanceRelative(int dataSize) {
  int ratio = 10;
  int smallTime = measureAlgorithm(dataSize);
  int largeTime = measureAlgorithm(dataSize * ratio);

  // Verify the algorithm is O(n)
  assertApproximateEquals(largeTime / smallTime, ratio);

}
```

This time, our test function takes no timing parameter, only the size of the sample to run the algorithm on. It invokes our code with this size, stores the timing in the variable `smallTime`, and then invokes the code a second time but on a sample ten times that size and stores the timing in the variable `largeTime`.

The important part is then the `assert` statement, which compares these two timings and makes sure they are in the proportion we expected.

In Listing 2–70b, we expect the algorithm to be O(n), so if we multiply the size of the input by ten, we should expect the response time to be multiplied by ten as well (approximately, see below).

If we wanted to verify that our algorithm was O(log(n)) instead, we would use the `assert` shown in Listing 2–70c.

Listing 2–70c Verifying the complexity

```
// Verify the algorithm is O(log(n))
assertApproximateEquals(largeTime / smallTime, Math.log(ratio));
```

Notice that this code is still missing one important method: `assertApproximateEquals()`. Because of the inherent uncertainty of performance measurements, we need to provide a margin for error when we are verifying our results, so there are various ways to approach this problem.

The simplest way is probably to implement this function in terms of percentage. For example, if we wanted to assert that a certain value is within 10% of another value, we could use the code shown in Listing 2–70d.

Listing 2–70d Verifying with percentages

```
public void assertApproximateEquals(float actual, float
  expected) {
  float min = expected * 0.9;
  float max = expected * 1.1;
  assert(min <= actual && actual <= max);
}
```

In this section, we have reviewed some of the main principles of measuring algorithm complexity, and we also established that testing performance is not just about testing raw speed but also about making sure that the speed of an application grows in a predictable fashion whenever its input grows as well.

Mocks and Stubs

In any software project, there are likely numerous subsystems and components. These components often have contractual boundaries that specify the contact points between them, as well as define the external interface to each component or subsystem.

Take any standard Web application, for example. There's likely to be a component that manages users, one that handles emails, another that manages presentation, and another that manages persistence. There are relationships between all of these, with components relying on others to perform their roles and in turn providing functionality for other components to fulfill their roles.

When it comes to testing, especially unit testing, it's crucial that we're able to isolate these components as much as possible. How our components are written can make this more or less difficult, due to how dependencies between components are managed. Are components looked up from a central registry? Do we have singletons? Are dependencies injected?

Regardless of which approach is used, our unit tests wouldn't be very good unit tests if they had to cart in the entire system to test any given part of it. So very shortly after the ideas around unit testing started to solidify, there was a recognized need to be able to provide the bare minimum of dependencies required in order to test effectively.

If we wanted to test our user manager component in the example Web application we just described, we should be able to do so without necessarily having to provide every other component as well, just because our user manager happens to use a `Mailer` object and a `UserDAO` object to perform its roles.

The solution in this case is to use stubs or mocks, depending on the situation. In this section we'll cover both, with examples highlighting the differences, as well as advice on when you should choose one over the other.

Mocks versus Stubs

Before we delve into the differences, let's first identify the common design pattern that these two approaches share in a trivial example, as illustrated in Figure 2–1.

In Figure 2–1, we have a `UserManager` object that creates a user through a `UserDAO` helper and, when that's done, emails the user with his or her login information.

A Data Access Object (DAO) is a pattern in which we encapsulate communication with an underlying data store in an object, which usually handles create/read/update/delete operations for a given entity.

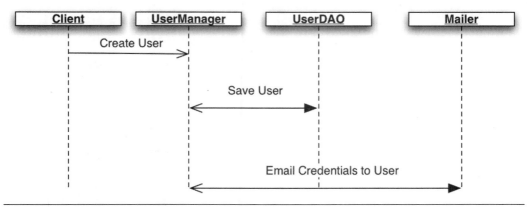

Figure 2–1 Sequence diagram for a component

We already have unit tests in place to ensure that emailing works and that the UserDAO object behaves as expected and saves users correctly in our data store. However, we'd like to test whether the UserManager behaves correctly and invokes the other two components correctly under all possible circumstances. How do we do so?

Since we know all about good design, all of the classes involved have interfaces for the other components to interact with. If that weren't the case, this would be a good point at which to introduce them as boundaries and contract definitions between our various components. When initially developing this code, it is entirely possible that we did not have any interfaces since there was a need for only a single implementation. The fact that we require multiple ones now means that the functionality should be abstracted into an interface.

A naive test case for our UserManager interface would create it as it is and simply give it full-blown UserDAO and Mailer objects. That's not quite what we need, so why should we have to bring in all that heavy baggage when all we want to test is UserManager?

This is where mocks and stubs come in handy. Instead of passing in our full-blown functional UserDAO and Mailer objects, we instead pass in a simple implementation that does the minimum possible to fulfill the contract with UserManager.

Mock/Stub Examples

Let us first examine the stub approach. In this case, we have lightweight implementations for our dependencies that we can supply the UserManager with that we can also query later for their state. This is shown in Listing 2–71.

Listing 2–71 Stub implementation

```
public class UserDAOStub implements UserDAO {
  public boolean saveUser(String name) {
    return true;
  }
}

public class MailerStub implements Mailer {
  private List<String> mails = new ArrayList<String>();

  public boolean sendMail(String to, String subject,
   String body)
  {
   mails.add(to);
   return true;
  }

  public List<String> getMails() {
    return mails;
  }
}
```

Since we have other tests that verify our UserDAO implementation, and since we are not concerned with it for this UserManager test, we provide a stub implementation that always returns true (to signal that the user has been created successfully).

For our Mailer stub, we do something similar. We also keep track of what emails we've sent, since we might like to query this stub later on to verify that it was invoked and that the email was sent to the right person.

Our test now looks like Listing 2–72.

Listing 2–72 Test using stubs

```
@Test
public void verifyCreateUser() {
  UserManager manager = new UserManagerImpl();
  MailerStub mailer = new MailerStub();
  manager.setMailer(mailer);
  manager.setDAO(new UserDAOStub());
  manager.createUser("tester");
  assert mailer.getMails().size() == 1;
}
```

We create our stub implementations, inject them into our `UserManager` instance, and finally verify that the mailer was invoked correctly.

The mock approach usually involves using an external library that does the grunt work of creating the interface implementation for us. Once that's done, we specify expectations on the mocked instance. Note that the next example uses pseudocode since, unfortunately, the exact syntax that mock libraries use can sometimes be somewhat awkward, thus disguising the intent and purpose of the test! This is shown in Listing 2–73.

Listing 2–73 Pseudocode using a mock library

```
@Test
public void createUser() {
  // create the instance we'd like to test
  UserManager manager = new UserManagerImpl();

  // create the dependencies we'd like mocked
  Mock mailer = mock(Mailer.class);
  Mock dao = mock(UserDAO.class);

  // wire them up to our primary component, the user manager
  manager.setMailer((Mailer)mailer.proxy());
  manager.setDAO((UserDAO)dao.proxy());

  // specify expectations
  dao.saveUser() must return true;
  expect invocation dao.saveUser() with parameter "tester";

  dao.sendMail must return true;
  expect invocation dao.sendMail with parameter "tester"

  // invoke our method
  manager.createUser("tester");
  // verify that expectations have been met
  verifyExpectations();
  }
```

Ignoring the specifics of this code (we'll discuss specific mock libraries later), the idea here is that we do not provide our own stub implementations of the components we'd like to swap in.

Instead, we use a mock library. The library will set up the mock object, on which we can then specify any number of expectations and behaviors.

In Listing 2–73, we specified that the `saveUser` method will be invoked, with a parameter of `tester`, and will return `true`. Similarly, we then specify that the mailer mock's `sendMail` method will also be invoked once, with the first parameter being `tester`, and that it will return `true` on this invocation.

Having set up our expectations, we invoke the `createUser` method on our manager object. If the expectations are matched, the test will pass. If they are not, the test will fail. The actual check for all the expectations being matched is done in the `verify` method, which will go over our mock objects and verify that their expectations have been met.

Based on the examples in Listings 2–72 and 2–73, the difference between mocks and stubs should be somewhat clearer now. Stubs replace a method with a specified result that is the bare minimum required. Mocks, on the other hand, are specified in terms of expectations from a particular method.

Certainly, there are a lot of concepts and ideas that make this differentiation somewhat tricky to conceptualize. For example, mocks are a specialized form of stubs. A stub can also fulfill a trivial expectation. In general, though, mocks are all about expectations and defining them, whereas stubs are more generic, rather than being structured around their expectations.

Mocks test the behavior and interactions between components, whereas stubs replace heavyweight processes that are not relevant to a particular test with simple implementations.

Naming Confusion

Unfortunately, while the two concepts are quite distinct, it's not uncommon to find a whole array of examples where they're used interchangeably. Many projects confuse stubs with mocks and refer to stub implementations as mock objects. The Spring framework's excellent test library, for example, is called `spring-mock`, despite the fact that it has no mocks (none of the classes in the library define expectations—all of them are in fact stubs for various Java Enterprise Edition APIs!)

The same issue plagues a number of other projects, where the name *mock* is used instead of *stub*, so make sure the distinction is clear in your mind.

To confuse the issue further, if we were to be stricter in terms of naming, the stub objects we defined above are *test doubles*. A test double is basically a dummy implementation used just to satisfy a dependency. The difference between a double and a stub is that a double is used purely to satisfy a dependency, while a stub has a bit more of an implementation and usually returns hardcoded data instead of going to a database, for example.

The testing crowd in fact has even finer-grained names, but in practice, we've found that these can be confusing. Although the difference between mocks and stubs is important, drilling down further can be an interesting exercise in naming things but isn't particularly important or useful when developing tests.

Designing for Mockability

In order to successfully use mock or stub objects, it's important to ensure that our code is designed in such a way as to make this easy and straightforward.

The most important aspect of that design is correctly identifying our component interactions and, from that, defining interface boundaries between components.

Practically speaking, if we have two components A and B, and A needs to use B, it should do so via B's interface, rather than the specific implementation of B. That way, we can trivially hand A a different implementation to work with.

Then it's important to be able to select what instance of B to provide A with. The more control we have over that process, the easier it is for us to specify implementations to suit various use cases. Component A could, for example, look up a static instance of B, as shown in Listing 2–74.

Listing 2–74 Singleton lookup

```
public void doWork1() {
  B b = B.getInstance();
  b.doSomething();
}
```

This approach would be problematic for us since we'd have no way to provide a new instance, short of modifying B's implementation. This is one of the fundamental flaws of using statics: There can be only one instance of a given object, which can (and often does) hinder its usage later in the project's lifecycle. While initially it might seem quite sensible that we'd have just one instance, we cannot be confident enough about how the project will evolve and what direction it will take to know that this will always be the case.

Component A could also use a Service Locator pattern to find an instance of B. Listing 2–75 shows an example using JNDI.

Listing 2–75 Service Locator via JNDI

```
public void doWork2() throws NamingException {
  B b = (B)new InitialContext().lookup("B");
  b.doSomething();
}
```

The problem with this approach is that it does not allow us to give A a specific instance of B that we control. There is one global instance, and that's what A gets.

The core concept here is that A should not decide how it gets B. Instead, we should tell A what instance of B it should use, as shown in Listing 2–76.

Listing 2–76 Refactoring to use injection

```
private B b;

public void setB(B b) {
  this.b = b;
}
```

In this case, we externally informed A what instance of B it should use. This gives us the flexibility to decide per instance of A what B to provide. In a test, for example, we could trivially provide A with a mock or stub of B.

The external dependency resolution can be performed by an Inversion of Control (IoC) container such as Spring or Guice, both discussed in Chapter 5, that takes care of wiring all our components together.

Mock Libraries

Two popular libraries take the hard work out of managing the definition of mock objects along with their expectations: EasyMock and jMock. The two libraries have a number of crucial differences, and which one you end up choosing (if any) is a matter of personal taste. We'll cover the main features and benefits of both. Based on our experience, many people find EasyMock simpler and more intuitive to use, so we'll cover that one first. Feel free to read up on both libraries, though, as which library to use does boil down to personal taste and programming style.

We also revisit the example we went through earlier with the `UserManager`, `UserDAO`, and `Mailer` objects, to show how one of these libraries can be used within our test case.

EasyMock

EasyMock is a mock library that allows us to set up expectations by invoking methods on our mock objects exactly as the primary test object would. Listing 2–77 shows an EasyMock example.

Listing 2–77 Test based on EasyMock

```
import static org.easymock.EasyMock.*;

public class EasyMockUserManagerTest {
  @Test
  public void createUser() {
    // create the instance we'd like to test
    UserManager manager = new UserManagerImpl();
    UserDAO dao = createMock(UserDAO.class);
    Mailer mailer = createMock(Mailer.class);
    manager.setDAO(dao);
    manager.setMailer(mailer);

    // record expectations
    expect(dao.saveUser("tester")).andReturn(true);
    expect(mailer.sendMail(eq("tester"), (String)notNull(),
                           (String)notNull())).andReturn(true);
    replay(dao, mailer);

    // invoke our method
    manager.createUser("tester");
    // verify that expectations have been met
    verify(mailer, dao);
  }
}
```

For any EasyMock test, we must follow four steps.

1. *Create mock objects*: The first step is to create mocks for all our secondary objects. This is done through the `createMock` method, with the parameter being the class we'd like to mock. Note that due to good use of generics, we don't need to cast the result to the type we expect. The mock objects are handed to the primary test object.

2. *Record expectations*: Recording expectations simply involves calling the methods we expect to be invoked. For cases where we have specific parameters we expect, we can simply pass them as is. In other cases, we need to specify argument matches, as we did in Listing 2–77 for the `sendMail` method.

3. *Invoke the primary test*: We invoke the method or methods on our primary test object that we expect will then make the right calls into the mock instances.

4. *Verify expectations:* Finally, we invoke `verify`, passing in all of our mock objects. Again, sensible use of the Java 5 varargs feature means we can pass in as many as we'd like.

jMock

jMock is a mock library that allows us to specify constraints programmatically. This allows us to use a rich API to develop flexible constraints for our mock objects and also use the same API to specify the number of invocations expected, return values, and so on.

Conceptually the approach is the same, except that instead of programmatic method invocation, jMock requires that we specify expectations using string method names, along with what we expect each to return, and so on.

Which Is Right for You?

There are a number of key practical differences between the two libraries, even though they address the same issues.

jMock uses strings for method names, and despite the protestation of its developers that this is still refactoring friendly, it is in fact a significant shortcoming. Not all refactorings will go through and modify all string occurrences.

The jMock syntax relies heavily on chained method calls, which some people might find difficult to debug or decipher. While verbosity is useful in code to ensure clarity, in jMock's case the verbosity can be difficult to work with.

Also, jMock requires a base class, which severely hampers test cases by imposing a superclass that must be extended. There's no clear reason for this awkwardness, and it is very clearly an antipattern; most of the methods provided by the base class are helper utility methods that could have just as easily been moved to a utility class to set up expectations. However, the latest version of jMock addresses this, so it is less of an issue.

Finally, at the time of writing, EasyMock seems far more in tune with the times and has received numerous updates that take full advantage of all the language features provided by Java 5, making the resultant mock code much clearer and more obvious. Again, though, jMock will have a new version out soon that will address many of these shortcomings, so the final answer is to pick the one that happens to match your personal taste and style. Both libraries achieve the same functionality; the differentiator lies mostly in the usage you anticipate and your programming style.

Selecting the Right Strategy

A number of factors determine whether we should use mock objects or stubs, or even whether we should avoid both.

Lack of Interfaces

Sometimes we inherit big, bulky legacy systems that aren't designed as optimally as we'd like. For example, sometimes there are no interfaces used between components. Most mock libraries now allow us to swap in classes, not just interfaces. The libraries work by generating a new class at runtime through bytecode manipulation that fulfills the contract we specify.

This is obviously not such a great approach; it is instead a clever hack. It can be useful, however, in certain situations where a redesign is not possible.

Complex Classes

It's not uncommon for manager type classes to grow uncontrollably. While we all know that this is a design smell and that classes should not have too many methods, it's much harder to achieve in practice.

So we end up with classes that have over 20 methods that interact with many other components and keep on getting more and more complex over time.

In this situation, it's not practical to keep maintaining a stub for this class. Every new method that's added will also have to be added to the stub. We'll also have to figure out what the appropriate stub implementation should do.

So for this scenario, dynamic mock object libraries can be useful since they allow us to define the behavior of single methods, rather than having to worry about all of them.

Of course, the right solution is to address the underlying design issue that's causing the problem. Ideally, we would refactor the manager class to more fine-grained role-based interfaces. So, for example, if we had a `UserManager`, we'd consider splitting this up into a `UserFinder`, a `UserPersistor`, a `UserPermissionManager`, and so on. While doing so might seem somewhat daunting initially, it's actually not that difficult in practice. In most cases, the new interfaces can be introduced and methods simply copied or moved over. The semantics and functionality are exactly the same, so it's not even a particularly risky refactoring. The benefit of this interface segregation is increased unit testability, where we can easily work with one interface at a time instead of having to view the `UserManager` as one big monolithic object to test.

Contract Capture

In terms of what we're trying to verify, is this for internal or external functionality? Internal subsystems interacting with each other inside one project are not good candidates for mocks since we control both sides, and they are both likely to evolve and change quite significantly over time.

Having said that, there are cases where using mocks is more useful since they enable us to capture more than simple method signatures to assert the validity of a contract over time. This is particularly useful when verifying protocols or documenting and testing standard APIs that need to adhere to certain behavior over time.

Test Goal

What is our test trying to achieve? Determining whether we should use a stub or a mock lies in the answer to that question.

The rule of thumb is that if we want to test interactions between components, mocks might be a better approach than stubs. Mock libraries allow us to specify the interactions in a concise and exact manner. Stubs, on the other hand, are more useful as scaffolding—dependencies that components expect to be present and to perform certain roles. Stubs should be used for secondary components used by the component under test. The test purpose in this case is to test the primary component itself, rather than its interactions with other components.

Mock Pitfalls

Mocks and stubs are powerful tools that can greatly help us with testing by reducing dependencies and ensuring we can test interactions between components in isolation.

However, many issues arise due to relying too much on mocks, and it's vital to keep in mind the flip side of using mock objects.

Mocking of External APIs

It might be tempting to mock external heavyweight libraries, simply to speed up a test and reduce its dependencies on a specific implementation. Whenever you're tempted to do so, think again.

You should rarely need to mock an API that is not owned by you. This includes all third-party libraries and APIs. To many newcomers to the mocking approach, this is surprisingly unintuitive. Many view mock objects as a way to stub out external dependencies, a way to get rid of that pesky database call or servlet invocation. Doing so is not only hugely inefficient compared to refactoring but also harmful, as the chances are minimal that said developer would come up with an implementation that's robust enough to replace the real thing.

In some cases, the external dependency is very trivial or easy to mock. If you can be confident that the implementation is indeed simple and lends itself well to being mocked, using mock objects would be a good fit. The peril of that approach, however, is that it is sometimes difficult to make that judgment.

False Sense of Security

Having huge swathes of mock tests is likely to give us a pretty good feeling in terms of the increased coverage of our code base. This is in fact a false sense of security, as we're not really testing how objects behave but are instead testing their interactions with one another. The interactions are also specified in the test. This means that, quite frequently, the expectations do not match what will actually happen in a production environment and are instead specified at the time of writing the test.

When the two are written together, it's almost impossible to resist the temptation to tweak one or the other just to get the test to pass! Therefore it's crucial that mock-based tests be complemented with coarser-grained functional tests to minimize the mismatch between the mock implementation and the real one.

Note that this also applies to stubs since our implementations do not match those used in production either. The risk is slightly lessened, though, since stubs are used to satisfy dependencies rather than encapsulate behavior, so we're making fewer fundamental assumptions about their implementation details than we are with mocks.

Maintenance Overhead

Mock objects are not refactoring friendly, so we have to constantly work to keep them up to date with any changes in implementation in primary test objects.

This is especially true for jMock, which uses strings for method names. However, it also applies to EasyMock since refactoring is more than simply renaming methods or classes. (In fact, that use case is too trivial to be called refactoring!)

For example, we might decide that our `UserManager` in the earlier example should not be responsible for sending the credentials email and that a layer above that should handle the mailing. As soon as we do that, our mock test becomes broken. Some might argue that it's a good thing that this test breaks since it forces us to find all usages of the `createUser` method in the manager and ensure that they now handle the email sending themselves. However, in most cases, a developer should be able to make such changes without having to worry about the brittle mock tests.

In addition to the potential refactoring issues, a common problem when using mock objects that results in maintenance headaches is overspecifying expectations just to get the test working. For example, just for the sake of testing, it's not uncommon to see that every method invocation is expected (since mock libraries are not so lenient about incidental calls that weren't explicitly expected). Since the ordering or method calls will change as part of refactoring, we have yet another location where we need to modify code to handle this.

Hierarchies and Complexity

Mock objects are also very susceptible to increasing complexity, especially when confronted by deep object hierarchies.

As methods do more and more, we have to either keep growing our expectations or just live with the false sense of security that underspecified expectations give us. Of course, it's also entirely possible to overexpect, thus making the tests more brittle in the face of refactoring. Test brittleness increases with expectations.

Hence there's always a tradeoff between overspecifying and underspecifying expectations. There's no good rule of thumb for how much we should expect, leaving it to the judgment of the individual developer. This in turn is usually a bad idea, as it's highly unlikely that many developers have a good feel for the right amount! Rather than being a flaw in developers, this is in fact one of the flaws of the whole mock object approach; it puts too much onus on the developer to have the right feel for the tool, instead of encouraging good practices by itself.

Dependent Testing

Consider the following scenario: We are trying to test a Web application and have the following test methods for:

- Launching the Web server (`launchServer()`)
- Deploying the application (`deploy()`)
- Testing the application (`test1()`, `test2()`, ..., `test20()`)

Let's assume that in our scenario, the Web server comes online but the application fails to deploy. Assuming that there is a way to tell JUnit how to order test methods, Listing 2–78 shows the output we'll see.

Listing 2–78 Sample output for single test failure without dependencies

```
1 SUCCESS (launchServer())
21 FAILURES (deploy(), test1(), test2(), etc.)
```

Naturally, it would be extremely worrying if we saw this sort of report; we could even enter a state of panic as we tried to decipher what went wrong and why everything seemed to be broken. Someone familiar with the code might immediately notice that `deploy()` failed and infer that the test report does not actually mean there were 21 failures, but more that there was 1 failure and 20 test methods that can't possibly succeed because there is no server to test on. Said developer might even suspect that once this single failure is fixed, the other 20 failures will go away as well.

This is an example of what we call a *cascade failure*: The failure of a test causes an entire section of tests to fail as well.

Wouldn't it be nice if the testing framework knew about this dependency, so that if ever `deploy()` failed, not only would it simply skip the next 20 methods that depend on it, but it would also reflect this fact in its report, which would therefore look like Listing 2–79.

Listing 2–79 Sample output for single test failure with dependencies

```
1 SUCCESS (launchServer())
1 FAILURE (deploy())
20 SKIPS (test1(), test2(), etc.)
```

This is exactly what TestNG allows you to do, but let's not get ahead of ourselves. First, we'll take a step back and think a little bit more about what dependent testing really means, and then we'll explain in detail how TestNG supports it.

Dependent Code

Dependent testing is a common need, and this shouldn't be surprising since even the simplest programming tasks are also fundamentally dependent on the ordering of their methods. For example, take a look at your own code, pick a section where two consecutive methods are invoked, and reverse their order. Your application will most likely break.

Most of the code we write every day is structured this way; some if not all of it is not going to run unless some previous variables have been set or some requirements have been met.

Having established this fact, it is quite natural to assume that our testing framework should make it easy for us to test dependent code, and our example shows what happens when a discrepancy in functionalities exists between the code and the testing framework.

It's fair to say that some developers in the testing community are strongly opposed to any hint of dependencies in tests. Their arguments usually come in two flavors.

1. As soon as test methods depend on other test methods, it becomes hard to run these methods in isolation.
2. Test methods that depend on each other usually do so because they share some state, and sharing state is a bad thing in tests.

While sharing state across test methods can be delicate, it can also be extremely useful when done properly. We will cover the concept of sharing state among test methods in Chapter 7, so we suggest you refer to that chapter if you are interested in an in-depth discussion of this important topic right now.

It is important to realize that while these two arguments look different, they are actually underpinned by the very same idea: You shouldn't use dependent testing because running test methods in isolation is no longer possible. Indeed, in the example shown in Listing 2–79, it wouldn't be possible to run the `deploy()` test by itself (since it depends on `launchServer()`). Therefore, to people hostile to dependent testing, the correct way to write the tests above would be as shown in Listing 2–80.

Listing 2–80 Manual dependency handling using duplicate method calls

```
public void test1() {
 launchServer();
  deploy();
  // implement test1
}
```

Similarly, all the other test methods (`test2()` to `test20()`) would have to invoke `launchServer()` themselves.

Indeed, these test methods are now completely isolated from each other, but this approach comes at an expensive price. Do we really want to launch the Web server for each test method? Do we really need to redeploy the Web application every time? Isn't this yet another good example where sharing some state would be a good thing, as discussed earlier?

If you are tempted to say, "Well, it's easy. Just put the initialization code in your `setUp()` method," we'll point out that you actually might want to run tests on this initialization phase, and therefore these methods need to be tests themselves—they can't be initialization methods. After all, there might be a bug in the deployment descriptor of your Web application, so you definitely want to write a test for this.

It turns out that the arguments against dependent testing are actually implementation-dependent arguments. They are not a condemnation of the idea, but just an observation that until now, there was no easy way to actually run dependent test methods easily.

What if it was actually possible to ask the testing framework to run `test1()`? Then it would automatically figure out the requirements (`launchServer()`, `deploy()`) and run them before finally invoking the method you requested.

Once you start looking at the problem this way, the answer is obvious: If the testing framework gives you a way to express these dependencies, it will have no problem calculating the requirements for any test method you want to run in isolation. We showed an example of this technique earlier in this chapter when we covered `testng-failed.xml`.

Dependent Testing with TestNG

Now that we have introduced the basic principles behind dependent testing, let's turn our attention to how TestNG actually implements it.

Dependent testing is enabled in TestNG with two attributes of the `@Test` annotation, `dependsOnGroups` and `dependsOnMethods`, which are described in the Javadocs shown in Listing 2–81.

Listing 2–81 Javadocs for dependency annotation

```
/**
 * The list of groups this method depends on.  Every method
 * member of one of these groups is guaranted to have been
 * invoked before this method.  Furthermore, if any of these
 * methods was not a SUCCESS, this test method will not be
 * run and will be flagged as a SKIP.
 */
public String[] dependsOnGroups() default {};

/**
 * The list of methods this method depends on.  There is
 * no guarante on the order on which the methods depended
 * upon will be run, but you are guaranteed that all these
 * methods will be run before the test method that
 * contains this annotation is run. Furthermore, if
 * any of these methods was not a SUCCESS, this test
 * method will not be run and will be flagged as a SKIP.
 *
 *  If some of these methods have been overloaded,
 * all the overloaded versions will be run.
 */
public String[] dependsOnMethods() default {};
```

These annotations are very similar to each other. One lets you specify an array of strings representing the names of the methods the test method depends on, and the other lets you specify an array of strings describing the groups your test method depends on.

Deciding Whether to Depend on Groups or on Methods

In order to illustrate the difference between these two attributes, let's implement our Web server example with `dependsOnMethods` first, as shown in Listing 2–82.

Listing 2–82 Tests using method dependency

```
@Test
public void launchServer() {}

@Test(dependsOnMethods = "launchServer")
public void deploy() {}

@Test(dependsOnMethods = "deploy")
public void test1() {}

@Test(dependsOnMethods = "deploy")
public void test2() {}
```

With this setup, TestNG will execute our test methods in the following order:

1. `launchServer()`
2. `deploy()`
3. `test1()` and then `test2()`, or the other way around

Listing 2–83 shows a sample output for this run.

Listing 2–83 Output of the tests using method dependency

```
PASSED: launchServer
FAILED: deploy
SKIPPED: test2
SKIPPED: test1
===============================================
Dependent Concurrent Suite
Total tests run: 4, Failures: 1, Skips: 2
===============================================
```

The first thing to notice is that when no order is specified (such as between `test1()` and `test2()`), TestNG will run these test methods in any order. In our example, `test2()` was run before `test1()`, but you should not rely on this kind of ordering unless you use `dependsOnMethods/dependsOnGroups`.

Here is how our sample ran.

- `launchServer()` succeeded.
- TestNG looked at the dependencies of `deploy()` (`launchServer`), verified that it had run and succeeded, and then ran it. `deploy()` failed.
- TestNG looked at the dependencies of `test1()`, noticed that they failed, and marked `test1()` as a `SKIP` without running it. Then it did the same with `test2()`.

This seems to solve our problem nicely, but using `dependsOnMethods` has a few problems.

First, notice that we are specifying method names with strings. This, in itself, is a design smell: Whenever you specify a Java element as a string (such as a class name in a `Class#forName` call, or a method name when you are trying to look it up), you are making it possible for this code to break later when you refactor it. Worse yet, even refactoring IDEs might miss this string. As a rule of thumb, you should specify Java elements in strings (whether in Java, XML, or any kind of files) only when you have no other choice.

Related to the previous point, we seem to be violating the Don't Repeat Yourself principle: Method names are used both as Java methods but also as strings. This is never a good sign.

But more importantly, consider the following scenario: A new requirement comes in, and our Web application now depends on another application (say, Authentication Server) to be launched first. Therefore, our test methods will not run unless this server is up and running as well. Figure 2–2 shows the new dependency.

In order to accommodate this new testing scenario, we need to add `deployAuthenticationServer` as a dependency to all our test methods, as shown in Listing 2–84.

Figure 2–2 New dependency order

Listing 2–84 Adding a new method dependency to tests

```
@Test
public void launchServer() {}

@Test(dependsOnMethods = "launchServer")
public void deploy() {}

@Test(dependsOnMethods = "launchServer")
public void deployAuthenticationServer() {}

@Test(dependsOnMethods = { "deploy",
    "deployAuthenticationServer" })
public void test1() {}

@Test(dependsOnMethods = { "deploy",
    "deployAuthenticationServer" })
public void test2() {}
```

Things are getting worse. Our violation of the DRY principle is increasing, our test class will collapse if ever we decide to rename `deploy` to `deployMyApp`, and finally, this test case is certainly not going to scale well as we keep adding new test methods.

As the old saying goes, "In computer science, all problems can be solved by adding a level of indirection." In this case, the level of indirection is to introduce groups.

Figure 2–2 already hinted that our test methods seem to fall into certain categories (one per box), so putting these methods in their own groups is a very natural thing to do. Let's create the following groups.

- `init`: Start the container(s).
- `deploy-apps`: Deploy all the applications we'll need.

We'll now rewrite our example with the following changes: We put our test methods in groups, and we use `dependsOnGroups` instead of `dependsOnMethods` (Listing 2–85).

Listing 2–85 Switching to group dependencies

```
@Test(groups = "init")
public void launchServer() {}
```

```
@Test(dependsOnGroups = "init", groups = "deploy-apps")
public void deploy() {}

@Test(dependsOnGroups = "init", groups = "deploy-apps")
public void deployAuthenticationServer() {}

@Test(dependsOnGroups = "deploy-apps")
public void test1() {}

@Test(dependsOnGroups = "deploy-apps")
public void test2() {}
```

As you can see, using groups to specify our dependencies has solved all the problems we encountered initially.

- We are no longer exposed to refactoring problems. We can change the names of our methods in any way we please, and as long as we don't modify the dependsOnGroups or groups attributes, our tests will keep running with the proper dependencies set up.
- We are no longer violating the DRY principle.
- Whenever a new method needs to be added in the dependency graph, all we need to do is put it in the right group and make sure it depends on the correct group. We don't need to modify any other method.

Dependent Testing and Threads

In order to respect the ordering that you are requesting, TestNG will automatically run methods that depend on each other (either with dependsOnMethods or dependsOnGroups) by running them in the same thread.

Therefore, whenever you are trying to run tests in parallel, keep in mind that one or more of the threads in the thread pool will be used to run each method in sequence. Relying excessively on dependent tests can therefore adversely impact the performances of your tests if you expect all of them to run in different threads.

Failures of Configuration Methods

You might not realize it, but you have already encountered dependent methods. If you think about it, all test methods depend on configuration methods (e.g., `@BeforeClass`). The only difference between dependent test methods and configuration methods is that test methods depend implicitly on configuration methods (we don't need to specify `dependsOnMethods`).

Let's see what happens when a configuration method fails, as shown in Listing 2–86.

Listing 2–86 Failing configuration method

```
@BeforeMethod
public void init() {
  throw new RuntimeException();
}

@Test
public void f() {
  System.out.println("Will I run?");
}
```

The result is shown in Listing 2–87.

Listing 2–87 Output of a failing configuration method

```
FAILED: init
java.lang.RuntimeException
... Removed 24 stack frames
SKIPPED: f
```

As expected, TestNG skipped the test method because its configuration method didn't run. This behavior is actually very useful: While configuration methods should in theory never fail (they don't contain code that is under test, they just initialize the entire system), they can very possibly fail, and when it happens, there is no point in running your test methods because your system is not in a stable state.

Having said that, there are several types of configuration methods, and their failure doesn't have the same meaning for your test methods. Table 2–6 shows what happens when a configuration method fails.

Table 2–6 Consequences of a configuration method failing

Configuration method	What happens when it fails
@BeforeMethod	All the test methods in the test class (and superclass) are skipped.
@BeforeClass	All the test methods in the test class (and superclass) are skipped.
@BeforeTest	All the test methods that belong in all the classes inside the <test> tag are skipped.
@BeforeSuite	All the test methods of the suites are skipped.
@BeforeGroups	All the test methods that belong to the same group as this configuration method are skipped.

The first thing to remember about dependent testing is that while dependsOnMethods is handy for simple tests, or when only one method depends on another method, most of the time, you should be using dependsOnGroups, which is easier to scale and more robust in the face of future refactorings.

Second, using dependencies with TestNG has several benefits.

- Since we are supplying precise dependency information, TestNG can run tests in the order expected, and because it has this knowledge, it can produce very accurate reports of what went wrong when tests start failing. This is illustrated by the two possible statuses of tests: FAILURE and SKIP.

- Test isolation is not compromised. Even though some of our test methods depend on others to run correctly, TestNG calculates those automatically, thereby allowing us to ask TestNG to "run this single test method" and have this executed without having to trace all the dependencies needed.

- Dependent tests can speed up test runs significantly when cascading errors appear. As soon as a central piece of the testing architecture fails, tests that depend on it will automatically be skipped by TestNG, therefore allowing us to get a very fast turnaround in the cycle of fixing tests, running tests, and debugging failures.

Inheritance and Annotation Scopes

In this section, we'll examine how we can leverage inheritance and TestNG annotation scopes to improve the modularity and structure of your tests.

The Problem

In the previous section, we took a close look at the hypothetical example of a Web application. Because it needs dependencies, this example introduced a set of groups and also contained several test methods that actually test the Web application. These methods were called `test1()`, `test2()`, and so on.

These test methods did not belong to any group because that wasn't necessary for our illustration of dependencies. However, in the context of an entire test structure, we would probably want to put them in at least one similar group (e.g., `web`, or `web.credit-card`) in order to make it possible to invoke only these test methods when changes are made to this particular Web application.

Listing 2–88 shows some code for putting those methods into a group.

Listing 2–88 Dependencies specified per test

```
public class CreditCardTest {
  @Test(groups = "web.credit-card")
  public void test1() {}

  @Test(groups = "web.credit-card")
  public void test2() {}
}
```

There are a few obvious problems with this code.

- It violates the Don't Repeat Yourself principle. We are repeating the name of the group for each method, which makes future refactorings problematic.
- It puts a burden on the developers who will be adding test methods. They will have to remember to put the new test methods in that group, or those methods will not be run the next time someone tries to test the `credit-card` application.

TestNG provides an easy solution to this problem: annotation scopes.

The definition of TestNG's `@Test` annotation is as shown in Listing 2–89.

Listing 2–89 `@Test` annotation definition

```
@Target({METHOD, TYPE, CONSTRUCTOR})
public @interface Test {
```

This shows that this annotation can be put on a method, a constructor, or a class.

When the `@Test` annotation is specified on the class level, it automatically applies to all the public methods of that test class, along with its attributes. We can therefore rewrite the test as shown in Listing 2–90.

Listing 2–90 Groups specified on a class-level annotation

```
@Test(groups = "web.credit-card ")
public class CreditCardTest {

public void test1() {}

public void test2() {}
```

This is an improvement: The name of the group is now mentioned only once, and every public test method that gets added to this class automatically becomes a member of that group.

Inheritance

But we can do better. In reality, it's very likely that some of the test methods that exercise a particular part of the system will span over several classes, not just one as shown in our example. While it might be conceivable to have all the tests of a Web application called `credit-card` in one class, consider a group `front-end`, which would exercise all the Web applications and maybe also HTML generation, HTTP connections, and other front-end-related code.

Again, we want to make sure that we don't violate the DRY principle (we only want to mention that group name in one place) and also that our test code base is very easy to maintain and to grow.

In order to make this possible, TestNG supports a mechanism called *annotation inheritance*. The idea is very simple—all TestNG annotations declared on a class will automatically be visible on all subclasses of this class.

Before we explore the consequences of this functionality, let's make a quick digression to emphasize an important point: Annotation inheritance is *not* supported by the JDK. Consider the code shown in Listing 2–91.

Listing 2–91 Example of Java's annotation inheritance behavior

```
@Test(groups = "web.credit-card")
class SuperA {}

public class A extends SuperA {
  public static void main(String[] argv) {
    Class[] classes = { SuperA.class, A.class };
    for (Class c : classes) {
      System.out.println("Annotations for " + c);
      for (Annotation a : c.getAnnotations()) {
        System.out.println(a);
      }
    }
  }
}
```

This code produces the output shown in Listing 2–92.

Listing 2–92 Output of the annotation introspection example

```
Annotations for class org.testngbook.SuperA
@org.testng.annotations.Test(groups=[web.credit-car], ...)
Annotations for class org.testngbook.A
<nothing>
```

Therefore, support for inheritance of annotations has to be supplied individually by each tool, and that's exactly what TestNG does. Just don't expect to find this behavior in other products, unless is it explicitly advertised.

Leveraging this support, we can create a base class with the correct annotation and simply have our main test class extend it. This is shown in Listing 2–93.

Listing 2–93 Dependencies defined in a base class

```
@Test(groups = "web.credit-card")
class BaseWebTest {
}

public class WebTest extends BaseWebTest {
  public void test1() {}
  public void test2() {}
}
```

Introducing annotation inheritance in our code has two very beneficial side effects.

1. Any class that extends `BaseWebTest` will see all its public methods automatically become part of the `web.credit-card` group. This makes it very trivial for anyone to add Web tests, and they don't even need to know TestNG or what a test group is.

2. More importantly, our class `WebTest` has become a plain old Java object (POJO) without even any annotations. Take a look at the code: There is no annotation, no imports, and, in effect, absolutely no reference whatsoever to anything related to TestNG. All the magic is happening in the `extends` clause.

In conclusion, annotation inheritance is a simple extension of Java inheritance, and when combining these two tools, we can create a very streamlined and easy-to-extend test code base that will stand the test of time.

However, misusing inheritance can sometimes create surprising results, as explained in the following section.

Pitfalls of Inheritance

Now that we've covered annotation inheritance, let's turn our attention to a more traditional way to use inheritance in Java.

Just as annotation inheritance turned out to be useful in our previous example, Java inheritance is also quite useful once we realize we want to share initialization code in our tests. For example, let's assume that we'd like to add a method that will test that a transaction to a bank works correctly. On top of that, this test will be used in other classes, so we decide to put it in a base class, as shown in Listing 2–94.

Listing 2–94 Tests declared in a base class

```
public class BaseWebTest {
  @Test
  public void verifyBankTransaction() {}
}

public class WebTest extends BaseWebTest {
  @Test
  public void verifyCreditCard() {}
}
```

Then we edit our `testng.xml` to reflect this change, as shown in Listing 2–95.

Listing 2–95 Configuration file including superclass and subclass

```
<!DOCTYPE suite SYSTEM "http://testng.org/testng-1.0.dtd">

<suite name="Web suite" >
  <test name="Web">
    <classes>
      <class name="org.testngbook.BaseWebTest" />
      <class name="org.testngbook.WebTest" />
    </classes>
  </test>
</suite>
```

And finally, we run it, and we get the output shown in Listing 2–96.

Listing 2–96 Output of running tests with superclass and subclass

```
PASSED: verifyBankTransaction
PASSED: verifyCreditCard
PASSED: verifyBankTransaction


===============================================
    Web suite
    Tests run: 3, Failures: 0, Skips: 0
===============================================
```

Something went wrong. Our `verifyBankTransaction()` method was invoked twice.

The problem is that when we included the base class of our tests in `testng.xml`, we included this method twice in our test run: once in the base class itself, and once in the subclass, where this method is visible as well because of the way Java inheritance works.

The simple fix to this problem is to remove the base class from `testng.xml`, as shown in Listing 2–97.

Listing 2–97 Configuration file modified to remove the base class

```
<classes>
  <class name="org.testngbook.WebTest" />
</classes>
```

And we now get the expected result, as Listing 2–98 shows.

Listing 2–98 Output of only the specifying subclass

```
PASSED: verifyCreditCard
PASSED: verifyBankTransaction


===============================================
    Web suite
    Tests run: 2, Failures: 0, Skips: 0
===============================================
```

In order to avoid this kind of problem, we suggest this simple rule of thumb:

Don't list test base classes in `testng.xml` *files.*

Since TestNG methods need to be public, methods declared in a base class will automatically be visible in subclasses, and they should never need to be listed explicitly as test classes. We also recommend that whenever you use a naming convention for test classes (e.g., saying all the names must end in `Test`), choose base classes names that don't match the given convention so you can avoid accidentally including them in the test run (e.g., the `ant` task might include the file pattern `**/*Test.class`). For example, we would therefore rename `BaseWebTest` to `BaseWeb` or `WebTestSupport` to make it clear that this class should not be listed as a test class.

Test Groups

In this section, we will discuss one of TestNG's main features: test groups.

Ever since programming languages have been in use, language creators have done their best to provide developers with the ability to keep their code bases ordered in a way that's as flexible as possible for them. One of the first popular breakthroughs in this area was made by C++ with the introduction of namespaces, which not only made it possible to avoid clashes between classes of similar names but also helped developers classify their classes and put them in locations shared with classes that cover similar functionalities.

Java's equivalent to namespaces is packages. Each Java class typically belongs to a package. (The use of the default package is completely deprecated by now; use it only when you need to write some quick throwaway code.) Just like namespaces, packages are hierarchical in nature, putting the developers in full control of how they want to organize their code bases.

Until recently, Java packages were the only way you could classify test classes as well, and while they work well for Java code in general, they suffer from several limitations for testing, including the following.

- A class can belong to only one package.
- Sometimes we want to be able to find test classes with loose package definitions.

■ Packages are part of the Java type system, and modifying them not only requires a recompilation but also can have ripple effects throughout the test code.

At about the same time that TestNG was created (about three years ago, at the time of writing), two new applications, Flickr and Gmail, were becoming extremely popular. These two next-generation Web applications introduced a simple idea that was immediately embraced by its users: tags. Users could go through their content (pictures or email messages) and add random words to describe them, which not only helped describe the data but, more importantly, made it very easy to search as well.

Thus was born the idea of test groups for TestNG.

Test groups solve the limitations we mentioned, and they actually further one of TestNG's main design goals: to create a clean separation between the static model (the code of your tests) and the runtime model (which tests get run). Once you start specifying that your test methods belong to one or more groups, it becomes possible to specify which methods to run in a totally dynamic manner and without having to recompile anything, thereby making it possible to compile once and run different configurations many times.

Let's start with a quick overview of how test groups are specified in TestNG, and then we'll carry on with a few general patterns and recommendations on how to use test groups.

Syntax

Both the `@Test` annotation and the configuration annotations (`@BeforeClass`, `@AfterClass`, `@BeforeMethod`, and so on) can belong to groups. Listing 2–99 shows the signature of the `groups()` attribute.

Listing 2–99 *groups()* annotation signature

```
/**
 * The list of groups this class/method belongs to.
 */
public String[] groups() default {};
```

The `groups()` attribute is an array of strings, and it can therefore be specified in any of the ways shown in Listing 2–100.

Listing 2–100 Specifying *groups()* on a test

```
@Test(groups = { "group1" })
@Test(groups = { "group1", "group2" })
@Test(groups = "group1")
```

The last version shown in the listing is a shortcut allowed by the annotations syntax of JDK 5 (see Appendix B for more details).

The `@Test` annotation can also be placed at the top of a test class, and the groups specified in it will then apply to all the public methods of the class, as shown in Listing 2–101.

Listing 2–101 Specifying *groups()* on a class

```
@Test(groups = "group1")
public class A {
  @Test
  public void test1() {
    // this test method belongs to "group1"
  }
}
```

There is one additional twist: Groups defined at the class level are cumulative with groups specified at the method level, as shown in Listing 2–102.

Listing 2–102 Specifying a group on a class and a method

```
@Test(groups = "group2")
public class B {
  @Test
  public void test2() {}

  @Test(groups = "group3")
  public void test3() {}
}
```

In this example, the method `test2()` belongs to the group `group2` (by virtue of the class annotation), and the method `test3()` belongs to both group2 and group3. This cumulative effect makes it possible to extend the coverage of a group to only a few methods in the class.

Groups and Runtime

Now that you know how to specify groups for your test methods, how do you actually use them?

Groups are used at runtime. When you are about to run your tests, TestNG gives you several options that allow you to be arbitrarily broad or restrictive in deciding which test methods should run. The main way to specify this at runtime is with the testng.xml (there are other ways, which we will cover shortly).

Listing 2–103 shows one of the simplest testng.xml files that uses groups.

Listing 2–103 *groups()* declared in a configuration file

```
<suite name="Simple suite">

  <test name="GroupTest">
    <groups>
      <run>
        <include name="group1"/>
      </run>
    </groups>
    <classes>
      <class name="com.example.A" />
    </classes>
  </test>
</suite>
```

This testng.xml instructs TestNG to run all the test methods that belong to the group group1 in the class com.example.A.

Two additional features make things more interesting.

1. You can exclude groups.
2. You can specify patterns (regular expressions) of groups to include or exclude.

You exclude groups similarly to the way you include them, as shown in Listing 2–104.

Listing 2–104 Specifying group inclusions and exclusions

```
<include name="database">
<exclude name="gui">
```

This is a good example of a `testng.xml` that could be used when you want to run only database tests (it would probably be called `testng-database.xml`). Conversely, you would probably want to define a `testng-gui.xml` file that would include the group `gui` and exclude `database`.

If a test method happens to be in a group that's both included and excluded, the exclusion prevails. While this scenario might strike you as a bit odd, you will see soon that it's actually quite common when your groups start describing different categories of tests.

In the absence of either an `include` or `exclude` directive, TestNG will simply ignore your groups and run all your test methods. As soon as either an `include` or an `exclude` is specified, groups become strictly enforced. This may sound very natural, but it has a side effect that you will probably trip over at least once: If a test method doesn't belong to any group and you suddenly decide to include a group, that test method will not be run. Keep this in mind the next time some of your test methods mysteriously stop being invoked after you change your runtime group configuration.

Another useful feature is that you can specify regular expressions[8] of groups in `testng.xml`, as shown in the following example.

Listing 2–105 shows a summary of the inclusion/exclusion rules as applied to the example code.

Listing 2–105 Sample code using multiple groups

```
@Test
public void noGroups() {}

@Test(groups = { "web", "servlet"})
public void servlet() {}

@Test(groups = { "web", "jsp"})
public void jsp() {}
```

8. Emphasis on the term *regular* expressions. These are different from the wildcards typically used in the command line or shell window. With regular expressions, "any character" is represented by the symbol "." and "anything" is ".*". Please look at the Javadocs for the package `java.util.regex` for more details.

```
@Test(groups = "broken")
public void broken() {}

@Test(groups =  {"web", "broken"})
public void webBroken() {}
@Test(groups = {"weekend"})
public void weekend() {}
```

Table 2–7 shows a list of the various methods from Listing 2–105 that get run depending on which groups you decide to include and exclude in your TestNG configuration.

Table 2–7 Methods that run depending on the groups specified

Groups specified in `testng.xml`	Methods run	Remarks

No include, no exclude	`broken()`
	`jsp()`
	`noGroups()`
	`servlet()`
	`webBroken()`
	`weekend()`
		All methods are run.

`<include name="web" >`	`webBroken()`
	`jsp()`
	`servlet()`
		`noGroups()` was not run because it doesn't belong to any group (therefore, it doesn't belong to the group that's included).

`<exclude name="broken" />`	`jsp()`
	`noGroups()`
	`servlet()`
	`weekend()`
		None of the methods belonging to the group `broken` are run.

`<include name="web " />` `<exclude name="broken" />`	`jsp()` `servlet()`	`webBroken()` belongs to both an included group and an excluded group; therefore, it gets excluded (exclusion wins).

`<include name="we.*" />`	`jsp()`
	`servlet()`
	`webBroken()`
	`weekend()`
		All the methods that belong to a group starting with the letters "we" are run.

(continued)

Table 2–7 Methods that run depending on the groups specified *(continued)*

Groups specified in `testng.xml`	Methods run	Remarks

`<include name="web" >`
`<include name="weekend" >`
	`jsp()`
	`servlet()`
	`webBroken()`
	`weekend()`
		All the methods that belong to either web or weekend are run.

We can also create new groups in the `testng.xml` file (Listing 2–106).

Listing 2–106 Defining new groups in the configuration file

```
<groups>
  <define name="all-web">
    <include name="jsp" />
    <include name="servlet" />
  </define>
  <run>
    <include name="all-web" />
  </run>
</groups>
```

In this example, we are defining a new group called `all-web`, which contains all the test methods that belong to either the group `jsp` or to the group `servlet`.

Being able to define new groups in `testng.xml` gives us a lot of flexibility when designing the group hierarchy: We can focus on using very granular groups in the code and then gather these narrow groups into bigger ones at runtime.

Running Groups

We don't need to use a `testng.xml` in order to specify groups for a TestNG run. Here are four more ways we can invoke TestNG with groups.

With the Command Line

TestNG's main class has two options to specify grouping: `-groups` (to include groups) and `-excludegroups` (to exclude groups). Either of these can occur multiple times on the command line. Listing 2–107 shows an example.

Listing 2–107 Command line to specify group settings

```
java org.testng.TestNG —groups jsp —groups ↵
    servlet —excludegroups broken com.example.MyTestClass
```

With `ant`

The `ant` task offers equivalent attributes to the command line options just described. Listing 2–108 shows an example.

Listing 2–108 Groups specified in *ant build.xml*

```
<testng groups="jsp, servlet" excludedgroups="broken">
  <classfileset dir="build">
    <include name="com/example/MyTestClass.class" />
  </classfileset>
</testng>
```

With the Java API

We can also specify groups directly on an instance of the TestNG class, as shown in Listing 2–109.

Listing 2–109 Groups specified programmatically

```
TestNG tng = new TestNG();
tng.setGroups("jsp, servlet");
tng.setExcludedGroups("broken");
// ...
```

The TestNG API is described in more detail in Appendix B.

With a Synthetic `testng.xml`

Just like any element present in `testng.xml`, it is possible to specify groups by using the Synthetic API, which is described in Chapter 6.

Using Groups Effectively

Over the years, several practices in how test groups can be used have emerged in the TestNG community. This section explores a few of them and also offers some suggestions in terms of how test code can be organized with regard to group definitions.

Excluding Broken Tests

Ideally, all tests should always pass. In reality, however, this is very unlikely to be the case. Every day, probably a small percentage of tests are broken for a variety of reasons, and while it is recommended to fix them as soon as possible, it is sometimes not an option because of external factors.

- There are more important things to do. (As important as tests are, you should always exercise common sense when prioritizing your tasks, and sometimes deadlines need to be met, even if it's at the expense of tests.)
- You depend on another developer's code before the test can be fixed.
- The code owner is not available immediately to address the test breakage.
- The test cannot pass because it's testing a feature that is currently being implemented or improved.

On the other hand, it is very important to avoid having recurring failures in your test reports because once you get used to seeing failures every morning, you stop paying attention to them. One morning, a very important test failure might appear, and it won't be noticed.

In summary: Tests should be green at all times, but red is unavoidable.

How do we solve this dilemma?

A traditional way to solve this problem has been to comment out the offending tests. The problem with this approach is that in the absence of some support from your testing framework, there is a very distinct possibility that you might forget to uncomment this test before you ship, therefore giving you the false impression that all tests currently pass. Indeed, all the tests that are run do indeed pass, you just happen not to run all the tests that should be run.

One approach to mitigate this problem with older testing frameworks is to add a comment with a TODO or FIXME notice, but this is very fragile and hard to enforce. (A developer could, for example, misspell the notice and call it FIX-ME, and it will be missed when trying to determine the set of all currently commented-out tests.)

TestNG offers an elegant solution to this problem with test groups: Just create a special group (e.g., `broken`). Whenever a test method starts failing, add it to this group, as shown in Listing 2–110.

Listing 2–110 Creating a special *broken* group

```
@Test(groups = { "web", "broken" }
```

Then exclude the group at runtime (Listing 2–111).

Listing 2–111 Excluding the *broken* group at runtime

```
<exclude name="broken" />
```

This technique has two advantages.

1. It makes it trivial to avoid running tests that you know are not passing, therefore keeping the test reports green.
2. Since TestNG generates reports that contain all the groups that were noticed during a test run, it is trivial to look up the group called `broken` and get the full list of all the test methods that belong to it.

You can find the list of groups in the upper left corner of the main report page, as shown in Figure 2–3.

Using this report, it is very easy for anyone to keep track of the list of test methods that are currently broken. Of course, you can choose to use more descriptive names for this category of groups, such as:

- `broken.unknown` (when you don't know why this test is failing)
- `broken.temporary` (when this failure is expected to disappear soon)
- `broken.fix-in-progress` (when someone is currently working on a fix)

You can even imagine having a more sophisticated strategy in which test methods will be ignored only for a certain period of time. (Chapter 6 explains how to achieve this result.)

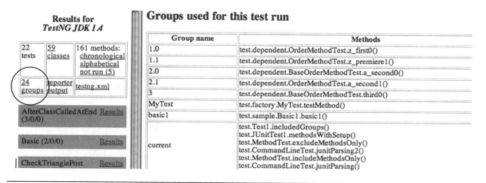

Figure 2–3 Locating the groups in the HTML reports

Group Categories

It is also possible to use groups to capture categories of tests. Organizations with elaborate code bases have usually developed their own terminology to describe their tests. Although the meaning of some adjectives is usually fairly agreed upon (such as *unit test*), the testing community as a whole is fairly divided on what the various test categories are.

Don't let that stop you. It's perfectly acceptable to come up with your own terminology as long as you make sure it's used consistently throughout your organization.

Here are a few ideas for group names.

- Test type: `unit, functional, integration, system, acceptance, performance`

   These names can be convenient if you manage to establish clear guidelines as to how a certain test method should be classified. In our experience, this classification doesn't work very well because it relies on vague and sometimes conflicting criteria.

- Test size: `small, medium, large`

   These names are a little easier to define. For example, a `small` test could be a unit test that is not supposed to access the network or use any business object (it would be using mocks). A `large` test method would use fully blown business objects and exercise real parts of your system. A `medium` test would fall in between, depending on what makes sense for your code base.

- Functional description: `web, gui, html, jsp, servlet, database, back-end`

   These names are also fairly easy to use and very descriptive, so we highly encourage their usage. You will most likely never have a lot of disagreement on whether a test should belong to the `database` or `web` group.

■ Speed of the test: `slow`, `fast`

We are also particularly fond of this kind of categorization. It's easy to draw a line that will decide which group a test method should belong to ("if it runs in less than a tenth of a second, it's fast; otherwise, it's slow"). Ultimately, it makes it very easy for developers to know which tests they should run and when.

■ Procedural description: `check-in`, `smoke-test`, `milestone`, `release`

This categorization gives developers indications about the moment where certain tests should be run. For example, you might want all your developers to make sure they are not breaking some vital functionalities of the system before checking in any code (hence the name *check-in test*, also known as a *smoke test*). Similarly, certain tests are so comprehensive that they should be run only before a main milestone or before a release gets shipped.

■ Platform: `os.win32`, `os.linux`, `os.mac-os`

Admittedly, since we are programming in Java, we should rarely need this kind of categorization, but we all know that operating-system-dependent code is sometimes a necessity. It is a good idea to tag tests that should run only on a certain platform with one of these names. For example, you might have a routine that creates file paths, and you need to make sure that on Windows, only backslashes (\) are used, while the Linux and Mac OS versions should use only forward slashes (/). Another example of platform-dependent tests would be when you launch processes or when you use a platform-specific external package.

■ Hardware: `single-core`, `multi-core`, `dual-cpu`, `memory.1gig`, `memory.10gig`

These groups should be fairly rare, but if your application tends to deal with heavy volumes of data or if it is heavily multithreaded, some of your tests might make sense only in the presence of certain hardware attributes. For example, a performance test that needs to manipulate gigabytes of data to be meaningful should probably be run only on a machine that meets a certain minimum memory requirement.

■ Runtime schedule: `week-days`, `weekends`, `nightly`, `monthly`

These groups can be used by an external scheduling facility (such as a continuous build system) so that tests get run only at certain times.

Of course, these groups are not mutually exclusive. You can very reasonably have test methods such as those shown in Listing 2–112.

Listing 2–112 Orthogonal test groups

```
@Test(groups = { "fast", "database" })
@Test(groups = { "slow", "database" })
@Test(groups = { "unit", "html" })
@Test(groups = { "functional", "nightly", "os.win32",
  "os.linux" })
```

One of the main benefits of being able to give names to groups of methods is that it makes it easy for developers to find out which tests they should be running. For this reason, we have found the names `slow` and `fast` to be particularly popular among developers because they don't make any assumptions about the contents of those tests or which parts of the system they exercise. Fast tests are simply guaranteed to run fast, making them attractive for developers to run before they commit any code to the repository.

Of course, no matter how fast tests are, they will take longer and longer as their number increases, so over time, it might be a good idea to couple this characterization with another one, so that developers who just modified some database code will know that they probably need to run only the groups `fast` and `database`.

Group Naming

Over time, we've observed that the TestNG community settled on a fairly regular naming pattern for groups. This pattern follows the notation popularized by Java packages and is represented by names separated by dots, starting from the most general category down to the most specific.

Listing 2–113 shows a few examples.

Listing 2–113 Example group names

```
@Test(groups = { "os.linux.debian" })
@Test(groups = { "database.table.ACCOUNTS" })
@Test(groups = { "database.ejb3.connection" })
```

This naming convention is particularly useful when coupled with TestNG's ability to parse regular expressions to locate the groups you want to run: running the groups `database.*` will run all the database tests, but you can still narrow the set of tests to `database.ejb3.*` if you want to be more specific.

Listing 2–114 shows a real-world example from the Harmony project that will run all the tests on the Win32 platform that are not broken. (You can find the full specification at http://wiki.apache.org/harmony/Testing_Convention.)

Listing 2–114 Specifying regular expression group patterns in the configuration file

```
<groups>
  <run>
    <exclude name="type.impl" />
    <exclude name="os\.(?!win\.IA32).*" />
    <exclude name="state.broken" />
    <exclude name="state.broken.win.IA32" />
  </run>
</groups>
```

Code Coverage

Code coverage is a measurement used to determine how much of the code the tests actually exercise. The idea is that by examining code coverage results, we can identify code paths that have not been executed and ensure that we write tests to test every branch.

High code coverage values are often associated with higher-quality code, since more of the code has been explicitly tested. As we will discuss later, this can be misleading and has its pitfalls.

This metric is a type of white-box testing. That is, we examine the coverage on the internals of the code being tested, rather than treating it as a black box.

The general approach taken with code coverage is to write a bunch of tests and run them, and then view the resulting coverage report. From the report, we would then write further tests to increase the coverage, repeating this until we have a suitably high coverage value. Hopefully that high value consists of useful code paths, rather than tests of trivial methods such as getters and setters.

In this section, we'll discuss an example of code coverage and examine a number of popular coverage tools. We'll also outline the integration approach that each tool requires in order to generate meaningful reports.

A Coverage Example

Let's examine a simple method that we will use to illustrate code coverage. We would like to test the method shown in Listing 2–115.

Listing 2–115 Sample method to test for coverage

```
public static boolean isNumber(String s) {
  try {
    Integer.parseInt(s);
    return true;
  } catch(NumberFormatException ex) {
    return false;
  }
}
```

Listing 2–116 shows our naive test implementation.

Listing 2–116 Initial test for the sample method

```
@Test
  public void testNumber() {
    assert isNumber("12");
  }
```

Using a coverage plug-in in our IDE, we run the test and then view the coverage report, shown in Figure 2–4.

```
public static boolean isNumber(String s) {
  try {
    Integer.parseInt(s);
    return true;
  } catch(NumberFormatException ex) {
    return false;
  }
}
```

Figure 2–4 IDE view of code coverage

This report shows us two important indicators. The thick dark gray bar denotes code that has been executed, and the thick black bar denotes code that has not.

So we can see from this view that though our test successfully verified that valid numbers are detected correctly, we did not actually confirm that invalid ones are also correctly identified.

Based on this information, we would now modify our test to test the untested code, as shown in Listing 2–117.

Listing 2–117 Updated test to increase coverage

```
@Test
public void testNumbers() {
  assert isNumber("12");
  assert !isNumber("foo");
}
```

Figure 2–5 shows how the coverage report now looks.

Note that we no longer have untested code in this method, as our test was modified to cover all branches of the code.

Obviously, this example is trivial, and it would have been obvious when writing the test that we should also verify invalid numbers. With more complex code, though, it becomes more and more difficult to intuitively spot code blocks that have not been executed by a test, and code coverage reports can help tremendously in identifying these blocks.

Coverage Metrics

Most coverage tools report different coverage percentage values depending on the coverage type. It's worth learning what the different types are in order to gain a better understanding of how good your code coverage actually is.

```
public static boolean isNumber(String s) {
  try {
    Integer.parseInt(s);
    return true;
  } catch(NumberFormatException ex) {
    return false;
  }
}
```

Figure 2–5 Updated IDE code coverage view

Class Coverage

Class coverage describes how many of the project's classes have been visited by the test suite. This is a useful metric for an overall view of how many areas of your code the tests cover. It also helps you identify classes or packages that are not tested at all.

Method Coverage

Method coverage is the percentage of methods that has been visited. This metric does not take into consideration the size of a given method, but rather whether or not the method has been invoked.

Statement Coverage

Statement coverage tracks the invocation of individual source code statements. This is an important coverage report to view as it allows you to pinpoint within a given source file what lines of code have not been executed, and to catch corner cases for your tests.

Block Coverage

Block coverage views code blocks as the basic unit for coverage, rather than individual statements. This is best illustrated with an example. We have an `Account` class with the method shown in Listing 2–118.

Listing 2–118 Example method to highlight block coverage

```
public boolean debitAccount(double amount) {
    if(amount <= 0) {
      log.warning("Cannot debit a negative amount");
      mailer.sendMail("accounts@acme.com", "Invalid debit",
                   "Attempt to debit " + amount);
      return false;
    } else {
      balance -= amount;
      return true;
    }
  }
```

The method returns `true` if the debit was successful and `false` if otherwise. If the latter happens, a message is logged and an email sent.

Our test appears in Listing 2–119.

Listing 2–119 Test for the block coverage method

```
@Test
public void verifyDebit() {
  Account manager = new Account();
  assert manager.debitAccount(-20);
}
```

The statement coverage for this test will be quite high, as we happen to exercise the code branch for handling invalid input. This branch happens to be larger than the other and has more statements. Thus, this test will show that we have high coverage.

However, the block coverage will be lower. The reason for this is that the code has two blocks. We test only one of these blocks.

Block coverage can be a more useful metric than line or statement coverage because it takes branching and conditions into consideration, rather than the single-line approach that can skew results.

Branch Coverage

Branch coverage is also known as decision coverage. This metric is calculated by measuring which branches in the code are executed. The coverage tool evaluates whether the Boolean value of a control structure is set to both `true` and `false`.

Coverage Tools

A number of code coverage tools are available to Java developers. Some of these tools are better than others, but ultimately they all work in a fairly similar manner. Deciding which tool to use depends on personal taste and which features are more useful to a given use case. However, it's reasonable to expect the following features from any mature coverage product.

- *IDE integration*: Being forced to leave the development environment in order to view coverage reports is irksome and interrupts the development flow. Any decent coverage tool should provide plug-ins for some subset of IDEs that are in popular usage.

- *Build tool integration*: Most coverage tools provide for varying levels of integration with ant (or maven). This integration also means that coverage reports can be run as part of a continuous integration build.

- *Report formats*: Textual output is not as useful as an HTML report for a high-level view. Different coverage tools have different levels of support for output formats. Some output plain text, and some support PDF and HTML, as well as plain text.

- *Historical coverage tracking*: It's useful to see how a project's coverage evolves over time. This is often helpful in flagging a decline in tests relative to functional code.

- *Report navigation*: While an overall view of coverage is useful, even more useful is the ability to drill down into the coverage data to actual source files, as well as being able to sort the data according to different criteria. In some cases, we might like to view package-level coverage reports, whereas in others, we're interested in method coverage for a specific class.

- *Coverage exclusion*: Invariably, we find trivial bits of code that shouldn't be taken into consideration for coverage reports. Some coverage tools allow us to add source-level comments around blocks we'd like to exclude from coverage reports.

We will discuss three of the more popular coverage tools. Clover by Cenqua is a commercial offering generally regarded as the best in the field. EMMA and Cobertura are both open source solutions that work reasonably well. We will cover the main features of each tool and show how to integrate it into your build process. For each of the examples, we will assume that you have an ant build file with a target of `compile` that compiles your sources to a `classes` directory and a TestNG task to run the tests, so the build file looks like Listing 2–120.

Listing 2–120 Base `build.xml` template for all the coverage tool examples

```
<project name="coverage" default="test">
  <taskdef resource="testngtasks" classpath="lib/testng.jar"/>
  <property name="reports" location="reports" />
  <property name="coverage" location="coverage" />
  <property name="coverage-output"
    location="coverage-classes" />
  <property name="output" location="classes" />
```

```
<path id="cp">
 <fileset dir="lib">
    <include name="*.jar" />
  </fileset>
  <pathelement location="${coverage-output}"/>
  <pathelement location="${output}" />
</path>

<target name="compile">
  <mkdir dir="${output}" />
  <mkdir dir="${coverage-output}" />
  <javac source="1.5" srcdir="src" debug="true"
         destdir="${output}" classpathref="cp">
    <include name="**/Coverage.java" />
  </javac>
</target>

<target name="test" depends="compile">
  <testng classpathref="cp" suitename="ant">
    <classfileset dir="${output}" includes="**/*.class" />
  </testng>
</target>
</project>
```

For each of the tools we'll cover in the following subsections, we will also go over the modifications that need to be made to this simple build file to generate coverage data. To ensure we're comparing similar approaches, we will use the offline instrumentation mode for all three tools. This means that the coverage tools will instrument our classes at compile time, rather than through using a custom classloader. The instrumented classes will be written to the `coverage-classes` directory.

In every case, we will output the coverage data store to a `coverage` directory and reports to a `reports` directory.

Note that we also specify a classpath that includes all our project jars and our output directories. The instrumented classes directory `coverage-classes` is included before the noninstrumented one, so that if it does contain instrumented classes, they are loaded first.

Clover

Clover was one of the earliest coverage tools available for Java. Developed by Cenqua, it is a commercial solution that is the most popular in terms of usage and deployment. Part of its success owes to the fact that Cenqua is an avid supporter of open source and provides free copies of most of its software for open source projects, thus helping its adoption significantly.

Clover supports a number of output formats for all its reports, including HTML and PDF. In addition to coverage reports, Clover can track coverage history over time, so a development team can keep an eye on whether the code base is growing faster than the tests and keep track of whether new tests are exercising previously untested code or simply going over the same covered code.

Clover also provides plug-ins for most major IDEs, ensuring that you can view coverage reports during the normal compile/build/test cycle, rather than having to drop to running a tool or an ant build file outside of the IDE.

One of the interesting features of Clover is that, rather than calculating separate percentages of the different metrics, it uses a formula to rank coverage, taking into account a variety of metrics, such as branch coverage and statement coverage. The final value is known as the Total Percentage Coverage (TPC).

Integrating Clover is fairly simple. The first step is to copy the `clover.jar` file to the `ant` home's `lib` directory. This can be quite annoying as that directory might be shared and write access to it might be restricted, so there are a number of other installation options available. One of these options enables you to include the clover jar within your build tree.

1. Copy the `clover.jar` file and the `cenquatasks.jar` file that comes with the download to your project's `lib` directory.
2. Define the Clover-specific tasks.

For the latter method of installation, you need to extend `ant`'s classpath using a Clover-specific task before declaring the Clover tasks, as shown in Listing 2–121.

Listing 2–121 Setting up Clover via `build.xml`

```
<taskdef resource="com/cenqua/ant/antlib.xml"
        classpath="lib/cenquatasks.jar"/>
<extendclasspath path="lib/clover.jar"/>
<taskdef resource="clovertasks" classpath="lib/clover.jar"/>
```

Defining the tasks is simpler, however, if you install Clover into `ant`'s `lib` directory:

```
<taskdef resource="clovertasks"/>
```

Having defined the Clover tasks, the next step is invoking Clover at the appropriate time. Clover works by modifying the source code directly, rather than through bytecode manipulation.

This is achieved through invoking a `clover-setup` task prior to compilation. So, for our example, you would create a new compilation task that compiles to the instrumented output directory and ensure that the `clover-setup` task is invoked first (Listing 2–122).

Listing 2–122 Compiling with Clover instrumentation enabled

```
<target name="clover" depends="compile">
  <clover-setup />
  <javac srcdir="src" source="1.5" debug="true"
         destdir="${coverage-output}" classpathref="cp" >
    <include name="**/*.java"/>
  </javac>
</target>
```

You now have compiled instrumented classes. The next step is to run your test suite against them. Since Clover does not require any extra settings for running, you can in fact leave your test task as it is. Note that earlier the classpath specified the instrumented classes directory before the uninstrumented ones, so the `testng` task will automatically end up loading these first and thus generating the coverage data.

The final step is to produce some reports for the coverage, as shown in Listing 2–123.

Listing 2–123 Generating the Clover report

```
<target name="clover.html">
  <clover-html-report outdir="${reports}"
                      title="My Project"/>
</target>
```

This code generates an HTML view of the coverage results. Clover's generated reports are very high quality and have features such as client-side sorting of results, code collapsing, and other useful navigational aids.

For our example, Clover generates the report shown in Figure 2–6.

```
Overview  Package  File          Stmts: 6    LOC: 24      Total cmp:    2  Stmts/Method: 6
  FRAMES  NO FRAMES  SHOW HELP   Branches: 2  NCLOC: 19    Cmp density: 0.33  Methods/Class: 1
                                 Methods: 1              Avg method cmp:  2
                                 Classes: 1

Expand All
⊞  Account      Line # 7  Total Statements  6  Complexity  2  TOTAL Coverage  55.6%  ▓▓▓▓▓▓▓▓▓▓▓▓▓▓▓▓

Show Tests  (1) Select All  Deselect All

Collapse All
  1         package com.testngbook.advanced;
  2
  3         import java.util.logging.Logger;
  4         import com.testngbook.patterns.mocks.Mailer;
  5
  6
  7         public class Account {
  8           private static final Logger log = Logger.getLogger("Account");
  9
 10           private Mailer mailer;
 11           private double balance;
 12
 13    1  ⊟   public boolean debitAccount(double amount) {
 14    1         if(amount >= 0) {
 15    0             log.warning("Cannot debit a negative amount");
 16    0             mailer.sendMail("accounts@acme.com", "Invalid debit",
 17                           "Attempt to debit " + amount);
 18    0             return false;
 19             } else {
 20    1             balance -= amount;
 21    1             return true;
 22             }
 23         }
 24       }
```

Figure 2–6 Coverage report in Clover

Clover also outputs an appealing dashboard view for your project that attempts to highlight classes that are problematic, as well as a number of statistics for the project as a whole (Figure 2–7).

```
Clover Coverage Report - My Project    Statistics for project coverage:
Coverage timestamp: Mon Jan 8 2007 11:30:39 GMT   Stmts: 11    LOC: 71      Total cmp:  3  Stmts/Method: 2.2
Overview  Package  File                Branches: 10  NCLOC: 49    Cmp density: 0.64  Methods/Class: 2.5
  FRAMES  NO FRAMES  SHOW HELP         Methods:  5   Files: 2  Avg method cmp: 1.4    Classes/Pkg:  2
                                       Classes:  2  Packages: 1


  Coverage  2 classes, 18 / 26 elements        Test Results  0 / 3 tests
  69.2% ▓▓▓▓▓▓▓▓▓▓▓▓▓▓▓                         0% ▓▓▓▓▓▓▓▓▓▓▓▓▓▓▓▓▓▓▓▓▓


  Most Complex Packages                        Top 20 Project Risks
  1. 69.2% ▓▓▓  com.testngbook.advanced (3)    Account


  Most Complex Classes
  1. 55.6% ▓▓▓  Account (2)
```

Figure 2–7 Project overview in Clover

EMMA

EMMA is a coverage tool that was created to fill a previously empty niche: an open source coverage tool that works well. It has a number of interesting features that make it worth considering, such as the following.

- *Offline or online mode*: Classes can be instrumented before they are loaded or on the fly by using an instrumenting classloader.
- *Different coverage types*: Class, method, and block coverage are all supported, as is the ability to detect partial coverage of a single source line.
- *Ability to merge multiple instrumentation data into one report*: This feature allows us to build up coverage reports over time, as well as merge reports from different test runs into one unified report.

Interestingly, EMMA was also chosen by JetBrains as the underlying coverage tool used by the code coverage support built in to IDEA.

In order to integrate EMMA into your build process, you need to add it to your classpath and import the tasks provided by the tool, as shown in Listing 2–124.

Listing 2–124 Defining the EMMA task in `build.xml`

```
<path id="emma.lib" >
  <pathelement location="lib/emma.jar" />
  <pathelement location="lib/emma_ant.jar" />
</path>

<taskdef resource="emma_ant.properties" classpathref="emma.lib" />
```

EMMA defines a top-level `<emma>` task that acts as a container to all its other subtasks. The general flow is to use the `<instr>` task to instrument the class files, then run the tests that would cause the coverage data to be generated, and finally generate some reports from the coverage data. This is shown in Listing 2–125.

Listing 2–125 Instrumenting classes using EMMA

```
<target name="emma" depends="compile">
  <emma>
```

```
    <instr instrpath="${output}"
           destdir="${coverage-output}"
           metadatafile="${coverage}/metadata.emma"
           merge="true"
    />
  </emma>
</target>
```

Having instrumented your classes, the next step is to modify your test run to use the instrumented classes (Listing 2–126).

Listing 2–126 Running instrumented classes

```
<target name="coverage-test" depends="emma">
  <testng classpathref="cp">
    <classfileset dir="${coverage-output}"
           includes="**/*.class"/>
    <jvmarg
      value="-Demma.coverage.out.file=${coverage}/ ↵
  coverage.emma" />
    <jvmarg value="-Demma.coverage.out.merge=true" />
  </testng>
</target>
```

We modified the test runner to include two JVM environment variables to let EMMA know where to generate the coverage data.

Finally, you can generate some reports, as shown in Listing 2–127.

Listing 2–127 Generating EMMA reports

```
<target name="emma.reports" depends="coverage-test">
  <emma>
    <report sourcepath="src">
      <fileset dir="${coverage}">
        <include name="*.emma"/>
      </fileset>

      <txt outfile="${reports}/coverage.txt"/>
      <html outfile="${reports}/coverage.html"/>
    </report>
```

```
</emma>
</target>
```

This code generates two reports, a plain text one and an HTML one. The plain text one is fairly useless, as it gives a high-level view (or a specific view, but for obvious reasons, that cannot be used to drill down into details). The HTML report, however, is more interesting as it shows a list of packages that were tested and makes it possible to drill down to the level of the individual source file to see the lines invoked. Figure 2–8 shows an example of an EMMA report for the `Account` class.

Cobertura

Cobertura is another open source coverage tool that allows for offline instrumentation of class files. One of its interesting features is the ability to fail a build if coverage falls below a certain percentage.

[all classes][com.testngbook.advanced]

COVERAGE SUMMARY FOR SOURCE FILE [Account.java]

name	class, %	method, %	block, %	line, %
Account.java	100% (1/1)	100% (3/3)	50% (19/38)	62% (5/8)

COVERAGE BREAKDOWN BY CLASS AND METHOD

name	class, %	method, %	block, %	line, %
class Account	100% (1/1)	100% (3/3)	50% (19/38)	62% (5/8)
debitAccount (double): boolean		100% (1/1)	39% (12/31)	50% (3/6)
<static initializer>		100% (1/1)	100% (4/4)	100% (1/1)
Account (): void		100% (1/1)	100% (3/3)	100% (1/1)

```
 1 package com.testngbook.advanced;
 2
 3 import java.util.logging.Logger;
 4 import com.testngbook.patterns.mocks.Mailer;
 5
 6
 7 public class Account {
 8   private static final Logger log = Logger.getLogger("Account");
 9
10   private Mailer mailer;
11   private double balance;
12
13   public boolean debitAccount(double amount) {
14     if(amount >= 0) {
15       log.warning("Cannot debit a negative amount");
16       mailer.sendMail("accounts@acme.com", "Invalid debit",
17                       "Attempt to debit " + amount);
18       return false;
19     } else {
20       balance -= amount;
21       return true;
22     }
23   }
24 }
```

Figure 2–8 EMMA coverage output

The steps for integrating Cobertura are very similar to those for EMMA. Assuming you have the same build file, the first change to make is to add in the task definitions:

```
<taskdef classpath="lib/cobertura.jar"
  resource="tasks.properties"/>
```

Having defined the tasks, you then instrument the compiled classes, as shown in Listing 2–128.

Listing 2–128 Instrumenting classes using Cobertura

```
<target name="cobertura" depends="compile">
  <cobertura-instrument todir="${coverage-output}">
    <fileset dir="${output}">
      <include name="*/**.class" />
    </fileset>
  </cobertura-instrument>
</target>
```

Once you have generated the instrumented classes, you can run your tests against them (Listing 2–129).

Listing 2–129 Running tests against the instrumented classes

```
<target name="coverage-test" depends="cobertura">
  <testng classpathref="cp">
    <classfileset dir="${coverage-output}"
    includes="**/*.class"/>
  </testng>
</target>
```

This will produce a `cobertura.ser` file. Note that if the file already exists, the new coverage information is merged into it, rather than overwriting the existing data. A clean run should therefore ensure that this file is removed.

Finally, having generated your coverage data, all that remains is to run a report to view it, as shown in Listing 2–130.

Listing 2–130 Generating the Cobertura report

```
<target name="cobertura.reports">
  <cobertura-report format="html" srcdir="src"
                    destdir="${reports}"/>
</target>
```

It is also possible to generate XML reports that can then be further processed for final presentation.

Implementation

On a side note, it's worth having a rough idea of how coverage tools actually do their work. Fundamentally, all approaches boil down to the same idea. Code needs to be modified so that every line has a callback to the coverage tool, to notify it that the given line has been executed. This can be done at the source level or at the binary level. The source approach involves generating an intermediary file with the coverage calls. Clover, for example, uses source instrumentation; an intermediate source file is generated based on the original sources, and that source is what is compiled.

For binary instrumenting, after the code is compiled, the coverage tool goes over the class file and identifies all lines of code. Each line is then wrapped in a callback to the coverage data store with the relevant invocation information. The new class file with all the modified bytecode is written out, and this is what is used for execution. Thus, when the class is invoked, the coverage data store is populated with all the lines that have been invoked.

There are two approaches for loading the modified class files.

1. *Custom classloader*: In this scenario, no preprocessing is needed, as a custom classloader is used to load all classes that need to be instrumented. The classloader works by loading in the class data for a given class, modifying its bytecode to include all the coverage code, and then defining a new class based on the modified bytecode and returning that to the user. All usages of this class will now correctly track coverage information.

2. *Static/source instrumentation*: In this case, the coverage tool is run as part of the build process. It can work on either the source code or the compiled code and might either generate a modified source file with the coverage code injected that is subsequently compiled or use the

same approach as above and inject the coverage bytecode into the compiled class files. These class files can then be loaded as is since they have the coverage code already injected—no custom classloader is required.

Beware!

We have often mentioned to any number of people that the red and green bars that coverage tools show us in all reports are one of the worst things to happen to coverage reports!

While that's an exaggeration, it really is astounding how many people live and die by these bars. It is not uncommon to see a point release of an open source project with one of the main new features being "increased coverage by 20%." Likewise, it's equally common to see source code littered with coverage exclusion comments, just to bump up the final coverage percentage.

There is something addictive about reducing the size of that red bar. It's a very simple, compelling representation of badness, so the urge to shrink it is very hard to resist. Many fail, sadly.

We cannot stress this enough: You must, absolutely must, resist falling into that trap. Code coverage is a useful tool in your arsenal, but it is not a measure of quality or how good your tests are. In any given code base, there are huge swaths of code that are trivial and simplistic and many helper methods that can be verified with the most cursory of glances. There is absolutely no benefit or point to ensuring that your test cases cover such code. You would in fact be wasting your time, time that is better spent on ensuring that other, more important parts of the code base have better tests. The law of diminishing returns is in full effect when it comes to that green bar, beyond a certain point; it's simply not worth the effort to make it inch up further.

Do not succumb to the allure of that shiny green bar!

A Guide to Successful Coverage

It turns out that there are a lot of good practices (and a great many bad ones) surrounding code coverage. Its current accessibility and popularity have made it an easy tool to integrate, and given the simplistic output and gratification it provides, everyone is now on board with the general principles. Sadly, this does mean that the finer points of the art of code coverage are lost.

Coverage Reports Don't Say What You Think They Say

We've run our test suite and now have a coverage report. We've identified a bunch of classes that have low or no coverage; what do we do? What is done currently on the whole involves running away to write more tests, ensuring the appropriate code paths are exercised. This is completely and utterly misguided, wrong, unhelpful, and deceptive!

Why? Well, what we've done is effectively masked the problem. We treated the most obvious symptoms without pausing to consider the root cause.

So what should we do? The first step is to identify what the untested code is supposed to do—not in terms of an API or actual method calls, but in terms of "What functionality or requirement does this code meet?"

Once we've identified the feature that hasn't been tested, and only then, we can go away and write that test we've been aching to write. It's crucial that we *not* look at the coverage report when writing the test. The goal is to test a feature, not to exercise the right code for the sake of coverage. The test should address the feature as best it can, without taking into consideration whatever else the coverage report says that is not directly related to an end-user feature.

Thus, we end up with new tests (or just as likely, redesigned old tests) that focus on missed functionality. Rerunning the coverage report will now hopefully yield a higher coverage percentage.

If the percentage has not changed, the test did not exercise the right feature, and it's time to redesign/rewrite it yet again, using the same approach. It's very likely that we simply did not correctly identify the feature to test, and we need to rethink it.

Coverage Is Hard

It's trivial to integrate a coverage tool, but to successfully use its results is far from easy. As we mentioned earlier, there is a strong urge to tweak a test or churn out a new one to bump up the percentage with little work. Far harder is making that mental pause, stepping back, and evaluating what the test should do instead, without taking the coverage into consideration.

Code coverage tools do not tell us what to do. They do not reveal acres of code that need tests written. Instead, they hint at problem areas. The tool is trying to say, "You should look at this code," rather than "Write a test for this block."

Percentages Are Irrelevant

It is fairly common to see a project declare as a goal that its test coverage should be 80%. Equally, it's common to see managers demand a certain percentage. In both cases, the product in question is considered incomplete until the target coverage percentage has been reached.

So what ends up happening in practice? In order to achieve the stated goal, developers will (sensibly) optimize for it. It's easy to look at a code base, identify large sections of code that are executed as part of normal operation, and write tests that exercise them. We can get high coverage surprisingly quickly through an almost mindless approach of rinse and repeat; look at code, find large chunks, write test, view coverage, and so on.

Designing for Coverage Is Evil

It's tempting, for the sake of that elusive 100% coverage mark, to decide that we're likely to save a lot of time and effort by thinking of coverage as we write the code, and ensure that all the code can be covered with simple tests.

Such thinking is to be avoided at all costs! The problem here is that all we end up achieving is more successfully disguising the weak points in our logic, by ensuring that a coverage tool cannot find them. We've effectively ruled out coverage as a useful indicator of functionality that needs rethinking or testing. This approach ensures we will not find faults of omission, cases where we've forgotten to handle a specific corner case or did not fully flesh out the functionality at a given point of the application.

A Little Is Better Than None

It's tempting given all the pitfalls surrounding coverage to give up on it altogether. It's equally disheartening to see a pitifully low coverage percentage that leaves us wondering why bother, given that going out to explicitly increase coverage is usually a bad idea.

It's crucial to keep in mind that coverage is a tool that tells us what direction we should think in; it doesn't tell us what to think. It's perfectly acceptable, given the constraints of delivery dates, the constant nagging by the business side to focus on functionality, and other such real-life concerns, to focus on a few high-value areas for coverage. These should be critical sections of code that cannot be verified with a glance. Ultimately, how much coverage we have is an ongoing battle, a tradeoff between delivering functionality and testing. All the stakeholders would be ill served if achieving a specific coverage percentage were a stated goal of any project.

Coverage Tools Don't Test Code That Doesn't Exist

Even if we were stupid enough to waste the time and effort to reach 100% coverage, we would still need some form of external testing in any serious product. This can mean a QA department or other developers who actually exercise the application we've developed. The reason for this is simple: Tests and coverage reports will not provide any information about missing functionality or let us know that the application runs suboptimally (for any value of suboptimal, such as performance, incorrect configuration, unexpected target platform, and so on).

Coverage History Tells Its Own Story

While it's useful to view coverage snapshots, an even more interesting metric is revealed through viewing coverage history reports.

A coverage history report shows how code coverage for the project evolves over time. This information is valuable because, regardless of the actual percentage values, it tells us important things about trends in the code.

For example, if coverage is dropping over time, that's a good indication that tests aren't being written for new functionality, something that would be quite difficult to detect otherwise. It's not unrealistic, for example, for tests to be written that don't happen to test any new code.

History will also spot some common developer mistakes. For example, it's surprisingly common for a developer to disable, comment out, or delete a test for various reasons (none of which are compelling, but it's a common mistake!). In such cases, a coverage history report will highlight this and will show a drop in coverage despite the fact that the code itself has not grown significantly.

Conclusion

Throughout this chapter, we have covered a wide variety of topics that represent various testing design patterns. We started by explaining the importance of making sure that your code works as advertised when the right conditions are met, but also that it fails in expected ways. We covered the usage of Factories and Data Providers, which help you create dynamic tests that can receive data from external sources.

Then we ventured into more advanced topics with asynchronous and multithreaded code testing and verification that the performance of code under test stays under well-defined boundaries. We spent some time explaining the concept of dependent testing and debunked some of the myths that surround it in order to show how useful it can be. We showed you how test groups could help you architect your testing code base in a very flexible and extensible way. Finally, we concluded by introducing two concepts that, while peripheral to the idea of testing, are good complements to testing techniques: mocks and coverage.

The goal of this chapter was to capture numerous testing patterns and design concerns that affect us on a daily basis as we write tests. To address many of these issues, it's important to enlist the help of the testing framework. Some things are much simpler with the right choice of tools.

Having said that, it is equally important to understand the patterns we've discussed on a more conceptual level and to always be on the lookout for when and where they apply. Choosing the right pattern to solve a particular testing problem will pay off tremendously in terms of clarity of code and intent, maintainability, and future enhancements.

While it's initially easier to write tests in a more brute force manner where we address only local concerns, it becomes more and more difficult to see the big picture or to spot emerging patterns as our test suites grow. Therefore, it is much easier to apply these patterns up front, instead of after the fact.

After such a deep dive into TestNG, it is now time to take a step back. In the next two chapters, TestNG will take more of backseat as we cover testing at a higher level, first by discussing enterprise testing and then by showing you various integration techniques.

CHAPTER 3

Enterprise Testing

Before we delve into the issues surrounding enterprise testing in Java, it's important to define exactly what we mean by *enterprise*.

It's hard to conceive of a word with as many meanings and connotations (and misconceptions!) as *enterprise* in Java. For many, this word is tied to the usage of the Java Enterprise Edition (J2EE, or its current incarnation, Java EE), whose APIs enable us to bless our applications with the enterprise stamp. For others, enterprise applications have specific features regardless of what APIs or even specific languages are used.

An example of using the enterprise API is an intranet application that manages a fixed set of entities, with its own backing store. It is likely that this application has a Web-based UI and that it uses some combination of servlets, JSP pages, and a persistence mechanism. In this example, the use of the ubiquitous term refers only to the API usage, and it is a relatively simple matter to ensure that this application can be tested easily, if one uses the right tools for the job.

Another example is an integration project in which a new middle tier is being added between two existing legacy systems, with the hope of slowly phasing out the old back end. This new layer has to be able to encapsulate the mapping between the two legacy systems, but more often than not, it is not allowed to modify either of the legacy systems. The mapping will likely be complex and require orchestration between a number of other external systems. In this case, we are much less likely to achieve our ideal of easy, quick-to-run unit tests and are far more likely to benefit from integration and functional tests.

That is not to say that enterprise projects cannot benefit from unit tests. It is also almost always possible to break down components into small enough pieces that meaningful unit tests can be derived, and all three types of tests go together hand in hand.

This chapter and the following one discuss testing issues with both definitions of *enterprise*. We need to be aware of a number of key concepts and issues when testing enterprise applications. These issues are not concerned with APIs but rather with the very nature of enterprise systems: complex

153

integration issues, legacy system support, black-box testing, and so on. Generally, the assumption is that we have either a body of existing code that we need to integrate with or a system that is already in use but needs tests. Once we've established this foundation, the following chapter will discuss how to test specific J2EE or Java EE components.

Before we start, here's a brief recap of the different types of tests.

- *Unit tests*: A unit test tests an individual unit in the system in isolation. Unit tests run very quickly since they have little to no start-up costs, and almost no external dependencies.

- *Functional tests*: A functional test focuses on one piece of functionality. This usually involves interactions between different components.

- *Integration tests*: An integration test is an end-to-end test that exercises the entire stack, including any external dependencies or systems.

A Typical Enterprise Scenario

To illustrate the concepts around enterprise integration and functional testing, it's helpful to examine a real-world example. Let's say that we're consulting for a financial institution that has a legacy back-end database that houses most of its financial data. This database is one of the major bottlenecks of the system. The database is the central point for all financial trade information and is directly read by a number of front- and back-office applications.

In addition to that, some of the newer applications talk to a recently implemented abstraction layer. The abstraction layer grew organically based on the needs of specific applications and was not designed up front to be a middle tier. It has many idiosyncrasies and is so convoluted and complicated right now that it is no longer possible for new applications to easily use it.

The company decides that it is time to revamp the system. The goal is to introduce a middle tier designed from the outset to service most if not all applications that need data from the database. The database is split into a number of smaller instances and the data partitioned according to business requirements.

After the new system is implemented, it quickly proves itself profitable. Due to the phased approach of development, some applications still talk to the old legacy database, but a number have been ported over to the new system. The new system acts as a mediator between the various components and includes transformation components to ensure the correct data is still fed to legacy systems that expect the old formats and schemas.

Participants

Confused yet? You shouldn't be. Chances are that most developers have been in this situation during one project or another. Is this project bizarre or extreme in its complexity? Perhaps in the details it is, but the overall issues confronting it are fairly standard and commonplace. Let us step back a bit and see if we can identify the main participants:

- The legacy database: the source of all evil
- The shiny new API: the source of all good
- Dozens of legacy systems: the nature of the business, neither good nor bad
- Transformers: a necessary evil to allow components to talk to one another

This probably is starting to sound more familiar. Most if not all enterprise applications have to deal with legacy data at some point. This could be a migration issue, it could be a transformation issue, or it could be simply the introduction of a new layer on top of existing systems.

Testing Methodology

So what testing methodology does this successful new project employ? Judging by its success, it must consist of rigorous unit tests, countless integration and functional tests, nightly builds, email notifications of test failures—all the good developer testing habits that every successful project has.

As a matter of fact, it has none of these. The testing methodology of this project consists mainly of developers writing the odd class with a `main(String[] args)` method, running that against their data, and eyeballing the results. If it looks good, the functionality is deemed complete, the code checked in, and that's the end of that. Before a production release, there is a one- or two-week period where a QA team goes through the application and tries to find bugs. This is a manual process, but by the time it's done, the production release is in pretty good shape. The code is deployed, and everyone is happy.

The developers involved in this project range from experienced team leads to average developers. Almost all of the developers know about unit testing and have written a unit test in the past. The project did not mandate formalized test code, so there was no requirement to develop a test harness or automated tests.

Furthermore, all the developers agreed that it does not make sense to unit test the code. It is an integration project and therefore impossible to capture the important business aspects that need to be tested in a single unit test. The tests written would violate any number of popular testing recommendations; they would take a long time to run (many seconds), have complicated setup requirements (a few more seconds), and require a specific environment in that they would be highly dependent on a specific database schema, with specific data and stored procedures.

We suspect that this conclusion is far more common than many testing advocates would like us to believe. It is tempting to dismiss developers who are not obsessive about writing tests as ignorant or incompetent. Both assumptions are rather incorrect. JUnit, for example, currently makes it difficult to think in terms of integration or functional testing; there is a stigma of sorts attached to tests that have complicated environment requirements (and as a byproduct, slow running tests). Developers shy away from them. Yet for enterprise projects, such tests are far more valuable than unit tests. An integration project, unsurprisingly one would think, is exactly what integration tests excel at.

Issues with the Current Approach

So where's the problem? The project works and is a success, and everyone is happy. As the popular saying goes, if it ain't broke, why fix it? However, it turns out that the current approach has a number of inefficiencies.

QA Cycle Is Too Long

Currently, every release requires one or two weeks of full-time testing. Bugs discovered during this testing phase are added to a list of issues that should always be tested. The testing cycle often runs late if many issues are found, as many things need to be retested once the first batch of issues has been resolved.

Poor Test Capture

Developers currently write plenty of tests that are discarded as soon as the functionality being tested starts working. The main method is simply rewritten, or code is commented out and commented back in to reconfirm a test. There is no growing body of tests, nor is there a way to automate these informal tests.

Regression Testing Effort Grows Linearly

With every QA cycle, issues found are added to a growing master list of issues that need to be tested for every release. It becomes the QA team's job to perform all regression testing. This isn't such a problem with just a handful of releases, but the new system in place is expected to have a lifetime of at least five years, with many more enhancements and changes to come in future releases. Within a year or two, the mountain of regression tests is very likely to have a significant negative impact on the manual test cycle.

Lack of Unit Tests

The developers often argue that the system is too complex to be tested usefully through unit tests. This could well be true, in the general case. However, it is highly likely that a number of components or pieces of functionality do lend themselves well to unit testing. In a large, complex system, it can be a daunting task to identify these components, so the tendency is to stick to integration and functional tests.

Once we do have integration tests, unit tests more often than not will naturally emerge. Because the testing infrastructure is already in place, debugging an integration test is quite likely to result in a unit test, simply to try to narrow the scope of the bug.

A Concrete Example

So where do we start? Let's look at a typical component of this system, identify what we want to test, and then choose a strategy of how to test.

A fairly typical component in this system receives a JMS message that contains a payload of an XML document. The XML document is fairly large (400K or so) and describes a financial transaction. The component's job is to read in the message, parse the XML, populate a couple of database tables based on the message contents, and then call a stored procedure that processes the tables.

The sequence diagram in Figure 3–1 helps illustrate the message flow for this component.

Listing 3–1 shows the rough outline of the code we'd like to test.

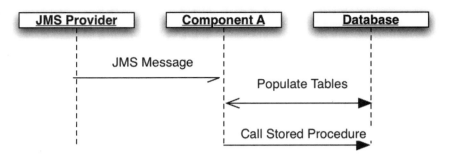

Figure 3–1 Sequence diagram for a typical component

Listing 3–1 Existing message processor for the legacy component

```
public class ComponentA implements javax.jms.MessageListener {
  private Log log = LogFactory.getLog(ComponentA.class);

  public void onMessage(Message message) {
    java.sql.Connection c = null;
    PreparedStatement ps = null;
    TextMessage tm = (TextMessage)message;
    String xml = null;
    try {
      xml = tm.getText();

      // XMLHelper is a util class that takes in an XML string
      // and parses it and returns a document
      Document doc = XMLHelper.parseDocument(xml);

      // manipulate the document to get at various elements
      // DatabaseHelper is a util class to look up and return a
      // database connection
      c = DatabaseHelper.getConnection();
      String sql = ""; // create SQL to call in db
      ps = c.prepareStatement(sql);
      // populate sql
      ps.executeUpdate();
      String spSql = "<sql to execute stored proc>";
      // call the stored procedure
      c.prepareCall(spSql).execute();
    }
```

```
catch(Exception ex) {
  log.error("Error processing message " + message
    + " with data " + xml,ex);
}
finally {
  if(c != null) {
    try {
      if(ps != null) {
        try {
          ps.close();
        }
        catch(SQLException e) {
          log.error("Error closing statement", e);
        }
      }
      c.close();
    }
    catch(SQLException e) {
      log.error("Error closing connection", e);
    }
  }
}
}
```

The focus of this exercise is to ensure that we test our component. A vital aspect of the process is also explicitly defining our test goals and non-goals up front, including the assumptions we're making.

Goals

Any functionality that we'd like to explicitly verify or check is considered one of the prime goals of the test process. For our specific case, we'd like to meet the following three goals.

1. We will create a success test. We want to ensure that if we receive a valid XML message, we process it correctly and update the correct database tables, and the stored procedure is also successfully called.

2. We will model different scenarios. We would like to be able to feed a variety of XML documents to our test to be able to easily add a growing body of sample data and use it for regression testing.

3. We will institute explicit failure tests. Failure behavior should be captured and tested so that the state of the component when it fails internally is predictable and easily captured.

Nongoals

Equally important as choosing goals is identifying nongoals. These are tasks that, if we're not careful, we might accidentally end up testing, thus having our tests focus on the wrong thing. We have three nongoals in our case.

1. We will not test the JMS provider functionality. We assume that it is a compliant implementation that has been correctly configured and will successfully deliver the intended message to us. The JMS API allows us to work with the `TextMessage` object. We can assume that this object allows us to get at the message contents without throwing any exceptions and that it will be correctly delivered. Finally, we can always have separate integration tests that verify the system's behavior end-to-end.

2. We will not perform catch-all error testing. Failure test should model explicit and reproducible failure modes. A failure test that, for example, checks what happens if a `NullPointerException` is thrown is somewhat useless.

3. We will not test APIs. The behavior of the JDBC driver is not the test subject, for example. It is also important to ensure that all our tests focus on our business functionality and to avoid tests that test Java language semantics. Therefore, we are not interested in verifying that the XML parser is able to parse XML; we assume it can.

Test Implementation

Based on our goals, we can now start to define a test for our component. The test definition involves going through each of our goals and enhancing the test so the goal is satisfied, while ensuring that we do not accidentally get distracted with any of the nongoals.

The first goal is to ensure that a valid XML document is processed correctly and the appropriate database calls made. Listing 3–2 shows the test skeleton.

Listing 3–2 Initial attempt at a functional test

```
@Test
public void componentAShouldUpdateDatabase() throws Exception {
    ComponentA component = new ComponentA();
    component.onMessage(...);
    Connection c = DatabaseHelper.getConnection();
    String verifySQL = ...;
    PreparedStatement ps = c.prepareStatement(verifySQL);
    // set parameters
    // read resultset and verify results match expectations
    String someValue = resultSet.getString(1);
    assert "foo".equals(someValue);
}
```

Testing for Success

As soon as we start to fill in our test code, we start running into problems. The first problem we have is that the component's only method is the onMessage method. This method takes in a JMSMessage. This class in the JMS API is in fact an interface, as is our expected message type, TextMessage. The API does not provide for an easy way to create instances of these interfaces (which, incidentally, is a good thing—an API should define contracts, not implementations). So how do we test our component?

There are two options for tackling this hurdle.

1. Use mock (or stub) objects to create our own implementation of TextMessage, represented by a simple POJO with setters for the message body and properties.

2. Refactor the component so the business functionality is not coupled to the JMS API.

The first approach is fairly popular but violates one of our nongoals, which is to not test external APIs. Strictly speaking, we'd be trying to use mock objects to refactor away the external API dependency. In practice, however, we'd have to model too much of it.

We would have to define a JMS message, and to ensure correctness, our implementation would have to be checked to ensure it matches the specification contract for TextMessage, if we hope to reuse it in any other tests that might expect different (and more compliant!) semantics of TextMessage. This extra code is another source of potential bugs and is yet more code to maintain. The mock object approach for external APIs should generally be used only for black-box testing, where we do not have access or rights to modify the source for the code being tested and so are forced to provide an environment that matches its expectations.

Although using mock or stub objects is the incorrect choice for our test, this is not always the case. For APIs that are complex or have very implementation-specific behavior, mocking of third-party dependencies should be avoided. However, there are times when the external API is trivial and easy to mock, in which case there is no harm in whipping up a quick stub for testing purposes.

The second approach is the correct one for our purposes. Since our goal is not to check whether we can retrieve text from a JMS message, we assume that functionality works and can be relied on. Our component should instead be modified so that the business functionality is decoupled from the incoming message. The decoupling gains us an important benefit: increased testability. We did make an implicit tradeoff in this decision, too. The modification to the code is the result not of a domain-based consideration (no business requirement is satisfied by this change) but of a testability one.

In Listing 3–3, the `onMessage` method handles all the JMS interaction and then passes the XML document string to the `processDocument` method, which then does all the work.

Listing 3–3 Refactoring component to decouple extraction from parsing

```
public void onMessage(Message message) {
  TextMessage tm = (TextMessage)message;
  processDocument(tm.getText());
}

public void processDocument(String xml) {
  // code previously in onMessage that updates DB
  // and calls stored procedure
}
```

We can now modify our functional test as shown in Listing 3–4 so that it no longer references JMS at all and instead simply passes the XML string to the `processDocument` method.

Listing 3–4 Refactored test to only test message processing

```
@Test
public void componentAUpdateDatabase() throws Exception {
  ComponentA component = new ComponentA();
  String xml = IOUtils.readFile(new File("trade.xml"));
  component.processDocument(xml);
  Connection c = DatabaseHelper.getConnection();
  String verifySQL = ...;
  PreparedStatement ps = c.prepareStatement(verifySQL);
  // set parameters
  // read resultSet and verify that results match expectations
  String someValue = resultSet.getString(1);
  assert "foo".equals(someValue);
}
```

Note how we load in the sample XML data from a file and then pass it to the component. The fact that the component happens to rely on JMS for message delivery is not relevant in terms of its business functionality, so we restructured the component to allow us to focus on testing the functionality rather than the JMS API.

An interesting side effect of this approach is that we made the processDocument method public. This method could well be an implementation detail that should not be exposed. To restrict its access level, we could make it protected or package protected and ensure that the test case is in the appropriate package. That way it can be invoked from the test but not from other clients.

As a side note, though we've moved the processing into another method, in practice we'd go a bit further than that and move it to another class altogether. That refactoring will result is a more reusable class that is not coupled to JMS at all.

At this point, we have a test that can verify that a sample XML file can be processed and that the database has been updated correctly.

Building Test Data

Now that we can consume a previously recorded XML file, we can easily grow the test input data and support as many files as we want. We can create a test for every file that ensures that all sorts of different input data can be verified.

Unfortunately, this approach very quickly proves itself to be rather cumbersome. The input XML files can vary significantly, and alarm bells should be going off anyway whenever we find ourselves copying and pasting, thus violating the Don't Repeat Yourself (DRY) principle.

As we have discussed previously, this is where it's useful for the testing framework to support Data-Driven Testing. We simply modify our test to use Data Providers, and parameterize the XML data as shown in Listing 3–5.

Listing 3–5 Refactored test using a Data Provider

```
@Test(dataProvider = "componentA-data-files")
public void componentAUpdateDatabase(String xml) throws Exception {
  ComponentA component = new ComponentA();
  component.processDocument(xml);
  // rest of test code
}

@DataProvider(name = "componentA-data-files")
public Iterator<Object[]> loadXML() throws Exception {
  // return data set
}
```

Note that our test now takes in a parameter and no longer has to concern itself with sourcing the sample data or determining how to load it in. All it does now is specify its Data Provider. The actual mechanism of loading the XML is now delegated to a separate loader. Our test is cleaner as a result since we have parameterized the variable data and can now invoke it multiple times for each of our sample XML files.

The type of the parameter is a `string`. Due to how the two methods are related, it is not possible to have a type-safe declaration for the method parameter. The Data Provider must return a type that matches that declared by the test method. For example, if the `loadXML` method were to return `Document` objects, we would get a runtime type mismatch exception.

The Data Provider itself can now deal with loading the XML file, as shown in Listing 3–6. Note that it does not need to have a hardcoded list. Instead it scans a specific directory and feeds all the files found to the test case. So the next time a new sample XML file needs to be added to the test suite, we just have to drop it in a specific directory and it will automatically be included, no coding or recompilation needed.

Listing 3–6 Refactored test to read in all data files from a specific directory

```
@DataProvider(name = "componentA-data-files")
  public Iterator<Object[]> loadXML() throws Exception {
    File[] f = new File("samples/ComponentA/trades").listFiles();
    final Iterator<File> files = Arrays.asList(f).iterator();
    return new Iterator<Object[]>() {

      public boolean hasNext() {
        return files.hasNext();
      }

      public Object[] next() {
        return new Object[]{IOUtils.readFile(files.next())};
      }

      public void remove() {
        throw new UnsupportedOperationException();
      }
    };
  }
```

The provider is fairly simple. It grabs a list of all the XML files in a specific directory and adds the file contents to the parameters. The file contents are added as an array of size 1 since the test method takes in just the one parameter. If we needed to parameterize other variables, that would be reflected in the array returned by the next() iterator method.

The provider method name does not matter at all; it can be whatever is most appropriate for a given case, as long as the @DataProvider annotation name matches what our test expects.

Of course, it is possible to return an array of Object[] from the Data Provider. However, that approach would mean that we would have to load all the file data in memory at once since the array has to be prepopulated. While this will work for a small data set, the memory requirements of the test will keep increasing over time, so the test will not scale with our data. Since this test is designed to grow over time, a little bit of upfront planning will head off this issue early on; we simply use lazy loading for the Data Provider so we only load one file's data at a time.

Test Setup Issues

Unfortunately, our test is not idempotent. An idempotent test is one where the result of running a test once is the same as running it multiple times. Describing something as idempotent is essentially saying that it does not alter state when it is invoked multiple times. So, for example, a method that reads data from a database is idempotent since calling it again will return the same data. On the other hand, a method that writes to a database may not be idempotent; invoking it again will likely result in an error since the state of the database has changed once the method has been invoked.

While we'll cover specific strategies for handling database setup and management, the concepts apply equally to any external stores we might need to interact with as part of the tests. These range from file systems to WebDAV resources to remote repositories of any format.

Not only is our test required to be idempotent, but the ordering of tests themselves shouldn't matter (assuming we haven't declared dependencies to enforce any ordering). So in addition to being idempotent, tests should not have any impact on other tests in terms of state or data.

Since the test performs a number of write operations, successive runs can easily be polluted from the results of previous runs. Any test that writes to a database will suffer from this problem, and while there is no ideal solution, a number of approaches can help us cope with this problem.

- Embedded databases
- Initialized data in the test setup
- Transaction rollbacks

Each of these approaches has its uses, and which combination of them we end up going with depends on the application and environment; some might not be options, and some might be more cumbersome than others.

Note that it might be tempting to consider using a mock library for the JDBC functionality. Resist that temptation! We discussed mocks earlier, and this is a great example of the urge and the need to resist it. A JDBC mock object would not (could not, even) cope with all the intricacies of database behavior, much less all the issues surrounding transactions or locking.

Embedded Databases

A number of Java-based database engines have been specifically designed with embedding support in mind. These databases can be created and initialized on the fly, from inside the test. They have low overhead in terms of setup costs and often perform very well.

The disadvantage of this approach, however, is that it deviates significantly from the environment the application will actually run in. There are also often significant differences between database features. While this approach is well suited to applications that use a database purely as a data store and restrict themselves to ANSI SQL database calls or use an abstraction layer (such as JPA or any similar object-relational mapping tool), it is not suitable for any applications (such as our example) that have application logic embedded in the database. Stored procedures are not portable across databases, and reimplementing them in our embedded database would be too much effort.

Initialized Data in the Test Setup

The next approach is to load our test database with a known quantity of test data. This would include all the data we'd like to manipulate, as well as any external references that our component relies on. For some tests, this might not even be sufficient, so in addition to loading data we'd have to ensure that extraneous data is also removed on start-up. While somewhat cumbersome, this approach can be combined with the embedded database engine to satisfy the needs of the component sufficiently for it to run successfully in any environment.

In practice, many tests rely on two different kinds of data. The first is *statics*. Statics are effectively constants stored in the database. For example, the list of U.S. states is considered a static, as is a list of currencies. If our test does its work against a shared remote database (a test instance, not the production one!), it can reasonably expect that the static data will be in place. After all, this information is constant across all tests, so there's no reason to load it in every run.

However, tests do also rely on data that is specific to their business functionality. For example, we might have a test that asserts that an audit trail for a financial transaction meets certain criteria, or that an invalid audit trail correctly raises the right alarms. In such cases, our test setup needs to load this test data into the database and then clear it out after the test run.

One downside of this approach is the difficulty of maintaining a robust data set that is meaningful enough to test. As the project progresses, there's a strong chance that data structures and schemas will change, and the test data can become stale. Updating the tests constantly in this situation can be quite unsatisfying as it involves duplicating the effort it has taken to implement the changes in the rest of the code base.

Thus, we have a tradeoff between capturing a meaningful data set and locking ourselves into a very specific snapshot of our model that will constantly need updating and modification to keep up to date. There is no right answer for which approach is best; the choice varies depending on the project and how much we expect the model to evolve over time.

Transaction Rollbacks

Another approach is to use Java APIs to prevent the data from being written out to the permanent data store. In both cases, the general idea is to start a transaction, perform all of our write operations, verify that everything works, and then roll back the transaction. The benefit of this approach is that we do not have to worry about cleanup; simply rolling back the transactions ensures that all the work is undone correctly, something that a manual cleanup operation might not do quite as thoroughly.

A manual rollback is also more brittle since it is more code to write and thus more code that could go wrong. Manual rollbacks becomes even trickier if we're testing multiple databases, and dealing with the hassles of ensuring that the databases are synchronized and the data is correctly cleaned up is too cumbersome for testing.

As with many of these approaches, there are disadvantages. Code that manipulates transactions or starts its own transactions cannot be tested this way without complicated nested transaction setups. For example, any code that calls `commit()` or `rollback()` should usually not be tested using this approach unless you're very clear on the semantics of what the code does and how having an external traction will impact its behavior.

Most applications will communicate with the database either through straight JDBC or through a `DataSource` implementation. The first approach involves manually working with `Driver` and `Connection` objects. Connections obtained through this mechanism are not transactional, so to prevent any writes to the database from taking place, our test would simply have to turn off autocommit, via the `Connection.setAutocommit(false)` method.

The other option is to perform database access through a `DataSource` object, which can integrate with a transaction manager and thus can be told to abort a transaction. We'll outline the specifics of this approach in Chapter 4.

Note that it is also important to ensure that the isolation level is set to READ UNCOMMITTED. Some databases (particularly embedded ones) have this as the default. The reason we need this is that we'd like to be able to verify some of the data we've attempted to write, and this isolation level allows us to read uncommitted data. Setting it to anything else means that we'd have to ensure that data is validated in the same transaction as it's being written, or else we'd never get to read it.

Having said that, it is important to understand the semantics of the isolation level we choose. It's very likely that in the production environment, a different isolation level is in place, and this subtle change in environments could result in some difficult-to-track bugs that do not manifest themselves in the test environment. Furthermore, this isolation level will cause issues when run in concurrent tests, as different tests might end up seeing the same data if there is just one transaction covering a particular set of tests.

Selecting the Right Strategy

For our component, we can go with disabling autocommit on the connection we obtain in the test. An embedded database is not an option since we rely on a database-specific stored procedure. So the test can expect to have a database that has been set up correctly to connect to.

Looking over the test code as we have it now, we currently obtain a database connection within the test method itself. The fact that we expect certain data to be available in the database opens us to the possibility of connecting to a database that does not have this data or, even worse, failing to connect to the database at all. In both cases, we don't get to test the business functionality, so we don't actually know if our business logic is correct or not.

In that case, our test will fail through not being tested, rather than through an explicit logic error. To distinguish between the two, another refactoring is called for.

We know that our test will be called multiple times, and we also know that it's fairly likely that we will end up with further tests that verify different aspects of our component, all of which are going to need access to the database. The database is an external dependency, so we model it accordingly in Listing 3–7, as part of the environment setup, rather than the test proper.

Listing 3–7 Extract database setup into configuration methods

```
private Connection connection;

@BeforeMethod
public void connect() throws SQLException {
  connection = DatabaseHelper.getConnection(...);
  connection.setAutoCommit(false);
}
```

```
@AfterMethod
public void rollback() throws SQLException {
  connection.rollback();
}
```

We've refactored the test to move the database connection handling into setup methods. The benefit of this approach is that if we do have an issue connecting to the database, we will get a more helpful error message that makes it clear that the failure is in setup and not in the tests themselves. We also ensure that the connection is rolled back after every test method invocation.

Of course, it might be desirable to perform a number of tests and then roll them back at the end. The rollback method can instead be marked with @AfterClass or @AfterSuite, depending on our needs.

An interesting problem we might face is that the code we're testing might explicitly call commit. How would we prevent the transaction from committing in this case?

To deal with this situation, we employ the Decorator pattern. We'll assume that the code has a connection provided to it. In Listing 3–8, we wrap the connection in a decorator that prevents calls to commit and pass that to the component instead of the real connection.

Listing 3–8 Disabling *commit* by using a wrapped connection

```
private WrappedConnection wrappedConnection;

@BeforeMethod
public void connect() throws SQLException {
  connection = DatabaseHelper.getConnection();
  connection.setAutoCommit(false);
  wrappedConnection = new WrappedConnection(connection);
  wrappedConnection.setSuppressCommit(true);
}
```

The WrappedConnection implementation is a decorator around the actual connection. It implements the Connection interface. The relevant parts are shown in Listing 3–9.

Listing 3-9 *WrappedConnection* implementation

```
public class WrappedConnection implements Connection {
  private Connection connection;
  private boolean suppressClose;
  private boolean suppressCommit;

  public WrappedConnection(Connection c) {
    this.connection = c;
  }

  public boolean isSuppressClose() {
    return suppressClose;
  }

  public void setSuppressClose(boolean suppressClose) {
    this.suppressClose = suppressClose;
  }

  public boolean isSuppressCommit() {
    return suppressCommit;
  }

  public void setSuppressCommit(boolean suppressCommit) {
    this.suppressCommit = suppressCommit;
  }

  public void commit() throws SQLException {
    if(!suppressCommit)
      connection.commit();
  }

  public void close() throws SQLException {
    if(!suppressClose)
      connection.close();
  }
  // rest of the methods all just delegate to the connection
  }
```

Using the wrapped connection now enables us to prevent any objects we use in our tests from calling `commit` or `close`, as needed.

Error Handling

At this point, we've achieved two of our stated goals, while reworking our code to ensure we don't pollute our tests with nongoals.

This test is valuable in that it successfully verifies that our component behaves the way we'd like it to, but an equally important part of testing is capturing boundary and error conditions. Invariably in the real world, things go wrong. They often go wrong in interesting and perplexing ways, and they often do so at fairly inconvenient times. What we'd like is to at least capture some of these failures and know what our code is going to do. It's fine if things blow up, as long as we know exactly what will blow up and how.

Of course, it's tempting to wrap the whole thing in a big `try`/`catch`, log the error, and forget about it. In fact, if we look at our component code, that's pretty much what it does. It's equally tempting to think that we can easily figure out all the failure points and account for them. Very, very few people can do this. It's important, in fact, not to get bogged down thinking of every possible thing that can go wrong and check for it. It's crucial that we remain pragmatic and practical and, at this point, handle only likely errors.

Our test will not capture everything that can go wrong. Things will go wrong over time that we did not anticipate. Some will be obvious, but others will be insidious and tricky. The crucial lesson in error handling then is to take back the feedback and results from a live run and feed them back into our tests. It's less important to have a comprehensive set of failure tests up front than it is to capture actual failures as they happen after the code has been deployed. The value of tests lies in their growth and evolution over time, not in the initial spurt, which in terms of the big picture is insignificant.

When capturing a bug that's found in production code, it's also important to label it correctly. The requirement that should always be satisfied is this: "If someone new joins the project six months after I leave, will he or she be able to look at this test case and know why it's here?" Comments in the test should include a link to the associated bug report. If that's not available, add a brief explanation of what functionality the test verifies beyond just the code.

So, what can go wrong with our component? The developer responsible for this component merrily yelled out "Nothing!" when asked. But he wasn't quite as accurate as we'd all hoped.

One interesting error that cropped up time and time again in the log files is the ubiquitous `NullPointerException`. On further investigation, it turns out that the processor extracts a currency code from the XML. It then looks up some rates associated with that currency. The problem? The currency wasn't listed in the database, hence a dazzling variety of long stack traces in the log files. No problem; the developer adds a check to verify that the currency is valid, and if not, to throw an exception.

Now that we have some tests in place, the first thing we need to do is model the failure before fixing it. Having an easy way to reproduce an error instead of clicking around a UI is a huge timesaver and is a very easy payoff for having gone to the bother of developing a testing strategy.

How do we model this failure? Thanks to our Data-Driven Testing, all we have to do is get the XML file with the invalid currency and drop it into our data directory. Running our test now will correctly show the `NullPointerException`.

We now have a reproducible error, and we know how to fix the code. The fix involves explicitly checking for invalid currencies and throwing an application-specific exception indicating invalid input data (e.g., `InvalidTradeException`). Putting that fix in shows that we correctly throw the exception, but, of course, our test will still fail since it does not expect this exception.

One option shown in Listing 3–10 is to catch the exception in the test.

Listing 3–10 Initial attempt to handle invalid data

```
@Test(dataProvider = "componentA-data-files")
public void componentAUpdateDatabase(String xml) throws Exception {
  ComponentA component = new ComponentA();
  try {
    component.processDocument(xml);
  }
  catch(InvalidTradeException e) {
    // this is OK
    return;
  }
  // rest of test code
}
```

As a side note, it's convenient to have tests declare that they throw an exception, as a reasonable catch-all mechanism for "anything that can go wrong." In production code, this is a bad idea, as it does not allow the caller to explicitly handle exceptions. Here we see yet another example of a pattern that is acceptable (and even recommended, for the sake of simplicity) in test code that should always be avoided in production code.

The problem with the approach is that it does not enable us to distinguish between the cases where that failure is expected and those where it isn't. Instead, what we should do is distinguish between expected successes and expected failures. The test as it stands can pass for two situations: It either passes when we have good data, or it passes when we have bad data. In either case, we can't make assertions about what actually happened; did we test the good data path or the bad data one? More importantly, what didn't we test?

The fact that the two paths happen to be "good data" and "bad data" in our case is a specific example. It's equally easy to accidentally write a test that has two or more conditions for passing, and we'd have the same issue with regard to what sort of assertions we can make about the success result.

The guideline to follow here is that a test shouldn't pass in more than one way. It's fine if the test verified different failure modes, but having one that can pass for both good and bad data is inviting subtle errors that are tricky and difficult to track down. We therefore define another directory and Data Provider in Listing 3–11 that handles failures, the same way as we do for valid input.

Listing 3–11 Defining a separate provider for invalid data

```
@DataProvider(name = "componentA-invalid-data-files")
  public Iterator<Object[]> loadInvalidXML() throws Exception {
    File dir = new File("samples/ComponentA/trades/invalid");
    File[] f = dir.listFiles();
    final Iterator<File> files = Arrays.asList(f).iterator();
    return new Iterator<Object[]>() {

      public boolean hasNext() {
        return files.hasNext();
      }

      public Object[] next() {
        return new Object[]{IOUtils.readFile(files.next())};
      }

      public void remove() {
        throw new UnsupportedOperationException();
      }
    };
  }
```

```
@Test(dataProvider = "componentA-invalid-data-files",
      expectedExceptions = InvalidTradeException.class)
public void componentAInvalidInput(String xml) throws Exception {
  ComponentA component = new ComponentA();
  component.processDocument(xml);
  // rest of test code
}
```

Here we defined another set of inputs with an associated test that always expects an exception to be thrown. If we do end up putting a valid XML file in the invalid `trades` directory, we will also correctly get a test failure since our `processDocument` method will not throw `InvalidTradeException` (since the input is valid).

Emerging Unit Tests

As we receive more bug reports from the QA team, our test sample grows steadily. Each sample will test a certain code branch. It won't be long, however, before we find that it's actually rather cumbersome to run the entire functional test to narrow an issue with our XML parsing.

The example of invalid data that we highlighted earlier demonstrates this perfectly. In this case, our first step in the functional test fails. We never even get to the database. Given that our problem is restricted to a small part of our functional test, it would be tremendously useful if we could isolate that one part and split it off into a unit test.

This highlights one of the important paths through which we can grow our unit tests; let them evolve naturally through functional tests. As we start to debug failures, unit tests will become more apparent as a quick and easy way to reproduce fast failures. This top-down approach is very useful in isolating bugs and in testing an existing code base. Once we're in the habit of testing, using the bottom-up approach of unit tests followed by functional tests is well suited when developing new functionality.

We have an important principle here. Unit tests do not necessarily have to be written before any other kind of test—they can be derived from functional tests. Particularly in large projects or an existing code base, writing useful unit tests at first can be tricky because, without an understanding of the bigger picture, they're likely to be too trivial or unimportant. They can instead be derived from meaningful functional tests intelligently, as the process of debugging and developing functional and integration tests will reveal their unit test components. Since functional tests are (hopefully!) derived from specifications and requirements, we know that they satisfy a core piece of functionality, whereas in a large project it might be difficult to immediately spot meaningful units that are relevant and in need of testing.

So, for our example, we will go through another round of refactoring. We need to split up the XML validation and database processing into separate methods so that we can invoke and test them separately.

Our component code now becomes something like Listing 3–12.

Listing 3–12 Refactored component to separate processing from validation

```
public void processDocument(String xml)
  throws InvalidDocumentException {
  Document doc = XMLHelper.parseDocument(xml);
  validateDocument(doc);
  // do DB work
}

public void validateDocument(Document doc)
  throws InvalidDocumentException {
  // perform constraint checks that can't be captured by XML
}
```

We separated the document validation from document processing so that we can test them separately. The upshot of this refactoring is that we now have a simple unit test that has very few (and more importantly, light and inexpensive) external dependencies that can be used to validate all our documents. This test does not require a database or much of an environment since all it does is look through our set of XML documents to ensure that any constraints that cannot be expressed via the document's DTD or schema are not violated.

Since we already have a good set of input XML, why not reuse it for our unit test, too? By the very nature of how we derived our unit test, we know that if it fails, the functional test will also fail. This is an important aspect of functional testing; a good functional test can be decomposed into a number of unit tests. And no matter what anyone tells you, the order in which you write them is not important at all. For new code, it's likely easier to start with unit tests and then develop functional tests that likely build on the rest of the unit tests. For existing code, the reverse is true. The principle remains the same in both cases.

Having said that, it is important to note that regardless of what order they're written in, functional and unit tests are complementary. A functional test is a more horizontal test that touches on many different components and exercises many portions of the code. A unit test, on the other hand, is more vertical in that it focuses on a narrow subject and tests far more exhaustively than a functional test would.

How do we express this relationship between functional tests and unit tests? We place them into logical groupings and explicitly specify the dependency. Putting these concepts together gives us the tests shown in Listing 3–13.

Listing 3–13 Dependency between unit and functional tests

```
@Test(dataProvider = "componentA-data-files", groups="unit-tests")
public void componentAValidateInput(String xml) throws Exception {
  ComponentA component = new ComponentA();
  component.validateDocument(XMLHelper.parseDocument(xml));
  // rest of test code
}

@Test(dataProvider = "componentA.xml", groups = "func-tests",
       dependsOnGroups = "unit-tests")
public void componentAUpdateDatabase(String xml) throws Exception {
  ComponentA component = new ComponentA();
  component.processDocument(xml);
  // rest of test code
}
```

Here we have two tests, one unit and one functional, both belonging to their respective groups, and the dependency between them is explicitly specified. Our test engine will ensure that they are run in the correct order. We can also use the same approach we did for our functional test to add a unit test that verifies that invalid inputs fail correctly as well.

Coping with In-Container Components

One thing we assumed in our test is that the component to be tested can be instantiated easily. Unfortunately, most code out in the real world isn't quite blessed with that convenience. In many cases, the component we dissected earlier would be a Message-Driven Bean (MDB), which runs in an application server. It could also be a servlet or any other managed component that expects a specific environment and cannot be easily instantiated.

We use the term *in-container* to denote that the code needs to be run and deployed into a container and so requires an expensive and heavy environment.

Obviously, this makes testing much trickier and more difficult, and a recurring theme of frameworks like Spring is to always try to abstract away the container dependency, to promote better reuse and code testability.

So, how do we test components in such situations? The answer lies in the same way we managed to get rid of the JMS dependency in our component test. The trick is to refactor the component so that its business functionality is isolated from its environment. The environment is either handled by an external class or injected into the component. For example, if our component were an MDB, we would have gone through the same approach as we did earlier to get rid of JMS. If it were a servlet, we would have used a delegate.

This is not to say that we should always avoid tests that have external dependencies or need to run inside of a server. Such tests are complimentary to our other unit and functional tests. For example, we do need a test at some point to verify that we don't have a typo in the code that reads a JMS message property, and such a test cannot be done without JMS in place.

The Delegate pattern means that the functionality of the component would have been moved away from the servlet class itself into a POJO that can be easily instantiated and tested. The servlet would act as a delegate, and all it would do is ensure that the actual component receives the correct environment and settings based on the request the servlet receives.

Having said that, components are sometimes more intimately tied to their environments and APIs. While it is possible to modify code that, for example, relies on JTA and JNDI, it might be more convenient to simulate that environment in our tests to minimize the testing impact on the code being tested. Chapter 4 will go through a number of Java EE APIs and outline approaches for simulating the correct test environment for them.

Another option that is worth considering is using an in-container test. We will explore this further Chapter 4. The main concept is that the test engine is embedded in the application server, so we can invoke tests that run in the actual deployment environment and interact with the results remotely.

Putting It All Together

We started out with a transformation component that was written without taking testing into consideration at all. It consisted of a monolithic method where a number of concerns and concepts were intertwined, without any clear separation of responsibility. More informally, it was what's often called messy code.

When we tried to test this code, we immediately ran into hurdles. The test encouraged us to shuffle things about a bit in the component itself to make it more easily testable. The shuffling about (or refactoring, as it's more politely known) resulted in a cleaner code base and a more testable one.

We defined our goals for the test and implemented them one by one. Putting together all our changes, Listing 3–14 shows our modified component.

Listing 3–14 Refactored component

```
public void onMessage(Message message) {
  TextMessage tm = (TextMessage)message;
  processDocument(tm.getText());
}

public void processDocument(String xml)
              throws InvalidTradeException {
  Document doc = XMLHelper.parseDocument(xml);
  validateDocument(doc);
  // do DB work
}

public void validateDocument(Document doc)
    throws InvalidTradeException {
  // perform constraint checks that can't be captured by XML
}
```

We also have three test classes in Listing 3–15, one to hold all our functional tests for this component, one to hold all the unit tests, and one to act as the Data Provider.

Listing 3–15 Test classes for the component

```
public class ComponentFunctionalTests {
  private Connection connection;

  @Test(dataProvider = "componentA-data-files",
        groups = "func-tests",
        dependsOnGroups = "unit-tests")
  public void componentAUpdateDatabase(String xml)
                              throws Exception {
    ComponentA component = new ComponentA();
    component.processDocument(xml);
    // rest of test code
  }
```

```java
@Test(dataProvider = "componentA-invalid-data-files",
        expectedExceptions = InvalidTradeException.class)
public void componentAInvalidInput(String xml)
                                throws Exception {
  ComponentA component = new ComponentA();
  component.processDocument(xml);
  // rest of test code
}

@BeforeMethod
public void connect() throws SQLException {
  connection = DatabaseHelper.getConnection();
  connection.setAutoCommit(false);
}

@AfterMethod
public void rollback() throws SQLException {
  connection.rollback();
}
}

public class ComponentUnitTests {
@Test(dataProvider = "componentA-data-files",
        groups="unit-tests")
  public void componentAValidateInput(String xml)
                                throws Exception {
  ComponentA component = new ComponentA();
  component.validateDocument(XMLHelper.parseDocument(xml));
  // rest of test code
}
}

public class ComponentDataProvider {
  @DataProvider(name = "componentA-invalid-data-files")
  public Iterator<Object[]> loadInvalidXML() throws Exception {
    return getPathContents("samples/ComponentA/trades/invalid");
  }

  @DataProvider(name = "componentA-data-files")
  public Iterator<Object[]> loadXML() throws Exception {
    String path = "samples/ComponentA/trades";
    return getPathContents(path);
  }
}
```

```
private Iterator<Object[]> getPathContents(String path) {
  File[] files = new File(path).listFiles(new XmlFileFilter());
  final Iterator<File> iter = Arrays.asList(files).iterator();
  return new FileContentsIterator(iter);
}

private static class XmlFileFilter implements FileFilter {
  public boolean accept(File file) {
    return !file.isDirectory() &&
            file.getName().endsWith(".xml");
  }
}

private static class FileContentsIterator
    implements Iterator<Object[]> {
  private final Iterator<File> iter;

  public FileContentsIterator(Iterator<File> iter) {
    this.iter = iter;
  }

  public boolean hasNext() {
    return iter.hasNext();
  }

  public Object[] next() {
    return new Object[]{IOUtils.readFile(iter.next())};
  }

  public void remove() {
    throw new UnsupportedOperationException();
  }
}
}
```

As we can see, the few small refactorings we performed on our component have paid off handsomely, and the code is now clearer and easier to test. Our tests now include a unit test as well as functional tests, both of which will hopefully grow over time.

Exploring the Competing Consumers Pattern

The example we concluded in the previous section tackled integration issues and how to handle external dependencies and enterprise environment test issues. We'll now visit a different example that explores an enterprise integration pattern.

The pattern we'll explore is explained in much greater detail in Gregor Hohpe and Bobby Woolf's excellent book *Enterprise Integration Patterns* (Addison-Wesley, 2004). We strongly recommend you get hold of a copy if you're serious about enterprise applications.

The Pattern

The pattern we'll examine is the *Competing Consumers* pattern. This pattern applies to message-driven applications. We have a queue that holds any number of messages that our application needs to process. To improve parallelism and efficiency, we'd like to process messages concurrently. This is particularly useful if message processing can be lengthy or expensive. By expensive processing, we generally mean something that is I/O bound or that involves blocking for a significant period waiting for some other part of the system to do its work while the CPU is idle. For instance, the component we explored in our earlier example communicates with a database and potentially a number of other external systems, so processing an individual message is fairly expensive.

The pattern name simply refers to what happens when firing up a number of instances to process messages. Each of the consumers will read messages off the queue and start processing. The consumers compete for messages since there is one source and more than one consumer.

Note that this approach obviously works only with message queues (point to point).[1] Obviously it would not work with topics since in that case all subscribers receive every message, and they do not need to compete for any single message.

We have to make some implicit assumptions to use the Competing Consumers pattern. The most important one is that we cannot guarantee message ordering. Since we are processing messages in parallel and the consumers

---

1. JMS supports two kinds of destinations, topics and queues. A topic can have multiple subscribers, and messages sent to it will be broadcast to all of them. A queue, on the other hand, allows only one client to consume any given message and is thus a point-to-point messaging destination.

are competing, we know that messages are not processed serially, and thus we can make no guarantees as to which messages will be processed first. Of course, we could add an ordering property to each message and introduce a buffering processor that holds onto messages until a contiguous sequence is received, then deliver them to the component. For the sake of simplicity, however, we'll instead assume that ordering does not matter.

The other important issue is that we would most likely want to consume the messages transactionally: if a message cannot be processed, we would want to roll back any partial changes we've made to any transactional resources and ensure the message is rolled back to the queue correctly.

Listing 3–16 shows the implementation outline of the processor.

Listing 3–16 Example of a competing consumer

```
public class MessageProcessor implements MessageListener {

  private Log log = LogFactory.getLog(MessageProcessor.class);

  public void onMessage(Message message) {
    TextMessage msg = (TextMessage)message;
    try {
      String value = msg.getText();
      String someProp = msg.getStringProperty("prop");
      process(value, someProp);
    }
    catch(JMSException e) {
      log.error("Error processing message", e);
    }
  }

  public void process(String value, String someProp) {
    // do a lot of expensive stuff, like a DB conversation
  }
}
```

Since this processor is a `MessageListener`, the JMS provider (or EJB container) will invoke it asynchronously, so each instance will run in its own thread.

The Test

Having implemented this pattern, how do we test it? Before we start writing a test, it's important to first decide what exactly we're trying to test.

The first issue is that the consumers run concurrently, so we'll have to somehow simulate that in the test to match what happens in production. Once we've done that, we'd also like to verify the results. It doesn't matter which consumer ran first or which completed first. We would like to assert that with a given number of consumers, we have a set of known results that we can verify. For the sake of simplicity, we'll assume that the results are entries in a database that we can query.

Using the techniques discussed earlier, we can use a clean database for our test. It doesn't need to be completely empty; it can contain enough static data so that our consumer can do its job. However, it should not be shared with other tests, so we can easily determine the changes that the test caused.

Also, from what we learned earlier, our goal is not to test JMS functionality. We know, for example, that JMS supports transactions, which ensures that a consumer is transactional. We also know that specifying the transactional behavior is a configuration issue. The test in this case focuses on the business functionality. Chapter 4 will cover the details of testing-specific APIs such as JMS.

The component is already refactored so that the business functionality is not coupled to JMS, so we can ignore that aspect of it for the purposes of our test.

Listing 3–17 shows the test for the component.

Listing 3–17 Test for Competing Consumers pattern

```
private final List<Object[]> data =
  Collections.synchronizedList(new ArrayList<Object[]>());

@BeforeClass
public void populateData() {
data.add(new Object[]{"value1", "prop1"});
  data.add(new Object[]{"value2", "prop2"});
  data.add(new Object[]{"value3", "prop3"});
}

@Test(threadPoolSize = 3, invocationCount = 3,
      dataProvider="concurrent-processor")
public void runConcurrentProcessors(String value,
                                  String someProp) {
```

```
    // create processor
    MessageProcessor processor = new MessageProcessor();
    // invoke method to test
    processor.process(value, someProp);
}

@Test(dependsOnMethods = "runConcurrentProcessors")
public void verifyConcurrentProcessors() {
    // load data from db
    // verify that we have 3 results
    // verify that each of the 3 results matches our 3 inputs
}

@DataProvider(name = "concurrent-processor")
public Object[][] getProcessorData() {
    return new Object[][]{data.remove(data.size() - 1)};
}
```

The test uses a number of interesting approaches, so it's worth spending some time exploring them. For one thing, since at runtime we expect that the container for our component is multithreaded, we don't need to worry about firing up multiple instances since the container will most likely handle that. For our test, however, since the test is effectively the container, we do need to explicitly specify that we'd like multiple threads.

Our test is split into two tests, one that handles running the consumers and one that then verifies the results. Why the split? The reason is that runConcurrentProcessors is invoked multiple times, and we only want to verify results once all invocations of that method have completed. To express this ordering, we use the dependsOnMethods annotation attribute.

To express the desired parallelism, we use the threadPoolSize and invocationCount annotation attributes. We specify that we'd like three threads to run our test three times.

Having done that, we next turn our attention to generating data for the consumers. The test class is initialized with a list of test data. The populateData() method is run before the test and fills the list with the values we'd like the consumer threads to use. Note that configuration methods are run once, and only tests are run in parallel.

The run test takes in two parameters, denoting the data we'd like to pass to each consumer. The data comes from the concurrent-processor Data Provider.

This Data Provider is fulfilled by the `getProcessorData()` method. However, instead of just returning the set of three data items we want, we're removing items from the data list one at a time. Why is this?

To see why this works, we need to understand how Data Providers interact with concurrent tests (or don't, more accurately). When TestNG sees a Data Provider, it invokes the test once for every data item returned. Similarly, when we specify an invocation count, TestNG invokes the test the specified number of times.

Therefore, if we were to return the three data items we have in our Data Provider, each thread would then invoke the test three times, once for each data item. This would result in the test being invoked nine times, something we definitely do not want.

The solution therefore is to use a stack structure, and for each time the Data Provider is invoked, return one item and remove it from the list. The Data Provider will be invoked three times (due to the specified `invocationCount`) and each time will return a unique data item for the test, thus ensuring that each thread gets its own parameters when invoking the test.

Of course, instead of all that work with the Data Provider, we could have just run all three instances ourselves inline. While that might have worked with three instances, it very quickly becomes unwieldy if we have more.

As a design principle, it is crucial that we separate data concerns from functional ones. In this case, the specific data that the consumer runs with should be orthogonal to the actual test. This approach means that as our data needs to evolve and become more complex, the test itself does not need to be modified. Of course, we also need to apply some common sense here: If a test has only one data item, there is no need to externalize that into a Data Provider.

The Role of Refactoring

A crucial point we touched on in a number of places is the importance of refactoring when testing enterprise applications.

The fundamental issue with many of these systems is that they are heavyweight processes that have many expectations about their environment. The environment doesn't just include containers and servers; it also includes APIs. For example, code that is coupled to `javax.servlet.HttpSession` is tricky to test because we'd have to lug in an implementation of that API along with its idiosyncrasies.

Likewise, a servlet is not easy to test. It needs to be deployed into a container, and we'd need to find a request and response to feed to it, and then even if we did manage all that in a test environment, the next problem we'd have to deal with is interrogating the response to a sufficient degree to obtain meaningful assertions that aren't fragile and susceptible to breaking from minor UI changes.

This issue crops up time and time again in almost all the enterprise APIs. EJB2 is a great (and horrific) example of components that are tightly controlled and managed by an expensive container (in terms of start-up and how difficult it is to embed). Similarly, JMS suffers from the same issues and requires a message broker to control the message flow.

The problem isn't restricted just to Java APIs. Enterprise systems often have to work with legacy applications, applications that are expensive and cumbersome to start up or use in a testing scenario.

Refactoring is that great wrench in our toolbox that can help attack all of these problems. Of course, there are many times when it's just not possible to sidestep that ugly, difficult API we need to work with. Refactoring might help minimize the pain, but sometimes there isn't really an easy way to avoid expensive, time-consuming tests, and that's fine, despite what you might read elsewhere!

A Concrete Example

Let's have a look at a concrete problem shown in Listing 3–18. We'd like to test a login servlet. The servlet takes in a request, checks the user name and password, and if they're valid, puts a token in the session denoting that the user is logged in.

Listing 3–18 Example of a login servlet

```
protected void doPost(HttpServletRequest req,
                      HttpServletResponse res)
          throws ServletException {
  String username = req.getParameter("username");
  String password = req.getParameter("password");
  LoginToken token;
  HttpSession session = req.getSession(false);
  if(session != null) {
    token = (LoginToken)session.getAttribute("logintoken");
    // if user is logged in, then we ignore the login attempt
    if(token.getUserName().equals(username)) {
```

```
        return;
      }
    }
    Connection c = null;
    try {
      Object o = new InitialContext().lookup("jdbc/MyDS");
      DataSource ds = (DataSource)o;
      c = ds.getConnection();
      // some SQL calls
      // manipulate the result set
      // extract data from the result set and verify password
      // assuming login is valid...
      token = new LoginToken(username);
    }
    catch(NamingException e) {
      throw new ServletException("Error looking up data source", e);
    }
    catch(SQLException e) {
      throw new ServletException("Error obtaining connection", e);
    }
    finally {
      if(c != null) {
        try {
          c.close();
        }
        catch(SQLException e) {
          // just log it, not much else we can do
          log.error("Error closing connection " + c, e);
        }
      }
    }
    if(token != null) {
      session = req.getSession(true);
      session.setAttribute("logintoken", token);
      // record other info too
      session.setAttribute("loginTime",
    System.currentTimeMillis());
    }
}
```

This code in Listing 3–18 is quite common. It should be fairly obvious
what it does from just glancing at it. The test approaches at our disposal are
these.

- Embed a servlet container.
- Test it in the container by remote invoking it once it's deployed.
- Refactor!

No prizes awarded for choosing the last option, given that that is what this section is about!

What's so bad about the other two options? They'd both work equally well; the problem is their overhead. For the embedding solution, we'd still have to go through all the servlet code just to get at the meat of our business functionality. The second approach is even worse; it's not possible to use it during rapid development, and it incurs a very expensive overhead for servlet container start-up. Also, both of these solutions have a lot of collateral damage, in terms of testing APIs and functionality, that's incidental to the desired testing.

We know we need to refactor; how do we do it?

Let's examine what the code does at a high level:

- Takes in a number of parameters
- Performs a check against the environment (in this case, the session)
- Uses the parameters to query a data source
- Creates a value to place in the environment, along with some extra information

The objective of the refactoring is to capture these goals without resorting to a servlet-specific implementation so that, having done so, the servlet can act as a simple shell to the object that will now encapsulate the functionality.

The object we'll create is a `LoginManager`. A first stab at this appears in Listing 3–19.

Listing 3–19 Initial attempt at a refactored *LoginManager*

```
public class LoginManager {
  public LoginToken login(String username, String password) {
    try {
      Object o = new InitialContext().lookup("jdbc/MyDS");
      DataSource ds = (DataSource)o;
      Connection c = ds.getConnection();
      // some SQL calls
      // manipulate the result set
      // extract data from the result set
```

```
      // assuming login is valid...
      return new LoginToken(username);
    }
    catch(Exception e) {
      throw new RuntimeException("Error looking up DataSource",
                                e);
    }
  }
}
```

We ripped out the database calls from the servlet into this new class, which takes in the parameters from the request. Note that this new class is quite testable—we can create an instance of it without any servlet or container dependency.

When we try to do so, Listing 3–20 shows the next container dependency.

Listing 3–20 Lookup code for the data source

```
new InitialContext().lookup("jdbc/MyDS");
```

This works only in an environment where JNDI is already configured. While this is easily doable in the test (as we'll see in Chapter 4), it's another tangential concern that we shouldn't need to worry about for the purposes of our test. The solution here is to switch from the Service Locator pattern (where objects look up their dependency) to a Dependency Injection pattern. This is achieved by adding a `DataSource` property (a field with a getter/setter pair) in our `UserManager` and having the caller set it.

In terms of database interaction, our test right now is good enough. There's no need to try to abstract away the database. We could employ any of the approaches we discussed earlier for handling database connectivity inside of tests. We'll focus the remainder of our discussion on the role of refactoring and how to identify abstractions through testing.

The test still doesn't quite handle all of the functionality we require. The servlet still has to take care of populating the environment (the HTTP session) with the right information. Whether this is a problem or not depends on our use case. Do we expect the implementation of the login method to require more information from its environment in the future?

Are we expecting that components other than the servlet will need to invoke `LoginManager`?

If we don't, then we're done, and we can stop refactoring now and start testing. However, assuming we do need to worry about the environment and abstracting that away, how do we achieve that?

The key issue here is that we're not really doing anything special with the HTTP session; we're simply treating it as a map of contextual information. It's not type safe, and pretty much anything can read attributes and dump others in. Ideally, we'd like to just pass in the session to the login method, but that would impose a servlet API burden.

Since all we do is use it as a map, we could instead add a `Map` parameter to the login method. This allows the implementation to manipulate the contents as needed. Listing 3–21 shows the new method signature.

Listing 3–21 Refactored signature of the login method

```
public LoginToken login(Map session, String username,
                        String password)
```

The method could even return void and deal with putting the login token in the session map itself.

However, this approach presents a problem for the servlet. How does it deal with this map and ensure that it corresponds to the session map? In an ideal world, `HttpSession` would implement `Map`, or we'd be able to make it extend `Map` as well; neither is realistic at this point, so instead we create a proxy wrapper that handles all the messy work of synchronizing the contents for us.

The proxy in Listing 3–22 is a map implementation that wraps the `javax.servlet.HttpSession` object.

Listing 3–22 *HttpSession*-backed *Map* implementation

```
public class SessionMap extends AbstractMap {
  private final HttpSession session;
  private Set entries;

  public SessionMap(HttpSession s) {
    this.session = s;
  }
```

```
public Set entrySet() {
  if(entries == null) {
    entries = new HashSet();
    // loop over session attribute names
    // create new Map.Entry anonymous inner class
    // with attribute name/value
    // ensure setValue on the entry modifies underlying session
    // add to entries
  }
  return entries;
}

public Object put(Object key, Object value) {
  entries = null;
  Object originalValue =
session.getAttribute(key.toString());
  session.setAttribute(key.toString(), value);
  return originalValue;
}

public Object get(Object key) {
  return session.getAttribute(key.toString());
}

public Object remove(Object key) {
  entries = null;

  Object value = get(key);
  session.removeAttribute(key.toString());

  return value;
}

public void clear() {
  entries = null;
  session.invalidate();
}
}
```

The entrySet() method is not implemented here (since it's quite verbose), but the idea is more important than the details.

Using the SessionMap class, our servlet can now easily pass in a map to the LoginManager, which can then make any reads/writes to the map that will be automatically reflected in the underlying HTTP session. This change now means that during testing, we can easily have the test supply a `HashMap` instead of the `SessionMap`, populate it with any values that need to be tested, and make assertions about its contents after invoking the `LoginManager`.

It can certainly be debated whether the `SessionMap` refactoring is the right approach or not; one could argue that we're mixing concerns here and having the login method do too much work by manipulating a map. It's also possible to argue that the loss of typing and weaker contract for callers means that it's more error prone. These are valid arguments, but the point of this exercise is to highlight an approach, not to specify a particular solution.

This example shows the power of refactoring as a testing aid and illustrates how even seemingly awkward APIs that need to be interacted with in complex ways can be abstracted away. The abstraction means that during testing, we can use simpler objects that are trivial to construct and thus test. A side effect of increasing testability is an improvement in the design. Refactoring for testability helps identify roles and concerns in a practical "in the code" way that's often much harder to spot when drawing design diagrams.

While the wrapper we created is verbose, it's something that we would write just once, and from then on it would become a valuable tool that could be reused many times. The time invested in writing it will pay off quickly in better code that is more testable.

An In-Container Approach

Servlets specifically can have an interesting in-container testing mechanism using the servlet API. This mechanism is Servlet Filters. It is possible, for example, to specify a test filter that can act on any requests to the servlet.

This approach allows us to noninvasively test a given servlet. The filter has access to the request before the servlet is invoked, so it can verify that the right parameters are specified. It can also interact with the request and response after the servlet has manipulated them and so is able to also make assertions about the state of the request, response, or session.

While this might not be as convenient from a testing standpoint as the earlier refactoring, it nevertheless introduces an important tool in our testing toolbox: the callback approach. Many APIs allow for custom code to be run before or after a component is invoked. Tests can take advantage of this mechanism and can thus get into locations where it's often difficult or tricky to have test code. A filter's access to `HttpServletRequest` and `HttpServletResponse` is one example of this since both of these objects are difficult to get outside of the servlet environment.

Conclusion

In this chapter, we examined a number of enterprise components and patterns, and we outlined the testing techniques and approaches that can be used to ensure that we develop a growing library of tests, both unit and functional. Different approaches were discussed to handle some common issues that get in the way of enterprise testing, such as expecting a heavyweight environment or a database with specific data.

The most important lesson we hope to impart is to take a practical and pragmatic approach to testing. We should not concern ourselves with coverage rates or tests of trivial code. Every test should test potential issues with the code, rather than basic Java semantics. Breaking down an enterprise component into more digestible pieces is a simple process provided it is tackled one goal at a time, rather than trying to convert the whole thing in one go. The value of our tests lies in their evolutionary nature, and their value is expected to increase over time. Based on that, it is vital that having too small a set to start with does not discourage you.

In addition to allowing tests to grow organically, diversifying the types of tests is also important. A project with nothing but unit tests is not very useful when it comes to being able to make confident assertions about how it will behave in a production environment. Likewise, a suite of tests with just functional or integration tests is very hard to debug or isolate specific issues in.

Furthermore, the order in which we write our tests is flexible. When tracking down a bug in a complex unfamiliar system, for example, a functional test might be easier to get us started. We can then break it down into unit tests as we focus on the specifics of the bug. When developing new functionality, on the other hand, starting off with unit tests will help ensure the component is designed correctly and lends itself to greater testability.

Many managers balk at the suggestion of spending two weeks writing tests. Deadlines have to be met, clients need to see new functionality, and a bunch of tests that prove everything works just as it currently does is a very hard sell. This isn't surprising and is in fact quite sensible. If testing is to be a goal, it needs to become part of development, not a separate concern that is tagged on at the end. Testing is just another facet of development, and it's crucial that developers adopt testing as part of both debugging and developing new functionality.

When it comes to integrating tests into an existing large code base, we should keep these ideas in mind. Spending weeks writing tests is unsatisfying and very susceptible to test rot, where tests are written once and then forgotten and neglected. A far better approach is to introduce new tests as needed and to let them grow organically over time. The history of test growth tells a far more compelling story that any sudden testing spike.

One of the most powerful tools available to us to promote testability is refactoring. Code that is easily testable is code that is better designed. It has more versatile and well-specified contracts and fewer dependencies—all of which happen as a side effect of increased testability.

A concrete application of these principles is when we find ourselves repeating a time-consuming task just to reproduce a bug, such as testing `HttpSession` and other similar objects. Stepping back and thinking about the functionality we're testing, it becomes obvious that all we care about, for example, is a `Map` implementation, so spending the 20 minutes to write an abstraction will save us hours of restarts and redeployments.

Ultimately, in an ideal world, development and testing go hand in hand. We must always think of them concurrently. Development testing's biggest payoffs manifest themselves only when it becomes an ingrained habit and an approach to development as well as maintenance.

CHAPTER 4

Java EE Testing

Having explored some of the issues surrounding enterprise testing in general, it is time to turn our attention to testing Java EE components. Testing Java EE applications imposes unique constraints on us. Ultimately, most of the issues boil down to the fact that Java EE applications run inside a container. The container provides a variety of services, as well as a rich environment for components. The container also handles component lifecycles and initialization.

At first glance, these issues make the idea of testing EE applications difficult at best. None of the current crop of containers are designed to be embedded, and even if they were, the start-up times are often prohibitive. Not to mention that even if it were possible to embed a container, we would run into deployment issues. Java EE likes to have components packaged up in jar (or war, ear, rar) files, which is an extra step we'd have to go through in testing and another impediment to fast tests.

Having said that, the importance of testability has had an impact on the EE specifications. The latest version (Java EE 5.0) goes a long way toward allowing components to be easily testable. Through the use of annotations and optional deployment descriptors, components can now be treated as simple POJOs that can be instantiated in tests. This chapter will show examples of how to write tests for these components and how to initialize them correctly to best simulate their actual usage at deployment time.

There still remains the issue of providing the right environment and services for our components. Fortunately, a number of open source solutions can help us tremendously in this regard. We will also go over some solutions for simulating common services that a compliant EE container is required to provide in a test environment.

In terms of deployments, there are currently thousands of J2EE 1.3 or 1.4 applications out there. Should we abandon testing them since they cannot be easily tested outside of the container? Absolutely not! We will also explore what our options are for that scenario and what can be done to test these components.

This chapter will address specific APIs, and the general approach will be to find an existing library or solution that enables us to test any given API. It's unlikely that you'll need to go through every single section, as it's quite rare to find an application using all these APIs! Far more likely is that you'll need to test one or two of them, so you can skip ahead to the relevant section.

Some sections build on others. For this reason, JNDI, the Java Naming and Directory Interface, is the first API we cover since it is (unfortunately) a common mechanism used by many components to find services to invoke, such as JMS, JDBC, and others. After delving into how best to test and model JNDI in tests, we move on to JDBC, which is another cornerstone on which many components rely.

The next building block is JTA, the Java Transaction API. While somewhat exotic and rarely used directly by end users, it's useful to learn how to set this up since it is another base service that others often rely on. While for the sake of completeness we cover how to use the API directly, in most cases it's sufficient to just set it up without worrying about how to call it. From there we move on to three popular APIs: JMS, JPA, and EJB3. All of these require JTA and so build on the other services we've encapsulated in our tests.

Finally, we move to the Web tier, where we cover JAX-WS (Web services) and servlets, highlighting how to develop stand-alone tests for them. The chapter concludes with a discussion of testing XML since it's such a ubiquitous format that runs through numerous EE components. A reference table (Table 4–2) at the end of the chapter outlines all the libraries used to implement and work with the APIs we cover. Feel free to cheat and skip ahead to that table if all you'd like to know is what to use to test components using API X!

Before delving into the details, we'll first outline the differences between in-container testing and out-of-container testing, along with the pros and cons of each approach.

In-Container versus Out-of-Container Testing

The two main approaches for testing Java EE components are (1) testing them in the container they are intended to run in and (2) testing them outside of it in a simulated environment. Testing in the container involves embedding the test engine and tests in the container along with the rest of the application. The test engine can be interacted with, usually through a

Web interface of some sort. The tests are then responsible for interacting with the components to be tested. Since the whole thing is running inside the container, all the services and environment the component expects are in place, exactly as they are when the component is deployed (since, of course, the component is deployed in a container!).

Testing out of the container usually means creating a minimal environment for the component to run in or, even better, not having to worry about the environment at all. For example, all the testing solutions and approaches we have encouraged you to use so far can be considered out-of-container testing. Each test does its own setup if needed, handling the creation of all the resources the component needs, as well as managing the component lifecycle and cleanup.

There are advantages and disadvantages to both approaches, as shown in Table 4–1. Deciding which approach to choose is a tradeoff, and the decision is likely to change depending on your specific use case. Of course, nothing stops you from doing both, using out-of-container tests as your unit/functional tests and using in-container tests for your integration testing.

Based on Table 4–1, it should be fairly clear that in terms of testing, it's far easier to use out-of-container testing. We have more fine-grained control over everything, and the fact that tests are so easy and fast to run ensures that we will be running them often—we can easily fall into the habit of writing them as a matter of course to help track down bugs. We will first tackle the in-container testing approach, then go through a selection of EE APIs and show how each of them can be tested outside of the container.

Table 4–1 Pros and cons of in-container versus out-of-container testing

	Pros	Cons
In-container testing	Exactly matches the runtime environment	Expensive to start up Difficult to deploy new tests Difficult to automate Increased complexity of cross-platform testing
Out-of-container testing	Provides relatively fast start-up Allows full control over environment Easy to automate Easy to debug	Mismatched against the runtime environment Implementations used for tests might come from different providers than runtime

In-Container Testing

To run tests inside the container, we need to programmatically invoke the test framework. Regardless of what framework is actually used, the principles and rough steps are the same.

1. Create an instance of the test environment.
2. Identify the tests.
3. Register the tests with the test framework.
4. Register a listener for the results (which can then generate reports as needed)

Beyond these simple steps, it's possible to add functionality to make the process more user friendly. For example, you can provide a page that allows users to specify what test classes or groups should be run, as well as allowing further configuration and fine-tuning of the test environment.

We'll go over how these steps can be implemented in the case of TestNG. First, we need to make a number of assumptions.

- We are testing a Web application.
- The test classes are packaged as part of the Web application.
- The test classes are in the `WEB-INF/classes` directory and not part of a jar file.

Creating a Test Environment

The main entry point to TestNG is the `TestNG` class. This class allows us to set up a specific test run, and it is what we will use to specify all the tests, listeners, and any other run-specific configuration. Since we would be creating a specific instance, each user will get his or her own test run. The benefit of this approach is that we do not have to worry about concurrency issues in the test framework, as we do not have any shared state via static instances or variables.

Of course, it is possible that the tests themselves rely on shared resources. In such cases, we must take care to ensure that there are no conflicts between parallel runs. For example, if a test writes to the file system, another test running concurrently might be trying to read or write to that same file, resulting in errors. It's important to keep this in mind when writing tests; tests that minimize shared state are far easier to distribute or run in parallel than ones that have to rely on tricky synchronization or locking.

Creating an instance of the test framework is trivial. We also specify a default suite name for our reporting in Listing 4–1.

Listing 4–1 Invoking TestNG programmatically

```
TestNG tester = new TestNG();
tester.setDefaultSuiteName("container-tests");
```

Identifying Tests

The next step is to identify test classes. When using other frameworks, this can be tricky, as it requires that we examine the structure of every class to check whether it contains a test. Fortunately, this is much simpler in the case of TestNG: We can simply pass in all the classes and let it worry about figuring out which contain tests and which don't.

Since one of our assumptions is that all of our test classes are under WEB-INF/classes, we recursively read this directory to find all the class files in it. The simple helper class in Listing 4–2 will return an array of all the classes within a given directory.

Listing 4–2 Scanner to find test classes

```
public class ClassScanner {
  private File rootDirectory;
  private FileFilter filter;
  private ClassLoader loader;

  private static final Logger log
      = Logger.getLogger(ClassScanner.class);
  private static final String CLASS_EXT = ".class";

  public void setLoader(ClassLoader loader) {
    this.loader = loader;
  }

  public ClassScanner(File root) {
    this.rootDirectory = root;
  }

  public void setFilter(FileFilter filter) {
    this.filter = filter;
  }
```

```java
public Class[] getClasses() {
  List<Class> list =  new ArrayList<Class>();
  getClasses(list, rootDirectory);
  return list.toArray(new Class[list.size()]);
}

private void loadClasses(List<Class> list, File directory) {
  // superfluous check, but being explicit is a good thing
  // as we ensure we don't blow up if passed an invalid value
  if(directory == null || !directory.isDirectory()) return;
  File[] files = directory.listFiles();
  for(File child : files) {

    // skip hidden files and dirs
    if(child.getName().charAt(0) == '.') continue;

    // we apply the filter manually because it's a very
    // common mistake for user-supplied filters to forget
    // about directories
    if(child.isDirectory()) {
      loadClasses(list, child);
    } else if(filter == null || filter.accept(child)) {
      // since we know the root, we trim the file name to
      // only include the path from the root
      // then we replace file separators with dots
      // to make a class name
      if(child.getName().endsWith(CLASS_EXT)) {
        int trim = rootDirectory.toString().length();
        String name = child.toString().substring(trim + 1);
        // get rid of the .class suffix
        name = name.substring(0, name.length()
                            - CLASS_EXT.length());
        name = name.replace(File.separatorChar, '.');
        try {
          Class clazz = loader == null ? Class.forName(name) :
               loader.loadClass(name);
          list.add(clazz);
        }
        catch(Exception e) {
          log.warn("Error loading class " + name, e);
        }
      }
    }
  }
}
}
```

The helper class also allows us to specify a file filter. The reason for specifying the filter is that without it, TestNG would have to examine every class file to see if it has any annotations. Since we've written the test classes, we know how best to restrict the set that should be scanned. For example, it is possible that all our classes have the word *Test* in them, in which case we would specify a filter to check for that. We might also have all of our tests under a `com.foo.tests` directory. Listing 4–3 shows how to use our scanner in this environment.

Listing 4–3 Scanner in a Web container

```
public static Class[] scan(ServletContext context) {
    String root = context.getRealPath("/WEB-INF/classes");
    ClassScanner scanner = new ClassScanner(new File(root));
    scanner.setLoader(ClassScanner.class.getClassLoader());
    // we pick a specific directory
    final File testsDir = new File(root, "com/foo/tests");
    scanner.setFilter(new FileFilter() {

      public boolean accept(File pathname) {
        // check that the file is anywhere inside of test root
        return pathname.getPath().startsWith(testsDir.getPath());
      }
    });
    Class[] classes = scanner.getClasses();
    return classes;
  }
```

In Listing 4–3, `context` is an instance of `ServletContext`, obtained from the invoking servlet or JSP page. For performance reasons, it's always a good idea to define a filter that cuts out as many classes as possible. This allows us to reduce the time spent introspecting into each class to discover its annotations (or lack thereof).

Registering Tests

Having discovered all the test classes, the next step is to register them with the test framework. Registering test classes informs TestNG of the base set of classes it should look at when evaluating what to run. It will examine each of the classes specified to determine whether it contains any tests or configuration methods. Once all the classes have been examined, a dependency graph is generated internally to determine the order of execution for the tests that were found.

Informing our TestNG instance of the classes is very simple, as shown in Listing 4–4.

Listing 4–4 Registering test classes with TestNG

```
tester.setTestClasses(classes);
```

The next step is to register a listener for test results.

Registering a Results Listener

The purpose of a results listener is to be notified of the test status by TestNG. The listener can then process or aggregate the results as needed. TestNG allows for a number of different listener types. They can be listeners that are notified of any state changes as they happen or reporters that are invoked once the test run has completed and we need to generate a report for the user. The former is useful when showing test progress; the IDE plug-ins for example, all use this approach to visually present current test progress and results while the tests are being run.

Though we'll focus on the reporting mechanism for this simple example, it's equally possible to use a test listener to show test progress as well. For example, it's not hard to implement an AJAX-based interface that would show a Web page and test results as they happen; however, explaining how to do so is beyond the scope of this book.

TestNG is bundled with three reporters by default.

- `SuiteHTMLReporter`: This is the default reporter; it outputs a directory of cross-linked HTML files enabling drill-down into specific test results.

- `FailedReporter`: This reporter generates a TestNG run configuration that includes all failed tests from the previous run. It is also run by default; its purpose is to allow us to quickly run only failed tests after a given test run.

- `EmailableReporter`: This one generates a report file that can be easily emailed to show test results.

Since we'd like to keep this as simple as possible, we'll extend the emailable report and modify it to generate a single page of results to present to the browser. We could also use the richer `SuiteHTMLReporter`, making sure to write to a specific temporary directory for each user, so as to guarantee that parallel runs do not get their results mixed up. The important thing, though, is to understand the basic concepts involved; once we understand those, the framework allows us to write a much richer client later.

By default, `EmailableReporter` generates a file on disk. This isn't quite what we need since we can send the results directly to the browser. We subclass it in Listing 4–5 to provide the custom behavior we need.

Listing 4–5 Customized reporter

```
public class SinglePageReporter extends EmailableReporter {
  private Writer writer;

  public SinglePageReporter(Writer writer) {
    this.writer = writer;
  }

  protected PrintWriter createWriter(String out) {
    return new PrintWriter(writer);
  }
}
```

Our servlet or JSP page would register this listener, so that after the test run, the results will be presented to the user without our intervention, as shown in Listing 4–6.

Listing 4–6 Registering the reporter with TestNG

```
  IReporter reporter =
          new SinglePageReporter(response.getWriter());
  tester.addListener(reporter);
```

The final step, of course, is to actually run the test, which is done by invoking the `run()` method on the TestNG instance.

Reviewing everything we've done, we can easily drop in the JSP file from Listing 4–7, which allows us to run any tests shipping with the application and will present the results in the browser.

Listing 4–7 JSP page to invoke TestNG

```
<%@ page import="org.testng.*, java.io.*" %><%
  TestNG tester = new TestNG();
  tester.setDefaultSuiteName("container-tests");
  String root = application.getRealPath("/WEB-INF/classes");
  ClassScanner scanner = new ClassScanner(new File(root));
  scanner.setLoader(getClass().getClassLoader());
  scanner.setFilter(new FileFilter() {

    public boolean accept(File pathname) {
      return pathname.getPath().indexOf("Test") > -1;
    }
  });
  Class[] classes = scanner.getClasses();
  tester.setTestClasses(classes);
  IReporter reporter = new SinglePageReporter(out);
  tester.addListener(reporter);
  tester.run();
%>
```

Obviously this isn't the most elegant solution (scriptlets never are!), but as we stated earlier, the goal is to show the principles of running tests inside of a container. Beyond the basics, it is easy to jazz up the output and display so that they're more useful and functional.

From all the different steps in the in-container embedding process outlined in this section, the key concept is to embed the testing framework inside of the container environment and from then on to invoke it programmatically. Beyond this basic principle, it's possible to use many enhancements to improve the functionality and usefulness of in-container tests, such as test autodiscovery, test selection, or even hot deployment via custom classloaders. The final step is to present the results to the user using a custom reporter.

Java Naming and Directory Interface (JNDI)

JNDI is an API for looking up resources in a global directory. Think of it as a big tree structure where we can look up a given node by its name. In this section, we'll delve into the details of how JNDI works so that we can understand how to hook into that mechanism so our tests can use a custom implementation outside of a container. As is common throughout this chapter, we will then present existing solutions that can be dropped in to do all the hard work for us. Listing 4–8 shows the common usage pattern of JNDI.

Listing 4–8 Sample JNDI usage

```
new InitialContext().lookup("someObject");
```

Listing 4–8 creates an `InitialContext` object that, when running inside a container, will use a vendor-specific implementation of the API that performs the lookup in whatever representation the container has internally of the naming directory. Having creating the context, we can now look up objects in it, list its contents, or traverse the tree. All of this is done though the JNDI API. The `InitialContext` constructor has an overloaded version that takes in a `Hashtable` object that contains various environment values to determine how the context should be created. For example, many implementations of JNDI allow us to look up resources remotely. In such a case, the environment `Hashtable` to pass in would contain the URL for the remote server, as well as login credentials.

In practice, JNDI is used to look up many of the resources that an application server provides. These range from `DataSource` objects to the `TransactionManager`. In the next section, we'll examine how JNDI's internals work and what an application server does in order to support JNDI lookups. Note that you can skip this section if you don't want to learn about how JNDI works!

Understanding JNDI's Bootstrapping

The main issue facing us is that we do not have access to the container's JNDI implementation. We have no way to know how it stores data internally, nor how we can use that mechanism independently of the container.

Thankfully, usage of the API does not require that we interact with the implementation. JNDI has a well-defined mechanism that allows the container to hook in its implementations, so we employ the simple trick of hooking our own implementation, which just happens to allow us to populate the tree, not just query it.

To understand how this can work, we need to understand the mechanism through which a JNDI provider is registered. The Service Provider Interface (SPI) for JNDI requires at least two classes, one that implements `javax.naming.Context` and an implementation of `javax.naming.⏎ InitialContextFactory`. The factory is responsible for creating the context implementation.

When we create an `InitialContext` and pass in the environment `Hashtable`, one option is to explicitly pass in the factory implementation we'd like it to use. This is the approach used when accessing JNDI remotely, for example. Listing 4–9 shows an example of a vendor-specific JNDI lookup.

Listing 4–9 Invoking JNDI with a custom provider

```
Hashtable env = new Hashtable();
env.put(Context.INITIAL_CONTEXT_FACTORY,
        "com.swiftmq.jndi.InitialContextFactoryImpl");
env.put(Context.PROVIDER_URL, "smqp://localhost:4001/");
Object topic = new InitialContext(env).lookup("myTopic");
```

We can see that a factory class is specified for the context. We also specified a URL since we are connecting to a remote directory. The URL is a custom one that the factory implementation understands and can use.

Using the exact same approach, we can create our `InitialContext` objects and specify our factory implementation.

Since we don't need any advanced features beyond the ability to look up and store objects, the factory is relatively simple to implement. All it would do is return an instance of our custom `Context` object that contains a tree structure to hold the directory information. This can be a simple `Map` of `Map` objects data structure, with appropriate methods for looking up objects at any given node. The vast majority of methods specified in the `Context` interface can simply throw `UnsupportedOperationException`. We can do so with confidence since we know how we'll be accessing our JNDI implementations and know which lookups work and which don't.

This is all well and good; we can now create a custom `InitialContext` outside of a container than will look up resources in our internal map. However, the problem is that in many cases, the components we are testing assume they are running inside a container and using code like `new`

`InitialContext().lookup("jdbc/MyDataSource")`. In this case, we have no easy way to populate the environment `Hashtable`. What can we do in this situation?

The answer lies in the JNDI API's default context discovery mechanism. Looking into the source for `InitialContext`, we see that it calls the protected method `getDefaultInitCtx()`. This method calls `NamingManager.getInitialContext(myProps)`, and in turn, this method calls `getInitialContextFactoryBuilder()`, which is where application servers usually hook themselves into the API.

Thus, a bit of digging around has shown us that the way to become the default JNDI provider is to call `javax.naming.spi.NamingManager.⏎` `setInitialContextFactoryBuilder(...)`. Unfortunately, this method can be called only once during the lifetime of the JVM. So it's something we would do at the beginning of a test run once only, and then throughout the test we would simply populate and look up resources as needed.

If all that sounds a little bit complicated, there is, conveniently, a rather popular open source library that does all the heavy lifting for us. Within the Spring framework's testing classes (in the `spring-mock.jar` file) there are a couple of very useful helpers that take care of doing all this work for us.

Spring's `SimpleNamingContextBuilder`

`SimpleNamingContextBuilder`, found in the `spring-mock.jar` library, has the few simple calls needed from a test perspective to get a JNDI environment up and running. Listing 4–10 shows its usage.

Listing 4–10 Spring JNDI test setup

```
@BeforeSuite
public void setUpJndi() throws NamingException {
  SimpleNamingContextBuilder builder =
      SimpleNamingContextBuilder.emptyActivatedContextBuilder();
  Object myResource = ...;
  builder.bind("myResource", myResource);
}
```

Here we populated a global resource that we'd like to make available to all our tests. In this specific case, we are also assuming that the JNDI context is to be shared across all tests. If, however, we wanted to ensure that for every test method a new and clean context would be obtained, the annotation would be changed to be `@BeforeMethod` instead. Then in any test (or more likely, within any component that relies on JNDI), the `new InitialContext().lookup(...)` method would succeed.

Avoiding JNDI

While we've shown how easy it is to test components that rely on JNDI (of which there are thousands upon thousands out in the wild, despite what everyone tells you!), JNDI is far from being the ideal mechanism for resource lookups.

JNDI lookups follow the Resource Locator pattern (also know as Service Locator). A component that requires a particular service or resource looks it up in a global registry. From a testing perspective, this is less than ideal, as it mandates some form of registry with all the baggage it brings along with it, such as having only one implementation available. The current trend is in fact to favor the exact opposite approach: Component Injection (also know as Dependency Injection, or Inversion of Control). In this case, resources are not looked up but are instead set on the component.

A component that looks up the `myResource` object used in Listing 4–10 would be modified to have a `setMyResource(...)` method instead. In the latter case, we don't need JNDI, and the component becomes easier to test because we then have better control over the lifecycle of the `myResource` object and can provide the component with a variety of implementations, should we so choose.

The other pain point with JNDI is the proliferation of checked exceptions, which makes any code using JNDI needlessly verbose and cluttered because of the exceptions that have to be caught with every invocation.

To summarize, component dependencies are satisfied through either service locators (commonly JNDI) or injection. If you have the choice, go down the injection route, as the testing overhead is minimal, and the approach allows for more flexibility.

Java Database Connectivity (JDBC)

Many (if not all!) of the components we'd like to test in an enterprise environment like to talk to databases. There is often an object-mapping abstraction layer between the application code and the database itself. This is usually in the form of an object-relational mapping (ORM) tool, such as Hibernate, EJB entity beans (JPA), TopLink, or some other mechanism.

However, there is also often a need to communicate directly with the database through straight JDBC queries.

As we did with JNDI, we'll first explore how JDBC connections are used inside of application servers and then outline solutions for simulating the same approach in a stand-alone test. Likewise, we'll also explore a couple of solutions we can use to do all the hard work for us.

Before delving into the details of testing data sources and setting JDBC in tests, it's worth mentioning DbUnit. DbUnit is designed specifically to deal with a number of common database issues in tests, and we discuss it in detail in Chapter 5.

Managing database connectivity in a stand-alone application is simple. We interact with the `DriverManager` core JDK class to get a connection, as shown in Listing 4–11.

Listing 4–11 Obtaining a JDBC connection in Java SE

```
Connection c
  = DriverManager.getConnection("jdbc:mydriver://server");
```

In an enterprise environment, it is a bit trickier. Database connections in such an environment have features that stand-alone connections do not since the container manages them. These features include connection pooling, auditing and manageability extensions, transaction enlisting, and so on.

The mechanism for obtaining a connection is also different from within the container. We could still use the `DriverManager` approach, but that would bypass all of the enhanced functionality the container provides for us, so it would be a fairly silly thing to do.

Listing 4–12 shows the typical JDBC connection lookup pattern in Java EE.

Listing 4–12 Obtaining a JDBC connection in Java EE

```
InitialContext context = new InitialContext();
DataSource ds = (DataSource)context.lookup("jdbc/MyDataSource");
Connection c = ds.getConnection();
```

Here we've created an `InitialContext` to look up a global resource, then looked up our `DataSource` object given its name, and finally obtained a connection. We depended on two container features, JNDI and `DataSource` support.

Why bother with `DataSource` objects anyway? The `javax.sql.DataSource` API was introduced as a successor to the more basic `java.sql.DriverManager` mechanism as the preferred way to obtain database connections. The `DataSource` API provides hooks to allow database driver vendors to provide pooling[1] support, as well as distributed transactions.

Back to our JDBC testing approach. Given that we'd like to test our component that runs in a container, how do we get ahold of a `DataSource`? Simulating the JNDI environment is easy; we covered that earlier. The next hurdle is figuring out how to obtain a `DataSource` object.

We could implement our own, as always. A `DataSource` implementation can simply wrap the legacy `DriverManager` API. This isn't such a bad thing to do in a testing environment since our test is not multithreaded (most of the time), so we don't need pooling. Likewise, we're very unlikely to need distributed transaction support.

Instead of writing our own, we can use a number of existing open source solutions that fit the bill perfectly. Let's go over three of the more popular solutions.

c3p0

c3p0 is a library that provides connection pooling as well as data source support that can be used outside of any container. The library is specification compliant and tries hard to adhere to the JDBC standards. To create a `DataSource` object using this library is very straightforward, as shown in Listing 4–13.

Listing 4–13 Obtaining a *DataSource* in c3p0

```
ComboPooledDataSource ds = new ComboPooledDataSource();
ds.setDriverClass("com.foo.Driver");
cpds.setJdbcUrl("jdbc:vendorName://localhost/testdb");
cpds.setUser(...);
cpds.setPassword(...);
```

---

1. A common misconception is that `DataSource` objects are automatically pooled. Not so! A more accurate description is that `DataSource` objects are *poolable*. In practice, this means that it is possible to decouple the pooling mechanism from the driver, and it enables a simple event listener mechanism for connections being closed or triggering connection-level errors.

This will create a `DataSource` object that is also pooled using the default settings (which are fine for our test). We could tweak the pool configuration (such as initial pool size, maximum/minimum connections, and so on) through the setters provided by the `ComboPooledDataSource` class.

Commons DBCP

Commons DBCP is a similar library provided by Apache. It is built on top of a more general pooling solution, commons-pooling. The documentation is what can be expected from an Apache Commons project, spotty and sporadic at best. The extra dependency might also be annoying to add in. The API, however, is very similar, as shown in Listing 4–14.

Listing 4–14 Obtaining a *DataSource* in Commons DBCP

```
BasicDataSource ds = new BasicDataSource();
ds.setDriverClassName("com.foo.Driver");
ds.setUrl("jdbc:vendorName://localhost/testdb");
ds.setUsername(...);
ds.setPassword(...);
```

Spring

The Spring framework also provides its own `DataSource` implementation. To specify it, we edit our `applicationContext.xml` file as shown in Listing 4–15.

Listing 4–15 Spring *DataSource* XML declaration

```
<bean id="DataSource" class=
"org.springframework.jdbc.datasource.SingleConnectionDataSource">
    <property name="driverClassName" value="com.foo.Driver" />
    <property name="password" value="mypassword" />
    <property name="username" value="myuser" />
    <property name="url"
        value="jdbc:vendorName://localhost/testdb" />
    <property name="suppressClose" value="true" />
  </bean>
```

Note that in this case, Spring will not perform pooling; it simply wraps a standard `DriverManager` connection with the `DataSource` API. What this object does is reuse a single connection for its lifetime. We also specify that all calls to the `close` method should be suppressed since we never want to actually close the connection.

Of course, it's entirely possible to combine one of the connection pooling libraries described earlier with Spring. However, since we are using this connection in a test case, we don't actually need a full-blown pool, and a single connection implementation suits us just fine.

Having created our `DataSource` via any of these libraries, all that remains is for us to bind it to JNDI, so our component can look it up, as shown in Listing 4–16.

Listing 4–16 Test setup for initializing the `DataSource`

```
@BeforeSuite(dependsOnGroups = "jndi", groups = "db")
public void bindDataSources() throws NamingException {
  // initialize DataSource
  DataSource ds = ...;
  new InitialContext().bind("jdbc/MyDataSource", ds);
}
```

Note that we specified some group information for our setup method. When setting up JNDI for our test environment, we had another setup method. Our `DataSource` setup requires that JNDI configuration has already been run, so we declare this dependency to ensure that our database configuration methods are always run after the JNDI ones.

Having gone through this setup, any components that require access to database resources will now be able to do so in the exact same manner as they would within a Java EE container. Furthermore, we can write our tests to use the same APIs that our components do, without having to use a different API to access database resources, for example.

Again, though, using the Service Locator pattern here is discouraged. It's far simpler, for example, to have the `DataSource` injected. Java EE does actually provide for resource injection of data sources, so any components written to that specification should favor that approach instead of using a JNDI lookup.

Java Transaction API (JTA)

The JTA specification is responsible for specifying how to create and manage transactions in an EE environment. It is a set of Java interfaces between a transaction manager, the application server, the resource manager, and transactional applications. The API allows for resources to participate in ongoing transactions, as well as components to start and stop transactions.

In practice, many applications don't interact directly with JTA. Most of the ORM tools, for example, interact with JTA behind the scenes, and all the application developer does is declaratively specify transaction boundaries. Once that's done, the libraries will interact with JTA and the transaction manager to ensure that all work is done atomically, without the application developer having to worry about explicitly enlisting every resource.

However, in some cases we would like to directly interact with JTA. We'd like to be able to start a transaction at arbitrary points in our code and commit it elsewhere, without having to restrict ourselves to method boundaries (most declarative transaction settings are on the method level).

In the past, JTA has been notoriously difficult to test. This is due to a number of reasons, among which is the lack of stand-alone JTA managers that can be embedded easily. Another issue is that JTA transactions are typically to a thread; the thread that starts a transaction must be the one that completes it.

In many cases, frameworks have defined abstraction layers over JTA just to be able to introduce another more testable API. One of the main issues has been the fact that there weren't any decent embeddable transaction managers. Even having overcome that hurdle, there is still the issue of how to obtain a handle onto the transaction manager. Spring, for example, has introduced its own transaction management API, via its `PlatformTransactionManager`, that supports multiple transaction strategies (including one backed by JTA) as well as performing exception translation from JTA's checked exceptions to Spring's unchecked exceptions. The goal is to be able to use the same mechanism for transaction management regardless of what environment you're running in.

Note that although we will show how to test programmatic transaction management, by far the best approach is to rely on declarative transaction management. That approach will free you from having to worry about all the checks and boilerplate code required when manually working with transactions. Listing 4–17 shows how a component typically interacts with JTA.

Listing 4–17 JTA usage example

```
InitialContext context = new InitialContext();
UserTransaction ut =
  (UserTransaction)context.lookup("java:/UserTransaction");
try {
  ut.begin();
  // perform transactional work
  // update a database
  // send a JMS message
  ut.commit();
} catch(Exception ex) {
  try {
    ut.rollback();
  } catch(SystemException ex2) {
    throw new RuntimeException("Rollback failed", ex2);
  }
  throw new RuntimeException("Transaction failed", ex);
}
```

Again, we have the ubiquitous JNDI lookup, followed by a `try/catch` block (due to the checked exceptions in the JTA API). We start our transaction, then interact with other container resources that are transactional (such as JDBC and JMS), and finally commit the transaction. If any of our application logic throws an exception, we catch it and explicitly roll back the transaction. We need more `try/catch` blocks since the rollback method throws a checked exception.

Of course, this code is far from ideal. For example, the JTA API's use of checked exceptions means that we have far more boilerplate code than we'd like. However, the goal is to show you how you can test this code. For better or worse, this is the real-world code we have now, and sadly, this pattern is used in too many places for refactoring to be a practical consideration at this point. So we don't give up, and instead we see how we can tackle the testing aspects of this component.

We've already covered JNDI in a testing environment; the tricky part in this case is being able to create a `UserTransaction` (or `TransactionManager`) and putting it in JNDI. Since application servers typically ship with their own transaction managers that cannot be embedded or used outside, we need to look elsewhere to find a stand-alone solution.

It turns out that currently two open source solutions fit the bill. One is Java Open Transaction Manager from ObjectWeb, and the other is Transaction-Essentials from Atomikos.

In both cases, integration into our tests is quite simple.

Java Open Transaction Manager (JOTM)

JOTM requires a number of jar files to be present in the test classpath to run, in addition to the JTA API classes:

- `jotm.jar`
- `jotm_jrmp_stubs.jar`
- `jotm_iiop_stubs.jar`
- `ow_carol.jar`
- `commons-logging.jar`
- `connector-1.5.jar`
- `howl.jar`
- `log4j.jar`

To set up JOTM as the transaction manager for tests, you can use the setup method shown in Listing 4–18.

Listing 4–18 Setting up JOTM

```
@BeforeSuite(groups = "jta", dependsOnGroups = "jndi")
public void setupJOTM() throws NamingException {
  Jotm jotm = new Jotm(true, true);
  InitialContext context = new InitialContext();
  context.bind("java:/UserTransaction",
    jotm.getUserTransaction());
  context.bind("java:/TransactionManager",
    jotm.getTransactionManager());
}
```

Similar to how we set up our `DataSource`, we depend on our JNDI group before trying to bind the transaction manager objects. Any of our transactional tests that require JTA can now be placed in the `jta` test group, and from then on they can access the `TransactionManager` or `UserTransaction` objects through the names they have been bound to in JNDI.

Atomikos TransactionEssentials

The following jars are required for the Atomikos TransactionEssentials transaction manager:

- `atomikos-util.jar`
- `transactions.jar`
- `transactions-api.jar`
- `transactions-jta.jar`

In addition to the jars, the library likes to have a configuration file called `transactions.properties`, which should be in your classpath somewhere. The library comes with a very well documented example that you can use. This file configures the logging levels and transaction log directory, along with various other settings. The setup code is equally simple, as shown in Listing 4–19.

Listing 4–19 Setting up Atomikos

```
@BeforeSuite(groups = "jta", dependsOnGroups = "jndi")
public void setupAtomikos() throws NamingException {
  InitialContext context = new InitialContext();
  context.bind("java:/UserTransaction",
      new com.atomikos.icatch.jta.UserTransactionImp());
  context.bind("java:/TransactionManager",
      new com.atomikos.icatch.jta.UserTransactionManager());
}
```

Of the two, we would recommend you use Atomikos TransactionEssentials. It has recently been open sourced and is a far more robust and reliable transaction manager. It supports many features that JOTM does not, including full support for JDBC and JMS, and superior performance. It is also slightly simpler to integrate into test suites and is production worthy, so it is a realistic option for deployment. JOTM's documentation is out of date, and the information in it is often inapplicable. The list of jars required no longer matches the list in the latest release, to cite one example. The Atomikos library also has out-of-the-box support for Spring, which makes integration a slightly easier experience.

Java Messaging Service (JMS)

Testing JMS can be tricky due to the asynchronous nature of the API. Messages are received asynchronously, so it is harder to coordinate between senders and receivers within a test.

Chapter 3 outlined one approach for dealing with JMS testing. The key goal there was to abstract away the business functionality from the JMS implementation, thus ensuring that we test the functionality of our code, rather than the transport mechanism. In this section, we will develop techniques and approaches for testing the JMS API itself and cover testing of message sending and receiving, as well as handling the asynchronous nature of the messages.

Creating a Sender/Receiver Test

Having said that, there are still times when we'd like to verify that we're reading a JMS message correctly and that a specific implementation behaves in a way that we expect. In that case, we follow the same approach as that for general asynchronous testing with TestNG, outlined in Chapter 2.

We define a pair of tests, one that sends the message and another that receives it, as shown in Listing 4–20.

Listing 4–20 JMS test pair

```
private Session session;
private Destination destination;

@BeforeClass(groups = "jms")
public void setupJMS() throws NamingException, JMSException {
   Hashtable env = new Hashtable();
   // populate environment for our specific provider
   InitialContext context = new InitialContext(env);
   ConnectionFactory factory =
      (ConnectionFactory)context.lookup("QueueConnectionFactory");
   Connection connection = factory.createConnection();
   session = connection.createSession(false,
                            Session.AUTO_ACKNOWLEDGE);
   destination = (Destination)context.lookup("TestQueue@router1");
}

@Test(groups = "jms")
public void sendMessage() throws JMSException {
```

```
    TextMessage msg = session.createTextMessage();
    msg.setText("hello!");
    session.createProducer(destination).send(msg);
}

@Test(groups = "jms", dependsOnMethods = "sendMessage",
        timeOut = 1000)
public void receiveMessage() throws JMSException {
    MessageConsumer consumer = session.createConsumer(destination);
    TextMessage msg = (TextMessage)consumer.receive();
    assert "hello!".equals(msg.getText());
}
```

The setup method here follows the same pattern as we have been for all our other EE API tests: Set up the environment first, and specify what group of tests it applies to. In this case, we also look up our JMS destination and create a JMS session. Since here we are looking up resources specific to this set of tests within this one class, our configuration method is applied only to this class, rather than the whole suite.

The test runner will realize that the `receiveMessage` test relies on `sendMessage`, so `sendMessage` will be run first.

The receiver test, for the sake of this example, specifies a timeout value. Note that in the case of the JMS API, it is also equally easy to specify a time-out parameter to the receive method, which will behave in the exact same way.

This test will then verify that the message that was received is the same one that was sent. Obviously, this example is trivial, and a real test would likely verify a whole number of other variables and conditions for the message.

One interesting difference between the JMS testing and all the other EE API tests is that we rely on an external JNDI provider to look up the JMS connection and destination. It would not be surprising if the code in our components assumed that those resources were registered in the default provider and simply used `new InitialContext()` to look them up. In this case, we'd go through our usual JNDI setup, and in our JMS setup we would simply populate the default context with the resources we had looked up from the external provider, as shown in Listing 4–21.

Listing 4–21 Setting up JMS in JNDI in the test setup

```
@BeforeClass(groups = "jms", dependsOnGroups = "jndi")
public void setupJMSInJNDI()
                throws NamingException, JMSException {
```

```
Hashtable env = new Hashtable();
// populate environment for our specific provider
InitialContext external = new InitialContext(env);
InitialContext context = new InitialContext();
context.bind("QueueConnectionFactory",
  external.lookup("QueueConnectionFactory"));
context.bind("TestQueue@router1",
  external.lookup("TestQueue@router1"));
}
```

We can see from our example that placing items into the default context is trivial; we simply look them up in the external context and bind them to the local one.

Of course, we have an external dependency running now on a separate system, which can be problematic for some tests. It is possible, via the ActiveMQ JMS library, to run JMS tests within a single JVM, without having to rely on an already running instance.

Using ActiveMQ for Tests

ActiveMQ is an Apache-licensed open source message broker solution that has a number of advanced features and supports a wide variety of cross language protocols and clients. It also supports clustering, persistence, and other features usually found in commercial message broker offerings.

ActiveMQ's Achilles heel lies in its documentation, which is poor at best and has often lagged behind the current feature set. The current version also has issues supporting large messages. ActiveMQ 5.0, however, does support them fully, including out-of-band delivery mechanisms (such as internal or external file servers).

However, it supports an in-memory broker, which is ideal for unit tests—just what we're going to use it for.

Downloading and Installing ActiveMQ

ActiveMQ can be downloaded from http://activemq.apache.org/download.html. Once you have unpacked the download, you will need the following jars in your classpath:

- `activemq-core-4.1.0-incubator.jar` (or whatever the latest release is)
- `backport-util-concurrent-2.1.jar`

- geronimo-j2ee-management_1.0_spec-1.0.jar (or equivalent)
- geronimo-jms_1.1_spec-1.0.jar (or equivalent jms.jar)

To run the in-memory broker, we need to disable broker persistence, so that settings and messages are not persisted across instances and we do not have to worry about queue flushing and suchlike. We also don't need to perform any monitoring, so we also disable the JMX (Java management API) support.

The first client to connect via the in-memory broker will initialize it. Subsequent connection will use the same broker. Once all clients have disconnected, the broker is automatically shut down. The broker's shutdown is performed by a shutdown hook, so we don't need to explicitly handle it ourselves, unless we want to create and destroy a new broker for every test to guarantee isolation.

Running ActiveMQ

ActiveMQ has a special protocol for intra-VM (client and server both running inside the same JVM) invocation. By specifying a certain JMS URL to connect to, the ActiveMQ provider can create a message broker inline that can be used in unit tests without us having to worry about persistence, socket connections, destination configuration, and other setup costs usually associated with JMS. Using the same example shown in Listing 4–21, our setup method for ActiveMQ becomes Listing 4–22.

Listing 4–22 Setting up ActiveMQ in tests

```
@BeforeClass(groups = "jms")
public void setupActiveMQ() throws Exception {
  BrokerService broker = new BrokerService();
  broker.setPersistent(false);
  broker.setUseJmx(false);
  broker.start();
  URI uri = broker.getVmConnectorURI();
  ConnectionFactory factory = new ActiveMQConnectionFactory(uri);
  Connection connection = factory.createConnection();
  connection.start();
  session = connection.createSession(false,
                       Session.AUTO_ACKNOWLEDGE);
  destination = session.createQueue("TestQueue@router1");
}
```

This code explicitly configures the broker by setting its properties. There is a shorthand solution, though, that allows us to specify all these properties in the URI. So we could replace the factory creation as shown in Listing 4–23.

Listing 4–23 Configuring the broker via URL

```
String uri = "vm://localhost?broker.persistent=false";
ConnectionFactory factory = new ActiveMQConnectionFactory(uri);
```

As an aside, one of the most common symptoms of writing JMS tests is that at first try, it doesn't work. Everything looks OK, but the messages being sent aren't received. The reason for this is that it's very common to forget to call `start()` on the connection. JMS will let you create a session and even interact with it on a closed connection, but nothing actually happens until you call `start()`. That's the first thing to double-check when writing JMS code.

Back to the code: We create a broker programmatically, disable persistence as well as JMX monitoring, and then create a connection factory for it.

Finally, we create the destinations we need for our test. As far as the actual JMS tests we have are concerned, they now have a complete JMS environment to work with, even though everything is now running in-memory.

The benefit of this approach is that we have managed to minimize yet another external dependency and have also removed the need for more JNDI lookups.

Furthermore, since we no longer have to create network connections, the speed at which the tests are completed is also drastically increased, making them more realistic to use when debugging or verifying behavior.

Handling State

An interesting issue arises once we have multiple tests in our JMS example. Since our tests are composed of pairs of methods, let's imagine another send/receive pair of tests in the same class.

On running this test, let's assume that the first receiver fails to consume the message from the queue. We have one failure now.

The next send test method is now invoked, and another message is put on the queue. Finally, our last receive test is invoked. What happens now?

The answer is that the receive test will fail. This is due to the fact that we're working with queues, so the message that is actually pulled off is the one that the first sender put on the queue. The queue contains two messages since the test to pull off the first one had failed; the next receiver ends up pulling that one instead of the one matching its sender.

However, there are a number of ways around this.

One approach is to combine the sending and receiving into one test and invoke the broker initialization before every test method. Note that these two go together since it would be quite tricky to have broker initialization go before pairs of methods. While the downside is that we end up mixing sending and receiving in the same method, when realistically they don't belong together, we do eliminate a potential source of errors, the refactoring-unfriendly method name listed as a string in the `dependsOnMethods` annotation attribute.

Another approach is to use message selectors. A JMS message selector enables us to filter received messages such that we receive only those that match the selector. Using this approach requires that we modify the sender to tag the outgoing message with something we can filter on and for the receiver to specify the selector when subscribing. Listing 4–24 shows the change needed in the sender.

Listing 4–24 Setting the test name in a JMS message

```
msg.setStringProperty("test", "test1");
```

On the receiving side, we specify the selector when creating the consumer, as shown in Listing 4–25.

Listing 4–25 Subscribing to a specific test

```
MessageConsumer consumer =
        session.createConsumer(destination, "test = 'test1'");
```

Finally, we can have each sender create a queue before sending. This way we can still share a broker and not have to recreate one for every test, but by ensuring that test pairs have their own unique destination, we isolate any failures from the rest of the JMS tests. This approach allows us to maintain the separation of sending and receiving but incurs some extra code in sending when we have to create a destination.

In both the latter cases, it's a good idea to pick strings that match the class or method names. This helps a bit with refactoring (hopefully you're using an IDE that handles class and method names in strings) as well as making the association between a given queue or message and its test more explicit.

Java Persistence API (JPA)

JPA is one of the more innovative APIs in Java EE 5.0. It draws from a number of popular persistence solutions, both open source and commercial. These include Hibernate, TopLink, and OpenJPA, among others. The standardized persistence API is a lightweight solution that addresses most if not all of the shortcomings of the previous persistence model, EJB2 entity beans.

Most of the benefits of JPA are derived from the fact that it is POJO based. Entities are regular Java objects that do not need to be abstract (as CMP did in EJB2), nor are their accessors abstract. Also, they are no longer required to extend or implement any specific classes or interfaces, either.

The other main innovation in simplifying persistence is in the use of sensible defaults and annotations. Instead of the reams of configuration previously required for EJB2, the current solution favors sensible defaults and optional configuration. There are many resources you can peruse to find out more about JPA. Here we will focus on how to best test JPA-based applications.

To start, one of the main goals of the JPA specification is to enable out-of-container testing. The use of POJO-based objects means that we can easily instantiate any entities within our testing environment. Furthermore, the support for using JPA within a Java SE environment means we do not require a full-blown container, either.

Let us start with a fairly trivial test. We have one entity and we want to verify its behavior, as shown in Listing 4–26.

Listing 4–26 Example of an entity bean

```
@Entity
public class Person {
  private String firstName;
  private String lastName;
  private String email;

  @Id
  @GeneratedValue
  private Long id;
```

```
public void setEmail(String email) {
  if(email == null || email.indexOf('@') == -1)
    throw new IllegalArgumentException("Invalid email");
  this.email = email;
}
// getters and setters for all fields...
}
```

We have a simple validation rule for emails that we'd like to test.[2] Since this is a POJO, we can very trivially create a test that simply calls `new Person()` and attempts to specify an invalid email, as shown in Listing 4–27.

Listing 4–27 Example of a test for an entity bean

```
@Test(expectedExceptions = IllegalArgumentException.class)
public void verifyEmail() {
  Person person = new Person();
  person.setEmail("wibble");
}
```

All very straightforward and trivial; in fact, you could argue it really is too trivial to write such a test, which would be an entirely valid complaint to make.

Things get a lot more interesting once we need to test the actual persistence mechanism. There are a number of issues to take into consideration:

- Deciding on a persistence store
- Configuring the JPA provider
- Making modifications for out-of-container testing
- Simulating an in-container environment

For the sake of completeness, we'll cover each of these issues. However, you can skip the manual configuration and wiring by jumping ahead to the Spring section, which will discuss how to achieve all of the above by using Spring.

---

2. Obviously, a real example would have a slightly more robust check for valid emails and would abstract out the validation logic into a separate helper class.

Let's tackle these issues one at a time. The first one is fairly simple: We need a database to store our entities. A number of open source embedded database engines fit the bill nicely here. One of the most popular is hsqldb. Another new up-and-comer is the h2 database engine, by one of the original authors of hsqldb. The configuration is fairly similar for both, so we'll cover h2 here, since it's faster and has more features. Using Derby (also called JavaDB) is another option. Running these embedded databases in-memory ensures that we can have very fast tests that are easy to run without the cost of starting up a database or going over the network to connect to one.

Configuring the Database

The first step is to download the latest h2 release from www.h2database.com. The database can be deployed with a single jar file, `h2.jar`.

The database can run in a number of modes, including server mode (where it listens to database connections through a socket, much like a standard database would) and in-memory mode. The latter is what we're interested in, as it enables us to bring up the database and shuffle data around very quickly, which is ideal for a testing environment.

To do so, we have to specify the correct URL for the JDBC connection. For an in-memory database, this URL is `jdbc:h2:mem:testdb`. We will configure the JPA provider with this URL in the next section.

Configuring the JPA Provider

To deploy a JPA persistence unit (a collection of entity classes), we need a `META-INF/persistence.xml` file in the classpath, shown in Listing 4–28. Typically, all jar files within a container that contain this marker file will be scanned for all annotated entity classes by the container. The file can be mostly empty; it is used just so the container knows what jar files to look through.

Listing 4–28 Example `persistence.xml` file

```
<persistence xmlns="http://java.sun.com/xml/ns/persistence"
        version="1.0">
  <persistence-unit name="UserManagement">
    <jta-data-source>jdbc/DefaultDS</jta-data-source>
  </persistence-unit>
</persistence>
```

This configuration file specifies a single persistence unit called `UserManagement`, along with the data source to use for the entities found within this unit. If we were running inside of the application server, the `jdbc/DefaultDS` data source would be mapped to a database, which is part of the server configuration (and is specific to the application server used).

Unfortunately, deploying our test with this configuration is problematic. The default transaction type for JPA is JTA, which, without our JTA implementation earlier, is likely to fail spectacularly. The issue applies for the data source, which requires not only JNDI and a `DataSource` implementation but also a JTA-aware `DataSource` that can talk to our JTA implementation.

Another approach is using the out-of-container functionality provided by JPA. In addition to running inside an application server, JPA can be run stand-alone in a plain Java SE environment without a container. In this case, more configuration needs to be done, and certain features that can be relied on in an application server are not available. While JPA is certainly testable in this mode, it is fairly cumbersome and awkward to set up. After we show this approach, we'll examine how some of this setup can be handled more easily and how we can more closely simulate the in-container mode.

We'd have to make two modifications to the persistence configuration to run it stand-alone.

1. Specify the JDBC information.
2. Use resource local transactions.

Unfortunately, the JDBC connection information specified for the stand-alone case is vendor specific, so we would need to consult vendor documentation to determine the names of the JDBC properties. For example, Listing 4–29 shows the TopLink configuration.

Listing 4–29 *persistence.xml* file for TopLink in Java SE

```
<persistence xmlns=http://java.sun.com/xml/ns/persistence
             version="1.0">
<persistence-unit name="UserManagement"
    transaction-type="RESOURCE_LOCAL">
  <provider>
  oracle.toplink.essentials.ejb.cmp3.EntityManagerFactoryProvider
  </provider>
  <class>Person</class>
  <properties>
    <property name="toplink.jdbc.driver" value="<driver class>"/>
    <property name="toplink.jdbc.url" value="<database url>"/>
```

```
        <property name="toplink.jdbc.user" value="<user>"/>
        <property name="toplink.jdbc.password" value="<password>"/>
        <property name="toplink.logging.level" value="INFO"/>
        <property name="toplink.ddl-generation" value="create-tables"/>
    </properties>
</persistence-unit>
</persistence>
```

Note that in this case we had to explicitly specify the class we'd like persisted. The JPA specification does not mandate scanning of jars when running in an SE environment, so while some implementations (e.g., Hibernate) will support it, we cannot guarantee that all implementations will. We also specify a logging level and a custom TopLink property to ensure that our tables are created automatically.

Now that we've finished the configuration for running our JPA test, the next step is writing the test itself.

Writing the Test

Our test needs to initialize the JPA provider and then invoke the JPA API, as shown in Listing 4–30.

Listing 4–30 JPA test

```
private EntityManagerFactory factory;

@BeforeClass
public void initStandaloneJPA() {
  factory =
    Persistence.createEntityManagerFactory("UserManagement");
}

@Test
public void savePerson() {
  Person p = new Person("Captain", "Crunch", "cc@heroes.com");
  EntityManager em = factory.createEntityManager();
  EntityTransaction tx = em.getTransaction();
  tx.begin();
  // this will assign an ID to person
  em.persist(p);
  tx.commit();
  em = factory.createEntityManager();
```

```
    Person saved = em.find(Person.class, p.getId());
    assert saved.getFirstName().equals("Captain");
}
```

There are a number of things to note about this test. First, we are using a different transaction type than we'd be likely using within a container. We are using resource local transactions, which means that our transaction is scoped for the entity manager only, rather than any other resources that might participate in the transaction. For our test, this is not an issue since we are only testing JPA in isolation anyway. So although the semantics of what we're doing are the same, the actual code is different from the one in our real component.

Second, we are initializing JPA ourselves, rather than allowing the container to do so. Again, we run the risk here of using a different configuration from that of a container.

Finally, we also recreate the entity manager when querying to ensure that we're not getting back a cached value from the first one.

These changes mean that while we can test JPA directly ourselves by using tests like this one, we can't actually write tests for components that rely on the in-container version of this code, which is significantly simpler.

Simulating a Container

To test components that use JPA themselves within a container, we'd have to create the correct environment for the JPA provider to convince it that it's running inside of a container. The bulk of the work lies in setting up JTA and a `DataSource` for the provider to use and ensuring that all the components can talk to each other.

Of course, this still doesn't quite get us all the way toward testing any JPA-based components. One of the important new features of Java EE 5.0 is resource injection. JPA's `EntityManager` and `EntityManagerFactory` classes are both considered resources that can be injected into components. So, for example, it's quite common to see code like that shown in Listing 4–31 within a session bean or servlet.

Listing 4–31 Example of an injected `EntityManager`

```
@PersistenceContext(name="UserManagement")
private EntityManager entityManager;
```

```
public Person getPerson(long id) {
  return entityManager.find(Person.class, id);
}
```

Even if we were to wire up everything manually, our solution wouldn't be quite sophisticated enough to examine this component class for injected fields and to then figure out what entity manager should be injected, as well as manage its lifecycle and so on.

The persistence configuration in `persistence.xml` is also likely to rely on a data source, rather than specifying the information inline. Specifying database connectivity within the `persistence.xml` file is used only when we want to run JPA within an SE environment, so code that is expected to run inside of an application server is going to use a data source reference instead.

Listing 4–32 shows the `persistence.xml` file for using JPA inside of the container.

Listing 4–32 `persistence.xml` file for Java EE

```
<persistence xmlns="http://java.sun.com/xml/ns/persistence"
             version="1.0">
  <persistence-unit name="UserManagement"
                    transaction-type="RESOURCE_LOCAL">
    <jta-data-source>jdbc/DefaultDS</jta-data-source>
  </persistence-unit>
</persistence>
```

As you can see, again this is another hurdle to overcome if we want to test the exact same code outside of a container.

Finally, the JPA specification does not require that a persistence provider instrument persistent classes when running in an SE environment; that feature is required only when running inside of a container.

Fortunately, someone else has figured out how to perform all that plumbing for us and can inject entity managers or entity manager factories into any class, as well as provide an appropriate data source for the persistence unit: the Spring framework.

Using Spring as the Container

Spring 2.0's JPA support allows us to get rid of all the plumbing code shown in the previous sections and have Spring manage it instead. Since all Spring does is provide the infrastructure needed for our components and tests, it's a noninvasive approach to using JPA outside of a container. The actual approach taken by Spring to integrate JPA is to simulate the calls that an actual container would make to initialize a JPA provider.

Stepping back a little, JPA has two modes of initialization, one for out-of-container usage, via the `Persistence` factory class, and an in-container SPI, via the `PersistenceUnitInfo` definitions. For any SE-based applications, it is expected that the former would be used, while application servers would use the latter.

Spring simulates the latter in an SE environment, so as far as the JPA implementation is concerned, it is in fact running inside of an application server. Why bother convincing it of that? There are actually several benefits to that approach.

- It allows the same code to be run inside and outside of the container, without changing any descriptors.
- It uses the same transaction strategy.
- It gives us the ability to use resource injection outside of a container.
- It provides autoscanning support for entities, so they do not need to be explicitly specified in `persistence.xml`. Autoscanning means that the provider will scan through the jar file to find all entities that need to be persisted automatically.

We need to define a number of beans in Spring to take full advantage of its JPA support.

First of all, we need to tell it about our persistence unit and allow it to configure our chosen JPA vendor implementation. The persistence unit itself has several dependencies that need to be fulfilled, such as a transaction manager and a data source.

Then we need to tell Spring to inject the persistence manager into any beans that need it. Listing 4–33 shows the full Spring configuration file for our example.

Listing 4–33 Spring JPA configuration

```
<?xml version="1.0" encoding="UTF-8"?>
<beans
    xmlns="http://www.springframework.org/schema/beans"
    xmlns:xsi="http://www.w3.org/2001/XMLSchema-instance"
    xsi:schemaLocation="http://www.springframework.org/schema/beans
```

```
        http://www.springframework.org/schema/beans/spring-beans-2.0.xsd
">

    <!-- define the data source -->
    <bean id="dataSource" class=
    "org.springframework.jdbc.datasource. ↵
SingleConnectionDataSource">
        <property name="driverClassName" value="org.h2.Driver" />
        <property name="password" value="" />
        <property name="username" value="sa" />
        <property name="url"
            value="jdbc:h2:mem:testdb;DB_CLOSE_DELAY=-1" />
        <property name="suppressClose" value="true" />
    </bean>


    <!-- configure the entity manager factory -->
    <bean id="entityManagerFactory"
        class="org.springframework.orm.jpa. ↵
LocalContainerEntityManagerFactoryBean">
        <property name="dataSource" ref="dataSource" />
        <property name="persistenceUnitName" value="UserManagement" />
        <property name="jpaVendorAdapter">
            <!-- we're using Hibernate for this example -->
            <bean class= "org.springframework.orm.jpa.vendor. ↵
HibernateJpaVendorAdapter">
                <!-- explicitly specify the h2 database dialect -->
                <property name="databasePlatform"
                        value="org.hibernate.dialect.H2Dialect" />
                <!-- create database tables automatically -->
                <property name="generateDdl" value="true" />
            </bean>
        </property>
    </bean>
    <!-- our bean that we'd like the entity manager injected to -->
    <bean class="com.testngbook.ee.api.ejb.PersonManager" />
    <!-- Scans beans for persistence annotations -->
    <bean class="org.springframework.orm.jpa.support. ↵
PersistenceAnnotationBeanPostProcessor" />
    <!-- we need a transaction manager for JPA -->
    <bean class="org.springframework.orm.jpa. ↵
JpaTransactionManager">
        <property name="entityManagerFactory"
                ref="entityManagerFactory" />
    </bean>
</beans>
```

While this might seem verbose, most of it is boilerplate configuration that we can write once and then hopefully not worry about. Unfortunately, there's no real way around this, due to Spring's XML syntax.

We create the data source and tell Spring to suppress any close calls since we are running in a test environment and don't want to worry about setting up a database connection pool; we simply reuse the same connection over and over.

After that, we define the Spring bean responsible for managing the persistence provider. We specify the name of the persistence unit, which should match the name specified in `persistence.xml`. In our case, it might seem odd to duplicate this information, but it's useful in case we had multiple persistence units in the classpath.

The entity manager factory bean is also configured with the Spring-specific vendor adapter, on which we can also specify vendor-specific properties such as the database platform to use. Spring ships with vendor adapters for the current three most popular JPA implementations: TopLink, Hibernate, and Apache's OpenJPA.

Following this is the only line that is specifically concerned with our JPA usage: the `PersonManager` bean. We register this in Spring since we'd like the persistence context to be injected into it, rather than having to worry about manually looking it up from Spring and setting it ourselves.

Of course, it's equally easy to not register this bean in Spring and instead perform the manual injection ourselves. In fact, there are cases where that approach is more appropriate than explicitly listing every bean that might need injection in a static Spring configuration file.

Finally, we specify a bean postprocessor and a transaction manager. The postprocessor is a special Spring bean that is notified whenever any other bean is registered and is able to perform further initialization on the bean.

In this specific case, the postprocessor will scan all beans for the `@PersistenceContext` and `@PersistenceUnit` annotations and inject the appropriate implementations into the fields or properties marked with these annotations.

The transaction manager we're using in this example is `JpaTransactionManager`, which is useful when using transactions that only span JPA resources, and we do not need to register other resources such as JMS.

Our test case can also take advantage of Spring's transaction-aware test base classes. This enables us to easily ensure that the JPA code runs in a transactional context. The reason for this is that all write operations in JPA must run inside of a transaction, so we have to ensure that the environment provides that in test cases.

In addition to handling the transactional requirement, the test case also needs to set up the data source for the Spring JPA container. Listing 4–34 shows the setup code for the test case.

Listing 4–34 Spring-based transactional test

```
public class PersonManagerTests
        extends AbstractTransactionalSpringContextTests {

  protected String[] getConfigLocations() {
    return new String[]{"/com/testngbook/ee/api/spring.xml"};
  }
}
```

The `spring.xml` specified is loaded from the classpath; its contents are shown in Listing 4–33.

`AbstractTransactionalSpringContextTests` also extends `Abstract ↵ DependencyInjectionSpringContextTests`. While both classes are quite the mouthful, the fact that one extends the other means that we get all sorts of other goodies as well as transaction handling. One of the most useful of these goodies is automatic Dependency Injection into our test class. So all we need to do is add Listing 4–35 to the test.

Listing 4–35 Injection of dependency into the Spring-based test

```
private PersonManager manager;

public void setManager(PersonManager manager) {
  this.manager = manager;
}
```

By modifying our test case to include this code, we ensure that Spring will automatically populate the test instance with an appropriate instance of `PersonManager`, as specified in our Spring configuration file.

Even more interesting is that `PersonManager` will be correctly populated with all its dependencies. So even though the code is written to run inside an application server, it is still initialized correctly in a test environment, including the resource injection it expects, as shown in Listing 4–36.

Listing 4–36 *PersonManager* with injected resources

```
public class PersonManager
{
  @PersistenceContext(name="UserManagement")
  private EntityManager entityManager;

  @TransactionAttribute
  public void savePerson(Person p) {
    entityManager.persist(p);
  }

  public Person getPerson(long id) {
    return entityManager.find(Person.class, id);
  }
}
```

Despite the fact that we never explicitly initialize the `entityManager` field, it will be initialized thanks to Spring. This is achieved through the use of the `PersistenceAnnotationBeanPostProcessor` bean specified in the configuration file. Any bean with a persistence context annotation will have the field or method populated appropriately based on the entity manager configuration.

Enterprise Java Beans 3.0 (EJB3)

While JPA seems to receive most of the attention, the rest of the EJB3 API is just as revolutionary and useful in an enterprise environment.

The same principles that have driven JPA development also drive the rest of the EJB3 API. Testability is a core concern, as is simplification and switching toward a POJO-based approach, rather than the bulky and verbose EJB2 component model, which required numerous descriptors and interfaces for the simplest of implementations. In addition to the traditional Service Locator pattern, whereby components look up resources in JNDI, the new model supports Dependency Injection of resources, another feature that facilitates improved testability. As discussed earlier, improved testability is a worthy goal as it improves the code base in numerous other ways, such as realistic separation of concerns, improved design, and more robustness in the face of future changes.

The main two component types available are Session Beans and Message-Driven Beans (MDBs). Session beans are simple service objects that coordinate a number of resources, and contain the business logic of the application, that, in turn, often interacts with entity beans. MDBs respond to external events delivered via JMS and can likewise invoke other EE APIs to process the message.

In both cases, a container provides the runtime environment. The container manages the lifecycle of the components, as well as injecting required resources.

Note that we will not cover EJB2 components in this section, as they were never designed to be testable, so providing an environment for them is too cumbersome and difficult. For those components, in-container testing is the recommended approach, along with refactoring to allow testing business functionality through unit tests that do not require a container.

Message-Driven Beans

In EJB3, MDBs are now POJOs, with a few simple annotations to declare them as such. A typical bean might look like Listing 4–37.

Listing 4–37 Example of a Message-Driven Bean

```
@MessageDriven
public class MessageHandler implements MessageListener {

  @PersistenceContext
  private EntityManager entityManager;

  public void onMessage(Message message) {
    // Extract info from message
    TextMessage tm = (TextMessage)message;
    try {
      String owner = tm.getStringProperty("owner");
      persistMessage(owner, tm.getText());
    }
    catch(JMSException e) {
      throw new IllegalArgumentException("Error getting owner",
            e);
    }
  }

  private void persistMessage(String owner, String text) {
    MyEntity entity = new MyEntity(owner, text);
```

```
      entityManager.persist(entity);
   }
}
```

Interestingly, in this case, our tests do not require any special awareness of the fact that this is an MDB. We can use the exact same approach we used for injecting the `entityManager` as we did in JPA earlier. Instead of letting the container create our `MessageHandler` bean, we would create it manually. Note that because we've placed the business processing into a method that has no JMS dependencies, our test can run without any JMS dependencies other than the API.

We would use the same Spring configuration as we did to support JPA tests. Listing 4–38 shows our test implementation.

Listing 4–38 Spring test for a Message-Driven Bean

```
public class MessageHandlerTests
   extends AbstractTransactionalSpringContextTests {

   private MessageHandler handler;

   public void setHandler(MessageHandler handler) {
     this.handler = handler;
   }

   @Test
   public void verifyEntity() {
     String owner = "ploppy";
     String text = "Some test text";
     handler.persistMessage(owner, text);
   }
}
```

For an explanation of `AbstractTransactionalSpringContextTests` and its usage, please see the Spring section in Chapter 5. Note that this superclass provides two important benefits to our test:

1. Dependency Injection of the handler we'd like to test
2. Transactional support so we can use JPA without having to explicitly specify transactional behavior

While this test will hopefully pass, there is something amiss: We don't seem to have any asserts, so how can we verify that the entity was persisted correctly?

This is a very common problem in testing, with no ideal solution. We need to have access to the private state of our `MessageHandler`, namely, the `EntityManager` field. Once we obtain it, we can then interact with it and assert that it contains our entity, as well as any other information we'd like to confirm in the persisted entity.

As for getting a hold of the entity manager, we have the following options.

1. *Reflection*: We explicitly look up the value of a private field using reflection. We would have to call `setAccessible(true)` on the field to allow us to read its value. The advantage of this approach is that we do not leak implementation details just to satisfy testability. The disadvantage, however, is that it's a fragile solution since it will have the field name as a string; if we were to rename it, our test would break.

2. *Expose implementation*: A simple getter for the `entityManager` would allow our test to call it to verify its state and use it for assertions. The advantage of this solution is that it's simple and straightforward; the disadvantage is that we're explicitly exposing a private implementation detail, and anyone who sees this method might be tempted to call it outside of a test.

3. *Injection*: The final solution is to rely on the container to inject the entity manager into the test. The benefit of this approach is that we do not modify our component, nor do we expose any more than we need to. The downside is that we have an increased dependency on the container, and must make assumptions about the semantics of injection. Namely, that the `entityManager` injected into our test is the same one that was injected into the handler.

The first solution is too fragile and should be avoided in this case. Whether we go with the second or third option is a matter of personal taste. The second one is likely the easiest and simplest to understand and does not rely on any container magic.

Ultimately, it's crucial to remain pragmatic when it comes to determining how much the implementation details should be exposed. Making all methods public is obviously going too far, using package-protected is preferred where possible, but then leaving everything private and making testing much more awkward is probably going too far the other way.

Session Beans

Session beans in EJB3 have been tremendously simplified as well. Whereas a deployment descriptor used to be required, along with home and business interfaces, it is now possible to have a session bean that is a simple service object that can be instantiated easily within a test.

Session beans can be stateful or stateless. In terms of testing, the approach is exactly the same. An example of a stateless session bean is the `PersonManager` service object we covered earlier, with a simple annotation to mark it as a stateless bean, as shown in Listing 4–39.

Listing 4–39 Example of a session bean

```
import javax.ejb.Stateless;
import javax.persistence.PersistenceContext;
import javax.persistence.EntityManager;

@Stateless
public class PersonManager
{
  @PersistenceContext
  private EntityManager entityManager;

  public void savePerson(Person p) {
    entityManager.persist(p);
  }

  public Person getPerson(long id) {
    return entityManager.find(Person.class, id);
  }
}
```

At first glance, we can see that in this case as well, we do not need to do anything special to handle the fact that this is a session bean. We can simply instantiate it via `new PersonManager()`, then invoke whatever methods we'd like on it in our tests.

Unfortunately, most session beans are very unlikely to be this simple. They are far more likely to take advantage of a number of additional annotations that the EJB3 specification supports. So instead of the example shown in Listing 4–39, we likely will have code like that shown in Listing 4–40.

Listing 4–40 Annotated EJB3 methods

```
@TransactionAttribute
public void savePerson(Person p) {
  entityManager.persist(p);
}

@PostConstruct
public void init() {
  // initialize the bean
}
```

The first annotation specifies that the `savePerson` method must run inside of a transaction (a JPA requirement, in fact). The second one is an initialization annotation; whenever the session bean is created, the container must invoke the `init()` method before the bean is considered ready to be invoked.

The `@PostConstruct` annotation is defined in the common annotations specification (JSR 250). The specification is used by a number of other EE APIs, such as Web Services (JAX-WS). The specification contains annotations that allow for lifecycle callbacks, as well as some security-related annotations.

Testing this is actually still quite simple. For the first annotation, thanks to Spring, all our test methods automatically run inside of a transaction. Therefore, the session bean's `savePerson` method is correctly invoked within a transaction, just as it would be were it running inside a container than had processed the annotation.

Handling the second annotation in our test is also quite simple; we explicitly invoke it before calling any other methods on the session bean. For example, in the case where Spring has injected the `PersonManager` into our test case, we put the initialization invocation inside of the setter, as shown in Listing 4–41.

Listing 4–41 Explicitly invoking lifecycle methods

```
public void setManager(PersonManager manager) {
    manager.init();
    this.manager = manager;
  }
```

With these simple changes, we can provide the right environment to test our session beans. However, there are some pitfalls associated with this approach. For example, what happens if the manager is injected into multiple tests? We would likely end up with the `init` method being called multiple times, something that the manager bean is likely not designed to handle. Let's also consider the refactoring shown in Listing 4–42.

Listing 4–42 Refactored lifecycle methods

```
public void savePerson(Person p) {
  validatePerson(p);
  persistAndNotify(p);
}

@TransactionAttribute
protected void persistAndNotify(Person p) {
  entityManager.persist(p);
  sendNotification();
}
```

Instead of specifying that `savePerson` must run inside of a transaction, we refactored the actual process of saving into the entity manager into a separate method. Since we are no longer working with the entity manager in the `savePerson` method, we also moved the transaction attribute to our new method.

What happens to our test now? Well, in all likelihood, it still passes. There is, however, an insidious difference between the environment provided for the session bean between our test and the real environment: The transaction scope is different and encompasses more code than it would.

Does this matter? In most cases, probably not. However, in cases where it does matter, our test will give us a false sense of security since it's possible that later, code that requires a transaction could sneak into the `savePerson` method directly. Our test would pass, but if the bean were deployed into an actual container, the method would not run correctly.

The cause of the issue is that our test was not aware of the refactoring; there is no synchronization between the transactional behavior of the test and that mandated by the session bean.

Similarly, let's consider another refactoring, as shown in Listing 4–43.

Listing 4–43 Another lifecycle method refactoring

```
public void init() {
  // initialize the bean
}

@PostConstruct
public void prepare() {
  init();
  loadSettings();
}
```

Again, our test will subtly break. If we're lucky, the session bean will blow up since the test does not call `loadSettings()`. We will realize that the bean has been refactored and update the test accordingly.

However, it's possible that the bean could handle empty settings and so would not blow up if the method were not invoked. The test would still pass, even though the deployed bean would have an additional method invocation that was not called during testing.

Just like the example shown in Listing 4–42, the issue boils down to the fact that the test is not aware of the refactoring that was done, nor will it reliably blow up to flag that it should be updated.

We need some way of more accurately capturing the semantics and behavior of the EJB3 container. Doing so manually is certainly possible but, as we've seen, can have its drawbacks and complications. Just as we did with JPA, it would be nice to offload the work to a container than we can run inside our tests. Again, Spring comes to the rescue.

Another Spring Container

Spring's project Pitchfork is a subproject that effectively adds an EJB3 layer on top of the core Spring functionality.

It turns out that EJB3 session beans aren't that different from Spring beans. They expect a more tightly controlled environment to run in and support a different method of wiring and declaring dependencies and transactions, but functionally they are very similar.

Pitchfork is a layer to handle the mapping from the EJB3 world into the Spring bean world.

Adding the Pitchfork library enables us to run our session beans just as they'd run in an application server. The process is quite straightforward; the Pitchfork download contains all the jars needed:

- `pitchfork.jar`: the Pitchfork implementation classes
- `jsr250-api.jar`: the annotations for common annotations (JSR 250)
- `ejb-3_0-api.jar`: the annotations for EJB3
- `aspectjweaver.jar`: used by Pitchfork to apply transactional behavior

Once we have added these to our classpath, we need to modify the Spring configuration file we used in our JPA example earlier to include the bean processor that reads in the EJB-specific annotations, as shown in Listing 4–44.

Listing 4–44 Spring EJB3 bean postprocessor declaration

```
<!-- scan beans for EJB 3.0 and JSR 250 annotations -->
  <bean
class="org.springframework.jee.ejb.config. ⌐
JeeEjbBeanFactoryPostProcessor">
</bean>
```

Adding this bean postprocessor allows Spring to check all the beans listed in the configuration file for the JSR 250 annotations (`@PostCreate`, `@PreDestroy`) and ensure they are called appropriately. Also, the postprocessor will scan the beans for the EJB3 annotations and will perform the correct injection for `@Resource` annotated properties, as well as handle the transactional annotations specified on any given method.

Our bean will now run in an environment that very closely matches the runtime container environment it expects. Our test no longer needs to rely on any specific transactional behavior because the container now manages this. As a result, our test superclass no longer needs to be `AbstractTransactionalSpringContextTests`; it can now be the more generic `AbstractDependencyInjectionSpringContextTests` since all we need now is to support injection into the test, rather than transaction control.

Disadvantages of a Full Container

While it may seem that this approach is always the preferred one, as it more closely models the runtime environment, it actually has a number of disadvantages that we need to be aware of when deciding to commit to this approach. Let us consider the example shown in Listing 4–45.

Listing 4–45 Stateless session bean example

```
@Stateless
public class AccountManager {

  @EJB
  private PersonManager personManager;

  @PersistenceContext
  private EntityManager entityManager;

  public Account getAccount(long id) {
    return entityManager.find(Account.class, id);
  }

  public void createAccount(long personId) {
    Person person = entityManager.find(Person.class, personId);
    Account account = new Account();
    account.setOwner(person);
    entityManager.persist(account);
  }
}
```

At first glance, the Spring Pitchfork container is perfect for testing this session bean. It will correctly wire everything up, enabling us to test all of its methods.

However, what if `PersonManager` is an expensive bean to create? What if it has dependencies on another persistence unit, which means going through another expensive JPA initialization? It might even need to subscribe to a JMS destination, another very expensive operation.

Let's now assume that all we want to do is test the `getAccount` method. This method does not actually depend on `personManager`. Our test doesn't care if one is available or not.

Unfortunately, if we're using Pitchfork, we don't have a choice in the matter. If the `personManager` bean is not available, the bean will not be initialized, and we'll get a runtime exception.

As we can see, this is one example where using a container that is configured to load every bean is not an ideal approach and results in too high an overhead for many of our tests.

We have two approaches to deal with this situation.

1. *Use dependency stubs*: We can still use Pitchfork, but instead of providing the real dependency, we instead write a trivial no-op session bean and register that in the Spring configuration file. The advantage of this approach is that it allows us to still rely on Pitchfork for all the other initialization goodies. The disadvantage, however, is that it requires a different Spring configuration file, possibly with a lot of duplication.

2. *Fall back to manual setup*: There's nothing stopping us from having both Pitchfork-based tests and ones where we construct the environment manually. For the example we just presented, we can have our test without worrying about satisfying any dependencies if we construct the `AccountManager` bean manually. While this approach would still suffer from potential issues with regard to class evolution, the fact that it exists alongside a richer Pitchfork-based test means that there is more scope for these errors to be caught in other tests.

Interestingly, the Pitchfork container isn't useful just for testing. It can be used to deploy EJB3-based applications into any container, including pure Web engines such as Jetty or Tomcat. In fact, it is used as a basis for BEA WebLogic's EJB3 implementation.

Java API for XML Web Services (JAX-WS)

This API enables easy building of both Web services and clients that communicate using XML over HTTP. A call between the two sides is usually in XML, using the SOAP protocol. SOAP defines the message structure and allows for a language-independent mechanism of remote procedure calls between clients and servers.

In terms of the server, the service is usually represented by an interface and an implementation. There is usually metadata associated with the class to specify service-specific information, such as namespaces, methods to expose, and so on.

The application server is responsible for deploying the service and exposing it for remote clients.

One of the most convenient ways to specify Web service metadata is JSR 181, which specifies a number of annotations that can be used. Listing 4–46 is an example of a JSR 181–based Web service.

Listing 4–46 Example of a JSR 181–based Web service

```
@WebService
public class MyService {
  @WebMethod
  public String getData() {
    return "Hello World!";
  }
}
```

On deployment, the container will process the `@WebService` annotation and expose `MyService` for remote calls via SOAP.

For unit testing, there is no issue here at all. It's very simple to instantiate our service directly via `new MyService()`, then to invoke the methods we'd like to test on it.

For integration testing, however, we have the usual problem confronting us with most EE APIs: simulating a container environment.

The Web services implementation we'll use in our tests is XFire. XFire is a Codehaus Web services project that provides an excellent implementation for us to use. It has a module and embeddable design that make it easy to integrate into any environment.

Before delving into the details of using XFire, it's important to decide on a testing strategy. Since our tests are integration tests, we're not worried about the Java implementation. We're reasonably sure that that side of things works fine (and we hopefully have a bunch of unit tests to confirm that!).

Instead, we'd like to test that the service invocation responses are what we'd expect. The service (being a Web service) can be invoked from a variety of clients, both Java and non-Java. We want to make sure that we're emitting the right response based on a variety of request formats.

Our test approach therefore is the following.

1. Generate a number of requests.

2. Record the requests from a variety of clients.

3. Set up the test environment to invoke services programmatically.

4. Create the service test.

5. Assert that the responses are valid,

Since we have the service deployed, all we have to do to generate requests is to invoke it. The next step is a little trickier, however.

Recording Requests

To record our Web service requests, we need to be able to place a proxy between the client and the server. The proxy's job is to relay any requests the client makes to the server and, along the way, record them.

There are a number of solutions available. One of the simplest is to use Apache Axis's tcpmon tool (TCP Monitor). The tool is included as part of the Apache Axis download. It can be started up from the command line, as shown in Listing 4–47.

Listing 4–47 Invoking TCP Monitor

```
java —cp axis.jar org.apache.axis.utils.tcpmon [listenPort ↵
targetHost targetPort]
```

The `listenPort` parameter is a port that the proxy will listen on. The `targetHost` and `targetPort` parameters are set to the host and port, respectively, that the destination service is hosted on.

Once the tool starts, it will show all requests and responses. We can select the requests of interest and save them to disk, so that they can be replayed later in tests.

Setting Up the Test Environment

The XFire documentation contains a dependency guide to explain which jars we need depending on what features we'd like to use. For our example, we will need the following jars:

- `xfire-all.jar`: the xfire binary containing all the modules
- `activation.jar`: the Java Activation Framework, from Sun
- `javamail.jar`: used for SOAP attachments
- `commons-logging.jar`: the ubiquitous logging library
- `jdom.jar`: used internally for XML manipulation
- `wsdl4j.jar`: used by XFire to generate WSDL documents
- `stax-api.jar`: the XML Pull API used for XML parsing (Streaming API for XML)
- `wstx-asl.jar`: Woodstox, a high-performance implementation of StAX
- `xfire-jsr-181.jar`: contains the JSR 181 annotations

Once XFire is installed, we can start using it in our integration tests. The first step is to initialize XFire. We can do so in a base class that all our Web service tests will extend. Of course, it is also possible to refactor this into a separate helper class. The superclass approach is easier to demonstrate, as shown in Listing 4–48.

Listing 4–48 Superclass for the Web service test

```
public abstract class AbstractWSTest {

  private XFire xfire;
  private Session session;
  private ServiceFactory factory;

  @BeforeClass(groups = "ws-init")
  public void setupXFire() {
    xfire = new DefaultXFire();
    session = new MapSession();
  }

  public XFire getXFire() {
    return xfire;
  }
}
```

This class creates a default XFire implementation, along with a session to use. `MapSession` is an XFire class that allows for storing a client/server conversation in-memory. We also ensure that the setup method is in a `ws-init` group; this is so that other setup methods can use this grouping to determine whether they should run before or after XFire setup.

Having initialized XFire, the next step is to register services with it, so that they can be invoked through the framework. This is done through XFire's `ServiceFactory` API. We need a getter for it for subclasses to use, as shown in Listing 4–49.

Listing 4–49 Implementation of the *ServiceFactory* getter

```
public ServiceFactory getServiceFactory() {
  if (factory == null) {
    TransportManager tm = xfire.getTransportManager();
```

```
  AnnotationServiceFactory sf =
              new AnnotationServiceFactory(tm);
    sf.setStyle(SoapConstants.STYLE_MESSAGE);
    factory = sf;
  }
  return factory;
}
```

AnnotationServiceFactory is a class that allows for registering annotated classes directly as services. XFire has a number of other implementations that allow for other service implementations, for example, ones backed
by XML metadata instead of annotations. Finally, we need to have some
methods to actually invoke a service, as shown in Listing 4–50.

Listing 4–50 Invoking a service

```
protected String invokeService(String service, String document)
    throws Exception {
    InputStream stream = getClass().getResourceAsStream(document);
    XMLStreamReader xr = STAXUtils.createXMLStreamReader(stream,
                                          "UTF-8", null);
    return invokeService(service, xr);
  }

  protected String invokeService(String service,
                              XMLStreamReader reader)
    throws Exception {
    ByteArrayOutputStream out = new ByteArrayOutputStream();
    MessageContext context = new MessageContext();
    context.setSession(session);
    context.setXFire(xfire);
    context.setProperty(Channel.BACKCHANNEL_URI, out);

    if(service != null) {
      ServiceRegistry registry = xfire.getServiceRegistry();
      context.setService(registry.getService(service));
    }

    InMessage msg = new InMessage(reader);

    TransportManager tm = xfire.getTransportManager();
    Transport t = tm.getTransport(LocalTransport.BINDING_ID);
```

```
Channel c = t.createChannel();

c.receive(context, msg);

String response = out.toString();
if(response == null || response.length() == 0) return null;
return response;
}
```

Though this code might look complicated, most of it is boilerplate and is written only once. The first `invokeService` method takes in a string that represents a resource on the classpath. This will be the request we recorded earlier. It also takes in the name of the service to invoke. The default value of the service name when we register one is the simple class name (in our case, `MyService`).

The `MessageContext` class holds contextual information about the current request, such as the input, output, and other environment settings. We finally obtain a transport mechanism and a channel for it, which in this case is a local in-memory transport mechanism since we're invoking our service inline.

The method finally returns the result of the service invocation. The string value is in fact an XML document that we can then parse and check for various values.

Creating the Service Test

Having set up the environment for fast Web Service invocation, all that remains now is to write the test to use it, as shown in Listing 4–51.

Listing 4–51 Web service test

```
public class MyServiceTests extends AbstractWSTest {

  @Test
  public void prepareMyService() {
    Service service =
  getServiceFactory().create(MyService.class);
    getXFire().getServiceRegistry().register(service);
  }
}
```

The first step in our test is registering the service class. We simply pass it to the service factory, which will return a `Service` instance. This instance can then be registered with the service registry. By default, the name of the service is the simple class name, `MyService`. We can then use the helper methods in the base class to invoke the service with the requests we had recorded earlier. Listing 4–52 shows a sample request.

Listing 4–52 Web service request document

```
<?xml version="1.0"?>
<env:Envelope
      xmlns:env="http://schemas.xmlsoap.org/soap/envelope/">
 <env:Header/>
  <env:Body xmlns:m="http://www.testng.org/book/samples">
    <m:helloWorld />
  </env:Body>
</env:Envelope>
```

We save this request as `myservice-req.xml` on the classpath. Listing 4–53 shows our test code to invoke the service.

Listing 4–53 Test to invoke a specific service

```
@Test(dependsOnMethods = "prepareMyService")
  public void invokeMyService() throws Exception {
    String result = invokeService("MyService",
                              "/myservice-req.xml");
    assert result.indexOf("Hello World!") > -1;
  }
```

The result of the service invocation when our test succeeds is shown in Listing 4–54.

Listing 4–54 Web service response document

```
<soap:Envelope
      xmlns:soap="http://schemas.xmlsoap.org/soap/envelope/"
      xmlns:xsd="http://www.w3.org/2001/XMLSchema"
      xmlns:xsi="http://www.w3.org/2001/XMLSchema-instance">
```

```
<soap:Body>
  <helloWorldResponse>Hello World!</helloWorldResponse>
</soap:Body>
</soap:Envelope>
```

Obviously, we'd have a more robust assertion in a real test; the one shown here is just for demonstration purposes.

The advantage of this approach is that it's very lightweight. There are no sockets involved, and we don't have to worry about starting up servers, generating stubs, or doing anything beyond the basic setup code we highlighted earlier.

XPath Testing

Testing XML documents has a number of pitfalls and issues. The DOM API is far from ideal when it comes to navigating a document tree, and both the XML Pull API and SAX API are designed for parsing a document, rather than navigating one.

Instead of using the awkward DOM API to navigate, it's far more comfortable to use XPath, which is designed for this sort of thing.

XPath is a query mechanism for XML. It allows us to query and navigate a document's contents using simple strings to specify what nodes we're interested in selecting based on a set of criteria. For example, the XPath expression `//myNode` will return all occurrences of the element named `myNode` anywhere in the document.

For the example XML document in Listing 4–54, for instance, verifying that we have the correct response can be done via an XPath assert. The first step is to convert the response string into a document. For the sake of this example, we'll use JDOM. JDOM is a Java API designed to make working with XML content much simpler and more intuitive than with DOM. It uses Java collections and so feels a lot more natural and comfortable to use. First we define the following simple helper method to create a `Document` object, as shown in Listing 4–55.

Listing 4–55 Helper method for reading a *Document*

```
protected Document readDocument(String text) {
  XMLInputFactory factory = XMLInputFactory.newInstance();
  try {
    StaxBuilder builder = new StaxBuilder(factory);
```

```
    return builder.build(new StringReader(text));
  }
  catch(XMLStreamException e) {
    throw new IllegalArgumentException("Invalid xml", e);
  }
}
```

From there, we can define another helper method that verifies whether a given XPath matches any nodes in the document, as shown in Listing 4–56.

Listing 4–56 XPath test assertion

```
public static void assertValid(Document doc, String selector)
      throws JDOMException {
  XPath xpath = XPath.newInstance(selector);
  List nodes = xpath.selectNodes(doc);
  assert nodes.size() > 0 : "No nodes matching xpath " +
  selector;
}
```

Assuming we've used a static import to easily access this assert call in our tests, we would test the response in the example by using the XPath shown in Listing 4–57.

Listing 4–57 XPath assertion

```
Document doc = readDocument(result);
assertValid(doc, "//helloWorldResponse[text()='Hello World']");
```

Testing Remote Services

In the enterprise environment, a fairly common feature for any application is as a Web Services consumer. In this case, the application communicates as a client to a remote Web service provided by a third party. This remote service is not under our control, nor are we able to modify it. We are provided an API (usually in the form of a WSDL) to communicate with the service.

Testing this service would fall under the integration tests umbrella. The testing approach is the same as the one we'd use for verifying any server response.

To invoke any remote HTTP server, we could work directly with the Java networking API (`URLConnection` and friends) or use one of the more popular open source libraries that take the pain out of this API. Jakarta's commons-httpclient is the most popular solution and is ideal for testing usage.

Having made a request and obtained a response, we can make any number of assertions on the response. We could also use the same approach for regression testing; the results would be saved in the test suite, and subsequent runs would verify that the results returned by the server matched those saved earlier.

Servlets

Testing servlets can be quite cumbersome for several reasons. For one, the service method relies on request and response objects that are very tricky to implement. Furthermore, it is difficult to verify that the response has been written correctly since there are many issues involved such as buffering, status codes, headers, and so on.

Also, there is the issue of servlet lifecycle to worry about, as well as providing the rich and complex environment a servlet expects (e.g., `ServletContext` and `ServletConfig` objects, `HttpSession`, and so on).

We can take several approaches to test our servlet code. Some are less optimal than others, and some are downright awkward and clumsy. For the sake of completeness, let's go through all our options.

In-Container Testing

One approach we covered earlier for testing servlets is to not worry about providing implementations for this environment and simply to use in-container testing. That way we're guaranteed to use the exact implementation that we'd be using in our production environment.

This approach is far from ideal as it has a high overhead, and deploying and running new tests is awkward, as we saw earlier.

Mock/Stub Objects

The mock/stub objects approach involves using custom implementations of the various parts of the Servlet API that we're interested in. Listing 4–58 shows the rough outline of this approach.

Listing 4–58 Using stubs to set up the servlet environment

```
@Test
public void verifyServlet() throws ServletException,
  IOException {
  MyServlet servlet = new MyServlet();
  MockServletContext context = new MockServletContext();
  MockServletConfig config = new MockServletConfig(context);
  servlet.init(config);
  MockHttpServletRequest req = new MockHttpServletRequest();
  req.setParameter("someparam", "hello");
  req.setRemoteUser("admin");
  MockHttpServletResponse res = new MockHttpServletResponse();
  servlet.service(req, res);
  assert res.getStatus() == 200;
}
```

Here we created a number of stubs that implement just enough of the Servlet API to be usable.

We instantiate our servlet, set up the environment, and then invoke its `service` method. Finally, we verify that we get what we expect in the response.

Note that in this case we are using stubs instead of mock objects. The example happens to use Spring's mock library, which is more accurately a stub library, hence the naming mix-up. The difference is important, as we discussed in Chapter 2; mock objects involve setting up expectations, and stubs are alternative implementations of an interface. The mock approach, for example, would specify an expectation on the mock response that `setStatus(200)` will be called as part of the `service` method.

This approach is in fact very fragile and not recommended for the following reasons.

- It does not simulate actual container behavior; instead, it simulates what we think is container behavior.
- It does not capture the API. It's susceptible to what we think the API should do rather than an officially compliant implementation.
- Populating the environment can be very cumbersome.
- It provides a false sense of security since we essentially cheat by being able to fine-tune the environment so specifically.
- It can grow to be a maintenance nightmare, as more and more of the environment needs to be populated over time.

Refactoring

Another approach is to refactor away the servlet-specific API into other more testable classes. This is in fact the ideal approach, whereby the actual servlet is simply a thin wrapper between the Web layer and our presentation mechanism.

Using this approach, it's possible to ensure that our components are more easily testable since they require much less of an environment than a full-blown servlet would. The role of the servlet in this case would simply be to marshal request parameters and act as a proxy for the response that the underlying component writes to.

This is the approach that most Web frameworks take these days. The central concept is that of one front-end controller servlet that then delegates to actions. These actions can be easily tested as they usually abstract away the presentation aspect of Web development and enable us to focus on functionality and application logic instead.

Having said that, as we delve deeper into the Servlet API, it becomes trickier to test. While we can easily model `javax.http.HttpSession` as a `Map`, there is no real abstraction to encapsulate a `javax.servlet.Cookie`, for example. In some of these cases, mock objects may prove a useful tool.

Embedded Container

The next-best approach to refactoring is to use an embedded container. An embedded container is a full-blown servlet engine that can be controlled programmatically, so we can trivially include it in our tests.

The advantage of this approach is that it frees us from having to worry about the subtleties and nuances of a servlet container. For example, we no longer need to worry about ensuring that our implementation handles buffering correctly; the embedded container does all that work for us.

The Server

The best-known example of such a container is Jetty. Jetty is a lightweight servlet engine that is ideal for embedding. It provides an open API that allows us to control it programmatically, as well as a stand-alone mode where it runs like any other container.

Jetty has also passed all the compatibility tests required for a servlet engine, so we can rely on it behaving very similarly (if not identically) to our production environment, compared to any implementations we might come up with.

Starting an embedded Jetty server is very simple, as shown in Listing 4–59.

Listing 4–59 Setting up Jetty in a test

```
private Server server;

@BeforeSuite
public void setupWebContainer() {
  server = new Server(8000);
  Context root = new Context(server, "/", Context.SESSIONS);

  MyServlet servlet = new MyServlet();
  ServletHolder holder = new ServletHolder(servlet);
  root.addServlet(holder, "/myservlet");
}

@BeforeSuite(dependsOnMethods = "setupWebContainer")
public void startServer() throws Exception {
  server.start();
}

@AfterSuite
public void stopServer() throws Exception {
  server.stop();
}
```

First, we create the server instance configured to listen to port 8000. Any client can now connect to port 8000 to communicate through HTTP with our server.

Next, we create our servlet and map it to a specific URL (usually done in `web.xml`), in this case, /myservlet. Clients can now access our servlet though the URL http://localhost:8000/myservlet.

Finally, we specify a pair of start/stop methods for our server. As usual, these can be scoped to be per test or per class, depending on our usage. In this example, they're scoped to run at the start and end, respectively, of our test suite.

Obviously, we can register as many servlets as we like. Even better, we can have the servlet registration be part of individual tests, so we don't end up with one centralized point that always has to be modified whenever a new servlet needs to be tested.

The Client

So far we've shown the server-side portion of our test, but how do we interact with it? We have a couple of options for our client-side interaction.

One approach is to test it as we would any other remote HTTP service. We would connect directly to it through a socket connection, send the appropriate headers, and then read the response. A number of libraries can help with this, such as Jakarta's commons-httpclient. We could also directly use Java's networking package and the URLConnection class to create the request and then read in the response.

The benefit of this approach is that we perform the exact same operations as a regular browser would, thus enabling a more accurate representation of how our code would run in a production environment.

Using Jakarta's commons-httpclient is quite simple, as shown in Listing 4–60.

Listing 4–60 Using commons-httpclient

```
@Test
public void checkResponse() throws IOException {
  HttpClient client = new HttpClient();
  HttpMethod get =
        new GetMethod("http://localhost:8000/myservlet");
  client.executeMethod(get);
  String response = get.getResponseBodyAsString();
  assert "<h1>Hello MyServlet</h1>".equals(response);
}
```

Listing 4–61 shows how we'd do the same thing using URLConnection. It is a little bit more verbose, but equally simple.

Listing 4–61 Using *URLConnection*

```
@Test
public void checkURLResponse() throws IOException {
  URL url = new URL("http://localhost:8000/myservlet");
  HttpURLConnection c =
  (HttpURLConnection)url.openConnection();
  assert c.getResponseCode() == 200;
  // can be in a utility method somewhere
  StringBuilder sb = new StringBuilder();
  InputStream in = c.getInputStream();
  ByteArrayOutputStream os = new ByteArrayOutputStream();
  byte[] buffer = new byte[1024];
  int len;
```

```
  while ((len = in.read(buffer,0,buffer.length )) >-1) {
    os.write(buffer,0,len);
  }
  // assume output is utf-8 for this example
  String response = new String(os.toByteArray(), "utf-8");
  assert "<h1>Hello MyServlet</h1>".equals(response);
}
```

Which approach we go with doesn't really matter. The idea is that we open a socket connection to the embedded server and then read the content that way.

Obviously, the assertion shown in Listings 4–60 and 4–61 is just for the sake of this example and should never be used against real code! Testing for specific strings in an HTML response is very fragile, as tests will start breaking due to the most trivial of HTML changes that have no impact on functionality or even presentation.

In-Memory Invocation

Another approach is to use a Jetty feature that allows us to bypass all the socket setup and connectivity and directly invoke a servlet through a simple custom API.

The advantage of this approach is that it is even more lightweight than the embedded server and does not require creating any sockets. Getting rid of the socket mechanism means we're further eliminating an environmental factor in our tests and invoking our servlet without having to worry about any sort of connectivity issues. This is ideal since, as we've stated previously, the goal of a test is to test our components, not the environment they run in.

To perform an in-memory test of a servlet, we again resort to Jetty, which has a convenient API for doing just this, as shown in Listing 4–62.

Listing 4–62 In-memory Jetty `ServletTester`

```
private ServletTester tester;

@BeforeSuite
public void setupMemoryTester() throws Exception {
  tester = new ServletTester();
  tester.setContextPath("");
  tester.addServlet(MyServlet.class, "/myservlet");
  tester.start();
}
```

We create an instance of `ServletTester`, then register our servlet along with the URL to map it to (the equivalent of `servlet-mapping` in `web.xml`).

Since we're using an in-memory servlet engine, there is no socket connectivity or port number involved.

Jetty also provides a simple API for invoking the servlets, so we can avoid the overhead of commons-httpclient or any associated network connectivity.

Raw HTTP Request

This approach allows us to specify a raw HTTP request to the container. It is useful in cases where we have a number of prerecorded requests to play back. An example of a raw request is shown in Listing 4–63.

Listing 4–63 Invoking a servlet using a raw HTTP request

```
@Test
public void verifyServletRaw() throws Exception {
  String response = tester.getResponses("GET /"
    + "myservlet?query=foo"
    + " HTTP/1.0\r\n\r\n");
  assert response.startsWith("HTTP/1.1 200 OK\r\n");
}
```

Note that the response string is the complete response, including headers. So to extract the response body from it, we'd have to parse this string and parse headers and body individually. If that sounds like too much work (and it is!) then thankfully there are some helper methods that'll do the work for us.

The Request API

The Request API allows us to specify a request programmatically and have a helper class take care of converting the request parameters and headers into a request string, as shown in Listing 4–64.

Listing 4–64 Invoking a servlet using Jetty's Request API

```
@Test
public void verifyServlet() throws Exception {
  HttpTester http = new HttpTester();
```

```
http.setMethod("GET");
http.setUri("/myservlet?query=foo");
http.setVersion("HTTP/1.0");
http.parse(tester.getResponses(http.generate()));
assert http.getStatus() == 200;
assert "<h1>Hello MyServlet</h1>".equals(http.getContent());
}
```

The `HttpTester` helper class enables construction of a request string, as well as parsing a response string to extract headers and content.

Note that we specifically are not discussing how to test the returned content. The content we check for in this example is clearly unrealistic, and in any real-world usage, we are likely to use something more elaborate than simple string comparisons.

XML

Invariably in the enterprise world, we'll run across XML—XML that needs to be parsed, sent, and dissected. This could be XML used for interoperability between two languages, XML used in a Web service, or any other of the myriad solutions that have managed to shoehorn XML in somewhere.

Testing XML is not as straightforward as it might seem at first glance. Consider the two snippets shown in Listing 4–65.

Listing 4–65 XML document example

```
<item>
  <type>12</type>
  <id>10</id>
</item>

<item>
  <id>10</id>
  <type>12</type>
</item>
```

It's obvious that for most intents and purposes, they're the same.[3] But how do we test for that? We cannot use string comparisons since the elements are ordered differently. We would have to compare the structure of the documents, rather than their literal representation.

To tackle this issue, we have to use an XML library that will help us in processing the documents. For the actual comparison, we can either handle it ourselves by comparing the existence of nodes and their values, or we can use a JUnit extension, called XMLUnit, which will do the work for us.

Using dom4j

Java allows us to work with XML via the DOM API. This API enables us to load a document, traverse its structure, and examine all of its contents. Unfortunately, the DOM API is cumbersome and unwieldy, to say the least. Because it was defined to be fairly language-agnostic, it's not very Java-like and can be awkward to invoke.

Addressing these issues are a couple of popular open source projects that provide a more native API around XML and its manipulation. JDOM and dom4j both provide an easy API for working with XML content. For the purposes of this example, we will use dom4j. JDOM is very similar, and the concepts are identical.

None of these APIs allows us to easily compare entire documents. Instead, we have to manually select the nodes of interest and validate their contents, as shown in Listing 4–66.

Listing 4–66 dom4j-based test

```
Element root = doc.getRootElement();
assert root.elements().size() == 2;
Element child = (Element)root.elements().get(1);
assert child.getTextTrim().equals("12");
```

This approach is obviously quite verbose and can be cumbersome. However, it does enable us to narrow in on sections of concern, rather than

---

3. The documents don't have a DTD or schema specified, and while element ordering is significant in XML, most parsing code is not sensitive to it, as we usually check for an element's name rather than assuming a strict sibling element ordering.

having to worry about other potentially unrelated sections of the documents interfering with the results.

Another useful tool for navigating and verifying XML document contents is XPath, whereby we can specify expressions to select a given document node in a simple string, and having selected one, we can go on to call any assertions required against the results. We covered this approach is more detail earlier when discussing JAX-WS testing.

Using XMLUnit

XMLUnit is a JUnit extension that was developed to ease some of the pain associated with comparing XML documents.

XMLUnit expects you to subclass its `XMLTestCase` class (which extends JUnit's `TestCase`) and then use all the helper methods it exposes, such as `assertXMLEqual` and others. The assertions it provides will allow you to easily compare documents and nodes from a variety of sources and will provide a detailed description of any differences found.

Obviously, using JUnit's `TestCase` class is problematic for us. We'd like to be able to write test cases that are not constricted by this superclass.

Fortunately, under the hood, all of the methods of this superclass delegate to other classes, and it exists as a convenience rather than a necessity. For our tests, then, we can bypass this superclass and invoke the comparison API directly, as shown in Listing 4–67.

Listing 4–67 Testing XML with XMLUnit

```
@Test
public void checkDocument() throws Exception {
  String doc1 = "<item><type>12</type><id>10</id></item>";
  String doc2 = "<item><id>10</id><type>12</type></item>";
  Diff diff = new Diff(doc1, doc2);
  assert diff.similar() : diff;
}
```

Note that we used the `similar` method, rather than the `identical` one. In our example, the two documents are not identical, so the test would fail. Two documents are considered identical if they have the same nodes, specified in the same order.

Also note that for our assert, the message we pass is simply `diff`. This is because the `Diff` class has overridden `toString()` to show meaningful information, so we don't have to bother with creating one ourselves.

Let's consider another example. We have two documents, as shown in Listings 4–68 and 4–69.

Listing 4–68 XML document with no whitespace

```
<item><type>10</type></item>
```

Listing 4–69 XML document with whitespace

```
<item>
  <type>10</type>
</item>
```

In this case, the only difference between the two documents is the insignificant whitespace. So what happens if we run these through our test?

Surprisingly, the test will fail. The documents are considered neither identical nor similar. The reason for this is that in XML, whitespace is not ignored—it is a specific type of content. The error message XMLUnit gives us will hint at that, as shown in Listing 4–70.

Listing 4–70 Output of the XMLUnit assert error

```
java.lang.AssertionError: org.custommonkey.xmlunit.Diff
[different] Expected number of child nodes '1' but was '3'
- comparing <item...> at /item[1] to <item...> at /item[1]
```

XMLUnit (or rather, the underlying parser it uses) correctly reports that the item node has three children in one case and one child in the other. Where have the extra two nodes come from?

The two extra nodes turn out to be the carriage return immediately following the `<item>` opening tag and the carriage return following the closing `</type>` tag in the second line.

Does this matter to us for testing purposes? Realistically, there are very few situations where this whitespace is significant. Unfortunately, this highlights some of the problems with XMLUnit, and any such strict XML document comparison tool.

Ultimately, both approaches can work well together, provided we are aware of the strengths and weaknesses of each.

Conclusion

This chapter covered most of the popular APIs in Java EE. When testing EE-based components, the first decision that needs to be made for any given test is whether it should run inside a container or outside. Though in-container testing more closely models the final runtime environment, it is a bulky and expensive approach that does not lend itself to quick and easy unit or functional testing.

On the other hand, out-of-container testing requires that we set up the environment manually, using a variety of third-party libraries.

Thankfully, the open source ecosystem provides solutions for every EE API. It is possible to create an almost complete EE container using a variety of third-party libraries. We covered how to handle JNDI dependencies, as well as data source and transaction management. We also covered APIs that depend on these core features, such as JMS, JPA, EJB3, and servlets. Hopefully now we can model an environment in which functional tests are easy to deploy and quick to run. Table 4–2 is a quick reference for which library to use for which API.

Table 4–2 Summary of testing approaches for Java EE APIs

Java EE API	Suggested library or framework
JNDI	Spring's `SimpleNamingContextBuilder`
JDBC	c3p0
	Jakarta commons-DBCP
	Spring's `SingleConnectionDataSource`

(continued)

Table 4–2 Summary of testing approaches for Java EE APIs *(continued)*

Java EE API	Suggested library or framework
JTA	Atomikos JOTM
JMS	ActiveMQ
JPA	Spring
EJB3	Spring Pitchfork
JAX-WS	XFire
Servlets	Jetty
XML	XMLUnit, dom4j, XPath

It's important to note that even though we are now able to run our EE components outside of a container, tests that rely on this are considered functional or integration tests, rather than unit tests. Finally, developing a suite of unit tests that have no container dependencies and can run in isolation without requiring a complex or expensive environment will pay off handsomely in terms of faster development, as well as encouraging developers to integrate testing as part of regular development, instead of viewing it as a separate and unrelated task.

Integration

We've previously covered many of the shortcomings of JUnit 3. It should be pretty obvious by now that it's not really a tool suitable for many types of testing. Yet it's wildly popular.

A large part of this popularity is due to the JUnit ecosystem. Despite its awkwardness and lack of extensibility, developers have come up with remarkable workarounds and extensions in order to twist JUnit's proverbial arms into satisfying more niche requirements than bare-bones unit testing.

Some of these extensions include frameworks that provide their own testing harnesses, such as the ubiquitous Spring framework. Others include base classes that enhance the set of asserts provided by JUnit. Many provide additional frameworks to ease the testing of certain APIs, such as JDBC, XML, and others.

TestNG would never have achieved its current level of success without leveraging the existing ecosystem of JUnit add-ons and ensuring a smooth migration path. At best, the add-on can be dropped in as is; at worst, some trivial changes are required to switch to TestNG's syntax. Appendix D explains the migration process in more detail.

For many cases, it is possible to use the add-on as is, without any modifications. Even if you're unsure, chances are that someone has already thought about the add-on you're considering, and either the framework itself was modified to ensure smooth integration with TestNG or the user posted about his or her experiences in integrating the framework.

In this chapter, we will cover integration solutions with a number of popular add-ons and testing frameworks, starting with Spring, going through DbUnit, and HtmlUnit, a unit testing framework to ease the pain of testing HTML content.

In each case, in addition to showing how best to integrate the framework with TestNG, we will also explore the usage and functionality provided. While we have selected some popular and common add-ons, it's worth nothing that this list is by no means exhaustive. The aim of the chapter is more to highlight some of these extensions. Ultimately, we encourage you to use any that you find useful. The migration and integration discussions here will hopefully give you a good sense of how to mix any JUnit add-on with TestNG.

Spring

The Spring framework's philosophy is to make enterprise Java simpler to use, more flexible, and less susceptible to vendor specifics or external API dependencies. This approach manifests itself by advocating and ensuring that all objects in the system are simple Java objects (POJOs). By following this approach, we ensure that it's very easy to develop unit tests for any component since we can control its lifecycle and invocation and ensure that it does not contain infrastructure-dependent code that cannot be easily tested or simulated.

When we're following the Inversion of Control (IoC) principles espoused by Spring, unit testing becomes much easier. Instead of having to worry about a central registry and an environment that provides dependencies, we can manually construct them as required and inject them into our primary test components. Our tests end up with few or no dependencies on any external containers, be it Spring or a full-blown Java EE container.

Our objects will naturally lend themselves toward easier testing if we follow a simple set of design principles. Therefore, when we can, we should take advantage of this and make sure that we have a robust set of unit tests that covers all basic usages of our objects.

This is all well and good for simple unit tests. As we've stressed time and time again, this is the very basic level of testing, and any serious project is likely to require a far more comprehensive test suite that includes functional and integration tests.

For such tests, our components expect more of an environment. For example, we should not be forced to manually resolve dependencies; that's what we expect our IoC container to do for us. Similarly, working with transactions can be a hassle, as is injecting external resources such as JDBC `DataSource` objects or persistence API implementations.

Spring recognizes the need for this functionality and contains a package that addresses most if not all of these needs. The spring-mock library contains a number of classes and helper objects that can be used to stub out APIs, in addition to providing infrastructure for wiring up dependencies and initializing Spring contexts.

Tests based on this package won't run as quickly as unit tests. The extra infrastructure provided comes at a cost. Reading in a Spring configuration file, initializing all the dependencies, and wiring them up obviously will consume some time. Having said that, they certainly are cheaper than running a full-blown container or invoking functionality remotely via an in-container solution.

Spring's Test Package Features

Firing up a container for every integration test we have is obviously too expensive. Waiting a few seconds is acceptable (for now); however, it is quite unreasonable to have to wait for a full application deployment every time we write a nontrivial test, so the middle ground of a Spring-based integration test gives us a bit of both worlds, a rich container environment along with reasonably fast running tests that can be used during development and debugging.

Spring's approach is centered on a number of JUnit-specific base classes residing in `org.springframework.test`. The base classes in this package are extended by tests in order to inherit all the scaffolding required by the container. Abstract methods are provided that the user is expected to implement.

The first hurdle that confronts us when attempting to use these classes with TestNG is their explicit dependency on JUnit. They all ultimately extend `junit.framework.TestCase` and rely on JUnit-specific behavior with regard to `setUp` and `tearDown`, as well as JUnit's peculiar test instantiation strategy.

TestNG addresses these issues with its own set of Spring-specific test classes, available as an extension. The `org.testng.spring.test` package contains all the classes that Spring provides in its own test package, modified for use with TestNG-based tests.

The feature set of these helper classes is identical to their Spring-developed counterparts.

- *Caching of the Spring container*: Starting up Spring can be expensive, due to the number of objects it needs to create. These will often contain persistence implementations and other third-party libraries that have very expensive start-up costs. Going through all these costs for every test is too time consuming, thus greatly hindering the ability to quickly run a large number of tests.

- *Transactional handling*: The test classes allow us to start or stop transactions and also provide hooks for rolling back a transaction after a given test to ensure that the permanent store is not modified in every test run.

- *Dependency Injection into the tests*: Integration tests almost always test interactions between different components. Spring allows us to write our tests so that, instead of the more fragile approach of looking up these components explicitly, they are injected into our tests. In essence, a test becomes just another component hooked into the system.

Test Class Hierarchy

Spring's test support class structure is based around the idea of specialization via subclassing. In practice, this means that each successive test class simply extends another, in order to enhance its functionality.

While this approach works reasonably well, it is not without its drawbacks. For one thing, it makes it very difficult to enhance a particular superclass. It also means that for TestNG migration purposes, you have to replicate the whole hierarchy, rather than simply modifying one or two base classes.

A better approach that is more amenable to reuse and modification would have been to provide a number of helper classes that can be invoked from anywhere, without having to impose a specific superclass just to gain functionality.

Interestingly, many of the classes attempt to cajole features into JUnit that are already provided by TestNG. For example, the classes all contain methods for enabling or disabling certain tests for certain environments. TestNG's runtime configuration support handles that problem by separating runtime from compile-time behavior, so your configuration file determines whether tests are run or not, rather than the source code itself.

Starting from the root base class, we'll examine each of the available classes for subclassing. It's crucial that, for a given test, we choose the appropriate superclass to ensure that we offload as much of the work as possible onto Spring. Note that all these classes are available in the `org.testng.spring.test` package. The classes discussed in the following subsections are listed in order of base class to subclass, so each successive class extends the previous one.

`AbstractSpringContextTests`

This is the base class for all the Spring tests. Its main role is to provide context management. It's rare that we would use this class directly and far more likely that we'd work with one of its subclasses.

The class's implementation contains a static map of all the registered Spring contexts. The benefit of this is that it avoids the potentially costly operation of loading a Spring context. Each context is therefore loaded once and stored by key, and further requests for that context are looked up via the static map.

Note that in an ideal world, these contexts would not be stored in a static map, as that approach has some downsides, including potential issues when running in a multithreaded environment, as well as test pollution, whereby one test can interact with another's context. This restriction is yet another hack that has been implemented to achieve the desired functionality with JUnit's limitations. For the sake of consistency between JUnit-based tests and TestNG ones, we've elected to retain this behavior just to make it easier to switch from one to the other.

This class also contains methods for explicitly marking a given context as dirty so as to ensure that it is reloaded instead of loaded from the cache.

AbstractSingleSpringContextTests

This class, which extends `AbstractSpringContextTests`, provides for hooks to load in a single `ApplicationContext` object.

The method that subclasses should implement is `getConfigLocation(String[] paths)`. This method returns an array of strings that point to locations to Spring configuration files, usually loaded from the classpath, as shown in Listing 5–1.

Listing 5–1 Spring-based test

```
import org.testng.annotations.Test;
import org.testng.spring.test.AbstractSingleSpringContextTests;

public class SpringContextTests
        extends AbstractSingleSpringContextTests {

  protected String[] getConfigLocations() {
    return new String[]{"/spring.xml"};
  }

  @Test
  public void beanDefined() {
    assert applicationContext.getBean("myBean") != null;
  }
}
```

We can see that the superclass performs all the setup and configuration needed from the location we've specified. Note also that in this case we are specifying a single file to be loaded from the classpath; it is also possible to use Spring-style URLs in the location, as well as wildcards. The superclass also exposes an `applicationContext` field that we can use to look up any beans defined.

Due to the lack of dependencies or ordering in JUnit, Spring has developed its own method of `setUp`/`tearDown` method decoration. Since many of the Spring test classes need to perform various tasks before and after a test run, the standard JUnit `setUp`/`tearDown` methods are declared as final, with a pair of new empty methods defined for subclasses called `onSetUp` and `onTearDown`.

This is all fine if subclasses have one method of configuration that has to run before a test, but in many cases, a number of things need to be done. TestNG's grouping and dependencies features mean that it's quite normal to have multiple setup methods that expect to be run in a certain order.

To allow for similar functionality when using the Spring test classes, the Spring setup methods are declared in a `spring-init` TestNG group.

Therefore, instead of having to rely on a single `onSetUp` or `onTearDown` method, we can declare as many `@BeforeMethod`/`@AfterMethod` configuration methods as we want and simply specify that they depend on `spring-init`, to ensure that they are invoked after Spring has performed its magic.

AbstractDependencyInjectionSpringContextTests

In practice, this is likely to be the class used most often in Spring-based integration tests. The most interesting feature provided by the class is injection into the tests themselves. The test's dependencies can be exposed as either setter methods or member fields. The test can also specify what type of autowiring Spring should perform on its properties.

This is best illustrated with an example, as shown in Listing 5–2. We will assume that our Spring configuration file is the same as the one used in Listing 5–1 and contains a `PersonManager` bean we'd like to test.

Listing 5–2 Dependency injected into a test

```
public class SpringInjectionTests
    extends AbstractDependencyInjectionSpringContextTests {

  private PersonManager manager;

  protected String[] getConfigLocations() {
    return new String[]{"/spring.xml"};
  }
```

```
  public void setManager(PersonManager manager) {
    this.manager = manager;
  }

  @Test
  public void verifyManager() {
    assert manager != null;
  }
}
```

In Listing 5–2, we provide a setter, and Spring will automatically wire the `personManager` bean. Note that, by default, Spring will perform autowiring by type, so we need to ensure that for every setter, we have defined a bean of the appropriate type.

In cases where multiple beans of the same type are defined, we would have to specify that we want autowiring by name. This can be done via the `setAutowireMode` method defined in the superclass, which accepts one of the following: `AUTOWIRE_BY_NAME`, `AUTOWIRE_BY_TYPE`, or `AUTOWIRE_NO`. Note that it is also possible to specify injection into fields. The field must be nonstatic and should be `protected`. Our example would, in that case, be simplified in that we no longer have to define a setter. In order to take advantage of field injection, we need to call `setPopulateProtectedVariables` in the test constructor. Listing 5–3 shows the modified version.

Listing 5–3 Field injected into a Spring test

```
public class SpringInjectionTests
    extends AbstractDependencyInjectionSpringContextTests {

  protected PersonManager manager;

  public SpringInjectionTests() {
    setPopulateProtectedVariables(true);
  }
  ...
}
```

We would also remove the setter since we are relying on field injection now instead of setter injection.

AbstractTransactionalSpringContextTests

Having managed to inject our dependencies into Spring-based tests, the next issue that arises is that of transaction handling. This class contains all of the plumbing required in order to ease the pain of working with transactions inside of integration and functional tests.

Being able to control transactions is very important in integration tests. Most ORM solutions require a transaction for any writes to the persistence store. Likewise, many objects behave differently depending on whether or not they are queries inside of a transaction. For example, we often cannot traverse the lazily loaded relations of a persistent entity outside of a transaction. Thus, it's important for us to have tests that check transaction-sensitive behavior, in terms of both methods that require transactions and ones that are expected to function well without a transaction.

The default mode of operation for tests based on this class is to start a transaction before every test, and then after every test, to roll back the transaction.

Of course, it is possible to configure the test so that transactions are committed after each individual test, too.

This class has a transaction manager property. Since it extends the injection-supporting test class, the configuration file must specify a `PlatformTransactionManager` to be injected. Listing 5–4 is an example test using this superclass, with our `PersonManager`.

Listing 5–4 Transaction spring test

```
public class SpringTransactionTests
   extends AbstractTransactionalSpringContextTests {

  private PersonManager manager;

  public void setManager(PersonManager manager) {
    this.manager = manager;
  }

  protected String[] getConfigLocations() {
    return new String[]{"/spring.xml"};
  }

  @Test
  public void savePerson() {
    Person p = new Person();
```

```
    manager.savePerson(p);
    assert p.getId() != null;
  }
}
```

Note that we did not specify any transactional behavior in the test; the superclass will automatically take care of that and ensure that every test is run in its own transaction, which is rolled back after the test is run.

This works well for tests when we have an external data source that should not be polluted with test data, but what happens if we are embedding our own database and want to do work transactionally?

We would modify our test as shown in Listing 5–5.

Listing 5–5 Committing a transaction in a Spring transactional test

```
@Test
public void savePerson() {
  Person p = new Person();
  manager.savePerson(p);
  assert p.getId() != null;
  setComplete();
}
```

The extra call to `setComplete` informs the superclass that the transaction should be committed, rather than rolled back after the test has run. Calling this method has an interesting side effect: All further tests in this class will also commit their transactions rather than rely on the default behavior.

Why is this? The answer lies in one of the subtle differences between JUnit and TestNG. The Spring tests assume JUnit semantics. Every test class is expected to be reinstantiated for every test method. Therefore, the tests all assume that instance state is reset across tests, which is not the case in TestNG.

In order to work around this issue, the TestNG version of this Spring class has an additional method; `setRollback()`. This method basically performs an undo of the `setComplete()` method, and any further tests that we want to revert to the "transaction should be rolled back after every test" behavior should call this method.

Just as we can specify default transaction behavior for our tests, it is also possible to manually start or end a transaction. This is useful in integration tests with persistence providers where entities have different semantics once they're outside of a transactional context. The pair of methods used to control this are `startNewTransaction()` and `endTransaction()`.

Note that in order to hook in extra behavior on test setup or teardown, the Spring `onSetUp()` and `onTearDown()` methods cannot be used. Instead, a number of methods allow us to perform setup or teardown before/after and inside a transaction, such as `onTearDownInTransaction()` and `onSetUpBeforeTransaction()`.

AbstractTransactionalDataSourceSpringContextTests

This class adds some JDBC-specific convenience methods in addition to the transactional behavior outlined earlier.

Specifically, it adds methods to allow for deleting table contents, counting the number of rows in a specific table, and running external SQL scripts. The only extra configuration required is a `java.sql.DataSource` bean specified in the Spring configuration file.

AbstractAnnotationAwareTransactionalTests

This class is specific to Java 5 and is not supported on earlier versions. In addition to all the features provided by the superclass hierarchy, this class allows us to specify Spring-specific transaction annotations on the test methods themselves rather than having to programmatically specify transactional behavior.

This approach is actually a lot more natural and intuitive and ensures that the test can focus on the actual content, instead of on secondary concerns such as transaction settings.

The Spring version of this class is interesting in that, for some reason, it duplicates a lot of the functionality already provided by TestNG. It's unclear why the Spring developers went down this route, but some of their annotations are directly supported by TestNG.

- `@Repeat`: Specifies that a test should be run multiple times. In TestNG, this is controlled via the `invocationCount` annotation attribute. Combining this with the parallelism support gives a much richer model and supports additional test scenarios.

- `@ExpectedException`: Allows a test to specify that it throws an exception on success. The TestNG equivalent is `@ExpectedExceptions`, also a richer version since it supports multiple values.

- @Timed: Enforces a time limit on the given test. If the test takes longer than the specified time, it is considered to fail. In TestNG, this is controlled by the `timeout` annotation attribute.

In order to avoid confusion and duplication of effort, the ported version of this class in the TestNG Spring support does not include support for these annotations since the TestNG ones are more consistent and provided by the framework anyway.

For our example earlier, instead of extending `AbstractTransactionalSpringContextTests`, we would extend `AbstractAnnotationAwareTransactionalTests`. The test method would also be modified to make use of the transactional annotation, as shown in Listing 5–6.

Listing 5–6 Transactional annotated Spring test

```
@Test
@Transactional
public void savePerson() {
  Person p = new Person();
  manager.savePerson(p);
  assert p.getId() != null;
}
```

The transactional annotation also supports several parameters, such as `isolation`, `propagation`, `readOnly`, and others. Consult the Spring documentation for a full discussion of the available settings.

Spring's test annotation support includes a couple of extra annotations that are useful and are supported by the TestNG Spring support.

- @DirtiesContext: Specifies that the current test modifies the Spring context in some way, so it should be marked dirty and reloaded for the next test. This effectively clears the cached application context, and the next interaction with it will result in it being reloaded rather than the cached value being used. It is the equivalent of calling `setDirty()` inside a test.

- @NotTransactional: Specifies that the current test should not be run inside a transactional context. This annotation is useful for cases where we'd like to specifically check how components behave when invoked outside a transaction.

Guice

While Spring offers powerful integration features, its IoC and bean-wiring capabilities are often either too much or too little. As an alternative, we will introduce an IoC framework from Google that can be embedded into applications and tests to perform all the wiring.

One of the advantages of using Guice (pronounced "juice") is that bean-wiring information goes where it belongs, in the source code, and will not grow out of control over time. Integrating Guice with TestNG involves using TestNG's `ObjectFactory` to control test instance creation, making it very simple and straightforward to integrate Guice into test suites.

For cases where we don't need all of Spring's EE integration features and where all we care about is Dependency Injection, Guice is worth a serious look. It has many more features than the basics we'll cover here that make it an ideal fit for any cases where an application needs to wire up components in an elegant and scalable way, without the burden of verbose XML files or awkward configuration.

The Issue with Spring

Spring has become a de facto standard and is used in thousands of projects. Its feature set and functionality are without parallel in Java currently and have encouraged a more elegant and scalable development style that benefits all developers. As an IoC container and for wiring up components, however, it has several drawbacks.

Chief among these drawbacks is the XML file usually used to configure Spring. While Spring 2.0 has made the syntax usable (in Spring 1.x, it was simply too verbose to use comfortably in any projects of significant size), it still has its issues. For example, it is not very refactoring friendly because it uses methods and properties listed as strings, and most refactoring tools will not correctly rename these when the source is modified. Spring does allow for programmatic configuration, but the API is also verbose and somewhat awkward.

In many ways, the XML configuration file suffers from the same issues that plagued J2EE: Descriptors contain source-specific information, yet they are decoupled from the sources they logically belong to. While it makes sense for some metadata to be externalized, there is no good reason to externalize metadata that is tightly coupled to the source and cannot be modified independently of the source.

In our opinion, Spring's strength is not in its wiring capabilities but in its integration and support infrastructure. Spring provides easy integration with a huge variety of APIs and frameworks, such as any number of persistence frameworks (including plain JDBC) and transaction handling, scheduling, and other such services that can be used across many applications. The value of using Spring lies in adding a friendly and modern layer on top of all these other frameworks, allowing us to easily switch implementations and encouraging good design principles such as loose coupling and testable code.

In terms of testing, Spring is a somewhat heavyweight solution. We have an XML file that has to be maintained or, if we try to do all the wiring programmatically, a ton of verbose code that grows steadily over time.

Spring's wiring support also suffers from extremes: We can use either manual wiring, which is very challenging to maintain in anything beyond trivial projects, or autowiring, which also ends up having undesirable side effects as the project code base grows.

Spring is in many ways a victim of its own success. It is deployed in so many places now that all changes have to be retrofitted, and it cannot drop support for old Java versions, which means that it is quite slow to move, with few radical changes or enhancements beyond support for new APIs and frameworks.

Having said that, Spring is still a superb framework that satisfies many needs, and its dominance of the marketplace is likely to continue for quite a while, certainly based on the strength of its integration features. Spring was the first framework to bring IoC to the mainstream and make it accessible and available to all, and as such, Spring is often seen as the pioneer of Dependency Injection. We've all learned a tremendous amount from it, and anything that follows cannot but build on the great work it's done so far. Future versions also promise better support for wiring beans and declaring them via annotations, thus further reducing the XML clutter.

Ideally, we'd be able to wire up our components easy and programmatically with minimal scaffolding code. In fact, we'd like to apply the same principles that drive the usage and design of TestNG itself to our tests and their wiring up.

For example, there's no reason to require a specific superclass, the way Spring's test integration does. Also, wiring should be driven by annotations within the source, rather than an external file. We should also be able to easily specify what implementation we'd like for a given test, while still avoiding the Service Locator pattern and instead relying on Dependency Injection.

Enter Guice

Fortunately, there's a new IoC container that gives us all of these features. Developed by Google, Guice is a truly lightweight container (in the sense that it has minimal dependencies, has a low footprint, a small jar size, and excellent performance) designed up front to take advantage of the latest language features to promote ease of use and to clear up cluttered code.

Guice does not impose or require XML files or any externalized configuration. Instead, all components are created and wired up at runtime. Instead of a single global registry, components are wired into module units. A module contains any number of wirings, and we can have as many modules as we'd like in a project, grouped in whatever way makes the most sense.

Having declared all our components, injection happens via an *injector*. Injectors are created by Guice and perform injections by examining components for annotations to determine what to inject.

A Typical Dependency Scenario

In order to illustrate how Guice works, we'll revisit an example we went through in Chapter 2 when we discussed mocks. As a brief recap, we have a number of interfaces: UserManager, UserDAO, and Mailer. The user manager works with the Data Access Object (DAO) to save and load users and uses the mailer to send emails when users are created.

For each of these interfaces, we have two implementations. One is the actual production implementation that will interact with external dependencies, such as a database for the UserDAO object, and an SMTP mail server for the mailer object. We also have stub implementations used for testing.

In our earlier example, since we were focusing on the mocking and stubbing aspect of these components, we performed all the wiring by hand. This means that we wrote code that explicitly set the mailer and DAO on the user manager, and we also created all those objects and the correct implementation ourselves inside of the test.

What we'd like to do is rewrite that test to let Guice handle all the messy details of wiring objects. Ideally, we would declare what objects we'd like, and Guice can figure out how to best service those needs. We want to migrate from the code shown in Listing 5–7 to that shown in Listing 5–8.

Listing 5–7 Manual DAO wiring test code

```
@Test
public void verifyCreateUser() {
  UserManager manager = new UserManagerImpl();
  MailerStub mailer = new MailerStub();
  manager.setMailer(mailer);
  manager.setDAO(new UserDAOStub());
  manager.createUser("tester");
  assert mailer.getMails().size() == 1;
}
```

Listing 5–8 Guice-injected test

```
@Inject private UserManager manager;
@Inject private MailerStub mailer;

@Test
public void verifyCreateUser() {
  manager.createUser("tester");
  assert mailer.getMails().size() == 1;
}
```

Of course, we could use Spring. Listing 5–9 shows the Spring version of the test.

Listing 5–9 Spring-injected test

```
private UserManager manager;
private MailerStub mailer;

@Test
public void verifyCreateUser() {
  manager.createUser("tester");
  assert mailer.getMails().size() == 1;
}

public void setManager(UserManager manager) {
  this.manager = manager;
}

public void setMailer(MailerStub mailer) {
  this.mailer = mailer;
}
```

This Spring version doesn't include the XML configuration we'll need. The reason we prefer the Guice approach is that it's a lot more obvious by just looking at the code to figure out what is being injected. The explicit field annotation is much clearer and less error prone that having the wiring done in an XML file that's far away from the source, with no strong explicit relationship between the two.

Before delving into the details of how to do so, let's examine a TestNG feature that we'll make use of shortly: the object factory. It's important that we understand the concept of the TestNG object factory so we control the creation of injected test instances.

The Object Factory

By default, TestNG will instantiate test objects for us through treating them as simple JavaBeans. This means that the test class is expected to have a no-argument constructor (or more commonly, no constructors) so it can be created at runtime through reflection using `Class.forName(...)`.

However, there are times when we'd like to apply some custom processing to tests before they're actually used. For such cases, we can use the object factory support in TestNG to specify a class that will take care of creating all tests. Listing 5–10 shows the interface that needs to be implemented.

Listing 5–10 Object factory interface

```
public interface IObjectFactory {
   Object newInstance(Constructor constructor,
                      Object... parameters);
}
```

By registering an implementation of this class with TestNG, we can add in test instance preprocessing. There are several uses for this feature, ranging from resource injection (which we'll get back to shortly) to adding AOP[1] functionality to even returning bytecode instrumented test classes.[2]

As mentioned earlier, if we don't specify an object factory, TestNG's default implementation will be used. The default implementation simply invokes the constructor with the parameters supplied, if any (usually, none are).

---

1. AOP stands for Aspect-Oriented Programming. The general concept is to identify aspects or concerns that apply across a number of classes, rather than being constrained to one class. Examples include logging or transactional behavior where we want to set up a transactional context for a given set of methods across a number of classes.

2. An instrumented class is a class that has had its bytecode modified in order to enhance it with particular functionality. Examples of instrumented or enhanced classes include ones that have had persistence code injected or that have logging calls added in every method entry/exit point.

How this works in practice is probably best illustrated with an example. Listing 5–11 defines an object factory that simply prints out a message every time a test class is instantiated.

Listing 5–11 Example of a logging object factory

```
public class LoggingObjectFactory implements IObjectFactory {

   private ObjectFactoryImpl wrapped = new ObjectFactoryImpl();

   public Object newInstance(Constructor constructor,
                             Object... objects) {
     Object o = wrapped.newInstance(constructor, objects);
     System.out.println("Created test " + o.getClass());
     return o;
   }
}
```

This object factory follows the Decorator pattern. It is a decorator that wraps the underlying default factory and adds behavior to it, namely, logging test instantiation.

The next step is to register the object factory. TestNG offers various ways to do this.

- Command line: On the command line, specifying -objectfactory *className* will instruct TestNG to create the object factory and use it.
- ant: An object factory attribute to the TestNG ant task can be specified with its value set to the fully qualified class name.
- testng.xml: On the top-level suite element, an object factory attribute can be specified to use a given object factory.
- Annotation: Within the test sources, an @ObjectFactory annotation can be specified on one method.

For the annotation approach, we need to be aware of some issues. For example, the method signature must specify org.testng.IObjectFactory as the return type. Listing 5–12 shows the method to register the object factory from Listing 5–11.

Listing 5–12 Object factory annotation registration

```
@ObjectFactory
public IObjectFactory createFactory() {
  return new LoggingObjectFactory();
}
```

We can place this method anywhere in our test suite, as long as we include the class containing it in TestNG's list of classes to examine. However, in order for us to be able to bootstrap the factory, we can't use it to load itself, and we have to rely on simple instantiation for the class that creates the object factory. What does this mean in practice? If the class with this method has any tests in it, they will not have any of the custom behavior that the object factory provides since it can't create its own instance.

The best approach to handling this restriction is to not have any tests in the class. So our `createFactory()` method, for example, could go in its own class: `FactorySetup`.

Finally, the test suite should contain only one method with this annotation. It doesn't make sense to have more than one object factory. TestNG won't report it as an error but can make no guarantees as to which method will actually be used for the factory; the rest will be ignored.

Why would we use the annotation approach? There are a couple of benefits to this approach over declaring the factory statically at invocation time. First, this approach enables us to pass state to the factory since we're responsible for constructing it programmatically. We could, for example, pass in a Spring `ApplicationContext` that we construct elsewhere.

Second, it keeps all the logic inside of the source code. In most cases, the factory used has a direct impact on what sort of features are supported by test objects, and it's rare that object factories would be swapped or random new ones plugged in.

Guice Configuration

Having gone through object factories, it's time to get back to Guice. We'd like to add a step in between the test classes being instantiated and actually being used. This intermediate step would allow Guice to work its magic on the test instances and take care of any wiring that needs to be done.

The object factory approach just covered is the ideal way to achieve this. Before introducing this custom factory, let's examine how we can use Guice for applications in general. As mentioned earlier, Guice wires all components inside of a `Module`. From the user perspective, all we need to do is provide Guice with a `Module` instance, and in turn it will return an `Injector`. The returned `Injector` is what we use from then on to construct and wire all objects. This is best illustrated with an example.

The `Module` implementation is very simple; all we need to do is specify our bindings, as shown in Listing 5–13.

Listing 5–13 Implementing a Guice `Module`

```
public class UserAppModule extends AbstractModule {

  protected void configure() {
    bind(UserManager.class).toInstance(new UserManagerImpl());
    bind(Mailer.class).to(MailerStub.class);
    bind(UserDAO.class).to(UserDAOStub.class);
  }
}
```

Wiring objects involves binding interfaces to implementations. In Listing 5–13, we used two different kinds of bindings supported by Guice: binding to a prototype class and binding to an instance.

Binding to a prototype means that we supply Guice with a class, and it will construct the class for us as needed. Binding to an instance allows us to manually instantiate the object we'd like bound, rather than having Guice create the instance for us. Though in our example it doesn't really matter which approach we use, it's not hard to imagine that in a more realistic situation, `UserManagerImpl` might require a lot more setup, so registering an instance would make more sense.

Having defined the module, the next step is to pass it to Guice so it can give us an `Injector` based on the bindings specified, as shown in Listing 5–14.

Listing 5–14 Creating a Guice `Injector`

```
private Injector createInjector() {
    return Guice.createInjector(new UserAppModule());
  }
```

Now that we have an injector, we can choose from two approaches. The first is to use the injector to create the root object in our object tree. Due to how Guice works, all objects referenced from there will have injection applied, so all we'd have to do is supply that one object. Guice will then examine that object for the `@Inject` annotation and transitively follow the object graph, performing injections for all related objects.

However, in many cases this isn't quite possible. For tests, for example, there is no real root—all tests are isolated and stand alone. In this case, we'd need to use the second approach: a central factory that is responsible for creating all objects (sound familiar?). Listing 5–15 shows a sample factory.

Listing 5–15 Factory for creating injected instances

```
public class UserAppFactory {
  private Injector injector;

  public UserAppFactory() {
    injector = createInjector();
  }

  public <T> T create(Class<T> c) {
    return injector.getInstance(c);
  }

  private Injector createInjector() {
    return Guice.createInjector(new UserAppModule());
  }
}
```

Note that it's crucial that we don't end up with classes directly referencing the injector (one is fine, more than three is way too many!). This would defeat the whole purpose of using IoC as we'd be using the Service Locator approach. The key is to register a few objects and have IoC behavior propagated automatically to the rest of the application.

Having configured Guice and bound all our components, the last step is to specify injections required on any objects in the application. Listing 5–16 shows an annotated version of the user manager implementation.

Listing 5–16 Annotated user manager

```
public class UserManagerImpl implements UserManager {
  @Inject private UserDAO dao;
  @Inject private Mailer mailer;
```

We can specify the `@Inject` annotation on fields or methods, there is no setter restriction, and any method can specify that it expects its parameter to be injected.

The final step is to combine the two approaches, that is, the Guice module configuration and the TestNG object factory. For the sake of reuse, we define an abstract base class that deals with the integration, as shown in Listing 5–17.

Listing 5–17 Base class for the TestNG Guice object factory

```
public abstract class GuiceObjectFactory extends AbstractModule
      implements IObjectFactory {

  private Injector injector;
  private ObjectFactoryImpl creator = new ObjectFactoryImpl();

  public GuiceObjectFactory() {
    injector = Guice.createInjector(this);
  }

  public Object newInstance(Constructor constructor,
                            Object... objects) {
    Object o = creator.newInstance(constructor, objects);
    injector.injectMembers(o);
    return o;
  }
}
```

For a given test suite, we'd subclass this to provide the bindings we need, as shown in Listing 5–18.

Listing 5–18 Guice factory for wiring user manager dependencies

```
public class UserAppObjectFactory extends GuiceObjectFactory {
  protected void configure() {
    bind(UserManager.class).toInstance(new UserManagerImpl());
    bind(Mailer.class).to(MailerStub.class);
    bind(UserDAO.class).to(UserDAOStub.class);
  }
}
```

We're now done configuring our object factory, so we can finally write some tests.

Guice-Based Test

Having configured Guice and created our custom object factory using it, it's time to finally reap the rewards! The final step is to use this injection goodness in our tests. Because our tests now have all dependencies injected, we no longer need to explicitly specify how to find a given object, nor do we care what implementation we're handed. Guice now controls all that wiring. As a reminder, the test we had earlier is shown in Listing 5–19.

Listing 5–19 Manual DAO wired test code

```
@Test
public void verifyCreateUser() {
  UserManager manager = new UserManagerImpl();
  MailerStub mailer = new MailerStub();
  manager.setMailer(mailer);
  manager.setDAO(new UserDAOStub());
  manager.createUser("tester");
  assert mailer.getMails().size() == 1;
}
```

This can now be rewritten as the much more elegant version shown in Listing 5–20.

Listing 5–20 Guice-injected test

```
@Inject private UserManager manager;
@Inject private MailerStub mailer;

@Test
public void verifyCreateUser() {
  manager.createUser("tester");
  assert mailer.getMails().size() == 1;
}
```

Note that because we actually care about the mailer implementation, we're injecting not the interface but the actual stub implementation. We need the stub since it has functionality that allows us to query the number of times it has sent emails. Guice will automatically do the right thing based on our field type declaration.

Grouping Test Dependencies

Hopefully by now we have shown the value of using Guice for our tests. However, what happens when our test suite grows over time, and our dependencies also keep growing? Wiring up a handful of objects, or even a dozen, is easy. What happens when we need to bind 30 or 40 objects?

Since TestNG can have only one object factory, this can get tricky, not to mention messy. We're back to a centralized configuration point, with every new binding requiring that we modify the one central `configure()` method in the factory.

How can we cope with this issue? There is no ideal solution, but we'd like to present an approach here that will work. Since we're creating our factory programmatically, there's no reason why we can't modify it as we go along, the idea being that each group of tests can specify its own bindings. So instead of one huge central configuration, we have tests clustered together around a configuration, with as many configurations as we'd like.

The downside of this approach is that it makes it very tricky to parallelize our tests. Since the object factory is now stateful, we can't have tests modifying it concurrently. For the flexibility this approach allows us, though, we think this isn't such an imposing restriction. Listing 5–21 shows a sample implementation of the stateful factory. Note that the injector can now be modified through the `setCurrentModule` method.

Listing 5–21 Stateful Guice object factory

```
public class GuiceModuleObjectFactory implements IObjectFactory
  {

  private Injector injector;
  private ObjectFactoryImpl creator = new ObjectFactoryImpl();

  public void setCurrentModule(Module module) {
    injector = Guice.createInjector(module);
  }

  public Object newInstance(Constructor constructor,
                            Object... objects) {
    Object o = creator.newInstance(constructor, objects);
```

```
    injector.injectMembers(o);
    return o;
  }
}
```

We've now removed the configuration responsibility from the factory, and allow callers instead to set it as needed. How best to do this? TestNG has an excellent way of specifying configuration information, based on groups of tests. We can do all the setup we need in a method annotated with `@BeforeGroups`.

Since we need access to the object factory, we can store it in `ITestContext`, as shown in Listing 5–22. Like any other TestNG annotated methods, the object factory creation method can also accept an optional `ITestContext` parameter, in case it needs to interact with TestNG.

Listing 5–22 Storing the object factory in the TestNG runtime context

```
@ObjectFactory
public IObjectFactory init(ITestContext context) {
  GuiceModuleObjectFactory factory =
                  new GuiceModuleObjectFactory();
  context.setAttribute("factory", factory);
  return factory;
}
```

Now that we've set the factory in the context, we can access it from any other method. This enables us to modify the factory from anywhere within our configuration or test methods and thus register different modules and bindings as needed.

Note that this approach highlights another interesting feature of TestNG: the ability to store global state in the context and easily access it later. This saves us the hassle of having to worry about using `ThreadLocal`, statics, or any other more cumbersome solutions for passing information around. Listing 5–23 shows an example configuration method for a given group.

Listing 5–23 Group-based dependency wiring

```
@BeforeGroups("user-manager")
public void bindDependencies(ITestContext context) {
```

```
GuiceModuleObjectFactory factory =
  (GuiceModuleObjectFactory)context.getAttribute("factory");
factory.setCurrentModule(new AbstractModule() {
  protected void configure() {
    bind(UserManager.class).toInstance(new
UserManagerImpl());
    bind(Mailer.class).toInstance(new MailerStub());
    bind(UserDAOStub.class);
  }
});
}
```

All tests that belong to the `user-manager` group will now be able to declare injected dependencies based on our bindings.

However, one caveat covered earlier applies here as well. Since the factory creates the class that contains this configuration method, it cannot itself have the bindings injected. Therefore, the class that contains the `bindDependencies` method should not have any injected fields, and the tests in that group should be specified in a different class.

The power of this approach lies in the fact that different groups can have different dependencies. For example, it's not hard to imagine a functional test that requires more dependencies or different implementations. By localizing bindings this way, we're able to create small clusters of tests that include just the right set of dependencies, rather than a huge global repository that grows uncontrollably over time.

Injecting Configuration

Obviously, some information does not belong in source code. While all component injection can and should be expressed in source, there are often environment parameters that should remain externalized. Let's consider a simple example where we'd like to provide different database connection properties in different environments. This information has to go in a text file somewhere. How can we achieve this using Guice?

Guice has support for easily binding `java.util.Properties` objects, so we can then inject any key/value pair from the properties file into components. The first step is to modify our `configure()` method to load and bind the properties in the module, as shown in Listing 5–24.

Listing 5–24 Loading properties into Guice

```
Properties p = new Properties();
try {
  p.load(getClass().getResourceAsStream("app.properties"));
}
catch(IOException e) {
  throw new RuntimeException("Error loading app.properties", e);
}
Names.bindProperties(binder(), p);
```

Note that since we're loading the properties file ourselves, it's equally easy to instead load the bindings from an XML file or any other source, for that matter. The `app.properties` file is shown in Listing 5–25.

Listing 5–25 Example properties to be loaded into Guice

```
db.driver=org.postgresql.Driver
db.url=jdbc:postgresql://127.0.0.1/mydb
db.user=webuser
db.pass=webpass
```

The final step is to access the named (the key is the name) values in our tests. In an injected class, for example, we could define this method to create the database connection, as shown in Listing 5–26.

Listing 5–26 Guice-injected parameters

```
public void setConnection(@Named("db.url") String url,
                          @Named("db.user") String user,
                          @Named("db.pass") String pass,
                          @Named("db.driver") String driver
  ) {
    // create connection based on parameters
}
```

Note that injection is not restricted to just fields and methods; we can also declare that a method parameter is injected, as we're doing here.

Using this approach allows us to easily specify environment-specific configuration information—since Guice does not mandate a specific format, it is very easy to integrate it into any existing configuration infrastructure we have, at the small cost of having to write a bit of code to wire the two together.

DbUnit

DbUnit is a JUnit add-on that helps with all manner of database-related tests. Here are some of the main features.

- *Easy preloading and dumping of bulk data*: DbUnit allows for a number of different implementations for preloading a database with data. It supports a simple XML format, where the data can be first exported to a file, then loaded by tests to provide the right set of basic data the test expects.
- *Helpers for querying databases*: A few simple helpers enable us to get data out of the database.
- *Helpers to clean up and manage database state*: Given a data set, DbUnit provides a set of database operations to delete or add the data, enabling easy cleanup after test runs.
- *Result comparisons*: DbUnit offers programmatic sorting and filtering support for results. For example, when comparing data sets, we can choose to either ignore certain columns or enforce a certain ordering for the comparison.

Configuration

DbUnit requires the following set of jar files:

- `dbunit.jar`: the DbUnit implementation classes
- `commons-collections.jar`: Jakarta's commons collections library
- `commons-lang`: Jakarta's commons language library
- `junit.jar`: the JUnit assert classes used by DbUnit to verify expectations

Once that's done, we need a baseline data set for us to work with. For our example, let's assume that our tests expect that the database contains a ROLES table, a USERS table, and a USER_ROLES join table. This is the schema handed to us, and the goal is to write tests to ensure that the JDBC code we use to interact with these tables functions correctly.

Before we get started on the tests, we need our baseline data, the set of data we will populate the table with. Ideally, it would be a subset of real data taken from a live database. Instead of writing this by hand (which we could do for this example, since it is trivial, but your sample data hopefully won't be!), we use DbUnit to export the data we want in its own native XML format. This format is a simple table/column/data XML file that's easy to edit or update later. Though DbUnit has a pluggable interface for data readers and writers, in this case the default XML flat file is sufficient for our needs. Listing 5–27 shows an example of dumping a set of existing tables.

Listing 5–27 Application for dumping tables to a file

```
public static void main(String[] args) throws Exception {
  JdbcDatabaseTester tester = new JdbcDatabaseTester(
  "org.postgresql.Driver",
  "jdbc:postgresql://127.0.0.1/userdb",
  "username", "pass");
  IDatabaseConnection c = tester.getConnection();
  String[] depTableNames = new String[]{"ROLES", "USERS"
                        "USER_ROLES"};
  IDataSet output = c.createDataSet( depTableNames );
  FileOutputStream fos = new FileOutputStream("user-roles.xml");
  FlatXmlDataSet.write(output, fos);
}
```

In Listing 5–27, we specify the JDBC data inline for the sake of simplicity. DbUnit also supports loading the connection information from a properties file, via `PropertiesBasedJdbcDatabaseTester`. Note that this class expects the database connection properties to be set as environment variables (accessed via `System.getProperty(...)`), so it is of limited use, and you are most likely better off writing your own mechanism for externalizing the database connection information (e.g., via Spring).

When we run our data dumper tool, the `user-roles.xml` output file will have the exported database data. Listing 5–28 shows the contents of the file.

Listing 5–28 XML file for the database export

```
<?xml version='1.0' encoding='UTF-8'?>
<dataset>
```

```
<roles id="1" name="AUTHOR" description="Book authors"/>
<roles id="2" name="EDITOR" description="Book editors"/>
<users id="1" first_name="Hani" last_name="Suleiman"/>
<users id="2" first_name="Cedric" last_name="Beust"/>
<users id="3" first_name="Eddy" last_name="Editor"/>
<user_roles user_id="1" role_id="1"/>
<user_roles user_id="2" role_id="1"/>
<user_roles user_id="3" role_id="2"/>
</dataset>
```

This is the export from our database. Each child node of the `dataset` element represents a row in the database. The child node name is the table name, and the attributes represent the column data; each attribute is one column, with its value being the data in that specific column. So from this export, we can see that the USERS table has three columns: id, first_name, and last_name.

Note that in our dumper utility, it is important to list the tables in the correct order. For example, we need to take foreign key constraints into consideration since when the data is loaded, it is done in the order in which entries appear in the export XML file.

Usage

At this point, we have some export data we'd like to preload, and it's time to write our test to verify that our application functions as expected. The first task is to load the test data using the exported file, as shown in Listing 5–29.

Listing 5–29 Setup method to populate the database from the file

```
private JdbcDatabaseTester dbTester;

  @BeforeClass
  public void loadDB() throws Exception {
    dbTester = new JdbcDatabaseTester(
    "org.postgresql.Driver",
    "jdbc:postgresql://127.0.0.1/userdb",
    "username", "pass");
    IDataSet dataSet =
        new FlatXmlDataSet(new File("user-roles.xml"));
    IDatabaseConnection connection = dbTester.getConnection();
    try {
      DatabaseOperation.CLEAN_INSERT.execute(connection,
        dataSet);
```

```
  } finally {
    connection.close();
  }
}
```

As earlier, the first step is to create a tester instance. Since we'll be using this tester in all our tests, we specify it as a field in the test class. The `loadDB()` configuration method will run once for the test class, so all subsequent tests can rely on the baseline data being present. Of course, it is entirely possible that for some cases, we'd like the data to be initialized for each test method, rather than for the test class. In that case, we'd use the `@BeforeMethod` configuration annotation instead of `@BeforeClass`.

The next step is to load the data set we exported earlier from the XML file. Having done so, we open a connection to the database and execute a `CLEAN_INSERT` operation with the data set.

DbUnit comes with several database operations that can be performed on data sets.

- UPDATE: Allows you to update all the items in the database with the values listed in the data set. Note that if an item exists in the data set but does not exist in the database, it will not be inserted; instead, you will get an error.

- INSERT: Goes through each row in the data set and inserts it into the database. If a row exists matching the one in the data set (e.g., they have the same primary key), it will not be updated; you will get an error message instead.

- REFRESH: Is useful in cases where you might have some existing data in the database and want to load the data set even if some of the data matches what exists already. For cases where a row already exists in the database, it is updated with the values from the data set.

- DELETE: Does exactly what it says: deletes the data specified in the data set from the database.

- DELETE_ALL: Removes all data from the tables in the data set. Note that this does not take into consideration what values the data set contains; only the full list of tables names is used.

- TRUNCATE_TABLE: Issues a `truncate table` statement for every table in the data set. While less portable than the DELETE_ALL operation (not all databases support `truncate table`), it is significantly faster.

- CLEAN_INSERT: Creates a clean insert, which is composed of a drop followed by an insert. This is useful for cases where you are unsure of whether or not the data exists in the database. Using this will first delete all the items listed in your data set and then insert them.

Verifying Results

Having loaded the test data, the next step is to run the tests against the current data set. DbUnit provides a number of base classes that tests can extend. These tests ultimately extend JUnit's `TestCase`, so unfortunately, in order to use them in TestNG, the `junit` jar file needs to be present in the classpath.

It is interesting to note here that even though the base class is a JUnit `TestCase` instance, nothing stops us from running it inside of TestNG. The reason this works is that a JUnit failure ultimately throws an exception, which would still be flagged as a failure by TestNG, so we can easily use the same base class.

However, since the base class relies on `setUp` and `tearDown` methods, we'd have to invoke them explicitly.

It is also possible to write our test classes so as not to rely on the base class. Ultimately, this is a cleaner and more robust approach. We'll demonstrate it soon.

First, let's examine the `DBTestCase`-based approach. The class we actually extend for our example is `JdbcBasedDBTestCase`, which is an instance of `DBTestCase` that allows us to specify database connectivity parameters via getters. Other subclasses provided are `DataSourceBasedDBTestCase`, which is useful if we have a `DataSource` implementation (e.g., if we were using Spring in our tests), and `JndiBasedDBTestCase`, which is used for JNDI lookups of `DataSource` objects, useful when running inside a container.

DBTestCase *Example*

Using the sample data set we saved earlier, Listing 5–30 shows an example implementation of our test case to verify the data.

Listing 5–30 Skeleton of a DbUnit-based test case

```
import static org.dbunit.Assertion.*;

public class DBUnitTests extends JdbcBasedDBTestCase {

  protected String getConnectionUrl() {
    return "jdbc:postgresql://127.0.0.1/userdb";
  }
```

```
protected String getPassword() {
  return "pass";
}

protected String getUsername() {
  return "username";
}

protected String getDriverClass() {
  return "org.postgresql.Driver";
}

protected IDataSet getDataSet() throws Exception {
  URL data = getClass().getResource("/user-roles.xml");
  return new FlatXmlDataSet(getClass().getResource(url));
}

@BeforeMethod
protected void setUp() throws Exception {
  super.setUp();
}

@AfterMethod
protected void tearDown() throws Exception {
  super.tearDown();
}
}
```

The first few methods here just handle the return connection information. The `getDataSet()` method deals with returning the data we'd like to prepopulate the database with. This is the data we saved earlier.

The superclass will take care of taking this data set and doing a clean insert into the database for it. If we wanted it to behave differently on test setup, we would override the `getSetUpOperation()` method to return a different operation.

Finally, we override `setUp` and `tearDown` just so we can annotate them, to ensure that TestNG calls them at the appropriate time.

So far we've covered all the setup code required. What about the actual test? Since the environment has been taken care of, the test implementation becomes quite simple. All we need to do is perform whatever operations we'd like on the database, using the data we've preloaded if needed, and then call whatever asserts we need, as shown in Listing 5–31.

Listing 5–31 Example DbUnit test

```
@Test
public void verifyRemove() throws Exception {
    // code to delete a user (ID 1), perhaps through an ORM tool
    // verify the results
    assert getConnection().getRowCount("USERS") == 2;
    // verify that the join table also had a row removed
    String whereClause = "user_id = 1";
    assert getConnection().getRowCount("USER_ROLES",
                                       whereClause) == 0;
}
```

DbUnit also provides a couple of assertions that are useful in verifying table or data set contents. We could, for example, store expected database contents (using the data dumper tool we discussed earlier in Listing 5–27) in a different file. Our test would then preload the database, perform whatever operations are under test, and then load the expected data and compare it to the actual table contents. Listing 5–32 shows the code for doing so.

Listing 5–32 Using table data assertions

```
@Test
public void verifyUserModification() throws Exception {
    URL url = getClass().getResource("/user-roles-expected.xml");
    IDataSet data = new FlatXmlDataSet(url);
    ITable expected = data.getTable("USERS");
    // we have the expected data,
    // next we perform operations on the db

    // code that results in USERS table changes...

    // check that our modifications match our expectations
    IDataSet dbSet = getConnection().createDataSet();
    assertEquals(expected, dbSet.getTable("USERS"));
}
```

Inline Setup Example

Another option when writing DbUnit-based tests is to perform all initialization data using our own base class, or to specify it inline in tests instead of relying on a superclass.

The advantage of doing so is that we would no longer rely on JUnit and can use the full power of TestNG for test initialization and lifecycle management. The setup performed for us by the DBTestCase superclass is fairly trivial.

1. Set up the IDatabaseTester instance. This is used in tests to obtain connections and is called in the getConnection() method.
2. Provide support for loading an initial data set, This is done via the getDataSet() abstract method that all test cases have to implement.
3. Initialize the database with the data set provided, and delete the data set at the end of each test case.

In this case, we'd use the loadDB() method we specified earlier in our test, along with the test itself. The setup method handles steps 1 and 2. The only remaining issue to deal with is removing the data set once the test has completed. We would do this in a configuration method that is run after all tests in the class have completed, as shown in Listing 5–33. We could of course have data inserted/removed for every test method, though this example shows it being done once per class, rather than per test method.

Listing 5–33 Test configuration for the DbUnit-based test

```
@Test(groups = "db")
public class DBTests {
  private JdbcDatabaseTester dbTester;
  private IDataSet initialDS;

  @BeforeClass
  public void loadDB() throws Exception {
    dbTester = new JdbcDatabaseTester(
    "org.postgresql.Driver",
    "jdbc:postgresql://127.0.0.1/userdb",
    "username", "pass");
    initialDataSet =
        new FlatXmlDataSet(new File("user-roles.xml"));
    IDatabaseConnection connection = getConnection();
    try {
      DatabaseOperation.CLEAN_INSERT.execute(connection,
                                             initialDS);
    } finally {
      connection.close();
    }
  }
}
```

```
@AfterClass
public void cleanDB() throws Exception {
  IDatabaseConnection connection = getConnection();
  try {
    DatabaseOperation.DELETE.execute(connection, initialDS);
  } finally {
    connection.close();
  }
}

protected IDatabaseConnection getConnection()
                  throws Exception {
  return dbTester.getConnection();
}
}
```

In this class, we can now add the same test we defined earlier—
verifyUserModification(). The advantage of course is that we no longer
require JUnit, nor is a particular superclass imposed on our tests.

HtmlUnit

HtmlUnit is a JUnit add-on for testing Web pages. It is specifically designed
to test Web pages, rather than any HTTP traffic. For the latter, there is
HttpUnit, another add-on that lets us deal directly with requests and
responses, rather than focusing on the actual content returned.

The benefit of using HtmlUnit is that it allows us to work with Web
pages via their contents, which makes it easy to drill down to a specific form
on the page, populate it, and then submit it.

HtmlUnit is also suited for conversational tests where we expect to go
through a series of Web pages (e.g., a signup process) within a test. Through
the conversation, we expect to maintain certain state (e.g., credentials, cook-
ies, and so on).

HtmlUnit handles the messy details of maintaining conversation state,
allowing us to focus on the page contents and the elements within.

In addition to working with HTML content, HtmlUnit actually has
some JavaScript support and also handles any JavaScript logic embedded in
the page contents. The JavaScript support is provided by the Mozilla Rhino
JavaScript engine, which is bundled.

Before we delve into the details of using HtmlUnit, it's important to keep in mind that testing presentation specifics such as HTML pages can be very fragile.

For example, if an element is moved or renamed, we'll likely have tests that start to fail. They're not failing for a good reason; there's nothing bad about renaming or moving an element, so having to keep the test updated is a maintenance cost that we can do without.

Keeping this in mind, even if we do decide to test the presentation layer like this, it's important that the tests try to make as few assumptions as possible about the structure of the page. For example, we can check that a page contains a form called `fooform`, but looking inside of two named divs for this form is a lot more fragile.

Configuration

As with too many Java projects, the list of dependencies can be formidable. Here are the jars you'll need, along with an explanation of the purpose of each one:

- `HtmlUnit.jar`: the implementation classes
- `jaxen.jar`: required for XPath support
- `commons-collections.jar`: Jakarta's commons-collections API, used internally
- `commons-logging.jar`: used for all logging purposes
- `commons-httpclient.jar`: used to handle the HTTP networking
- `commons-codec.jar`: required by commons-httpclient
- `js.jar`: the Rhino JavaScript engine, required for parsing and executing JavaScript
- `commons-io.jar`: Jakarta's commons-io API, used internally

Along with these, there are also three jar files used for parsing HTML:

- `xercesImpl.jar`
- `xmlParserAPIs.jar`
- `nekohtml.jar`

While it's usually fairly easy to see missing dependencies, you'll find that in the case of HtmlUnit, you won't get sensible exceptions pointing out missing dependencies; instead, you'll see random instances of `XNIException` being thrown. This is because, in their infinite wisdom, the authors of the HTML parser used in HtmlUnit (nekohtml) commit one of the cardinal sins of Java library development: They catch an exception too broadly and then throw a custom one instead of letting it bubble back up.

If you do run into this issue, you'll need to explicitly catch XNIException in your test and use the code shown in Listing 5–34 to unwrap it into something useful.[3]

Listing 5–34 Unwrapping a Xerces XNIException

```
static Throwable extractNestedException(final XNIException e) {
  Throwable originalException = e;
  Throwable cause = e.getException();
  while (cause != null) {
    originalException = cause;
    if (cause instanceof XNIException) {
      cause = ((XNIException)cause).getException();
    } else if (cause instanceof InvocationTargetException) {
      cause = cause.getCause();
    } else {
      cause = null;
    }
  }
  return originalException;
}
```

Usage

Once all the jar files are added to your classpath, it's time to write some tests. HtmlUnit, unlike many other frameworks that piggyback on the JUnit name, is interestingly not built on top of JUnit. It is a stand-alone framework that doesn't really have any dependencies on JUnit: It does not impose a specific superclass, nor does it expect you to use any asserts it provides.

Even more perplexing: It's not for unit testing at all! The developers likely went for the Unit part of the name just to hook in the testing crowd!

---

3. This is an example of bad exception handling, where the underlying cause is obscured and makes debugging much trickier than it needs to be. For more information on exception handling and common misconceptions and mistakes, please see Chapter 7.

As usual, we will first consider the setup work needed before we write any actual tests. In this case, we need to create a `WebClient` instance, as shown in Listing 5–35. This is the main entry point to HtmlUnit and will enable us to make requests for specific Web pages and to get at the results.

Listing 5–35 Initializing a `WebClient`

```
public class BasicHtmlTest {
  private WebClient client;
  private URL baseURL;

  @BeforeClass
  public void initClient() {
    client = new WebClient();
    baseURL = new URL("http://localhost:8000/");
  }
}
```

Having created the Web client, we also specify a base URL. This is useful since it enables our tests to be easily used across different servers, instead of having to specify the host name for every page request. Since all our tests are against one server (most likely), we perform this setup work once for the test class. Note that it's also possible to define this as a system environment variable when invoking the test, as shown in Listing 5–36.

Listing 5–36 Using a system property to specify the target host

```
Private static final URL baseURL =
  new URL(System.getProperty("test.url"));
```

When invoking the test, we would specify a `—Dtest.url=http://localhost:8000` environment variable.

However, the instance field gives us more flexibility than a global static. We could, for example, combine this approach with a Data Provider to perform the same test against a number of servers, maybe to ensure that the application has been deployed correctly across a cluster. TestNG allows us to correctly scope variables, unlike the strictly global approach that JUnit mandates.

For our first test, we verify that the home page loads and find the Apply for Account link, as shown in Listing 5–37.

Listing 5–37 Example test for clicking a link

```
@Test
public void clickApplyLink() throws IOException {
  URL home = new URL(baseURL, "/index.jsp");
  HtmlPage homePage = (HtmlPage)client.getPage(home);
  String text = "Apply for Account";
  HtmlAnchor anchor = homePage.getFirstAnchorByText(text);
  assert anchor != null;
  HtmlPage nextPage = (HtmlPage)anchor.click();
  assert nextPage.getTitleText().equals("Apply for Account");
}
```

Having found the link, we proceed to click on it. Clicking on links works just as it would in a browser: A request is sent behind the scenes, and we're presented with the result. In this case, the result is another `HtmlPage` instance.

Finally, we verify that this second page has the expected title: "Apply for Account."

While this test is a good introduction to HtmlUnit usage, it actually is somewhat problematic in its implementation. The issue isn't with the API usage, but rather with the specifics of what we're testing.

The specific trouble lies with looking up links via their text. Though HtmlUnit makes this very easy, this is in fact a problematic approach due to a couple of reasons.

1. Text on pages changes often. The link might become an image at some point, for example.
2. The lookup is not friendly to internationalization. If at some point we were to develop multilingual versions of this page, the test might start failing.

A better approach when looking up links (and elements in general, in fact) is to do so via their `id` attribute. So the `getFirstAnchorByText` lookup in Listing 5–37, for example, would be changed to a different one, as shown in Listing 5–38.

Listing 5–38 Finding an anchor via its ID

```
HtmlElement element = homePage.getHtmlElementById("apply-link");
HtmlAnchor anchor = (HtmlAnchor)element;
```

This is less brittle because we're relying on the `apply` element having a specific ID. If this ID were changed, we would want to see the test break since it would signal that we should check for any other usage of this ID (e.g., in CSS or JavaScript) and ensure it is updated correctly to the new value. This is a case where a test is beneficial not just in highlighting issues in the logic but also in signaling that other code that is far more difficult to test (such as CSS) should also be fixed.

A More Complex Example

In order to highlight the power and functionality of HtmlUnit, let's test a more complicated interaction. In this case, we'd like to submit a form. We also want to verify that the page performs input validation and shows an alert message if the email address input field is left blank.

Before we write our test case, we need to consider some additional setup. HtmlUnit has a number of handlers that can be specified to deal with certain HTML elements. For example, we can use an `AlertHandler` to determine what should be done with any alerts shown. Another example of a handler is a `StatusHandler`, used when JavaScript on the page sets the browser status bar to a specific value.

For our test case, we need to register an `AlertHandler`. We would modify our test setup code as shown in Listing 5–39 to add support for alerts without tests having to explicitly set it up every time.

Listing 5–39 Verifying HTML alerts

```
private WebClient client;
private URL baseURL;
private List<String> alerts = new ArrayList<String>();

@BeforeClass
public void initClient() throws MalformedURLException {
  client = new WebClient();
  client.setAlertHandler(new CollectingAlertHandler(alerts));
  baseURL = new URL("http://localhost:8000/");
}
```

```
@AfterMethod
public void clearAlerts() {
  alerts.clear();
}
```

The setup code registers `CollectingAlertHandler`, an `AlertHandler` implementation that stores all alerts in a list. The list is a field in our test class, so we can access it from any test.

To ensure that alerts with each test are isolated and do not impact other tests, we also register an `@AfterMethod` configuration method `clearAlerts()` that is run after every test, to clear any collected alerts. Having dealt with alert handling, our test implementation is fairly straightforward, as shown in Listing 5–40.

Listing 5–40 Test case for verifying bad input

```
@Test
public void submitEmailForm() throws IOException {
  URL url = new URL(baseURL, "/email.jsp");
  HtmlPage page = (HtmlPage)client.getPage(url);
  HtmlForm form = page.getFormByName("emailform");
  HtmlInput input = form.getInputByName("email");
  // set empty value and check that we get a validation error
  input.setValueAttribute("");
  assert form.submit().equals(page);
  assert alerts.contains("You must specify an email address");
}
```

The test here loads the page, finds the right form, populates it, and finally attempts to submit it. We have a couple of asserts.

1. Verify that the page returned from the submit attempt is not a new page, signifying that we've remained on the same page.
2. Verify that the alerts list contains the alert we expect from having an empty email input field.

As you can see from these examples, HtmlUnit provides a rich API for interacting with Web pages. Note that it's important to write tests that are robust in the face of an evolving UI. When writing tests for HTML pages, focus on functionality rather than presentation. The UI will change often over time, and it would be a frustrating waste of time to have to constantly rework tests due to nonfunctional changes. Changing functionality, however, should be caught be broken tests, which will at least notify you that you have a regression issue. You can then make a better-informed decision as to whether the new functionality should be modified or the test updated.

Selenium

An interesting alternative to HtmlUnit is another open source framework: Selenium. Instead of simulating a browser, Selenium uses an actual browser to perform its tests. This makes it ideal for testing browser quirks and developing acceptance tests that match exactly what end users see and do.

We'll cover Selenium RC (Remote Control), one of the Selenium subprojects that allows us to interact easily with remote sites in a way similar to HtmlUnit, with the key difference of using a real browser instead of a simulated one.

Selenium RC has two components to it, a server component and a client one. The server is responsible for interactions with the target site that needs to be tested through firing up and interacting with a browser, and the client issues commands to the server to request that actions be performed on the browser.

While it is possible to write tests in a variety of languages (including JavaScript), we will focus here on a Java-based test, as shown in Listing 5–41. The concept is the same regardless of what language we choose to use.

Listing 5–41 Selenium-based test case

```
private Selenium selenium;

@BeforeSuite
public void startServer() throws Exception {
  SeleniumServer server = new SeleniumServer(8080);
  server.start();
}

@BeforeClass
public void startClient() {
  selenium = new DefaultSelenium("localhost", 8080, "*safari",
                      "http://localhost:8000");
  selenium.start();
}
```

```
@Test
public void verifyLogin() {
  selenium.open("http://localhost:8000/index.jsp");
  assert "Welcome!".equals(selenium.getTitle());
  selenium.type("j_username", "adminuser");
  selenium.type("j_password", "mypass");
  selenium.click("login");
  selenium.waitForPageToLoad("2000");
  assert selenium.isTextPresent("Logged in as: adminuser");
}
```

We can see here that our test performs the setup for both the client and the server. The `startServer()` method instantiates a `SeleniumServer` instance and binds it to port 8080. The `startClient()` method fired the client portion of the test and specifies the address of the server to connect to as well as the remote host.

Obviously, for our test to pass, it is expected that our Web application is already running on localhost port 8000.

Finally, the test itself opens up the index page, enters the user login information, submits the page, and finally verifies that certain text is available in the response.

The main value Selenium offers is that it uses the browser itself for all communication. It supports most of the major browsers (in theory) on various platforms (also in theory!). It works by setting itself up as a Web proxy and configuring the specified browser to use it as the proxy. This allows it to easily inject custom resources that can help us with testing.

Unfortunately, the product suffers from some problems that make it annoying and cumbersome to use.

For example, the ability to launch browsers on various platforms isn't robust or even functional, in many cases. On OS X for example, we have to perform some fairly complicated contortions to get it to work smoothly with any of the supported browsers (Firefox, Safari, and others).

Furthermore, the Selenium Java RC API is not quite as well designed or clear as its HtmlUnit counterpart and requires many trips to the documentation to decipher.

The documentation is also sadly of very low quality. It is difficult to navigate, and what exists of it is often scattered about haphazardly.

Despite these detractions, Selenium is an interesting approach that can be quite useful in various situations, so it is worth knowing about as a tool in our testing arsenal.

Swing UI Testing

One of the trickier aspects of an application to test is the user interface. After all, it requires a user, and those are fairly difficult to embed in a few lines of code. We looked at how we might test an HTML user interface via HtmlUnit. Parsing HTML is a fairly well understood field, and given that it's vaguely XMLish, it doesn't take much to be able to slurp in an HTML page and then navigate it programmatically.

On the other hand, Swing UIs are a bit trickier. For one thing, they aren't quite as common. It's also a bit trickier to capture one to file and then make assertions about it.

JDK 1.3, however, brought us a new class that makes all this much simpler. The `java.awt.Robot` class exposes all user interactions programmatically and enables us to simulate mouse moves, clicks, drags, and anything else the user might be able to do.

Instead of using that class directly, we'll use a framework specifically designed to ease UI testing. The Abbot framework proves a friendlier and higher-level API than that provided by `java.awt.Robot`. It takes care of a lot of the setup and infrastructure associated with GUI testing, including some helper methods to navigate components and easily drill down to the area to be tested.

Testing Approach

Interestingly, the approach we use is the exact same one as for HtmlUnit. Not so surprising since in both cases we're testing a user interface with a number of components, along with their interactions and relationships.

This parallel means that almost all of the same issues apply. First is that of identifying the component we're interested in. Analogous to the HTML `id` attribute is the component name property in Swing. So one approach would be to ensure that you name all your components, then directly access them by name.

This can be quite onerous since these names are largely useless in Swing, and there's not much point or incentive to set them (aside from better testability).

Another approach is to name the higher-level components and then drill down by type or label. We know, for example, that our `EditUserDetailsPanel` has a Cancel button that we can access by label. Likewise, we know that it has one `JTextArea` for the user notes that we can access by type.

Ultimately, there is no One True Way to access components. A measure of judgment is involved, and if we think a panel is likely to get more components of the same type, we don't rely on type for access. Likewise, if we think the component is likely to be internationalized, we don't rely on component labels.

Similar to the Spring integration, Abbot has a TestNG add-on that allows us to write TestNG-based Abbot tests with minimal effort.

Configuration

We'll need to download two components. One is Abbot itself, and one is the testng-abbot integration library. Here's the list of jars:

- `abbot.jar`: the Abbot implementation classes
- `testng-abbot.jar`: the integration library
- `jdom.jar`: required for Abbot scripting support

For our example, we'll assume that we have a simple `JPanel` that prompts the user for his or her user name and password. The panel also has Login and Cancel buttons, as well as an initially hidden error label, for showing any error messages during the login process. The label is also used for validation errors, for example, if the user did not specify a user name. Listing 5–42 shows an abbreviated version of the class (as abbreviated as Swing code can be!).

Listing 5–42 Example of a Swing component

```
public class UserLoginPanel extends JPanel {

    private JTextField userField = new JTextField(10);
    private JLabel errorLabel = new JLabel();
    private JButton loginButton = new JButton("Login");
    private JPasswordField passField = new JPasswordField(10);

    private class ConvertActionListener implements ActionListener {
        public void actionPerformed(ActionEvent event) {
            if(event.getSource() == loginButton) {
                if(userField.getText().trim().length() == 0) {
                    errorLabel.setText("Missing username");
                } else {
                    // do login stuff
                }
            }
        }
    }
}
```

```
public UserLoginPanel() {
  addComponents();
  setLayout(new GridLayout(3, 2));
}

private void addComponents() {
  JLabel userLabel = new JLabel("Username", LEFT);
  userLabel.setName("user_label");
  add(userLabel);

  userField.setName("user_input");
  add(userField);

  JLabel passLabel = new JLabel("Password", LEFT);
  add(passLabel);

  passField.setName("pass_input");
  add(passField);

  errorLabel.setName("error_label");
  add(errorLabel);
  loginButton.addActionListener(new ConvertActionListener());
  add(loginButton);
  }
}
```

Note that we're perfectly aware of the fact that this code, by any modern standard, would be considered awful Swing code. It doesn't use actions, it's not internationalized, it has very bare-bones validation support, and it uses a fairly horrific layout. Having said all that, none of it matters for our purpose, which is testing the component.

Usage

As usual, the first step is to take care of any initialization required. In Abbot's case, we need to create an instance of AbbotFixture. This class is responsible for providing containers for any components we'd like to test. It has a number of methods that allow us to test a variety of cases. Initially, it would be used to display a Window object. Once that's done, the fixture allows us to navigate the component and narrow in on a specific child component by name or type. The fixture class also internally manages the java.awt.Robot class and uses that to do all the heavy lifting.

The first thing we'd need is a helper method to wrap any component we'd like to test in a frame, so we can pass a Window to the fixture class to work with, as shown in Listing 5–43.

Listing 5–43 Helper method to create a component frame

```
public static Window createWindow(Component c) {
  JFrame frame = new JFrame("Test Frame");
  frame.setDefaultCloseOperation(JFrame.EXIT_ON_CLOSE);
  JPanel pane = (JPanel)frame.getContentPane();
  pane.setBorder(new EmptyBorder(10, 10, 10, 10));
  pane.add(c);
  return frame;
}
```

Listing 5–44 shows the rest of the setup code.

Listing 5–44 Abbot-based test skeleton

```
public class UserLoginPanelTest {
  private AbbotFixture fixture;

  @BeforeMethod
  public void initFixture() {
    fixture = new AbbotFixture();
    fixture.showWindow(createWindow(new UserLoginPanel()));
  }

  @AfterMethod
  public void destroyFixture() {
    fixture.cleanUp();
  }
}
```

For the purpose of our test, we'll also create a helper method that takes care of creating a ComponentTester for our component, as shown in Listing 5–45.

Listing 5–45 Creating an Abbot tester

```
private ComponentTester getTester() {
  Component panel = fixture.findByType(JPanel.class);
  return ComponentTester.getTester(panel);
}
```

`ComponentTester` is the main interface between our tests and the component under test. It allows us to easily simulate any user interaction with the application, including clicks, mouse actions, keyboard activity, interactions with application menus, and so on. The actual test appears in Listing 5–46.

Listing 5–46 Abbot-based Swing component test

```
@Test
public void emptyInputShowsError() {
  ComponentTester tester = tester();
  tester.actionKeyString("");
  Component button = fixture.findByType(JButton.class);
  tester.actionClick(button);
  JLabel label = fixture.findByName("error_label", JLabel.class);
  assert label.getText().equals("Missing username");
}
```

The test creates a `ComponentTester` for the panel, types in some text, then clicks the button. The second half of the test then verifies that the label is updated correctly with the right error message.

We can see here that, again, the environment setup and configuration we performed pays off when writing individual tests. Very little code is required, which lowers the barrier to testing and in turn encourages us to write more tests.

Tests for Painting Code

While testing the functionality of Swing components can be done via Abbot, which removes a lot of the pain involved in the process, that approach is not without its flaws. For one thing, it's not possible to run these tests in a headless environment, where there is no display facility.

Also, the framework takes over the display since the robot class manually moves the mouse cursor around to perform clicks and so on; thus, in many cases these tests cannot be run easily. Obviously, they also cannot be parallelized.

Abbot-based tests are, on the whole, functional tests. They focus on the interactions between components and also allow us to verify that they call our models and domain objects correctly.

On the other side of testing UI code is verifying painting behavior. This is particularly useful in cases where we have custom components and we'd like to see if it's possible to make any assertions about whether the painting code runs and modifies any pixels.

Let's examine a typical custom component first in order to determine the important methods that relate to our test. For this example, we'll assume we have a custom component that simply shows a faded-out icon. Listing 5–47 shows the relevant code for the component.

Listing 5–47 Example of graphics code

```
public class FadedIcon extends JComponent {
  private Icon icon;

  public FadedIcon(Icon icon) {
    this.icon = icon;
  }

  public Dimension getPreferredSize() {
    return new Dimension(icon.getIconWidth(),
                         icon.getIconHeight());
  }

  protected void paintComponent(Graphics g) {
    Graphics2D g2d = (Graphics2D)g;
    g2d.setComposite(AlphaComposite.getInstance(
            AlphaComposite.SRC_OVER, 0.2f));
    icon.paintIcon(this, g, 0, 0);
  }
}
```

This somewhat contrived example sets an alpha composite that specifies that all pixels to be drawn should have an alpha map applied. The end result is that the icon will show up with a faded look.

The tricky part now is testing this code. How do we do that? It's a bit tricky because there isn't really a good way to test it without eyeballing the results in an example class that uses it.

However, we could make use of some interesting approaches that allow us to at least make some assertions about the painting.

For example, we can check that *something* is painted, even if we can't quite verify what. The trick here is to use `java.awt.image.BufferedImage`. This allows us to use a graphics context in a headless environment, without popping up any GUI elements on the screen. A buffered image is essentially image data that is stored in memory and can be manipulated without requiring a screen representation.

All we have to do then is paint our component into this memory image representation. Once that's achieved, we can look through the image data and develop assertions to match what we'd like to verify.

Painting the component into a `BufferedImage` is fairly straightforward. We first create an instance of the memory image and paint it white, as shown in Listing 5–48. The reason we paint it white is to have a fixed starting point. Later, when we make assertions about what has been painted, we can check for white pixels to see if anything has been painted at all.

Listing 5–48 Creating a blank memory image to draw into

```
private BufferedImage createWhiteImage(int width, int height) {
  BufferedImage img =
    new BufferedImage(width, height,
                      BufferedImage.TYPE_INT_ARGB);
  Graphics g = img.createGraphics();
  g.setColor(Color.WHITE);
  g.fillRect(0, 0, width, height);
  return img;
}
```

Having created an image to paint into, the next step is to paint the component into this area, as shown in Listing 5–49.

Listing 5–49 Test to write the image data to memory

```
@Test
public void verifyIconPainting() {
  FadedIcon icon =
        new FadedIcon(new ImageIcon("images/icon.gif"));
```

```
    Dimension size = icon.getPreferredSize();
    BufferedImage img = createWhiteImage(size.width,
    size.height);
    icon.paintComponent(img.createGraphics());
    // check the image data for contents
}
```

We now have an in-memory representation of our faded icon component. All that remains is to see what sort of assertions we can make about it.

We have a number of options here, some of which are fairly simple and straightforward, and others of which are more complex and brittle but would give us more confidence about the image data that was painted.

The simplest assertion we could make is to verify that something was painted. Since we know that the baseline image is all white pixels, any nonwhite pixels we find must indicate that the component did draw something into the image. Listing 5–50 shows the verification method.

Listing 5–50 Assert to check that a nonwhite pixel exists

```
private void verifySomethingWasPainted(BufferedImage img) {
    int whiteRGB = Color.WHITE.getRGB();
    for(int x = 0; x < img.getWidth(); x++) {
        for(int y = 0; y < img.getHeight(); y++) {
            if(img.getRGB(x, y) != whiteRGB) return;
        }
    }
    assert false : "No modified pixels found";
}
```

We could get much fancier. For example, we could view the UI for our sample component, verify that it's exactly what we need, and save the image. Our assertions then would do a comparison of the saved image (which we know to be correct) and the generated one. This would be a useful regression test to ensure that any tweaks to the painting code (e.g., any optimization work) have no impact on the resulting image.

Another case where this approach would be useful is in ensuring platform fidelity. For example, if we were working on a component designed to mimic a native component to the pixel, having a saved native instance to compare against would be quite useful.

This approach is not without its pitfalls. For one, it's cumbersome to have to create the baseline images to compare to. Also, it's a fragile test as components do often change their painting code and visual appearance as they evolve. Even the most minor of painting tweaks would result in a test failure.

Continuous Integration

Continuous integration (CI) is the practice of integrating developer changes into the build as part of the regular development process. In practice, this means that the project relies on an automated build process that is triggered with some regularity; this could be on every developer check-in (usually followed by an idle period) or at a scheduled time (or times!) every day.

Why Bother?

There are several benefits to using a CI solution as part of the development process. One of the main ones is that it makes the process more predictable and ensures that teams are not drifting too far apart.

Traditionally, many large projects are split up into smaller chunks that separate teams work on. The idea is that as the ship date approaches, all these pieces can be easily jammed together to produce the final result.

In practice, this almost always results in nasty surprises, where different components don't get along very well with each other. The CI approach ensures that these surprises are found during development, not during a separate integration phase later when it might be too late to revisit design or architectural decisions.

The value of a CI solution increases with the number of tests the project has. Part of the CI tool's responsibility is to also run all tests in the project. This removes from individual developers the onus of running cumbersome and time-consuming functional or integration tests and ensures that even though these tests take too long to run during development, they're still being run on a daily (at least) basis.

CI Server Features

The landscape of CI servers has changed quite a bit since the early days of this concept. Initially there was just CruiseControl, a tool developed internally by a consulting company and then open sourced.

Since then, a number of far more usable, useful, and friendly products have shown up:

- *Luntbuild*: an open source solution
- *Anthill*: a very robust commercial solution based on plug-ins
- *Bamboo*: a product developed by Atlassian software, with very pleasant UI and some interesting historical data features
- *TeamCity*: a tool by the makers of the IDEA IDE, JetBrains
- *Continuum*: an open source solution developed by the maven team
- *Hudson*: an offering from Sun, probably the best of the open source solutions

We can expect several features as standard now from any CI server:

- *Email notifications*: Emails can alert the appropriate people about failed builds, successful ones, or status changes (e.g., from failed to success).
- *Build triggering*: In addition to running a build on a timed scheduled, it should also be possible to specify that a build should be triggered on commits. This is usually done after five minutes of no commits rather than instantly, to ensure that we don't build while someone is in the middle of different commits.
- *Project artifacts*: The build usually generates artifacts, and a CI server is expected to allow users to download these as nightly builds of the product, for example.
- *Build system integration*: CI servers usually support a number of build tools; at the very minimum, there is ant. Others also support maven, .NET projects, Makefiles, as well as regular build shell scripts.
- *Dependency management*: The more sophisticated servers allow for specifying dependencies between different projects and ensuring that they are built in the correct order.
- *Dashboard view and reporting*: The servers also usually provide a UI (varying in quality) for viewing the current build status. This often includes a list of projects, the current build status of every project, and drill-down links into specific projects, build logs, and artifacts.

TestNG Integration

In terms of integration with TestNG, usually nothing explicit is required by the CI server. Since TestNG can be invoked via ant, all the server has to do is invoke the ant build file. The target invoked should call the TestNG tasks to run all the project's tests. If any tests fail, the server will detect that because ant will return with a failure exit code, so the tool knows that the build did not succeed.

In order to expose the test results, the TestNG HTML output directory (`test-output` by default) should be specified as a project artifact. This allows for viewing the test results after a build is done.

Of the tools mentioned earlier, TeamCity (by JetBrains) and Hudson both natively support TestNG. These tools will detect that TestNG is being used to run the tests and so will know how to interpret the results and show them using the server's UI rather than having to rely on TestNG's HTML output. The build report will also show the test results inline as part of the general build information, as opposed to a separate artifact.

The way this works is that the build tool parses ant's `build.xml` file, and when it sees a TestNG invocation, it registers its own build listeners with TestNG and then receives callbacks when tests are run, as well as information about test results.

Ultimately, it doesn't matter which of the solutions we use, as long as we use one! Continuous integration is a crucial part of development; it is a valuable tool that ensures that the running of tests is not left to developer whimsy and that all tests are run often, with breakages being reported in a timely manner.

Using a CI tool also reduces the heartache of integration. It becomes part of the regular development cycle instead of an isolated task that's always underestimated and done at the very tail end of the project.

Finally, a word of warning: It's very tempting once a build breaks and starts spamming you with "broken build" emails to disable these notifications. Don't! Doing so greatly diminishes the value of having an automated build in the first place. The build is breaking for a good reason, and someone is trying to tell you that. Ignoring the complaints doesn't address them; you'd just be shooting the messenger instead of dealing with the root cause.

Conclusion

In this chapter, we examined several popular and different frameworks designed to work on top of or with JUnit and also discussed various testing approaches for common situations. It should be obvious by now that no matter how much the framework relies on JUnit, it is a fairly simple process to make it play nice with TestNG.

There are many different approaches to integrating all these third-party tools. In the worst-case scenario, as with Spring, we would have to define a set of parallel classes that use TestNG's annotations for test fixture setup and teardown.

In many other cases, however, we can simply fold in the superclass functionality into a helper class. A well-designed add-on will usually provide the base class as a matter of convenience rather than mandating it. The base class will usually call out to the framework itself. With TestNG, we'd simply bypass the superclass middleman and invoke the framework directly. Fortunately, many frameworks and add-ons are recognizing the need to redesign their APIs to allow for different testing frameworks, and newer versions will often be refactored to make integration with TestNG simpler.

Of course, many of the add-ons are only very loosely related to JUnit, such as HtmlUnit. In such cases, there is little to no work required in order to integrate with TestNG; the framework can be used out of the box.

CHAPTER 6

Extending TestNG

Now that we have discussed and explored many of the TestNG features, this chapter will focus on taking the next step and adding custom handling for various aspects of TestNG.

We recognize that there is no one-size-fits-all solution, and many aspects of TestNG are potentially interesting in terms of notifications, reports, and test behavior. One of the goals of TestNG is to enable large teams to define a common testing strategy and infrastructure. Since no two teams will have the exact same requirements or needs, it's vital that TestNG allows for as much customization as possible. This chapter will focus on some of the more common needs and how to best interact with the API to satisfy these needs.

The TestNG API

This section will explain how to use the TestNG API to create our own TestNG objects. This is particularly useful if we need to run TestNG inside a container (e.g., as a servlet or a Web application) or if the available invocation options do not fit the needs of the project.

With a few exceptions, the TestNG API is essentially made of interfaces in order to make it easy to mock the objects that get returned by TestNG.

`org.testng.TestNG, ITestResult, ITestListener, ITestNGMethod`

The `TestNG` class is the main entry point to TestNG. It lets us specify test classes, groups to include or exclude, XML files to run, and so on.

Listing 6–1 shows a simple example.

Listing 6–1 Running TestNG programmatically

```
public static void main(String[] argv) {
    TestNG tng = new TestNG();
    tng.setTestClasses(new Class[] { MyTest.class });
    TestListenerAdapter listener = new TestListenerAdapter();
    tng.addListener(listener);
    tng.run();

    log("PASSED:" + listener.getPassedTests().size());
}
```

We create a `TestNG` object, specify which test classes we want to run, add a listener, and invoke the `run()` method. The `TestListenerAdapter` class provides a simple implementation of the `ITestListener` interface. In this example, we're using another functionality of this class: It records all the tests that were passed, failed, and skipped in order to make it easy to access this information.

The `TestNG` class allows us to set anything that can be configured on the command line or in a `testng.xml` file, such as what directory to use for output, what groups to include or exclude, whether the test execution should run in parallel or sequential mode, how many threads to use, whether this run should be in JUnit mode, and so on. The Javadocs API is available in Appendix B.

As you can see, `TestListenerAdapter` can be useful on its own since it gives us convenient access to the lists of test results. If we decide to add functionality to this class while keeping these lists, it's important to remember to call the `super()` version of the method being overridden, as shown in Listing 6–2.

Listing 6–2 Calling `super()`

```
public class MyTestListener extends TestListenerAdapter {
    public void onTestSuccess(ITestResult result) {
        super.onTestSuccess(result);
        // do your own processing
    }
```

`TestListenerAdapter` stores the test results, as shown in Listing 6–3.

Listing 6–3 Accessing the test results

```
public List<ITestResult> getPassedTests()
public List<ITestResult> getFailedTests()
public List<ITestResult> getSkippedTests()
```

The `ITestResult` interface gives access to the status of a test, the test method, its parameters, and its start and end times (Listing 6–4).

Listing 6–4 Accessing the status of a test

```
public void onTestSuccess(ITestResult result) {
  long time =
    (result.getEndMillis() - result.getStartMillis());
  log("Success, method:" + result.getMethod()
      + " #parameters:" + result.getParameters().length
      + " time: " + time);
}
```

`ITestResult#getResult` returns an `ITestNGMethod`, which is TestNG's view of the test method. From this object, we can access the original `java.lang.reflect.Method` that the `TestNG` object is currently invoking, along with other TestNG-specific information, such as:

- Group/method information (the groups this method belongs to, the groups and methods it depends on)
- The number of invocations, the thread pool size, and the timeout
- If this method is a configuration method (`@Before`/`@After`), which kind it is

Listing 6–5 shows an example of this.

Listing 6–5 Other values accessible from the test result

```
ITestNGMethod method = result.getMethod();
log("  Method:" + method.getMethodName()
    + " invocationCount:" + method.getInvocationCount()
```

```
+ " #groups:" + method.getGroups().length
+ " timeOut:" + method.getTimeOut());
```

A Concrete Example

Let's illustrate some of these concepts with a test example from the TestNG code base itself.

In this test, we want to verify that the annotation transformer functionality is working as expected. We start by creating the following test class (Listing 6–6).

Listing 6–6 Simple test class

```
@Test(timeOut = 1000)
public class AnnotationTransformerClassSampleTest {
  public void one() {
    try {
      Thread.sleep(2000);
    }
    catch (InterruptedException e) {
      // ignore
    }
  }
}
```

If we run this class as is, it will obviously fail since the test method one() will be sleeping for two seconds, but the timeout specified at the class level is telling TestNG to interrupt all the test methods on this class if they haven't finished within one second.

In order to test annotation transformers, we are going to create a TestNG instance and install an annotation transformer that will override the class timeout to five seconds, therefore giving the test method enough time to complete. Finally, we will verify that the test results report one success (Listing 6–7).

Listing 6–7 Verifying the test result

```
public class MyTimeOutTransformer {
  implements IAnnotationTransformer {
```

```
public void transform(ITest annotation, Class testClass,
        Constructor testConstructor, Method testMethod)
{
  annotation.setTimeOut(5000); // 5 seconds
}
}

@Test
public void verifyAnnotationTransformerClass() {
  TestNG tng = new TestNG();
  tng.setVerbose(0);
  tng.setAnnotationTransformer(new MyTimeOutTransformer());
  tng.setTestClasses(new Class[] {
    AnnotationTransformerClassSampleTest.class});
  TestListenerAdapter tla = new TestListenerAdapter();
  tng.addListener(tla);

  tng.run();

  List<ITestResult> passed = tla.getPassedTests();
  Assert.assertEquals(passed.size(), 1);
  Assert.assertEquals("one",
    passed.get(0).getMethod().getMethodName());
}
```

The first class is the annotation transformer, which will override the timeout on all the test methods invoked during this run. In a case where the test includes more than one method, we might want to make the transformer more specific and ensure that it overrides only the annotations placed on the methods we are interested in, but since we are running only one test method in this example, this is not necessary.

The test method creates a TestNG object, removes all output, installs the annotation transformer, declares the test class, adds a listener, and then runs the test. Once we have the result, we make sure that our test method (and only that one) succeeded.

In order to be thorough, we should also verify our initial assumption (that this test will fail in the absence of an annotation transformer). Therefore, we can refactor our code and introduce the following utility method, which captures the logic common to both the positive and negative aspects of our test (Listing 6–8).

Listing 6–8 Introducing a utility method

```
private void runTest(IAnnotationTransformer transformer,
    String passedName, String failedName)
{
  TestNG tng = new TestNG();
  tng.setVerbose(0);
  if (transformer != null) {
    tng.setAnnotationTransformer(transformer);
  }
  tng.setTestClasses(new Class[] {
    AnnotationTransformerClassSampleTest.class});
  TestListenerAdapter tla = new TestListenerAdapter();
  tng.addListener(tla);

  tng.run();

  List<ITestResult> results =
    passedName != null ? tla.getPassedTests()
                       : tla.getFailedTests();
  String name = passedName != null ? passedName : failedName;

  Assert.assertEquals(results.size(), 1);
  Assert.assertEquals(name,
    results.get(0).getMethod().getMethodName());
}
```

This method receives an optional annotation transformer, the name of
the expected passed test method, and the name of the expected failed test
method. We install the annotation transformer if we received one, and once
the tests are run, we compare the results to what we expect: If `passedName`
is not null, we use `getPassedTests()`, and if `failedName` is not null, we
look in `getFailedTests()`.

We can now write the two tests shown in Listing 6–9.

Listing 6–9 Two simple tests

```
/**
 * Without an annotation transformer, we should have zero
 * passed tests and one failed test called "one".
 */
```

```
@Test
public void verifyAnnotationTransformerClass2() {
  runTest(null, null, "one");
}

/**
 * With an annotation transformer, we should have one passed
 * test called "one" and zero failed tests.
 */
@Test
public void verifyAnnotationTransformerClass() {
  runTest(new MyTimeOutTransformer(), "one", null);
}
```

The XML API

TestNG offers a simple interface that allows us to access and even create our own `testng.xml` file from scratch. The classes that handle the XML API are located in the `org.testng.xml` package, and each XML tag has a corresponding class (see Table 6–1).

The mapping between the XML file and the Java representation follows the JavaBeans convention: Each property can be accessed with a getter, and collections are stored as typed lists.

Listing 6–10 shows a sample `testng.xml` file.

Table 6–1 Tags and corresponding classes

Tag	Class name
`<suite>`	XmlSuite
`<test>`	XmlTest
`<package>`	XmlPackage
`<class>`	XmlClass
`<method-selector>`	XmlMethodSelector

Listing 6–10 Sample `testng.xml`

```
<suite name="TestNG JDK 1.5" verbose="1" thread-count="2">

  <parameter name="first-name" value="Cedric" />

  <test name="Regression1" >
    <groups>
      <run>
        <exclude name="excludeThisGroup" />
      </run>
    </groups>

    <classes>
      <class name="test.parameters.ParameterSample" />
      <class name="test.parameters.ParameterTest" />
    </classes>
  </test>
</suite>
```

The `XmlSuite` object will represent this file as shown in Table 6–2.

If we retrieve the first element of the `suite.getTests()` list, we get an `XmlTest` object with the values shown in Table 6–3.

Table 6–2 `XmlSuite` values

Method	Result
getName()	"TestNG JDK 1.5"
getVerbose()	true
getThreadCount()	2

getParameters()	Map<String, String> : {
	    "first-name" => "Cedric"
	}

getTests()	List<XmlTest>

Table 6–3 XmlTest values

Method	Result
getName()	"Regression1"
getIncludedGroups()	{}
getExcludedGroups()	List<String> : { "excludeThisGroup" }

getXmlClasses()	List<XmlClass> : {
	    "test.parameters.ParameterSample",
	    "test.parameters.ParameterTest"
	}

The XML API comes in particularly handy when it allows you to create synthetic XML files from scratch, which is what we discuss in the following section.

Synthetic XML Files

We can specify the path of a `testng.xml` file on a `TestNG` object as shown in Listing 6–11.

Listing 6–11 Specifying a path in `testng.xml`

```
TestNG tng = new TestNG();
tng.setTestSuites(Arrays.asList(new String[] {
  "testng.xml",
  "test-15/testng.xml"
}));
```

This can be useful when we need to generate these names programmatically, such as by finding them recursively in a directory or retrieving them from a Microsoft Excel spreadsheet or a database.

Consider the situation where the content of these files themselves should be dynamically generated. For example, there are hundreds of test classes called `Test1.class`, `Test2.class`, and so on, and their number is growing daily (this is particularly common when test classes are generated by automated tools). Another use case is when running TestNG inside a container or a Web application and referring to a physical XML file is problematic for various reasons (e.g., the application is clustered, there is no shared file system, the Web server doesn't have write access on the file system).

In such a case, we can create a synthetic XML file programmatically. As long as we create a valid `XmlSuite` object, TestNG doesn't care whether this object was created from parsing a real XML file or was just created programmatically.

Listing 6–12 shows how we can create an `XmlSuite` object that corresponds to the XML file shown previously.

Listing 6–12 Creating an `XmlSuite` object

```
XmlSuite suite = new XmlSuite();
suite.setName("TestNG JDK 1.5");
suite.setVerbose(1);
suite.setThreadCount(2);
Map<String, String> parameters = new HashMap<String, String>();
parameters.put("first-name", "Cedric");
suite.setParameters(parameters);

XmlTest test = new XmlTest(suite);
test.setName("Regression1");
test.setExcludedGroups(Arrays.asList(
 new String[] { "excludedGroup}"}));

XmlClass[] classes = new XmlClass[] {
  new XmlClass("test.parameters.ParameterSample"),
  new XmlClass("test.parameters.ParameterTest"),
};
test.setXmlClasses(Arrays.asList(classes));

// Now that we have a valid XmlSuite, we can pass it directly
// to TestNG
TestNG tng = new TestNG();
tng.setXmlSuites(Arrays.asList(new XmlSuite[] { suite }));
tng.run();
```

BeanShell

As the previous sections demonstrate, TestNG provides a lot of flexibility for determining which test to run. Depending on how the tests were designed, we can do the following:

- Include methods
- Exclude methods
- Include groups
- Exclude groups
- Any combination of these

However, in some situations, even this amount of flexibility is not enough.

- What if we want to run methods that belong to two groups? (The format of group inclusion in `testng.xml` supports only a union of the groups mentioned; if we include the groups `functional` and `fast`, methods that belong to either of these groups will be run.)
- What if we want to include and exclude methods programmatically, depending on certain conditions calculated in code?

In such cases, it is no longer enough to be able to specify inclusion and exclusion patterns: We need to run code to determine what methods or groups should be included or excluded in a run.

TestNG provides several solutions to solve this problem: BeanShell, annotation transformers, and method selectors. This section explains how TestNG leverages BeanShell to give you a way to implement your own runtime policies.

BeanShell Overview

BeanShell is an open source scripting language whose syntax is extremely close to Java's. It features a small and memory-efficient interpreter that can be easily embedded in Java applications. When inside a Java application, the interpreter can freely invoke Java code (and vice versa) as well as share state, making it very easy to extend Java code without requiring any compilation.

BeanShell not only parses any regular Java program but also offers a few extra features that make it easier to write short snippets of code, among which are the following.

- Variables do not necessarily need to have a type.
- Methods do not need to declare what type they return.

Listing 6–13 shows a few BeanShell snippets.

Listing 6–13 BeanShell examples

```
foo = "Foo";
four = (2 + 2)*2/2;
print( foo + " = " + four );   // print() is a BeanShell command

// Do a loop
for (i=0; i<5; i++)
    print(i);

// Pop up a frame with a button in it
button = new JButton( "My Button" );
frame = new JFrame( "My Frame" );
frame.getContentPane().add( button, "Center" );
frame.pack();
frame.setVisible(true);
```

Embedding an interpreter in applications makes it possible to:

- Evaluate full Java expressions at runtime, possibly input by users (particularly useful in applications that require user input, such as rule systems, financial/mathematical/numerical applications, and spreadsheets)
- Debug applications remotely, by making the entire Java runtime available for inspection by a remote application
- Script applications for easy testing, automation, or macro creation

As applications require more and more adaptability, we are seeing an increasing number of frameworks and products embedding scripting languages to give users and developers as much power as possible.

The need for embedding interpreters has sparked two initiatives.

- *Jakarta's Bean Scripting Framework (BSF)*: This framework contains a set of APIs to standardize the interface between scripting engines and their hosting environment.
- *Scripting Language Support for the JDK*: This work has been included in JDK 6.

For more details, please refer to the BeanShell Web site at http://beanshell.org.

TestNG and BeanShell

As mentioned earlier, TestNG uses BeanShell to give developers full control on what methods and groups get included during a run. In those cases where the default include and exclude functionalities are not sufficient, the developer can include a BeanShell script in the `testng.xml` file that decides programmatically whether a method should be included.

For example, let's assume that we want to run test methods depending on the day of the week: On weekdays, only methods that belong to the group `week` should be run, while methods in the group `weekend` should run on weekends.

We implement this logic in BeanShell, which we insert in our `testng.xml`, as shown in Listing 6–14.

Listing 6–14 BeanShell in `testng.xml`

```
<test name="Test2">
  <method-selectors>
    <method-selector>
      <script language="beanshell"><![CDATA[
        day = Calendar.getInstance().get(Calendar.DAY_OF_WEEK);
        group = day ==
          Calendar.SATURDAY || day == Calendar.SUNDAY
               ? "weekend" : "week";
        test = method.
          getAnnotation(org.testng.annotations.Test.class);
        if (test != null) {
          groups = ((org.testng.annotations.Test)
           test).groups();
          for (int i = 0; i < groups.length; i++) {
```

```
        if (groups[i].equals(group)) {
          return true;
        }
      }
    }
    return false;
    ]]>
    </script>
  </method-selector>
 </method-selectors>
</test>
```

The BeanShell script is included in tags called `<method-selectors>` and `<method-selector>`. We'll discuss method selectors in a later section, so let's just ignore them for now.

The BeanShell script is enclosed in a `<script>` tag, and since it uses characters that might be interpreted literally by the XML parser (such as <), we put it in a `CDATA` section.

The code itself is very much like Java, and it is fairly self-explanatory: Depending on the day of the week, we assign the value `week` or `weekend` to the variable group. After that, we retrieve the annotations found on the current test method, and if we find an `@Test` annotation, we look up the value of its `groups()` attribute. If any of them is equal to the group variable, we return `true`. Otherwise, we return `false`.

Here are some additional observations about the BeanShell-specific parts of this code.

- Variables do not need to be typed. You will notice that neither `groups` nor `test` have been declared or typed, but BeanShell doesn't mind as it will infer this type when it runs the code.

- The code specified in the `<script>` tag is expected to return a Boolean that tells TestNG whether or not the test method being considered should be included in the test run. We can either explicitly return that Boolean, as we did in Listing 6–14, or we can just make sure the last statement of the script is a Boolean expression.

You might have noticed that this code references a variable called `method` that is not declared anywhere. Before invoking your BeanShell code, TestNG automatically sets the values of a few predetermined variables (shown in Table 6–4) to make your job easier.

Table 6–4 Variables available in BeanShell

Variable name	Variable type	Role
method	java.lang.reflect.Method	The test method currently being considered. Returning true from your BeanShell code will cause this test method to be invoked, and it will not be run if you return false.
testngMethod	org.testng.ITestNGMethod	The corresponding method object with extra TestNG-specific information. This object allows you to find out more information about the test method under scrutiny, such as which groups it depends on.
groups	Map<String, String>	A map of the groups this method belongs to. This is a simple convenience variable to make it easier to manipulate groups. Each group is mapped to itself as a key/value pair.

Part of the code from Listing 6–14 can be rewritten by using the groups variable, as shown in Listing 6–15.

Listing 6–15 Running tests on weekends

```
day = Calendar.getInstance().get(Calendar.DAY_OF_WEEK);
group = day == Calendar.SATURDAY || day == Calendar.SUNDAY ?
  "weekend" : "week";
groups.containsKey(group);
```

Interactive Execution

The fact that we can get TestNG to invoke any BeanShell code written during the execution of the test provides a tremendous amount of flexibility. For example, how about adding some interactivity to our code run?

Let's assume that some of the test methods are part of a special group ask-developer, and we want to ask the developer interactively whether methods that belong to this group should be run.

In Listing 6–16, we add a bit of Swing in our BeanShell in order to ask the developer.

Listing 6–16 Combining BeanShell and Swing

```
boolean result = false;
if (groups.containsKey("ask-developer")) {
  result =
    0 == JOptionPane.showConfirmDialog(
      new JFrame(),
      "Run this method?\n" + method,
      "TestNG",
      JOptionPane.YES_NO_OPTION);
}
return result;
```

With this BeanShell script, TestNG will prompt with the dialog box shown in Figure 6–1 for each test method that belongs to the group `ask-developer`.

Note: As a rule of thumb, we should avoid making tests interactive since this will preclude them from running on a dedicated build machine or a continuous integration solution. This was just an example to show that it is easy to add custom running policies to TestNG.

BeanShell provides a simple way to implement our own inclusion and exclusion policies, but there might be times where the code that needs to be implemented for the runtime logic becomes quite complex. In such situations, BeanShell might not be the right approach for two reasons.

1. We don't want to have to include too much code in the `testng.xml` file.

2. The logic might need some of our own application code, which will not be accessible to BeanShell by default (we would have to add the

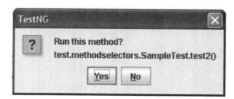

Figure 6–1 Output of the BeanShell and Swing example

relevant classes to the TestNG classpath, which introduces some fragility in the system).

When BeanShell is no longer practical, we can use another TestNG feature called method selectors, described in the next section.

Method Selectors

The previous section introduced an easy way to implement a custom policy to determine which methods get included in a test run with BeanShell. The BeanShell interpreter is actually a method selector implementation, which is a more generic mechanism that TestNG provides to achieve this goal. In this section, we'll examine in detail how we can implement our own method selector and when we should do so.

A method selector is a class that implements the interface shown in Listing 6–17.

Listing 6–17 The `IMethodSelector` interface

```
/**
 * This interface is used to augment or replace
 * TestNG's algorithm to decide whether a test method
 * should be included in a test run.
 */
public interface IMethodSelector extends Serializable {
  public boolean includeMethod(
    IMethodSelectorContext context,
    ITestNGMethod method, boolean isTestMethod);

  public void setTestMethods(List<ITestNGMethod> testMethods);
}
```

`includeMethod` is the main method that needs to be implemented. It needs to return `true` for test methods that should be included in this test run. Also, the Boolean parameter `isTestMethod` gives us a quick way to know whether this is an `@Test` or an `@After`/`@Before` method.

The parameter `context` is passed to all the method selectors in the chain and allows us to perform the following operations.

- Instruct TestNG to not call any method selector after the current one (by calling `setHalted(true)` on the context object).

- Share information with other method selectors by using the `Map` returned by `getUserData()`.

The method `setTestMethods` will be invoked before any test method is run, giving us a chance to store all the test methods that are considered for inclusion in this run. This might be useful if we need this information before making a decision about which methods should be included. Most of the time, we can leave the implementation of this method empty.

Once we have a class that implements this method, we need to tell TestNG about it by specifying it in our `testng.xml`, as shown in Listing 6–18.

Finally, this class needs to be associated with a priority number, which tells TestNG at which moment the method selector should be invoked with respect to the other possible selectors.

TestNG has a default method selector called `XmlMethodSelector`, which is responsible for implementing the deciding logic based on the content of `testng.xml`. This selector has a priority of 10, so if we want our selector to be invoked first, we need to use a priority between 0 and 9; we would use a priority greater than 10 if we want the `testng.xml` file to be considered first.

Finally, if we want our method selector to replace all the default ones, we would use a negative number for this priority. In this case, only selectors with a negative priority would be considered.

Note that method selectors are OR'd with each other: As soon as one of them returns `true` for a test method, that test method will be included in the run. If a selector returns `false`, the next one in order of increasing priority will be invoked (0 will be run before 10). If no selector returns `true`, the method does not get run.

Let's implement the BeanShell example with a method selector this time. The following selector will return `true` if the method under consideration is part of the group `weekend` and the current day is Saturday or Sunday, and it will also return `true` if the method is part of the group `week` and the current day is a weekday. Any method that doesn't meet these two criteria will not get run.

Listing 6–18 shows an example of a method selector implementing this logic.

Listing 6–18 Example of a method selector

```java
public class MethodSelector implements IMethodSelector {
  public boolean includeMethod(IMethodSelectorContext context,
                      ITestNGMethod method, boolean isTest)
  {
    int day = Calendar.getInstance().get(Calendar.DAY_OF_WEEK);
    String group =
      day == Calendar.SATURDAY || day == Calendar.SUNDAY ?
        "weekend" : "week";

    System.out.println(method.getMethodName());
    Method tm = method.getMethod();
    Annotation a = tm.getAnnotation(Test.class);
    if (a != null) {
      Test test = (Test) a;
      String[] groups = test.groups();
      for (String g : groups) {
        if (g.equals(group)) {
          System.out.println(": method selector returning true");
          return true;
        }
      }
    }
    System.out.println(": method selector returning false");
    return false;
  }

  public void setTestMethods(List<ITestNGMethod> methods) {
    // empty
  }
}
```

This code is slightly more complex than its BeanShell equivalent
because not only do we need to declare and type all the variables we use
(this is standard Java), but we also don't have the convenience methods that
the BeanShell integration gives us for free. Therefore, we need to look up
the groups() attribute of the @Test annotation manually and then see if the
correct group is listed there.

Listing 6–19 shows how to declare this class in our testng.xml.

Listing 6–19 Declaring a method selector in `testng.xml`

```
<suite name="Main suite" verbose="2" >
  <test name="Selector">
    <method-selectors>
      <method-selector>
        <selector-class name="org.testngbook.MethodSelector"
                        priority="2"/>
      </method-selector>
    </method-selectors>
    <classes>
      <class name="org.testngbook.A" />
    </classes>
  </test>
</suite>
```

And finally, when we run the code, we get the output shown in Listing 6–20.

Listing 6–20 Result of running with a method selector

```
weekend2: method selector returning false
weekend1: method selector returning false
week: method selector returning true
PASSED: weekend1
PASSED: weekend2
PASSED: week
```

Something went wrong: Even though our selector was invoked and correctly returned `false` for the two weekend test methods (we are running this on a weekday) and true for the week method, our three test methods ended up being run anyway.

This is because once our method selector was run, TestNG ran the default ones, including the one that parses the `testng.xml` file. Since this file doesn't contain any `<include>` or `<exclude>` tag, TestNG includes all the test methods that belong to the classes listed in this file, hence this result.

There are two ways to fix this problem.

First, we could call `setHalted(true)` in our selector, which will instruct TestNG to not run any other selectors. Since our selector has a priority of 2, it's being run before the default ones (at priority 10), and therefore we are guaranteed that TestNG will not run them.

Second, we can exclude all the groups in `testng.xml`, so that when the default selector gets run, it doesn't include any method. Listing 6–21 shows this approach.

Listing 6–21 Excluding all groups

```
<groups>
  <run>
    <exclude name=".*" />
  </run>
</groups>
```

Of course, this is a less efficient approach since the default selector will basically be invoked for every single test method, and it will return `false` for each of them.

Either of these approaches will produce the expected result, as shown in Listing 6–22.

Listing 6–22 Correct output

```
weekend2: method selector returning false
weekend1: method selector returning false
week: method selector returning true
PASSED: week


===============================================
    Main suite
    Tests run: 1, Failures: 0, Skips: 0
===============================================
```

BeanShell and method selectors serve the same purpose: to give us a way to override TestNG's default mechanism for inclusion and exclusion of groups and methods.

While BeanShell is convenient for simple scripts where the logic can be captured in a few lines, it will not scale well to more complex implementations. In these cases, we should write a class implementing the interface `IMethodSelector` and declare it in `testng.xml` with the appropriate priority. Keep in mind that TestNG has already installed at least one method selector itself (the one that parses the `testng.xml` file) with a positive priority, and that if we want to replace it completely, we should either use a negative priority for the method selector or exclude all groups and methods in the `testng.xml` file.

Annotation Transformers

Annotation transformers are classes that users can implement in order to completely override the annotations that TestNG sees at runtime. We will start by giving a quick history of annotations and then by taking a look at the pros and cons of the current annotation-based approach. Then we'll explain in detail how annotation transformers work by showing a few examples where they can be a very useful tool.

Annotation History

After JDK 1.4 came out, the increasing complexity at which the Java Enterprise Edition (Java EE, formerly known as J2EE) was growing started a new trend in software tools that developers turned to in order to make their work easier. One of the characteristics of Java EE's various specifications is that they heavily leverage XML in order to express constraints and configurations that couldn't be properly described in Java.

XML turned out to be a very powerful syntax to express complex and deeply hierarchical configuration files, but it also came with a few shortcomings that made Java development harder than it could have been. For example, the Java EE XML configuration files need to be tightly synchronized with the Java classes they extend, and as such, they find themselves having to invent a syntax that lets them pinpoint very specific Java elements (e.g., a method inside a class inside a package) in order to attach metadata to these elements.

For instance, Listing 6–23 shows a fragment of a deployment descriptor for EJBs that attaches a transaction attribute to the method `withdraw()`.

Listing 6–23 EJB deployment descriptor

```
<container-transaction>
   <method>
      <ejb-name>CartEJB</ejb-name>
      <method-name>withdraw</method-name>
   </method>
   <trans-attribute>Required</trans-attribute>
</container-transaction>
```

This format is very verbose, and it is also error prone in the sense that even the simplest refactoring (renaming the method or moving it to a different class) is guaranteed to break the application in very mysterious ways (the alteration of a transaction attribute might not show any hostile effects for a long time).

The increasing complexity and fragility of this approach resulted in the emergence of a new class of tools that tried to solve this particular problem. The idea was that any configuration element that needs to reference a Java symbol should ideally be placed as close as possible to this element in the source file, instead of being located in an XML file placed in some random directory on the file system. Two tools implementing this approach have become especially popular: XDoclet and EJBGen.

XDoclet is a generic engine that allows any Javadocs syntax to be implemented and retrieved at runtime, while EJBGen solves this problem only for Enterprise JavaBeans. Listing 6–24 shows the EJBGen equivalent to the XML fragment shown in Listing 6–23.

Listing 6–24 EJB example using EJBGen

```
abstract public class CartEJB implements EntityBean {
   /**
    * @ejbgen:remote-method transaction-attribute = Required
    */
   abstract public void withdraw());
```

Javadocs annotations were a big improvement over XML files in terms of readability because of one important characteristic: They put the relevant data next to the Java element that they annotate, making it very easy for programmers to make modifications and to know which annotations need to be updated whenever they modify their Java code.

Pros and Cons

Annotations were such a success that a JSR (175) was created shortly after the release of JDK 1.4 to make them part of the language for the next release. JSR 175 released a specification with JDK 5, and this feature is now known as annotations for Java.

Annotations are being widely embraced, and more and more Java frameworks use them every day. However, they are not perfect, having a few limitations of their own, among which are the following.

1. Any change requires recompiling source files, a problem that XML files didn't have.

2. Annotations are very static in the sense that very rigid definitions exist for the values they can take and how these values can be calculated (the values have to be Java constants). For example, it is not possible to set an integer attribute to the returned value of a Java method.

3. Although developers would like to be able to do so, they cannot override Java annotations at runtime.

Problem 1 is due to the very nature (and design goal) of annotations for Java. A solution to Problem 3 is still under consideration at the time of this writing, and a few frameworks have come up with solutions of their own until a standard approach is decided. Typically, the idea is to use annotations for as much configuration as possible and then use an XML file (but a much smaller one than if we didn't have annotations at all) to make runtime overrides.

TestNG offers a very convenient solution to problem 2, to which we will now turn our attention.

Using TestNG Annotation Transformers

As usual, let's start with a simple testing problem to solve.

Suppose that our continuous build machine is constantly running thousands of tests and that these tests spawn multiple threads and also exercise multithreaded code (therefore, there are multiple uses of the `timeOut` attribute). As the code grows, we notice that the load of this machine is slowly increasing, until we reach a point where it can no longer run the tests within the timeouts that were initially set. Now we start noticing sporadic failures (tests timing out randomly), which indicate that the tests rely too much on the load of our machine.

Of course, we could consider going through all our `@Test(timeOut = ...)` annotations and increasing the timeout value, but this approach has a few obvious flaws.

- It won't scale easily, and if we have hundreds of tests that use this attribute, it would take a while to adjust them all.
- What timeout value should we use? What if we upgrade the machine to a faster CPU one day—won't the value need to be decreased as well? And what happens one year from now, when the number of new tests is bringing the machine to a crawl again?
- In cases where the machine is not under heavy load, we'd like these timeouts to be considerably lowered so that failures don't take forever to be reported.

In short, it looks like our ideal solution would be a programmatic way to set the value of these timeouts, and that's exactly what annotation transformers do.

An annotation transformer is a class that the developer provides and that implements the interface shown in Listing 6–25.

Listing 6–25 The `IAnnotationTransformer` interface

```
public interface IAnnotationTransformer {
  public void transform(ITest annotation, Class testClass,
     Constructor testConstructor, Method testMethod);
}
```

The last three parameters tell us on which Java element the annotation was found: a class, a constructor, or a method. These three parameters are mutually exclusive. Only one of them will be non-null.

The first parameter is an abstract representation of the `@Test` annotation. Remember that TestNG supports both JDK 1.4 and JDK 5 annotation, and this representation is captured in the interface `org.testng.internal.annotations.ITest`. This interface is a simple JavaBean that contains getters and setters for each possible attribute of the `@Test` annotation.

Listing 6–26 shows a simplified and abridged version of this interface.

Listing 6–26 Abridged version of the `ITest` interface

```
/**
 * This interface encapsulates the @Test annotation.
 */
public interface ITest {
  /**
   * @return the maximum number of milliseconds this test
   * should take in milliseconds. If it hasn't returned
   * after this time, it will be marked as a failure.
   */
  public long getTimeOut();
  public void setTimeOut(long l);

  /**
   * @return the number of times this method should be invoked.
   */
  public int getInvocationCount();
  public void setInvocationCount(int l);

// ... more
```

When the annotation transformer is invoked, we have all the information we need to determine the content of the annotation and on which Java element it was found.

In order to solve our problem, all we need to do is implement the method `convertLoadToTimeOut()`, which will look at the current load of the computer and return an appropriate timeout value (the higher the load, the higher the timeout). Listing 6–27 shows our annotation transformer.

Listing 6–27 Changing the timeout in an annotation transformer

```
public class LoadTransformer implements IAnnotationTransformer
  {
  public void transform(ITest test, Class cls,
      Constructor constructor, Method method)
  {
    test.setTimeOut(convertLoadToTimeOut());
  }
}
```

Let's illustrate the entire process of implementing an annotation transformer with an example that has more visible results. The annotation transformer shown in Listing 6–28 will modify the number of times a test method is invoked depending on its name.

Listing 6–28 Changing the invocation count in an annotation transformer

```
public class InvocationTransformer
  implements IAnnotationTransformer
{
  public void transform(ITest test, Class cls,
      Constructor constructor, Method method)
  {
    if ("two".equals(method.getName())) {
      test.setInvocationCount(2);
    }
    else if ("three".equals(method.getName())) {
      test.setInvocationCount(3);
    }
  }
}
```

We'll run it on the test class shown in Listing 6–29.

Listing 6–29 Testing the annotation transformer

```
public class A {
  @Test
  public void one() {
    System.out.println("One");
  }

  @Test
  public void two() {
    System.out.println("Two");
  }

  @Test
  public void three() {
    System.out.println("Three");
  }
}
```

A simple run without specifying this transformer produces the result shown in Listing 6–30.

Listing 6–30 Output without the annotation transformer

```
Two
One
Three
```

In order to pass our annotation transformer to TestNG, we use the `-listener` parameter, either on the command line (we're using `-testclass` here, but we can also specify a `testng.xml`) or in `ant`. Listing 6–31 shows the first option.

Listing 6–31 Invoking TestNG with an annotation transformer from the command line

```
java org.testng.TestNG -listener ⏎
org.testngbook.InvocationTransformer -testclass ⏎
build/org/testngbook/A.class
```

Listing 6–32 shows the second option, using the TestNG `ant` task.

Listing 6–32 Invoking TestNG with an annotation transformer from `ant`

```
<project name="TestNG Book" default="all">

  <property name="build.jdk15.dir"
   value="/Users/cbeust/java/testng/testng-5.5beta-jdk15.jar" />

  <taskdef name="testng"
           classname="org.testng.TestNGAntTask"
           classpath="${build.jdk15.dir}"/>

  <target name="all">
    <testng classpath="${build.jdk15.dir};build"
         listener="org.testngbook.InvocationTransformer">
      <classfileset dir="build" includes="**/A.class" />
```

```
      </testng>
    </target>
</project>
```

In both cases, the output is now as shown in Listing 6–33.

Listing 6–33 Output of the annotation transformer

```
Two
Two
One
Three
Three
Three


=================================================
    Ant suite
    Tests run: 6, Failures: 0, Skips: 0
=================================================
```

Possible Uses of Annotation Transformers

Here are a few examples of when annotation transformers can be used to alter @Test attributes dynamically.

- timeOut: As we just saw, modifying the timeout for the test methods can come in handy if we can determine whether the running environment of the tests is subject to certain constraints (e.g., load, network traffic, running low on swap or memory, excess of running processes). We can also use this feature to determine with precision what the best timeout for the tests would be. There is no point in specifying a sixty-second timeout if most of the tests seem to finish in less than five seconds.
- enabled: Modifying the enabled flag on an @Test annotation lets us exclude or include a test method at runtime. TestNG already offers a variety of ways we can pick which test methods get run (include/ exclude, BeanShell), but if we need to have full control over this flag at runtime, using annotation transformers is probably the most flexible way to do so.

- `invocationCount`: This attribute is commonly used for load testing or in multithreaded environments, where we want several test methods to be invoked from different threads in order to determine whether the code under test is multithread safe, so it's also a good candidate for annotation transformers since we might want to adjust its value based on external factors. For example, we might want to query the application server being tested with JMX in order to get some information (such as the number of applications currently deployed or in activity) and then decide how many times the test method should run.

- `threadPoolSize`: This attribute can also be very environment dependent, but it depends more on the status of the machine the test is currently running on, as opposed to `invocationCount`, which can possibly impact a remote machine. An annotation transformer could query local information such as the number of processors, the amount of heap currently available, or the load of the computer before increasing or decreasing the default thread pool size.

- `successPercentage`: When used in conjunction with `invocationCount`, this attribute lets us allow for a certain percentage of test invocations to fail. It is possible, for example, to set it dynamically depending on the required reliability of the network (or whatever other transport is being tested). For example, while testing the sending of SMS messages, we could require the amount of successful messages to vary based on the provider being used. If we are testing a UDP connection, we could also vary this percentage depending on what network interface we are running the test on.

- `dataProvider/dataProviderClass`: Being able to change the name of the Data Provider at runtime is probably less interesting because the Data Providers themselves can perform dynamic decisions, sometimes even based on the test method they are about to feed data to. Still, annotation transformers can be convenient in this case as well since they can operate on the entire code base, therefore allowing us to make massive changes to Data Provider names with very little work.

- `description`: This attribute is used only in the HTML reports generated by TestNG, and again, they could benefit from runtime information as well, such as the host name on which the test was run and other information not included by default in the report. (The date and the thread identity are automatically included in the report.)

- `groups`: Modifying this attribute with annotation transformers is a bit delicate because it can complicate the logic of the tests quite a bit. However, we've seen users implement annotation transformers that dynamically altered group names based on environment variables, which make it easy for developers in various departments (e.g., QA, engineering, front end) to automatically run the right kind of groups without having to know too much about the testing infrastructure.

- `dependsOnGroups/dependsOnMethods/alwaysRun`: Since these attributes directly influence the order in which tests are run, you should avoid modifying them with annotation transformers and design the test infrastructure to make sure that the running order is defined statically. This will make it easier to understand and follow the logic of the tests whenever something doesn't work as expected.

Reports

Being able to browse the results of tests easily is an important aspect of testing, especially when we are trying to pinpoint why a particular test failed. TestNG creates a default set of reports that we will examine in this section. We will also review how we can leverage the Reporter API to add custom reports to the default ones and, finally, how we can write our own report plug-in.

Default Reports

Whenever TestNG is run, the reports are created by default in the directory `./test-output`. This directory can be modified via either the flag –d on the command line or `outputDir` in the `ant` task. This directory contains an `index.html` file that is the entry point to the reports.

In Listing 6–34, we are running two suites and then viewing the generated report.

Listing 6–34 Viewing the generated report

```
$ java org.testng.TestNG test/testng.xml test/testng-single.xml

$ open test-output/index.html [Mac OS]
    [or]
C:\> start test-output/index.html [Windows]
```

Test results

Suite	Passed	Failed	Skipped	testng.xml
Total	297	12	0	
TestNG JDK 1.5	292	12	0	Link
Single	5	0	0	Link

Figure 6–2 Report showing the suite results

Figure 6–2 shows the report created by this test run.

The top-level report gives us a list of all the suites that were just run, along with an individual and compound total for each passed, failed, and skipped test. We can also take a look at the `testng.xml` file used for each suite.

Clicking on the TestNG JDK 1.5 suite link brings up the main suite report (Figure 6–3).

The left pane shows a list of all the `<test>` tags found in this suite. Clicking on the Results link for a particular test brings up a detailed output, window similar to the one shown in the right pane of Figure 6–3 for the test called `AfterClassCalledAtEnd`. While the methods are shown only by name, we can see the fully qualified class names by hovering the mouse over them. Also, note that some of these methods have some text in bold. This text was inserted by the developer through the `org.testng.Reporter` API, which is discussed soon.

If we use `@DataProvider` or `@Parameters` in the tests, the reports will show an entry for each set of parameters that was passed to the test methods. Listing 6–35 shows an example of using `@DataProvider`.

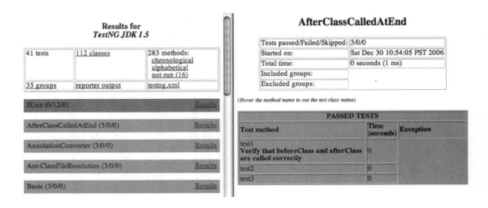

Figure 6–3 Main suite report

Listing 6–35 Using a Data Provider

```
@DataProvider(name = "dp1")
public Object[][] createData(Method m) {
  return new Object[][] {
    new Object[] { "Cedric" },
    new Object[] { "Alois" },
  };
}

@Test(dataProvider = "dp1")
public void test1(String s) {
}
```

Figure 6–4 shows the resulting report.

There can be more than one table in the result pane. If a few tests failed, the failed tests will be shown first with a red background, and if some tests were skipped, they will be shown second with a yellow background. Successful tests appear with a green background. (These colors are unfortunately shown as shades of grey in the book you're holding.) The idea behind this layout is that the information we are the most interested in will always be shown first (failures first, skips second, and successful tests last).

Also, failed tests will be reported with a stack trace that is initially presented abridged. Clicking on the link to show all stack frames (shown at the bottom of Figure 6–5) gives the entire stack trace. (Most of the time, these extra frames will not be relevant to the failure, which is why they are not shown in the first place.)

Figure 6–6 shows the portion of the reports that gives a summary of the previous test run.

This table appears in the upper left corner of the individual suite result and shows various aspects of the test run.

Figure 6–7 shows the groups used in the test run. This view shows all the groups that were found in this run along with all the methods that belong to them. Since groups are usually scattered throughout different test

| test1
Parameters: Cedric | 0 | |
| test1
Parameters: Alois | 0 | |

Figure 6–4 Parameters in the reports

Figure 6–5 Stack traces in the reports

Figure 6–6 Test summary table

Groups used for this test run

Group name	Methods
1.0	test.dependent.OrderMethodTest.z_first0()
1.1	test.dependent.OrderMethodTest.z_premiere1()
2.0	test.dependent.BaseOrderMethodTest.a_second0()
2.1	test.dependent.OrderMethodTest.a_second1()
3	test.dependent.BaseOrderMethodTest.third0()
A	test.configuration.ConfigurationGroups8SampleTest.testSomething() test.configuration.ConfigurationGroups8SampleTest.testSomethingMore() test.configuration.ConfigurationGroups7SampleTest.testSomethingMore() test.configuration.ConfigurationGroups7SampleTest.testSomething()
B	test.configuration.ConfigurationGroups8SampleTest.verify()
MyTest	test.factory.MyTest.testMethod()

Figure 6–7 Groups and the methods that belong to them

classes, it's not always easy to learn which groups contain which methods, so the alphabetical view shown in Figure 6–7 can be useful for finding this information.

Test Classes

The Test Classes view provides a TestNG view of the Java classes: what test methods were found on each class, along with the groups they belong to. Each class is categorized as an @Test, @BeforeClass, @BeforeTest, and so on.

The Reporter Output window shows a combined view of all the strings that were issued using the Reporter API. These strings are not limited to just one method but are presented as a whole, which might come in handy when we want to log information over several test or business methods (Figure 6–8).

This view shows all the methods that were run during this test, either in chronological or alphabetical order. The table also includes all the configuration methods, which show a clear view of the order of their invocation. Finally, we can also get a list of all the methods that were not run (either because they're part of a group that was not included or maybe because they were disabled). The color coding shows the methods that belong to the same class in the same color.

testng.xml

This is a similar link to the one we saw on the top-level page, and it shows the content of the testng.xml file that was used for this run.

Methods run, sorted chronologically

>> means before, << means after

TestNG JDK 1.5

(Hover the method name to see the test class name)

Time	Delta (ms)	Suite configuration	Test configuration	Class configuration	Groups configuration	Method configuration
06/12/30 12:27:30	0					
06/12/30 12:27:30	0					<<after
06/12/30 12:27:31	65					
06/12/30 12:27:31	65					
06/12/30 12:27:31	65					

Test method	Thread	Instances
test	main@12426614	
	main@12426614	
testMethod1	main@12426614	
testMethod3	main@12426614	
testMethod2	main@12426614	

Figure 6–8 Report showing the test methods

The Reporter API

We can add custom information to the default reports with the class org.testng.Reporter. The class shown in Listing 6–36 contains several static log() methods, which are all variations of the log() method with different parameters present.

Listing 6–36 log() method from the Reporter class

```
public static void log(String logMessage, int level,
                       boolean logToStandardOut)
```

Any string that we pass as logMessage will be shown in bold in the report under that method's name, as shown in the previous section. Also, if we pass true for logToStandardOut, that string will also be shown on the console. (And if we supply a verbosity level, that string will be output only if the verbosity of the current run is greater than that number.)

Test classes can also implement the interface org.testng.ITest, as shown in Listing 6–37.

Listing 6–37 Implementing the ITest interface

```
public interface ITest {
  public String getTestName();
}
```

Whenever TestNG displays the report for a specific test class instance, it will check whether that instance implements this interface, and if it does, the name of the test will be shown next to the instance hash code. This is particularly useful for distinguishing instances from the same class created with an @Factory.

The Report Plug-in API

If the default reports do not look good enough or contain enough information, TestNG provides a flexible API that makes if easy to write custom reporters. These reporters are not necessarily limited to generate HTML reports—they can also be used to report progress, store logs in a database, email the results automatically, and so on.

Two kinds of classes provide reporting abilities: listeners and reporters.

1. Listeners are notified in real time as the tests progress (e.g., when a configuration method is invoked, when a test passes or fails). They are well suited to report progress of a test run incrementally.
2. Reporters are invoked only once, at the end of a test run, and they receive the entire result information of the test run. Reporters are typically used to generate files based on these test runs.

TestNG itself uses these interfaces to achieve some of the tasks we have seen so far: generating the HTML files, displaying progress as the suites are run, generating the `testng-failed.xml` file that contains a subset of `testng.xml` to rerun just the failed tests, and so on.

Also, users have been writing plug-ins such as the following to meet their own needs:

■ A PDF report generator, which outputs a PDF file that can be printed and included in paper reports.
■ A JUnitReport plug-in, which generates a JUnitReport-compatible XML file that can then be given as is to JUnitReport for a similar result. JUnitReport is a JUnit plug-in that takes as a parameter an XML file that represents the result of the test files and creates a nice-looking HTML report.
■ A reporter that generates one big HTML file that's easy to email to coworkers (shown partially in Figure 6–9).

ITestListener

A test listener is a class that implements the `org.testng.ITestListener` interface (Listing 6–38).

Listing 6–38 `ITestListener` interface

```
public interface ITestListener {
  void onStart(ITestContext context);
  void onFinish(ITestContext context);
  void onTestStart(ITestResult result);
  void onTestSuccess(ITestResult result);
  void onTestFailure(ITestResult result);
  void onTestSkipped(ITestResult result);
}
```

Test	Methods Passed	Scenarios Passed	# skipped	# failed	Total Time	Included Groups	Excluded Groups
Regression2	46	55	0	0	1.7 seconds		
Triangle	3	3	0	0	0.0 seconds		
Skip	5	5	0	0	0.3 seconds		
Dependents	32	33	0	0	0.6 seconds		
DataProvider	15	26	0	0	0.0 seconds		
Parameters for constructors	1	1	0	0	0.0 seconds		
Regression1	20	20	0	0	1.0 seconds		excludeThisGroup
AfterClassCalledAtEnd	3	3	0	0	0.0 seconds		
Test class groups 1	3	3	0	0	0.0 seconds		
Inheritance	2	2	0	0	0.0 seconds		
Test outer scope	2	2	0	0	0.0 seconds	outer-group	
TimeOut	1	1	0	0	1.1 seconds		

Class	Method	# of Scenarios	Time (Msecs)
Regression2 — passed			
test.CommandLineTest	junitParsing (current)	1	80
	junitParsing2 (current)	1	81
test.MethodTest	excludeMethodsOnly (current)	1	56
	excludePackage	1	14
	includeMethodsOnly (current)	1	13
test.Test1	excludedGroups	1	43
	groupsOfGroupsSimple	1	30
	groupsOfGroupsWithCycle	1	32
	groupsOfGroupsWithIndirections	1	31
	includedGroups (current)	1	27

Figure 6–9 A custom HTML report made of only one file

The methods onStart() and onFinish() are invoked at the very beginning and end of the suite, respectively. The methods starting with onTest* are invoked each time a test method is run. We can inspect the ITestResult parameter to find out what method was run, whether it was passed parameters, and so on.

Listing 6–39 shows a listener that displays a period (.) for each passed test, an F for each failure, and an S for each skip.

Listing 6–39 Simple test listener

```
public class DotTestListener extends TestListenerAdapter {
  private int m_count = 0;

  @Override
  public void onTestFailure(ITestResult tr) {
    log("F");
  }
}
```

```
@Override
public void onTestSkipped(ITestResult tr) {
  log("S");
}

@Override
public void onTestSuccess(ITestResult tr) {
  log(".");
}

private void log(String string) {
  System.out.print(".");
  if (m_count++ % 40 == 0) {
    System.out.println("");
  }
}
}
}
```

Like all listeners used in TestNG, we pass this class to TestNG with the
—listener command line parameter (Listing 6–40).

Listing 6–40 Invoking TestNG with a test listener

```
java org.testng.TestNG —listener ↵
  com.example.DotTestListener testng.xml
```

Listing 6–41 shows the output.

Listing 6–41 Output of the test listener

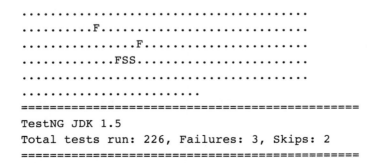

```
.........................................
..........F.............................
...............F........................
...............FSS......................
.........................................
.......................
=========================================
TestNG JDK 1.5
Total tests run: 226, Failures: 3, Skips: 2
=========================================
```

Note that this listener extends a class called `org.testng.⏎TestListenerAdapter`. This class implements `ITestListener` and provides empty bodies for all its methods, making it easy to just implement the methods that are needed for this specific report. `TestListenerAdapter` is part of the public TestNG API.

This listener doesn't do anything fancy with the parameters passed to its methods; it simply outputs the expected character and makes sure to wrap all its lines at 40 columns in the `log()` method.

IReporter

A reporter is a class that implements the interface `org.testng.IReporter` (Listing 6–42).

Listing 6–42 `IReporter` interface

```
public interface IReporter {
  void generateReport(List<XmlSuite> xmlSuites, ⏎
    List<ISuite> suites, String outputDirectory);
}
```

`XmlSuite` is a class that represents the `testng.xml` file and is documented in Appendix B. `ISuite` is a fairly comprehensive interface that provides access to the full information on the result of a suite. The indices of these two `List` commands correspond to the same XML file. For example, let's say that we invoke TestNG as shown in Listing 6–43.

Listing 6–43 Sample TestNG invocation

```
java org.testng.TestNG testng1.xml testng2.xml
```

Then `xmlSuites.get(0)` will represent `testng1.xml`, and `suites.get(0)` will correspond to the result of that suite. Index 1 will represent `testng2.xml` and its result.

Listing 6–44 shows a simple reporter that displays the number of passed and failed tests.

Listing 6–44 Sample reporter

```
public class MyReporter implements IReporter {
  public void generateReport(List<XmlSuite> xmlSuites,
      List<ISuite> suites,
      String output)
  {
    for (int i = 0; i< xmlSuites.size(); i++) {
      XmlSuite xmlSuite = xmlSuites.get(i);
      ISuite suite = suites.get(i);
      log("Suite:" + xmlSuite.getName());

      for (ISuiteResult result : suite.getResults().values()) {
        ITestContext tc = result.getTestContext();
        log("  Passed:" + tc.getPassedTests().size());
        log("  Failed:" + tc.getFailedTests().size());
      }
    }
  }

  private void log(String string) {
    System.out.println(string);
  }
}
```

Listing 6–45 shows the output.

Listing 6–45 Output of the sample reporter

```
=================================================
Main suite
Total tests run: 2, Failures: 0, Skips: 0
=================================================

Suite:Main suite
  Passed: 2
  Failed: 0
```

Notice that any custom listeners/reporters are added to the default ones that TestNG uses, which can sometimes create confusing output. The example shows that both the custom `MyReporter` and TestNG's text reporter provide outputs that are fairly similar. If we need to make sure that only custom listeners/reporters are run, we would use the –`useDefaultListeners` toggle (Listing 6–46).

Listing 6–46 Invoking TestNG without any default listener

```
java org.testng.TestNG —useDefaultListeners false testng.xml
```

In this section, we reviewed three important aspects of TestNG's reporting system:

- How to navigate and understand the information shown in the default HTML reports
- How to add custom traces to these HTML reports
- How to implement custom reports by using either `ITestListener` or `IReporter`, which allow us to act on the tests either as they are happening or once they have all run

Writing Custom Annotations

We conclude this chapter with an example that ties together all the concepts explained in the previous sections.

Consider the following situation. A test method exercises a part of the code that is currently broken. This is not an accident; this part of the code is currently being rewritten, and since the amount of work is significant, the functionalities it implements are expected to remain broken for several days, therefore breaking all the tests that exercise it for that period of time.

Undoubtedly, certain people will loudly proclaim that such a state of affairs is unacceptable, that tests should never stay broken for long periods of time, that making them pass should be the utmost priority at all times. But we all know better: In the real world, developers are constantly faced with important choices, and sometimes one of them is to choose whether to give precedence to fixing a bug, adding a feature, or pleasing a customer instead of fixing the tests.

Don't feel bad for having to break your tests once in a while, but do keep in mind that these tests need to be fixed eventually.

While it's acceptable to knowingly have broken tests in the code base, care should be taken to ensure that tests don't remain broken long enough for them to be ignored when they show in the daily reports—the more we get used to seeing failures in the daily tests runs, the more likely we are to miss an important failure. Therefore, we must be able to tell between a well-known failure and an unexpected failure.

TestNG helps us achieve this goal with groups. Whenever a test is expected to be broken, we can put it in a special group that is always excluded from all the runs, guaranteeing the following.

- Test runs continue to pass.
- We don't lose track of the test methods that are currently not run since they all belong to a specifically excluded group. Of course, we will need to make sure that by the time we ship or hit a milestone, all the broken tests have been fixed and that this `broken` group has become empty again, but in the meantime, it's acceptable to tolerate these failures while the code is being refactored.

While this approach helps, there is still a manual part to it that we'd like to get rid of: Someone needs to make sure that the group that contains all these broken methods eventually gets emptied. Concretely, this means that someone (probably the tech lead) needs to remember to make sure that this group is empty before the shipping date. If it's not, he or she will have to find out who's in charge of the respective test methods and ask them to fix every single method currently in that group.

An important aspect of good testing is automation, so we'd like to find a way to make sure that a disabled test doesn't stay disabled forever. A simple way to address this problem is to introduce a date that would let us specify for how long an `@Test` should be disabled.

This section will describe how you can create your own annotation, add it to TestNG, and then use TestNG's API to implement tests that guarantee that the new annotation works as expected.

Implementation

The first step is to define what we want in our annotation. For the sake of simplicity, we will use only one attribute, called `activeAfter`, which indicates after what date a certain test method should be enabled again. Of course, it's possible to introduce variations of this idea, such as specifying a duration instead of an absolute date ("ignore this test method for three days") or a date that indicates when a test method should no longer be run (probably more questionable; if we are going to stop using a test method, we should probably remove it from our code base instead of disabling it).

Listing 6–47 shows a possible implementation for our annotation, which is called `@ScheduledTest`.

Listing 6–47 `@ScheduledTest` annotation

```
import static java.lang.annotation.ElementType.CONSTRUCTOR;
import static java.lang.annotation.ElementType.METHOD;
import static java.lang.annotation.ElementType.TYPE;
import static java.lang.annotation.RetentionPolicy.RUNTIME;

import java.lang.annotation.Retention;
import java.lang.annotation.Target;

@Retention(RUNTIME)
@Target({METHOD, TYPE, CONSTRUCTOR})
public @interface ScheduledTest {
  /**
    * @return the date after which this test method should be
    * enabled again.  The format of the string must be
    * "yyyy-mm-dd hh:mm"
    */
  String activeAfter() default "";
}
```

If you are not familiar with how annotations are defined, refer to Appendix B. For now, here are a few observations about this code.

- We make extensive use of static imports, which improves the readability of our code by allowing us to use shorter names.
- We declare the annotation to be RUNTIME because we want it to be persisted in the class file, so we can use reflection to query the value of its attributes.
- Just like `@Test`, this annotation can be found on either a method, a class, or a constructor.
- The type of `activeAfter()` is `String`. Since annotations have to be either primitive objects or strings, we don't have much choice here if we want to specify a date. We need to explain in the Javadocs of our annotation what format is expected, and of course, we will have to

implement a parser that turns this string into a `Date` object, which will be easier to manipulate internally.

■ Only constants can be used for default values, so null is not an option. We use "" (the empty string) in this example, so our code will have to account for this special case.

The next step is to implement our method selector. This class will look up the test method currently under consideration and will see if it has an `@ScheduledTest` annotation. If it does, it will check to see if `activeAfter()` was specified (it is optional since it has a default value, so programmers can specify `@ScheduledTest` without any attribute if they so desire). If `activeAfter()` was specified, we retrieve its value, convert it to a `Date` object, compare it to the current date, and return `true` if the current time is after the `activeAfter()` date.

Listing 6–48 shows our method selector.

Listing 6–48 Method selector using the `@ScheduledTest` annotation

```
import org.testng.IMethodSelector;
import org.testng.ITestNGMethod;

public class ScheduledTestSelector implements IMethodSelector {

  /**
   * Create a Date representing the format passed in parameter.
   * @param format Must be formatted as "yyyy-mm-dd hh:mm"
   */
  private Date parse(String dateString) {
    SimpleDateFormat formatter =
      new SimpleDateFormat("yyyy-MM-dd HH:mm");
    return formatter.parse(dateString);
  }

  /**
   * @return true if either of the following conditions is true:
   * - method doesn't have an @ScheduledTest annotation
   * - method has an @ScheduledTest annotation whose activeAfter
   * attribute is equal to a date in the past.
   */
  public boolean includeMethod(IMethodSelectorContext context,
      ITestNGMethod method,
      boolean isTestMethod)
```

```
    {
      Method method = method.getMethod();
      Annotation annotation =
        method.getAnnotation(ScheduledTest.class);
      if (annotation != null) {
        Date now = Calendar.getInstance().getTime();
        ScheduledTest st = (ScheduledTest) annotation;
        Date activeAfter = null;
        String activeAfterString = st.activeAfter();
        if (activeAfterString != null &&
            ! "".equals(activeAfterString))
        {
          activeAfter = parse(activeAfterString);
          // Only include this method if now is after the
          // "activeAfter" date
          if (now.before(activeAfter)) {
            // We don't want that method
            return false;
          }
        }
        // else run if no date was specified
      }

      return true;
    }

    public void setTestMethods(List<ITestNGMethod> testMethods) {
      // empty
    }
  }
```

Finally, we take our new feature for a quick run. Listing 6–49 shows a sample class.

Listing 6–49 Test class for the `@ScheduledTest` annotation

```
public class QuickSelectedTest {
  @Test
  @ScheduledTest(activeAfter = "2006-01-30 11:10")
  public void shouldRun() {
}
```

Listing 6–50 shows our `testng.xml`.

Listing 6–50 Specifying the test class in `testng.xml`

```
<!DOCTYPE suite SYSTEM "http://testng.org/testng-1.0.dtd">

<suite name="Main suite"  >

  <test name="ScheduledTest">
    <method-selectors>
      <method-selector>
        <selector-class
          name="org.testngbook.ScheduledTestSelector"
          priority="15"/>
      </method-selector>
    </method-selectors>

    <classes>
      <class name="org.testngbook.QuickSelectedTest" />
    </classes>
  </test>

</suite>
```

The only thing left to explain is the priority we used: 15. This number guarantees that our method selector will be run after TestNG's default one (the one that parses the `testng.xml` file). We could specify a priority of 5, therefore making our selector run before TestNG's, but then we would have to make it call `setHalted(true)` after it has excluded a method. If we failed to do so, our selector would return `false`, and then TestNG would invoke the next selector, which would return `true` since all our methods also have the `@Test` annotation.

Since we are running this example in 2007, we verify that this test method is correctly invoked. Then we change the `activeAfter` value to the year 2008 (in the future), and we confirm that the test method is now excluded.

Everything seems to be working, but we're not quite done yet.

Testing

Since our code base is most likely going to rely on this new feature, it is very important to make sure it works as expected, so it has to be tested like everything else.

The first thing to do is to enumerate the possible use cases. It turns out that even such a simple feature has quite a few of them, listed here with their corresponding test classes:

- `@ScheduledTest` with no attribute (`ScheduledDefaultValue`)
- `@ScheduledTest` with `activeAfter` set to a date in the past (`ScheduledInThePast`)
- `@ScheduledTest` with `activeAfter` set to a date in the future (`ScheduledInTheFuture`)
- `@ScheduledTest` with `activeAfter` set to an invalid date (`ScheduledInvalidDate`)

These four classes are very simple, and we use a date far in the future to guarantee that it will be a while before they start failing (Listing 6–51).

Listing 6–51 Testing the four cases

```
public class ScheduledDefaultValue {
  @Test
  @ScheduledTest
  public void defaultValue() {}
}

public class ScheduledInThePast {
  @Test
  @ScheduledTest(activeAfter = "2004-01-01 08:00")
  public void inThePast() {}
}

public class ScheduledInTheFuture {
  @Test
  @ScheduledTest(activeAfter = "2010-01-01 08:00")
  public void inThefuture() {}
}

public class ScheduledInvalidDate {
  @Test
  @ScheduledTest(activeAfter = "2004")
  public void invalidDate() {}
}
```

Next, we implement our real test. Note that these four tests differ by only two parameters: the name of the class and the test methods expected to run. We can therefore centralize the testing logic in a helper method, as shown in Listing 6–52.

Listing 6–52 Running the test

```
private void runTest(Class testClass,
                     String[] expectedPassedTests) {
  TestNG tng = new TestNG();
  tng.setTestClasses(new Class[] { testClass });
  tng.addMethodSelector(
    "org.testngbook.ScheduledTestSelector", 15);
  TestListenerAdapter tla = new TestListenerAdapter();
  tng.addListener(tla);

  tng.run();

  List<ITestResult> passedTests = tla.getPassedTests();

  // Put the test names into a String[] so we can sort them
  // and compare them to the expected names
  String[] passedNames = new String[passedTests.size()];
  for (int i = 0; i < passedNames.length; i++) {
    passedNames[i] = passedTests.get(i).getName();
  }
  Arrays.sort(passedNames);
  Arrays.sort(expectedPassedTests);

  // Compare the tests that were run with those we expect
  Assert.assertEquals(passedTests.size(),
                      expectedPassedTests.length);
  for (int i = 0; i < passedTests.size(); i++) {
    Assert.assertEquals(passedNames[i],
  expectedPassedTests[i]);
  }
}
```

We start by creating a TestNG object and configuring it with our method selector and also the class that we received in parameter. Once we have run our test, we take the array of ITestResult from the test listener, convert it to an array of strings (in order to compare it with the expected array), and, just to make sure our code will keep working if several test methods are present on the class, we sort the two arrays. Then we compare them.

Finally, Listing 6–53 shows our four test methods, one per use case.

Listing 6–53 Full test case

```
@Test
public void inThePast() {
  runTest(ScheduledInThePast.class, new String[] { "inThePast"});
}

@Test
public void inTheFuture() {
  runTest(ScheduledInTheFuture.class, new String[] { });
}

@Test
public void withDefaultValue() {
  runTest(ScheduledDefaultValue.class,
    new String[] { "defaultValue" });
}

@Test(expectedExceptions = RuntimeException.class)
public void withInvalidValue() {
  runTest(ScheduledInvalidDate.class, new String[] { });
}
```

This code tests that the following things happen correctly.

- A test method that is active after a date in the past should be run.
- A method with an `activeAfter` set in the future should not run.
- A method with an `@ScheduledTest` without any attribute should run.
- A method with in invalid date should throw an exception, which we capture with the `expectedExceptions` attribute of `@Test`.

In this section, we used several concepts covered in the previous section in order to extend TestNG with a brand new annotation that introduces a time dimension to our tests. We used a method selector to achieve that goal, and once we were done, we thoroughly tested all the possible use cases by using the TestNG API.

Conclusion

While there is always hope that the framework will be complete enough to cover all our needs without having to extend TestNG, we obviously believe that there are countless testing scenarios, configurations, and goals. So it is important to make sure that users can take the framework in whatever direction they need, should they ever find themselves needing to do so.

This chapter gave an extensive coverage of the various ways in which you can extend TestNG. We explained how you can use BeanShell to extend the method selection mechanism and how annotation transformers allow you to introduce some dynamism to the discovery of annotations. We also showed how you can implement your own annotations and described how to write your own report generators.

CHAPTER 7

Digressions

This chapter contains all of our pet peeves, rants, annoyances, and musings that took place behind the scenes while writing this book. Much of it is only very tangentially relevant, some of it is outright irrelevant, and yes, some of it is even on topic and relevant.

This material landed here because it didn't fit in anywhere else, or because it wasn't appropriate in the main body of the book, or because it simply is personal opinion and should not be treated quite as authoritatively as the rest of the book. It's unlikely that you'll agree with all of it, just as it's equally unlikely that you'll disagree with all of it. Some things will resonate, some won't. Either way, we hope you find it an enjoyable ride, if somewhat bumpy and maybe even occasionally uncomfortable.

Motivation

If you are reading this book, chances are good that you are fairly familiar with JUnit, and whether you already knew TestNG or not, you probably wondered in what ways the two frameworks differ.

Chapter 1 gave you an idea of the problems that TestNG solves and that we believe are not addressed properly with JUnit today, and the rest of this book was dedicated to explaining the technical differences between these two testing frameworks. Now we'd like to emphasize a few key points that are more philosophical than technical in how TestNG and JUnit differ.

Essentially, TestNG addresses problems in a very practical manner, and it captures the realization that while JUnit made testing widely popular on the Java platform, it failed to bridge the last mile, that final step that makes the programmer's life not just easier but really *comfortable*.

For example, while JUnit has a lot of ways to report which tests failed and which ones passed, it doesn't actually provide any help in rerunning these failed tests and only these ones. In short, if we see a result like "999 PASSED, 1 FAILURE," we'd like to be able to tell JUnit, "I want to run my tests again, but only those that failed." This is just one of the many road-blocks we encountered in our testing activities that led to the creation of a testing framework that would not just automate the configuration and execution of Java tests but also make sure that developers need to do as little work as possible to reach their goals.

The TestNG Philosophy

As you read through this book, you hopefully realized that a lot of the features offered by TestNG derive from very concrete use cases and real-world scenarios. Not only do we believe that a testing framework should mimic the programming language we are using as closely as possible (e.g., by letting us share state using nonstatic fields or by passing parameters to our test methods), we actually believe that developers should be trusted to use these features responsibly.

TestNG gives you choices and doesn't attempt to impose certain views or principles on your programming style. We believe that if you know how to program with Java, you also know that a field modified in a test method will be seen with this new value in another testing method invoked later. In short, TestNG is designed to be extremely nonintrusive, and when designed properly, tests barely show any hint that the code you are writing is TestNG code. With a little practice, your code looks like simple Java, and your test classes look like simple POJOs: no forced inheritance, no forced named conventions, and with some practice, even TestNG annotations can become all but invisible.

In the rest of this chapter, we'll go over several topics, myths, misconceptions, and controversial ideas about testing, and we'll explain why, at the end of the day, you should trust your own judgment to make decisions and not one-liners taken from random books (not even this one!).

The Care and Feeding of Exceptions

It is perplexing how many frameworks and libraries get exception handling completely and utterly wrong. There are so many prevalent bad practices, so many misapplications, that these approaches are considered sane and should be emulated when writing software.

Before we delve into why this area is such a disaster, let's first take a brief detour into history. Once upon a time, there was the Java exception mechanism. Said mechanism allowed us to merrily toss up exceptions when things went wrong. In the same playground, we also had this idea of object-oriented code, whereby we split things up into different tiers, depending on what they do. So one tier calls down to the next, which is lower level, and so on. Each layer has a contract between it and the others above and below, and part of this contract is error handling.

Things go wrong all the time in various tiers. A tier encounters an unexpected error and has no idea how to handle it. So the tier merrily tosses it upward in the hope that the poor exception will eventually bump into someone who knows what to do.

In theory, this is great. In practice, it never quite works that way. A number of common, misguided patterns crop up. These are, in no particular order:

- Swallow and throw
- Log and rethrow
- Nest and throw

(We're excluding the obviously foolish "catch and do nothing" pattern because everyone agrees that that's a terrible idea.) We'll go over these patterns (or more accurately, antipatterns), and then go through some ideas on how exception handling should be done.

Listing 7–1 shows the first antipattern.

Listing 7–1 Exception handling antipattern: swallow and throw

```
try {
  callBackend();
} catch(SQLException ex) {
  throw new BackendException("Error in backend");
}
```

The problem with this approach is that we have now effectively lost any meaningful information we had about the actual error. When we do eventually get around to dealing with this exception, the information we have is that something went wrong in a tier, but we have no idea whether it's a problem within that tier itself or an issue at a lower level. Even if we did somehow know where the trouble originated, debugging would be largely a matter of flailing about helplessly and hoping we somehow stumble onto the answer. The lack of a sensible stack trace is all the more galling given that we do actually have a stack trace; it's just completely useless.

The second antipattern, shown in Listing 7–2, is the darling of a perplexing number of products and frameworks.

Listing 7–2 Exception handling antipattern: log and rethrow

```
try {
  callBackend();
} catch(SQLException ex) {
  log.error("Error calling backend", ex);
  throw ex;
}
```

If you've ever tried to use the JBoss Application Server, to name one example at random, you've probably spent a few days suffering at the hands of this antipattern.

So what's so evil here? The problem is something that often plagues stack traces: information hiding. Imagine an application with three or four layers, each of which logs every exception it handles, then shrugs and passes it on. How does the output look? For someone trying to debug the root cause, looking through eight pages of stack traces is not the most optimal approach. On the bright side, we know that somewhere in those eight pages are three lines that tell us the exact problem. We can't help but wonder why those three lines need to have four pages on either side of them, though.

The problem is made much worse when we consider the next antipattern. This one was the inspiration for this digression, in fact, since it resulted in an hour of effort wasted when trying to figure out why HtmlUnit was giving an internal Xerces error on parsing the simplest of pages. The main villain here is none other than the XML library, Apache Xerces. This pattern is illustrated in Listing 7–3.

Listing 7–3 Exception handling antipattern: nest and throw

```
try {
  callBackend();
} catch(SQLException ex) {
  throw new BackendException("Error in backend", ex);
}
```

In this case, we mix up both antipatterns and come up with something that sort of works. The problem, however, occurs when the developer forgets that some poor sap somewhere has to actually get at the information he or she is so kindly passing up.

Xerces, for example, wraps any unexpected errors in `XNIException`. The problem is that by the time this stack trace is shown, there is no hint of what the underlying cause is. You'd have to programmatically write a helper method to cajole the actual underlying exception from the outermost wrapped one. This process is made a lot more fun by the fact that you can't just unwrap one layer of exceptions—it's a veritable onion of errors that has to be carefully peeled until we finally find something of value.

This is less of an issue if developers use JDK 1.4 wrapped exceptions, which wisely print out root causes. Unfortunately, many frameworks that need to run in a JDK 1.3 environment (such as Xerces) completely botch that aspect of wrapping exceptions and do not override the stack trace printing method to at least hint at the underlying cause.

All is not lost, however; we have two solutions at our disposal.

1. Avoid checked exceptions. Runtime exceptions are perfectly useful for this sort of thing. Declaring them in the method signature as well as documenting in the Javadocs ensures that the caller can decide whether to handle the exception or let it bubble up. If the caller chooses the latter, there's no longer a need to explicitly catch the exception, so it's one less place botch it up.

2. Wrap exceptions. Wrapping exceptions is fine if you are absolutely sure that by the time a stack trace is printed, the underlying cause is shown. This is important since by the time such an exception is thrown, it's too late to plug in custom code to decipher it, and all you'll have to go by is a log file.

As with all rules of thumb, there are exceptions (no pun intended!). For the first solution above, for example, there are cases where checked exceptions are indeed useful. When making the decision, ask this question: "Can the caller do something about the exception?" In this case, doing something involves a nongeneric handling, such as deciding to retry, presenting the user with options on how to proceed, or trying an alternative call when this exception is raised.

We cannot provide a strict guideline on which solution to choose because the decision does depend on the application more than anything else. For example, in some cases, a generic data access exception from the database is nothing that can be handled on a component-by-component basis, and it's best to let it bubble up. In other cases, a certain foreign key constraint violation is something that can be handled by, for example, the user electing to do something differently.

Stateful Tests

As you may remember, Chapter 1 opened with a listing that illustrates sharing state among test methods.

If you have been in touch with the testing community, you are probably aware that sharing state across tests has been widely vilified and stamped as a terrible practice that should be avoided at all costs. Indeed, the fact that JUnit reinstantiates your class before every invocation is a stark reminder of how seriously a lot of testers take this issue. It's not just that you shouldn't share state—they just don't want you to, and they will go to great lengths to enforce this principle.

In fact, a measure of hypocrisy is involved. The same people who will scorn any hint of state in tests are likely to cunningly turn off JUnit's one-JVM-per-test behavior when invoking it through ant, in the name of faster tests. However, doing so just pushes the state further down into the JVM level, where statics will retain state across invocations. Of course, if one were to be purist about it, it's possible to go insane with state obsession and demand that every test be run in its own VM imaged environment (where the whole operating system is booted up once per test!).

But here is the simple truth: Sharing state among tests not only is an acceptable practice but also can lead to faster and better-designed tests.

The problem with the discussions about state is that a lot of developers fail to categorize which state they are talking about. There are two very distinct categories of state, which alter radically the problem at hand:

- Immutable state
- Mutable state

Let's go through these in order.

Immutable State

Immutable state is typically stored in fields that can be declared final (they get assigned once and only once), and while you actually don't need to declare that field final, it's a good practice to attempt to do so since it will allow the compiler to keep you honest by showing you a compile-time error if you attempt to alter the state of that field inside your class after it has been set.

You don't have to initialize your immutable state at the declaration level—you can perform this initialization inside the constructor or even inside a TestNG configuration method (e.g., `@BeforeClass`). Again, the only important thing is that this initialization must be performed only once.

Immutable state has a lot of great properties that are useful for testing (e.g., code that accesses immutable state exclusively is automatically multi-thread safe). But for testing, the one lesson you need to remember is the following:

Test methods that access shared immutable state are independent of each other.

This should be fairly obvious, but it's surprising how many advocates of the idea that state should be completely reset between test invocations tend to forget this simple idea. Since none of these methods can modify the state they are reading, they can be invoked in any order, and therefore they are not violating the principle that test methods should be independent of each other.

We've shown various examples of shared immutable state earlier in the book, but just to refresh your memory, a good example can be any object that is expensive to create (or destroy), such as the DOM version of a big XML file, a JDBC driver (the lookup of the class and its subsequent initialization can be costly), a database table being fetched into memory, and so on.

Mutable State

Mutable state is a little bit trickier to handle, and again, we've found that the debate is often clouded by emotions more than rational thought.

Listing 7–4 revisits the example we used in Chapter 1.

Listing 7–4 Test with mutable state

```
public class MyTest extends TestCase {
  private int count = 0;

  public void test1() {
    count++;
    assertEquals(1, count);
  }
}
```

```
public void test2() {
  count++;
  assertEquals(1, count);
  }
}
```

This test case is a good example of shared mutable state. The state is shared because both test methods reference the field count, and the state is mutable because it is modified by at least one of these methods (in this example, both).

As pointed out in Chapter 1, JUnit will pass this test, but TestNG won't. Does this mean that TestNG is wrong?

Well, not exactly because, to be honest, this piece of code doesn't make sense.

Look at it from a simple Java perspective: Can you really predict the value of a field after incrementing it if you don't know what value you started with? Of course not. And do you know in which order the test methods are going to be invoked? Again, no. (This is a behavior that both TestNG and JUnit share: Simple test methods can be invoked in any order.)

This observation brings us to an important fact:

Sharing mutable state makes sense only if you know the order in which the test methods are invoked.

In turn, this leads us to another important difference between TestNG and JUnit: TestNG gives you the option to specify in which order your tests will be executed. By default, the order of execution of test methods in TestNG is nondeterministic (as is the case with JUnit), but if you use the special annotations `dependsOnMethods` or `dependsOnGroups`, you can fully specify this order. Having covered dependency testing, we can safely challenge the following claim:

You should never share state among your test methods. (Wrong!)

Table 7–1 explains when it's safe to share data.

Next time you hear people say that state should never be shared among tests, make sure to ask them to clarify which kind of state they are referring to, and once they do, point them to this table.

Table 7–1 Sharing data safely

Type of shared data	Status
Immutable state	Safe
Mutable state with dependencies fully specified	Safe
Mutable state with no dependencies specified	Unsafe

The Pitfalls of Test-Driven Development

We basically have two objections to Test-Driven Development (TDD).

1. It promotes microdesign over macrodesign.
2. It's hard to apply in practice.

Let's go over these points one by one.

TDD Promotes Microdesign over Macrodesign

Imagine that you ask a famous builder and architect to construct a sky-scraper. After a month, that person comes back to you and says, "The first floor is done. It looks gorgeous; all the apartments are in perfect, livable condition. The bathrooms have marble floors and beautiful mirrors, the hallways are carpeted and decorated with the best art."

"However," the builder adds, "I just realized that the walls I built won't be able to support a second floor, so I need to take everything down and rebuild with stronger walls. Once I'm done, I guarantee that the first two floors will look great."

In a sense, this is what some premises of Test-Driven Development encourage, especially aggravated by the mantra "Do the simplest thing that could possibly work," which we often hear from Extreme Programming proponents. It's a nice thought but one that tends to lead to very myopic designs and, worst of all, to a lot of churn as you constantly revisit and refactor the choices you made initially so they can encompass the next milestone that you purposefully ignored because you were too busy applying another widespread principle known as "You aren't going to need it" (YAGNI).

Basically, we are afraid that focusing exclusively on Test-Driven Development will make programmers disregard the practice of large- or medium-scale design, just because it is no longer "the simplest thing that could possibly work." We claim that sometimes it does pay off to start including provisions in your code for future work and extensions, such as empty or lightweight classes, listeners, hooks, or factories, even though at the moment you are, for example, using only one implementation of a certain interface.

Another factor to take into consideration is whether the code you are writing is for a closed application (a client or a Web application) or a library (to be used by developers or included in a framework). Obviously, developers of the latter type of software have a much higher incentive to empower their users as much as possible, or their library will probably never gain any acceptance because it doesn't give users enough extensibility. Test-Driven Development might be a better match for developers of the first kind.

We all know that software is a very iterative process, and throwing away entire portions of code is not only common but encouraged (as long as you have tests to validate your redesign, of course). With that in mind, and with the full knowledge that your first version will most likely be rewritten completely, why bother writing tests for it? Isn't it a waste of time? Why not wait until you've come to at least a second internal version, when you will have a much better idea of what you need, to actually write tests?

At any rate, test-driven developers and pragmatist testers are trying to achieve the same goal: Write the best tests possible. Ideally, whenever you write tests, you want to make sure that these tests will remain valid no matter how the code underneath changes. Identifying such tests is difficult, though, and the ability to do so probably comes only with experience, so consider this a warning against testing silver bullets.

Yes, Test-Driven Development can lead to more robust software, but it can also lead to needless churn and a tendency to over-refactor that can negatively impact your software, your design, and your deadlines. Use it wisely, not unconditionally.

TDD Is Hard to Apply

We noticed a worrisome trend in the Test-Driven Development reading material that we have seen over the years. A lot of it focuses on very simple, textbook problems such as:

- A scorecard for bowling
- A simple container (`Stack` or `List`)

- A `Money` class
- A templating system

There is no question in our minds that Test-Driven Development works wonders on these examples, and the articles describing this practice usually do a good job of showing why and how.

What these articles don't do, though, is help programmers dealing with very complex code bases perform Test-Driven Development. In the real world, programmers deal with code bases comprised of millions of lines of code. They also have to work with source code that not only was never designed to be tested in the first place but also interacts with legacy systems (often not written in Java), user interfaces, graphics, or code that outputs on all kinds of hardware devices, processes running under very stringent real time, memory, network or performance constraints, faulty hardware, and so on.

Notice that none of the examples from the TDD reading materials falls in any of this category, and because we have yet to see a concrete illustration of how to use Test-Driven Development to test a back-end system interacting with a 20-year-old mainframe validating credit card transactions, we certainly share the perplexity of developers who like the idea of Test-Driven Development but can't find any reasonable way to apply it to their day jobs.

TestNG itself is a very good candidate for Test-Driven Development: It doesn't have any graphics, it provides a rich programmatic API that makes it easy to probe in various ways, and its output is highly deterministic and very easy to query. On top of that, it's an open source project that is not subject to any deadlines except for the whims of its developers.

Yet, for all its qualities, only about 10% to 15% of the tests validating TestNG have been written in a TDD fashion. This certainly got us to pause and reflect.

This low percentage is not due to an underappreciation of the TDD practice. Every new feature implemented and tested with TDD was certainly met with the satisfied feeling that developers have when they know they delivered solid, quality code.

It's just that code written with TDD was not necessarily of higher quality than if it was delivered "tests last." It was also not clear at all that code produced with TDD ended up being better designed.

No matter what Test-Driven Developers keep saying, code produced this way is not intrinsically better than traditionally tested code. And looking back, it actually was a little harder to produce, if only because of dealing with code that didn't compile and tests that didn't pass for quite a while.

In summary, Test-Driven Development left us with mixed feelings and conflicting signals.

Extracting the Good from Test-Driven Development

Now that we've stated our skepticism, we have to say that not all is bad about Test-Driven Development, and we'd like to close this section with a few constructive thoughts.

First of all, the goal of any testing practice is to produce tests. Even though we are firmly convinced that code produced with TDD is not necessarily better than code produced the traditional way, it is still much better than code produced without any tests. And this is the number one lesson we'd like everybody to keep in mind: It doesn't matter *how* you create your tests as long as you do create them.

Another good quality of Test-Driven Development is that it forces you to think of the exit criteria that your code has to meet before you even start coding. We certainly applaud this focus on concrete results, and we encourage any professional developer to do the same. We simply argue that there are other ways to phrase these criteria than writing tests first, and sometimes even a simple text file with a list of goals is a very decent way to get started. Just make sure that, by the time you are done with an initial version, you have written tests for every single item on your list.

Testing Private Methods

We actually agree with the rule of thumb that testing private methods is wrong, but we would also like to point out a few notable exceptions to its application.

Let's remember one of the guiding principles of effective testing: If it can break, you should test it. The fact that a method is private should certainly not make it exempt to thorough testing, but a private method is also not very easy to access by code outside the class it belongs to, by definition, so we are confronted with a difficult problem.

The usual response from people who claim that private methods should not be tested goes as follows. Your private method is being used by some protected or public code (otherwise, it's useless and should therefore be deleted). In order to test your private method, you should test your protected or public method, but not the private method directly.

The idea behind this approach is that since we can't test the private method directly, we are going to test it indirectly through a more public interface.

First, it is actually possible to test private methods, as we will show soon.

Second, the flaw in this reasoning is that it subtly implies that unit testing is optional since functional testing will exercise the underlying methods just the same. If we go down that route, why bother with unit testing at all?

Consider the following example. A feature of your application is to display a sorted list of items in an HTML page. One day, a user reports that the list shown in the Web browser is not sorted. When you learn about this bug report, you immediately think that the bug is most likely in one of the following two places:

1. In the sorting code (which is private)
2. In the code that generated the HTML

Intuitively, you probably already see that these two sections of code belong to different abstraction layers. The traditional way to leverage this distinction is to realize that the sorting code can easily be tested in isolation from the rest of the application (and it would therefore qualify as a unit test), while the display logic requires more components to interact with each other before it can be run and would therefore be categorized as a functional test.

At the end of the day, the only thing that matters to your customer is that the browser display the correct list, so you might be tempted to think that you need only functional tests. In a way, this is correct, and as long as your functional tests cover the entirety of the requirements from your users, you can safely assume that your code delivers exactly what's expected.

The problem is that foregoing unit tests (sometimes including the choice of not testing private methods) will make your life as a programmer more difficult. Ideally, you want to have not only tests that guarantee that the application works as advertised but also tests that are fine-grained enough, so that if ever they fail, the failure report will give an instantaneous idea of where the problem is. We'll come back to this important idea shortly, in the section about encapsulation.

In the meantime, let's get back to the original question: How do we test private methods?

The preferred way to address this question is to make your method more visible, for example, to make it protected or package protected. The latter is a little better since it lets you put your tests in the same package as the class you are testing (which is perfectly acceptable), and from there, you have full access to all its fields.

If neither of these approaches are an option, the way we test a private method is by using reflection.

Consider the class shown in Listing 7–5.

Listing 7–5 Example of a private method

```
public class LoginController {
  private String userName;

  private void init() {
    System.out.println("Initializing");
    this.userName = getUserNameFromCookie();
  }
}
```

In order to test this private method, we need to make sure that it initializes the userName field to some value. Listing 7–6 shows a test for this method. Another thing to note in Listing 7–6 is the invocation of setAccessible() on the Method object, which instructs the JVM to bypass a security check that would otherwise cause this call to fail (because the method is private).

Listing 7–6 Test for private method

```
@Test
public void verifyInit()
  // throws clause omitted
{
  LoginController lc = new LoginController();

  // Verify that the field is null
  Field f = lc.getClass().getField("userName");
  Object valueBefore = f.get(lc);
  Assert.assertNull(valueBefore);

  // Invoke the method
  Method m = lc.getClass().getDeclaredMethod("init", null);
  m.setAccessible(true);
  m.invoke(lc);

  // Verify that the field is no longer null
  Object valueAfter = f.get(lc);
  Assert.assertNotNull(valueAfter);
}
}
```

We'd like to emphasize one last time the dangers of this approach, which this code should make clear. Here are two red flags we see in the code.

1. We are using strings to describe Java elements (the field name and the method name). This is a dangerous practice that is guaranteed to break if you ever rename either of these elements.

2. We are leveraging a dangerously intimate knowledge of the class. Not only are we assuming the existence of specific private methods and fields, we are also implying that this method will modify a field in a certain way. When doing this kind of manipulation, you are breaking a fundamental trust in a programmer's mind, which is that private fields and methods can usually be very easily refactored without much impact on the outside world.

In summary, whenever you are tempted to test a private code, consider making it package protected first, and if this is not an option, then use code like that just shown to access the private method and invoke it via reflection.

Testing versus Encapsulation

The previous section on testing private methods should have given you a hint where we stand on that matter, but let's make this point very clear: Don't be afraid to break encapsulation if it makes your code more testable. Testability should trump encapsulation.

Increasing the surface covered by tests is a very concrete benefit that will contribute to making code more robust. However, the quality that we lose by loosening the visibility of certain elements is harder to quantify and probably not worth worrying about in the long run. We should also probably remember that this decision is not necessarily so clear-cut in the case of an API or a library, where exposing members carries a heavier price in maintenance and documentation.

Of course, there are limits to the amount that you should open your classes and methods, and while we don't advocate making all your methods public, the following actions are acceptable as long as you use them with caution.

- Making a private method (or a field) `package protected`, `protected`, or `public`. We list these scopes in order of decreasing preferences.

Package protected (meaning that we don't put any qualifier before the return type of the method) is our preferred way to handle this situation because it doesn't loosen up the scope visibility of the method by much while still giving the test code full access to the classes under test.

- Removing `final` from a method (or a class). This gives test classes the option to extend these classes or override these methods to mock them or slightly change their implementation in order to make the rest of the system more testable.

Remember: Most of the time, testability trumps encapsulation.

The Power of Debuggers

Surely you've heard one of these before: "If you write tests, you no longer need to debug," or "Stop debugging, start testing."

This outrageous claim has been used extensively to encourage developers to test their code more often. While we sympathize with the intent, we can't condone this attitude because it is extremely specious and actually quite harmful to the practice of software engineering in general.

The reasoning used by proponents of this myth goes along these lines. Whenever you are debugging code (setting breakpoints, inspecting variables, and so on), you are creating a one-time-only test case that will be lost once you are done. On the other hand, if you capture this activity in a test, not only does it get saved on your hard drive but developers other than yourself can reuse it as well.

This is actually a very good argument in favor of writing tests, but positioning this activity as being mutually exclusive with the act of debugging is extremely misleading.

Let's start by making the following point clear: We love debuggers, and we believe that if you are not using one, purposely or out of habit, you are not as productive as you could be.

You will find quantities of developers who basically think that they are too good for debuggers. They believe that the code they write is bug-free, but whenever a few bugs creep in, they think that sprinkling a few `System.out.println` statements here and there is always good enough to find and fix their bugs. These developers are missing out on an extremely powerful tool that, if used in a careful and timely way, can save countless hours of bug chasing.

We use debuggers all the time—we even use them when we're not chasing for bugs. When writing a new piece of code, it's often useful to set up breakpoints in various places in the code just to make sure that all the local variables, parameters, and fields contain the values we expect. Eventually, some of this logic will be captured in a test case, but we can't always write test cases that capture these values, and when implementing new functionality, we are typically more interested in getting a rough first version up and running as soon as possible rather than writing tests. (See also the earlier section on Test-Driven Development.)

Using a debugger and inspecting variables also allow us to find bugs that we hadn't considered when the code was written. When stepping through the code, the branches and the various Boolean expressions, we can suddenly see possible code pathways that we hadn't considered before. Of course, the best thing to do when making such an observation is to make a mental note not only to verify that the code works as advertised but also to write tests later that will cover these new code paths.

Unfortunately, many developers think that debuggers are only good at finding bugs, whereas we see them as tools to make sure that bugs don't happen in the first place. While we can easily understand code and have an idea of the various paths that it can take based on the inputs it received, it would be foolish to rely only on your eyes and your brain to verify that a piece of code does what it's supposed to do, especially if it's your own code.

`println` debugging, which is the usual name given to the alternative to using debuggers, is flawed in many respects.

- You should pretty much never use `println`; use a logging API instead.
- A `println` is tedious and error prone. You need to know exactly where to insert your `println` and make sure you remove it before you ship. It also needs to be well formatted and to display the correct variables.
- A `println` is human, hence fragile. This debugging method is only as good as your eyes or your brain. No matter how good you are at reading scrolling consoles or log files, your eyes will get tired. Really quickly. And at some point, you will miss something essential.
- A `println` cannot be automatically tested. Whenever you feel the need for `println` debugging, you should write a regression test to make sure the bug is fixed.
- A `println` carries your bias. This is the worst thing about a `println`: You typically find one only in places where you think there might be

a bug. If you created three variables in a method, it's pretty common to print only one or two of them because you think you don't really need to check that third variable—but you just *think* you know it contains the right value.

On the other hand, a debugger shows no mercy. It will expose every single variable you created, including arrays, hash tables, or properties. When you are running your code through a debugger, you don't just think it's working. You know it.

Don't underestimate the power of debuggers; they play a huge part in the software quality cycle.

Logging Best Practices

During TestNG's development, it was always a conscious decision to not require an external logging library. In fact, a couple of user contributions for integration with logging frameworks have been soundly rejected.

Nowadays, it's hard to find a project without the ubiquitous and insidious commons-logging (also know as clogging, more aptly) dependency. While in some rare cases that does make sense, on the whole it's bizarre to see how many people think this is a good idea and have blithely hopped onto that bandwagon.

Before we debate the uselessness of clogging, it's best to step back and try to understand the purpose of logging in the first place. It's somewhat galling to have to explain this since it seems to be such a trivial subject; yet the proliferation of logging libraries and people who are obsessed with logging tools clearly shows that, for inexplicable reasons, this is a subject matter near and dear to many people's hearts.

The two broad questions to ask with regard to logging are *how* to log and *when* to log. The "how" deals with the mechanism of logging itself, whereas the "when" deals with things that are worth logging.

Tackling the "when" first, we would assert that for a library or embedded framework, the answer is . . . never. By default, if nothing goes wrong, there is no reason at all for a framework to emit junk into log files. Why would it? Either a call succeeded or not. The user knows what they've done—why do they need to be informed of it again? The irony of many projects is that they're written in the hope of being adopted, yet the logging seems to cater only to the original developer. For some reason, the users' needs are never considered when it comes to deciding whether to log or not, or how much to log.

For example, a reasonably sized Spring-based project usually emits a page or two of output on start-up, as Spring informs you of what you're trying to do and how you're doing it. Why? Some might argue that this is to help you debug, but how often are you trying to debug Spring's internals? It's fine if you had to toggle a switch in order to see all this junk, but no, the toggle is to disable it. It's curious that, in a world that's rediscovering the joys of sane defaults across the platform, logging remains immune.

All is not lost, though. One of Spring 2.0.3's changes is this: "overall startup/shutdown logging at info level is less verbose (activate debug log level for more config details)."[1] Excellent! It took only a few years to get there, but it's nice that someone did.

However, things look significantly less rosy when we look at some versions of the JBoss Application Server, for example. The start-up usually manages to fill a small forest of pages, with information that most JBoss developers themselves (let alone users) couldn't possibly care about. Of course, when things do go wrong (and they do, often), you're again presented with reams and reams of stack traces and have to play "find the needle in the haystack" to get at any information that hints at the cause of the issue. Even more perplexing, shutting down the server again results in a page or two of information.

Logging is useful only when things go wrong, not when things are going well. Applications should not be generating gigabytes of log file data (along with the associated maintenance overhead for these files) if there are no problems. After all, you're never going to review data that you know is perfectly healthy—why would you?

When things do go wrong, it's reasonable to emit errors or warnings. Again, though, it's important to decide, in the case of warnings, whether it's the right thing to do. Every useless log message that we add will obscure a useful one, so it pays to be picky.

For debugging needs, logging is useful. However, with a toggle to turn it on or off, most logging needs are satisfied, and a complex solution is not required, something that most developers are keen to forget or ignore.

TestNG, for example, allows for a verbosity setting, which is a number between 1 and 10. Setting it higher will show you more and more debug information. Most users need never bother with it and can live perfectly happy, fulfilling lives never learning about it.

When it comes to the "how" of logging, the solution is invariably some kind of logging library. While this can be justified somewhat in bigger

---

1. "Spring Framework Changelog" for version 2.0.3. from http://static.springframework.org/ spring/docs/2.0.3/changelog.txt.

frameworks or libraries, there is absolutely no point in sucking in such a dependency for smaller things. A global debug flag is perfectly sufficient and saves the user the heartache of deciphering the rules and regulations governing the behavior of the logging library.

Of course, this also saves us from the disaster that is global logging, which can occur on two levels: the dependency/versioning level and the configuration level.

In terms of dependencies, reliance on clogging will invariably result in a headlong rush toward the brick wall that is classloader issues. The issue is that clogging tries to be useful by autodiscovering logging implementations. Without going into details, this approach has been somewhat of an abysmal failure. It works well enough in small projects where you control everything, but it spirals alarmingly out of control as you suck in more and more dependencies. Memory will leak, class cast/not found exceptions will kick off, and life will generally be miserable for everyone involved.

In terms of configuration, there is often one file used to configure logging. The problem occurs when some projects feel they can be helpful by providing this file (since, idiotically enough, log4j won't have any sane defaults). Suddenly, there are multiple versions of this file with different ideas of what should and shouldn't be logged. Since this file is loaded from the classpath, and your project has about 50 jars, it's time to play "hunt the file," a game that's tedious and frustrating at best.

Conceptually, there is absolutely no reason for clogging to exist. The use case it was developed for is an embedded component that needs to allow for being used with a variety of logging toolkits. It's a ridiculous use case since the component could have simply used its own logging mechanism that's configured programmatically, thus saving the world many hours of heartache.

What's the solution then? First and foremost, avoid commons-logging like the plague. It's pointless and just adds complexity with no discernible benefits. If you must use a logging library, stick to either log4j or the built-in `java.util.logging` framework. log4j has widespread adoption, is well understood by everyone, and provides a pleasant logging API to work with. It's also stable and has few releases, so it is not much of a moving target.

The built-in logging framework, ridiculous as its package name is (what next? `java.xmling`? `javax.jsp.readingandwriting`?), is something you can count on being there. Of course, for reasons inexplicable to many, Sun chose to ignore the community and came up with something that is more awkward to configure and has a less pleasant API, but the fact that it is a standard carries a lot of weight and saves you from having to lug in yet another dependency.

Ultimately, think carefully about your logging needs. The prevalent approach is sadly the wrong one, and simply tossing in clogging is similar to putting out a fire by chucking in a few batteries.

The Value of Time

It's surprising how many practices and goals of any software project fail to consider the cost of time invested.

There are plenty of examples showing that appalling lack of regard for the value of one's time. Many of these time-wasting practices are conducted under the general umbrella of improving quality, but in practice said benefit is so intangible that it's perplexing that time still continues to be poured in.

Let's go through a brief tour of some of these awful ideas disguised as clever solutions in the realm of testing. First up, we have coverage reports. A coverage report shows what percentage of your code is exercised through your tests. This useful tool can help with identifying functional gaps in tests. However, the actual percentage value is utterly, completely, and thoroughly meaningless.

Yet many projects attach religious value to this magic number. One doesn't have to look far (and certainly not far at all if one is just looking at agile/TDD-based projects) to find such ludicrous claims as "This project is not complete until it has 85% coverage."

What does that actually mean? The code is 85% good enough? What about the other 15%? Is it all trivial code? Does it matter which 85% is covered? Obviously, nobody will insist that 85% is the magical value, that said requirement is reasonable, or that 84% or 86% are equally acceptable, in a pitiful attempt to disguise the dysfunction with logic and pragmatism.

A popular open source product recently noted, as one of the most prominent items in the release notes, the following crucial functionality: "achieved 90% coverage."

Sure, it's perfectly possible to strive for such a value and reach it, if one has infinite time and runs out of useful things to do. In the real world, however, there are functional specifications to be met, real deadlines, and users with an endless stream of complaints. Wasting time on bumping up coverage percentages is somewhat similar to a certain Roman emperor fiddling while his city was getting a little too warm for comfort.

Similarly, the XP methodology offers up some excellent examples of idiotic time distribution. Much has been made of pair programming, and it's not hard to find crazy XP-obsessed people who insist that no project could possibly succeed without it (neglecting every project in history except for the handful that they happen to be making a ton of money consulting on).

Pair programming certainly is a novel approach. That it results in better code is not really under dispute—two pairs of eyes are always better than one, and when one person is typing and the other is thinking and looking at the bigger picture (hopefully), code quality should go up, even if marginally.

The problem is, nobody finishes the sentence. Pair programming is better than solitary programming—*if you can double your resources for zero cost*.

It's not surprising that the biggest advocates are consulting companies. After all, the goal there is to jam as many warm bodies down the poor client's throat as possible. Said consultants will croon endlessly about the joys of pair programming and about how, if you're not doing it, you clearly are missing out on something very important. To do it, you naturally need to hire some experts to show you how.

That's not to say it's all bad. Certainly, it's possible to see situations where this can work, for example, if a consultant is paired with an employee to ensure knowledge transfer. That can work quite well, despite the fact that it's against the spirit of pair programming and should better be called mentoring.

Pair programming also works in some situations, with a pair shown to be more productive than two individuals. These cases, however, are limited to novice–novice pairs against a solo novice developer. There is no evidence that a pair of experts, for example, will outperform a solo expert sufficiently to justify the cost increase. This is even setting aside the fact that in a novice–expert pair, the expert is likely to lose patience and feel intense boredom, with the accompanying drop in productivity and morale.

The corollary to the time-wasting practices is the time pressure to deliver. In terms of testing, this usually manifests in a lack of tests or very minimal automated formalized testing.

Of all the developers out there who know about unit testing, we'd be surprised if more than 10% routinely write unit tests (or any kind of tests). Why is that? The reason is that testing has traditionally been overlooked as a part of the development process. It's hard to justify to the business side that even though the project is done, it will not be delivered for another week or so, so that tests can be written. The response is, quite sensibly, "But it works now—let's roll it out."

How to tackle this situation? Obviously, doing what some testing zealots do and proclaiming that the lack of testing denotes that the project simply does not work (when it very blatantly does, as far as the customer is concerned) is idiotic and unlikely to get us very far.

The solution is twofold.

The first half is to make testing part of the development process, not a separate stage. This means that as bugs crop up, we quickly whip up a test to trigger it and then fix the code until the test passes. Writing tests becomes a debugging tool, one that is just as efficient as any other debugging technique. The same approach to verifying new functionality also means that writing tests becomes part and parcel of the rest of development, and so no longer needs to be justified as a separate (and time-consuming) activity.

The other approach, as with all things, has to do with moderation. Obsessively writing tests for every little thing might be a satisfying and suitable sacrifice on the altar of the gods of testing, but it's likely to result in very irate project managers as you constantly slip further and further behind on your deliverables relative to your (less obsessive) teammates.

Testing indiscriminately is foolish: It's much wiser to decide what needs to be tested and what doesn't. As we've stated time and time again, the value of a test suite is not the chunk of work done at any given time—it's the fact that the tests grow and increase over time, thus slowly testing more and more functionality. It's far more important to write a couple of tests occasionally but consistently than to write fifty tests once and then not bother with any new ones for months.

Ultimately, it's vital that the cost of time in any project be explicit and well defined. Far too much of it is lost due to building the wrong thing, testing the wrong thing, or naively following a given methodology without any real thought as to the best way to take advantage of it.

Conclusion

We hope these rants have been entertaining and, ideally, somewhat informative. Keep in mind that they're what we think: personal opinions that should be taken as such. In fact, feel free to disagree as strongly as you like, since the goal is the same theme we've tried to hammer home time and time again: Think, think, think!

Decide for yourself. There are no shortcuts, and as our industry progresses, it's crucial that we approach everything with an open mind and a willingness to question. Ultimately, what are taken as accepted truths in everything we do are determined by all of us, so it's up to us to ensure that those truths are fair and accurate.

IDE Integration

This appendix includes a couple of guides for integrating TestNG into the two most popular Java IDEs: Eclipse and JetBrains' IDEA. Both guides are a walkthrough starting from plug-in installation, moving through usage, and finally discussing other plug-in features such as refactoring support and any other TestNG-specific conveniences they add. TestNG has plug-ins for some of the other popular IDEs, but unfortunately, at the time of writing, none are as mature as the two we discuss here.

Eclipse

The TestNG Eclipse plug-in allows you to run TestNG tests from inside Eclipse in a convenient way. It leverages standard Eclipse functionalities (Quick Fixes, launch configuration, and so on) to make it easy to implement, run, debug, and inspect the results of tests.

Installing the Plug-in

You can install the plug-in in two different ways: by using the update site or by downloading it manually.

The Update Site

The TestNG team maintains an Eclipse update site that gets updated whenever a new TestNG version is released. The numbering of the Eclipse plug-in usually follows the one from the distribution. At the time of writing, the TestNG version is 5.6 and the Eclipse plug-in is 5.6.0.0. Subsequent versions of the Eclipse plug-in that still use the 5.5 TestNG distribution will be called 5.5.0.1, 5.5.0.2, and so on.

The update site's address is http://beust.com/eclipse, and here is how to use it.

1. Select the menu Help → Software Updates → Find and Install. This will bring up the dialog shown in Figure A–1.

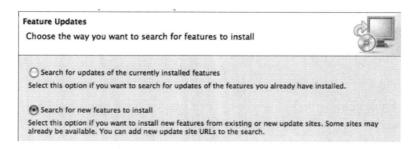

Feature Updates
Choose the way you want to search for features to install

○ Search for updates of the currently installed features
Select this option if you want to search for updates of the features you already have installed.

◉ Search for new features to install
Select this option if you want to install new features from existing or new update sites. Some sites may already be available. You can add new update site URLs to the search.

Figure A–1 Install plug-in wizard

2. Select the radio button labeled Search for new features to install. The dialog shown in Figure A–2 will appear.

Update sites to visit
Select update sites to visit while looking for new features.

Sites to include in search:
☐ Europa Discovery Site
☐ Subclipse update site
☐ Subversive update site
☐ The Eclipse Project Updates

New Remote Site...
New Local Site...
New Archived Site...

Figure A–2 Adding an update site

3. Click on the New Remote Site button, and enter the update site address along with a description of your choice, as shown in Figure A–3.

Name: TestNG
URL: http://beust.com/eclipse

Cancel   OK

Figure A–3 Specifying the TestNG update site

4. Check the new TestNG site you just created in the list and press Finish. Follow the directions, making sure that you check the plug-in to download once Eclipse has discovered it. The update site will show the TestNG plug-in available (Figure A–4).

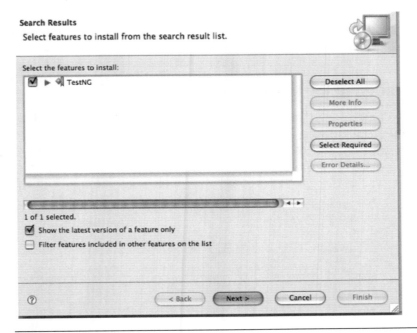

Search Results
Select features to install from the search result list.

Select the features to install:

☑ ▶ ⬦ TestNG

Deselect All

More Info

Properties

Select Required

Error Details...

1 of 1 selected.
☑ Show the latest version of a feature only
☐ Filter features included in other features on the list

⑦   < Back   Next >   Cancel   Finish

Figure A–4 Selecting the TestNG update site plug-in

5. Once you press Next, you will be prompted to accept the license (which is the standard Eclipse license), and after the download, you will be recommended to restart Eclipse.

Manual Download

Using Eclipse's download manager is the recommended way to keep your plug-ins updated because Eclipse takes care of downloading and putting the files in the correct place. If you can't use this method, you can download the plug-in manually and install it yourself.

In order to do this, go to http://testng.org, click on Download in the top banner, and click on the link labeled Download the plug-in directly. This will start the download of a `.zip` file.

Once you have retrieved this `.zip` file, locate the directory where you installed Eclipse (let's call it `$ECLIPSE`) and extract the content of that `.zip` file into `$ECLIPSE/eclipse/plugins`.

Note that this approach has a downside: Since you just installed the plug-in inside the Eclipse installation directory, you will have to reinstall it if you upgrade to a new version of Eclipse and put it in a different directory. To address this problem, Eclipse offers the possibility to look up plug-ins in an external directory, which guarantees that even if you upgrade your IDE, it will automatically find all your plug-ins right away. If you want to find out how you can achieve this, simply search on Google for "managing multiple Eclipse installations."

Verifying the Installation

To make sure that the TestNG plug-in was correctly installed, select the menu Window → Show View → Other..., and you should see a new TestNG view available in the Java category, as shown in Figure A–5.

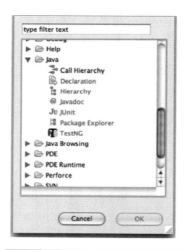

Figure A–5 Verifying the TestNG plug-in installation

Creating a Launch Configuration

The first thing to do to run your TestNG tests is to create a launch configuration. Select the Run → Debug... menu, and the left pane will show you a new TestNG category. Right-click on it and select New. The window shown in Figure A–6 will appear.

Make sure that you type a name in the box called Name and that the name in the Project box corresponds to the project you want to run your tests in. This window gives you three different ways you can run your tests.

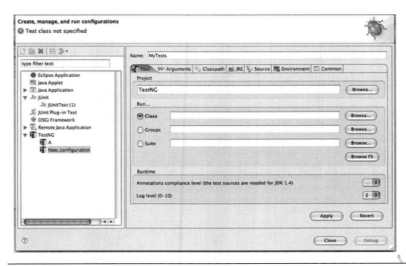

Figure A–6 TestNG launch configuration

Running a Class

You can either type the fully qualified name of your class in this text box or click on the Browse… button, which will bring up the window shown in Figure A–7.

    This window lists all the classes that contain TestNG annotation. Select the one you want to run, and press OK.

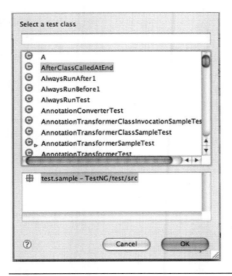

Figure A–7 Specifying a test class

Running Groups

Similarly, you can either type in the names of one or several groups (separated by spaces) or click on the Browse... button, which will bring up the window shown in Figure A–8.

This window contains all the groups that the plug-in found on your test classes. Select one or more, then click OK.

Figure A–8 Specifying a test group

Running a Suite

Finally, you can run an XML file, either by typing its name directly or by selecting it from the Browse... window, as shown in Figure A–9.

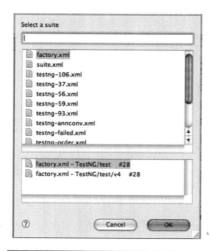

Figure A–9 Specifying a test suite file

Running a Method

Running a single test method is accomplished not from the Launch Configuration screen but directly from the Outline view. Once you are editing the test class you are interested in, and right-click on the method you want to run, select Run As or Debug As. You'll see TestNG in the resulting menu, as shown in Figure A–10.

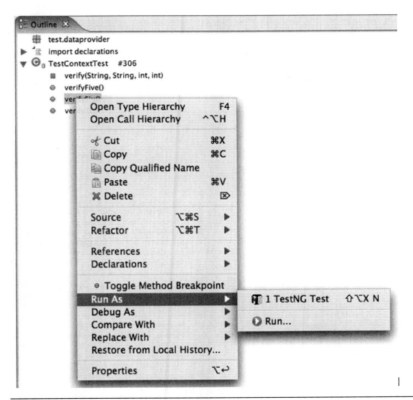

Figure A–10 Specifying a test method

A similar menu can also be used from the Package Explorer view and from the Java Browser perspective.

Runtime Parameters

You can configure two more settings from the main launch window:

1. The annotation compliance level, which can be either JDK (using Java 5 annotations) or Javadocs (Javadocs annotations)
2. The log level, which can range from 0 (no output at all) to 10 (full output level, usually necessary only when you report a bug)

Once you are satisfied with the launch configuration settings, you can press Run (or Debug).

Viewing the Test Results

Launching a test run will cause the view shown in Figure A–11 to open.

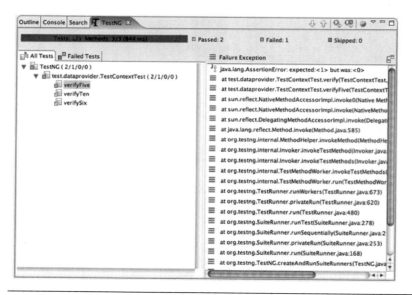

Figure A–11 Test results view

Let's examine the various elements of this window in turn, starting with the upper-right corner, shown in Figure A–12.

Figure A–12 Test results navigation toolbar

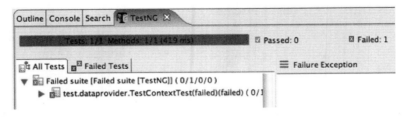

Figure A–13 Rerunning a single test

- The up and down arrows let you navigate from one test to the next.
- The first arrow in a green circle lets you rerun the last test, while the arrow next to it with a red cross will run only the failed method. The example in Figure A–11 shows that three test methods were run, but one failed (verifyFive). Pressing the red cross button will therefore rerun only that method, as shown in Figure A–13.
- The earth icon will load the HTML reports in a Web view, therefore allowing you to dig into more details in a particular test run.
- The other three icons are standard Eclipse icons, which let you orient the view differently, minimize it, and maximize it.

The top of the view shows a banner giving you a readable summary of the last run, in order, the total number of tests (and methods) and how many tests passed, failed, and were skipped, as shown in Figure A–14.

The main window has two panes.

- The left pane shows a list of the test methods that ran. One tab allows you to see all the tests that ran, and the other tab lists only the tests that failed (this is convenient when your test suite has thousands of tests but only a few failed).
- The right pane shows either nothing, if the tests passed, or the stack trace, if the test failed. In this case, you can double-click on any stack frame, and the editor will take you directly to where the failure occurred.

Figure A–14 Summary banner view

Configuring Preferences

You can configure TestNG by selecting the general Eclipse preferences and selecting the TestNG tab on the left pane, as shown in Figure A–15.

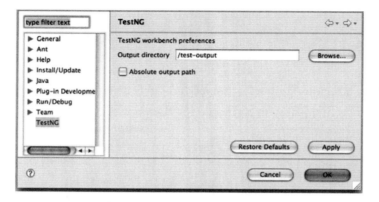

Figure A–15 Selecting a TestNG output directory

This panel lets you configure where you would like the HTML reports generated by TestNG to go.

Converting JUnit Tests

The TestNG Eclipse plug-in leverages Eclipse's support for Quick Fixes and refactorings to make it easy to convert a JUnit class to TestNG.

Whenever you are editing a JUnit class, you can invoke the Quick Fix command (Ctrl-1 on Windows and Linux, Option-1 on Mac OS). You will see two available fixes, one for each annotation type. The annotation-based conversion along with the change preview is shown in Figure A–16, while the Javadocs-based conversion is shown in Figure A–17.

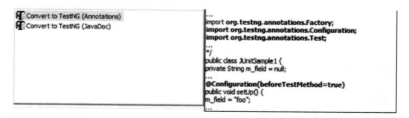

Figure A–16 Quick Fixes available in JUnit files (annotation)

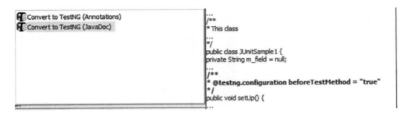

Figure A–17 Quick Fixes available in JUnit files (Javadocs)

The preview on the right-hand side gives you an idea of what the new source will look like. Keep in mind that if you accept this change but don't like the result, a simple Undo will revert the entire modification.

IntelliJ IDEA

TestNG fully supports IDE integration with IntelliJ IDEA, from JetBrains. The plug-in allows you to run tests, define new tests, and present statistics and a visual progress of currently running tests.

Installing the Plug-in

The TestNG plug-in is bundled with IDEA as of version 7.0 onward, so nothing needs to be done to start using it. With earlier versions, however, the plug-in must be installed via the plug-in manager.

The plug-in manager is launched from the preferences page via the Plugins icon. Going to the Available tab, you can scroll down to the TestNG-J plug-in, and click on the Install icon at the top of the dialog box.

IDEA will then prompt you to restart in order to load the plug-in. Once that's done, you can verify that the plug-in has been installed correctly by again going to the plug-in manager and verifying that TestNG-J is listed under the Installed plugins tab, as shown in Figure A–18.

Once the plug-in has been installed, you can start using it.

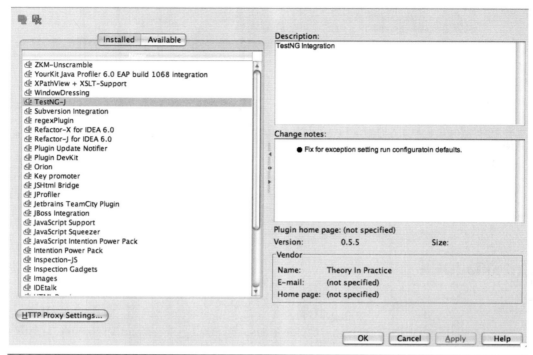

Figure A–18 IDEA plug-in manager dialog

Running Tests

Having defined a number of tests in a project, you can run through the IDE by using the regular Run/Debug dialog.

From the main menu, click on Run/Edit Configurations to bring up the dialog. The first step is to add a TestNG configuration, as shown in Figure A–19.

Once you create a run configuration, you will see an empty configuration page for TestNG, as shown in Figure A–20.

By default, the run configuration is set to run a single class. It is possible to configure, through the radio buttons at the top of this configuration editor, exactly what tests you'd like to run.

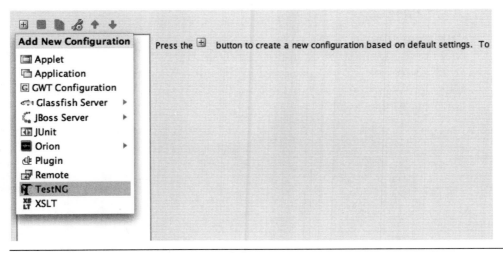

Figure A–19 Add New Configuration dialog

Name: Unnamed

Configuration | Startup/Connection

Configuration | Code Coverage

Test: ○ All in Package ○ Suite ○ Group ⊙ Class ○ Method

Test
Class:

Output Directory:

JDK Settings | Test Parameters

VM parameters:

Test runner parameters:

Working directory:
/Users/hani/projects/testng-book/hani/code

Use classpath and JDK of module:
tng-book

☐ Use alternative JRE:

Figure A–20 Default TestNG configuration view

All in Package

This configuration allows you to run all the tests in a given package. Note that due to the module definitions in IDEA, you would also have to specify whether to look for test packages in the entire project or within a specific module. When you select this option, the dialog will change accordingly, as shown in Figure A–21.

Figure A–21 Specifying a test package

If you select the option for searching across module dependencies, IDEA will look for packages by taking into consideration the currently selected module's specified dependency list.

Realistically, if you've defined your modules correctly and have ensured that modules are self-contained, the most common scenario is to select a package from within a single module.

Suite

A suite in this case, using TestNG terminology, is a `testng.xml` configuration file that defines all the test classes and groups as well as what the current runtime configuration is. When selecting this option, you are required to then select or type in the specific suite definition file to use, as shown in Figure A–22.

Figure A–22 Specifying a suite file

This approach is useful for cases where you already have a configured `testng.xml` (or a number of them!) used for building from the command line or for a continuous integration tool. Using this suite definition inside of the IDE allows you to run the test suite with the same configuration.

While this approach enables you to run the same set of tests across different environments, it's not well suited for rapid development. It's a lot more useful to instead run a specific class or method when inside of the IDE and during development.

Group

This option allows you to run a specific group. Selecting it will allow you to either enter the group name manually or select one from a list of all the groups the plug-in discovered in the project, as shown in Figure A–23.

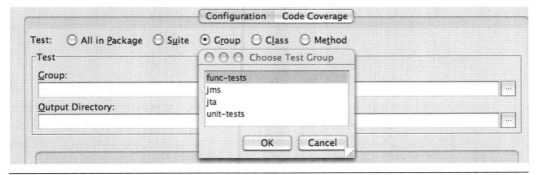

Figure A–23 Specifying a test group

Note that while the plug-in will attempt to perform dependency resolution (so that if group A depends on group B, group B's tests will run first), it's likely that it won't be able to perform an exhaustive search. For such cases, it is probably safest instead to use a suite definition file to explicitly list what to include or not include.

Class

Running an individual test class is likely the most common option used during development. Selecting it will present you with a choice of entering the class name in a field or selecting the class to run from the popup list, as shown in Figure A–24.

Figure A–24 Specifying a test class

If the selected class has any dependencies, the plug-in will automatically include those tests. However, the dependency resolution, much like the group-based one, is not exhaustive, and if your dependency graph is complex, it is safer to define the test using a `testng.xml` suite definition file.

Method

This option enables you to run a single test method. This is the fastest and most convenient approach during development; it ensures that you can run tests very quickly and with minimal waiting or disruption to development. That in turn ensures that writing tests is not an onerous task and is something that can be done as part of development.

Specifying the method to run involves first selecting the class, as described previously, then using the method selector to pick the specific method to run, as shown in Figure A–25.

Figure A–25 Specifying a test method

Running Shortcuts

For cases where you'd quickly like to run a particular class or method, there is a shortcut to do so without having to go through the Run Configuration dialog.

The context menu for any test class will have entries to run or debug the class, as shown in Figure A–26.

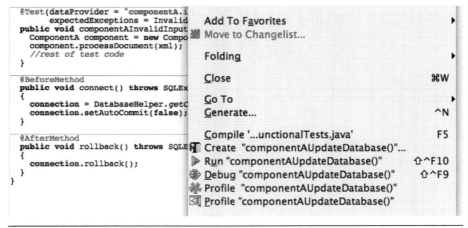

Figure A–26 Context menu for a test class

Selecting any of these shortcuts will automatically populate the configuration dialog with the test information. Note that in the case shown in Figure A–26, we right-clicked on a test method. Had we clicked on the class name itself, the suggested configuration would be for the whole class, rather than just one method.

If you select any of the autocreation options, a temporary run configuration will be created, as shown in Figure A–27. The faded-out TestNG icon indicates that the configuration is temporary. The distinction is to allow you to recognize test runs that were created during development and ones that you'd like persisted and reused regularly.

Note that the test name is created dynamically based on what you selected to run.

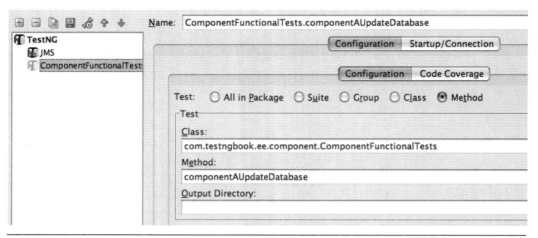

Figure A–27 Temporary method run configuration

Viewing Test Results

When running tests, IDEA will present a visual tool window showing test progress, as well as test output, as shown in Figure A–28.

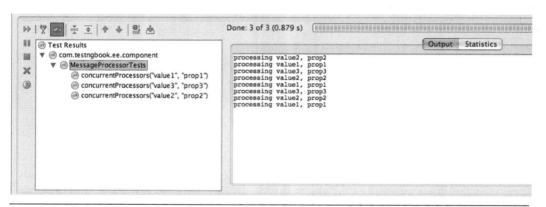

Figure A–28 Test run results view

The output window has a number of useful features for debugging tests; many of these mirror the built-in functionality that IDEA has for JUnit-based tests, including hiding passed tests from results, rerunning failed tests, and enabling source navigation for any of the test nodes in the tree.

Also, it is possible to filter output for a specific test method by clicking on it in the test results tree, as well as rerunning the current test configuration.

Status	Test	Time
	Output Statistics	
Pass	concurrentProcessors	0.333 s
Pass	concurrentProcessors	0.335 s
Pass	concurrentProcessors	0.334 s

Figure A–29 Test statistics view

The Statistics window shown in Figure A–29 shows information in a table format for the current test run.

Running Plug-in Refactorings

In addition to running and debugging tests, the plug-in also offers a number of refactorings that can be run on test code.

Migrate JUnit Code

This intention action is shown whenever a JUnit-based test class is open in the editor. It is covered in more detail in Appendix D.

Switch Annotation Style

TestNG supports both JDK 1.4 and JDK 1.5. The difference between the two lies in how the TestNG metadata is specified.

In the case of JDK 1.5, annotations are used. For 1.4, Javadocs-style annotation, comments are used. This intention allows you to easily switch from one to the other within a given test class.

Upgrade Deprecated Annotations

TestNG versions prior to 5.0 used a different style of annotations for configuring before/after test methods. Instead of the current `Before/After` set of annotations, there was a single `@Configuration` annotation to cover all cases.

This intention allows you to migrate code based on the old `@Configuration` annotation to the new ones.

TestNG Javadocs

This appendix contains a list of the important Javadocs TestNG classes. Only a few selected classes are presented here:

- Annotations
- The `TestNG` class
- The `Xml` classes

Since this kind of documentation tends to get out of date, we encourage you to refer to the online documentation or, better, to trust your IDE to give you the correct completions and latest documentation when you are developing.

JDK 1.4 and JDK 5

TestNG supports both JDK 1.4 and JDK 5. Since annotations are not supported on JDK 1.4, TestNG uses an alternative syntax to allow developers to annotate methods. This syntax is based on Javadocs tags, with each JDK 5 annotation matched with an equivalent Javadocs one. Each annotation described here is shown under its JDK 5 name (e.g., `@Test`) and JDK 1.4 equivalent (e.g., `@testng.test`). As a rule of thumb, the naming conventions for JDK 1.4 tags are as follows.

- Each annotation starts with `@testng`.
- The name of the annotation is converted to lowercase from its JDK5 equivalent: `@Test` becomes `@testng.test`.
- Multiword annotations are separated by a hyphen: `@BeforeClass` becomes `@testng.before-class`.
- The names of the attributes are unchanged: `@Test(dataProvider = "dp")` becomes `@testng.test dataProvider = "dp"`.

■ Multivalued attributes are separated by spaces: `@Test(groups = { "g1", "g2"})` becomes `@testng.test groups = "g1 g2"`

Since they are not enforced by the compiler, JDK 1.4 annotations are very error prone, so whenever you see behavior that is not what you expected, verify the following conditions.

■ The tags are in a real Javadocs comment, which must start with `/**` and end with `*/`.
■ Only one Javadocs comment is allowed per method or class. If you want to include both a comment and a TestNG annotation, put them in one Javadocs comment.
■ Make sure you spelled the annotations and attributes correctly.

Finally, here is a full example, expressed with JDK 5 annotations first.

```
public class MyTest {
  @BeforeClass
  public void setUp() {
  }

  @Test(invocationCount = 10, threadPoolSize = 3)
  public void f1() {
  }

  @Test(groups = { "unit", "functional" }
  public void f2() {
  }
}
```

Here's the version with JDK 1.4 annotations.

```
public class MyTest {
  /**
   * @testng.before-class
   */
  public void setUp() {
  }
```

```
/**
 * @testng.test invocationCount = "10" threadPoolSize = "3"
 */
public void f1() {
}

/**
 * @testng.test groups = "unit functional"
 */
public void f2() {
}
}
```

Shortcut Syntax for JDK 5 Annotations

JDK 5 annotations allow you to use a shortcut whenever you are trying to set an array attribute to only one element. The following syntaxes are therefore equivalent.

```
@Test(groups = { "unit" }) // is equivalent to
@Test(groups = "unit")
```

We mention this syntax because we use it throughout the book.

Annotation Javadocs

All the configuration methods (methods with an annotation that starts with @After or @Before) share the same attributes. Table B–1 gives a list of all these annotations, and Table B–2 shows all the attributes that each of these annotations supports.

Table B–1 Annotations for configuration methods

JDK 5 name	JDK 1.4 name	Documentation
@AfterClass	@testng.after-class	Annotates methods that will be run after the last test method on the current class is run.
@AfterGroups	@testng.after-groups	Annotates methods that will be run after the last test method belonging to the groups specified in its `value` attribute has been run. The annotated method is automatically put into these specified groups.
@AfterMethod	@testng.after-method	Annotates methods that will be run after every test method.
@AfterSuite	@testng.after-suite	Annotates methods that will be run after all the test methods in a given `<suite>` have been run.
@AfterTest	@testng.after-test	Annotates methods that will be run after all the test methods in a given `<test>` have been run.
@BeforeClass	@testng.before-class	Annotates methods that will be run before the first method on the current test class is run.
@BeforeGroups	@testng.before-groups	Annotates methods that will be run before the first method in any of the specified groups is run.
@BeforeMethod	@testng.before-method	Annotates methods that will be run before each test method.
@BeforeTest	@testng.before-test	Annotates methods that will be run before any method in a given `<test>` is run.
@BeforeSuite	@testng.before-suite	Annotates methods that will be run before any method in a given `<suite>` is run.

Table B–2 Attributes for configuration annotations

Attribute	Type	Documentation	Default value
alwaysRun	boolean	For before methods (@BeforeSuite, @BeforeTest, @BeforeTestClass, and @BeforeTestMethod, but not @BeforeGroups): If set to true, this configuration method will be run regardless of what groups it belongs to.	true
dependsOnGroups	String[]	The list of groups this method depends on.	—
dependsOnMethods	String[]	The list of methods this method depends on.	—
description	String	The description for this method (it will appear in the reports).	—
enabled	boolean	Whether this method is enabled.	true
groups	String[]	The list of groups this method belongs to.	—
inheritGroups	boolean	Whether this method should belong to the groups that are listed in the @Test annotation at the class level.	false

@DataProvider/@testng.data-provider

This annotation lets you specify a method that will supply arguments to an @Test method. Table B–3 lists the attribute available on the @DataProvider annotation.

Table B–3 Attribute for `@DataProvider`/`@testng.data-provider`

Attribute	Type	Documentation	Default value
name	String	The name of this Data Provider. The annotated method must return an `Object[][]` or an `Iterator<Object[]>`. Each row of objects will be cast into the corresponding type of the parameter found on the `@Test` method.	The name of the annotated method

@Factory/@testng.factory

This annotation specifies a method that must return `Object[][]`. Each object returned is in turn considered to represent a test class. No errors will be reported if some of these instances do not contain any TestNG annotations. These instances can contain `@Factory` annotations as well, in which case the process is repeated until no more new instances are found.

@Parameters/@testng.parameters

This annotation declares which parameters should be passed to the method. Each name supplied in its value will be looked up in the current `testng.xml` file, and if a corresponding `<parameters>` tag is found with a matching name, its value will be passed to the Java method. Table B–4 lists the attribute for `@Parameters`.

Table B–4 Attribute for `@Parameters`/`@testng.parameters`

Attribute	Type	Documentation	Default value
value	String[]	The list of parameter names to be looked up in `testng.xml`.	—

@Test/@testng.test

This annotation specifies a method as a test method. Table B–5 lists the attributes for @Test.

Table B–5 Attributes for @Test/@testng.test

Attribute	Type	Documentation	Default value
alwaysRun	boolean	If set to true, this test method will always be run even if it depends on a method that failed.	false
dataProvider	String	The name of the Data Provider for this test method.	—
dataProviderClass	Class	The class where to look for the Data Provider.	—
dependsOnGroups	String[]	The list of groups this method depends on.	—
dependsOnMethods	String[]	The list of methods this method depends on.	—
description	String	The description for this method (it will be included in the reports).	—
enabled	boolean	Whether this test method is enabled.	—
expectedExceptions	Class[]	The list of exceptions that a test method is expected to throw.	—
groups	String[]	The list of groups this class/method belongs to.	—
invocationCount	int	The number of times this method should be invoked.	—

(continued)

Table B–5 Attributes for `@Test`/`@testng.test` *(continued)*

Attribute	Type	Documentation	Default value
sequential	boolean	If set to `true`, all the methods on this test class are guaranteed to run sequentially, even if the tests are currently being run with `parallel="true"`.	—
successPercentage	int (0..100)	The percentage of success expected from this method.	100
suiteName	String	The name of the suite this test class should be placed in.	—
testName	String	The name of the test this test class should be placed in.	—
threadPoolSize	int	The size of the thread pool for this method.	—
timeout	int (ms)	The maximum number of milliseconds this test should take before being aborted and marked as a failure.	—

The `org.testng.TestNG` Class

If you want to run TestNG in your own code (such as in a servlet or in a Java EE container), you will need to instantiate and operate on the `org.testng.TestNG` class. This class makes it easy to set up tests, parameters, and listeners so that you can have the entire execution of your tests under control.

The `TestNG` class can run either `testng.xml` files or direct test classes. Additionally, the XML API (described in the next section) allows you to create virtual XML files programmatically. Table B–6 lists all the methods available on the class `org.testng.TestNG`.

Table B–6 `org.testng.TestNG` methods

Name	Documentation
`void addListener(IReporter listener)`	Adds an `IReporter`, a listener that will be invoked once at the end of all the tests.
`void addListener(ISuiteListener listener)`	Adds an `ISuiteListener`, a listener that will receive callbacks during the execution of a suite.
`void addListener(ITestListener listener)`	Adds an `ITestListener`, a listener that will receive callbacks during the execution of a test.
`void addMethodSelector(java.lang.String className, int priority)`	Adds a method selector, along with its priority. Method selectors implement the interface `IMethodSelector` and are used to complement or replace TestNG's algorithm to select test methods.
`IAnnotationTransformer getAnnotationTransformer()`	Returns the annotation transformer for this instance, or null if none was specified.
`String getDefaultSuiteName()`	Returns the default suite name. This name is used by TestNG whenever it is running tests that weren't specified in a `testng.xml` file (such as when invoked directly on test classes).
`String getDefaultTestName()`	Returns the default test name. This name is used by TestNG whenever it is running tests that weren't specified in a `testng.xml` file (such as when invoked directly on test classes).
`String getOutputDirectory()`	Returns the directory where all the reports will be generated. The HTML report index file can be found in this directory in `index.html`.

(continued)

Table B–6 org.testng.TestNG methods *(continued)*

Name	Documentation
List<IReporter> getReporters()	Returns a list of all the reporters declared on this instance.
List<ISuiteListener> getSuiteListeners()	Returns a list of all the suite listeners declared on this instance.
List<ITestListener> getTestListeners()	Returns a list of all the test listeners declared on this instance.
boolean hasFailure()	Returns true if the execution of the tests contained at least one failure (undefined if invoked before run()).
boolean hasSkip()	Returns true if the execution of the tests contained at least one skipped test (undefined if invoked before run()).
void run()	Runs TestNG.
void setAnnotations(String annotationType)	Sets the annotation type, which has to be either TestNG.JAVADOC_ANNOTATION_TYPE (JDK 1.4) or TestNG.JDK_ANNOTATION_TYPE (JDK5).
void setAnnotationTransformer(IAnnotationTransformer t)	Sets the annotation transformer.
void setDefaultSuiteName(String defaultSuiteName)	Sets the default suite name.
void setDefaultTestName(String defaultTestName)	Sets the default test name.
void setExcludedGroups(String groups)	Sets the list of groups to be excluded for this run. The group names must be separated by spaces.

(continued)

Table B–6 `org.testng.TestNG` methods *(continued)*

Name	Documentation
`void setGroups(String groups)`	Sets the list of groups to be included for this run. The group names must be separated by spaces.
`void setJUnit(Boolean isJUnit)`	Sets the JUnit mode. Pass `true` to this method to run JUnit tests.
`void setOutputDirectory(String outputdir)`	Sets the output directory where reports and other files will be generated.
`void setParallel(String parallel)`	Defines whether this run should be in parallel. Allowed values are `XmlSuite.PARALLEL_METHODS` and `XmlSuite.PARALLEL_TESTS`.
`void setSourcePath(String sourcePaths)`	Sets the source paths. This option can only be used in Javadocs mode, and it is mandatory then. Failure to set this option correctly will lead to TestNG not being able to find any Javadocs annotation on your tests.
`void setTestClasses(Class[] classes)`	Sets the test classes to be run.
`void setTestJar(String jarPath)`	Sets the jar file for this run. The parameter needs to be a valid path to a jar file that contains a `testng.xml` file at its root.
`void setTestSuites(List<String> suites)`	Sets the list of `testng.xml` files to run. Each member of the list needs to be a valid path to a `testng.xml` file.
`void setThreadCount(int threadCount)`	Sets the number of threads that TestNG is allowed to use to run your tests. This value will be ignored if parallel mode is not equal to one of the valid values described in `TestNG#setParallel`.

(continued)

Table B–6 `org.testng.TestNG` methods *(continued)*

Name	Documentation
`void setUseDefaultListeners(boolean useDefaultListeners)`	Defines whether TestNG should run default listeners. Pass this method `false` if you don't want TestNG to run any of its default listeners (assuming you added your own and you want them to be run at the exclusion of all others).
`void setVerbose(int verbose)`	Sets the verbose mode, a value between 0 and 10. You will typically not use any value greater than 2, unless instructed by the TestNG team to provide a more verbose feedback.
`void setXmlSuites(List<XmlSuite> suites)`	Sets the `testng.xml` files to run in the form of `XmlSuite` objects.

The XML API

The XML API allows you to create XML files programmatically. This is particularly useful for tools (e.g., all the TestNG IDE plug-ins use this API to run TestNG based on the configuration entered by the user), but it can also be convenient for anyone using the TestNG API.

The entirety of a `testng.xml` file can be described by classes contained in the package `org.testng.xml`. All the class names start with `Xml` and are full-fledged JavaBeans offering getters and setters for each tag and attribute available in the XML file.

Appendix C describes in depth how this API works and how you can use it, and the JavaBean aspect of these classes makes a full reproduction of their Javadocs API not very useful in a book, so we will just give a list of the available `Xml` classes and their corresponding XML tags. Please refer to the online documentation for more details about these classes. Table B–7 lists all the classes in the TestNG API that you can use to manipulate or create a `testng.xml` file.

Table B–7 TestNG classes used to manipulate XML

Class name	Tag name
XmlClass	<class>
XmlMethodSelector	<method-selector>
XmlPackage	<package>
XmlSuite	<suite>
XmlTest	<test>

testng.xml

testng.xml is an XML file that describes the runtime definition of a test suite. While its syntax is fairly simple (the DTD is less than 150 lines, most of them comments), it can describe complex test definitions while still remaining legible and easy to edit. In this appendix, we'll examine the structure of this file in detail, and we'll show how changing certain parameters affects how tests are run.

TestNG enforces a strict separation between the static model (the business logic of your tests) and its runtime (which tests get run). For example, you should be able to run front-end tests and then back-end tests without having to recompile anything in the code base in between.

TestNG offers the following mechanisms to enforce this separation:

- Test groups, which enable you to place methods in one or more groups and then decide which groups to run
- testng.xml,[1] an XML file that captures a given configuration of classes, tests, methods, parameters, exclusions, and so on

While it is easy to run tests without using a testng.xml file at all (you can specify classes directly or, if you're using ant, entire directories or classes matching a certain pattern), you will probably discover that as the test code base grows, testng.xml offers a convenient place to store all the runtime configuration of a suite that can easily be shared, emailed, or customized (e.g., testng-database.xml, testng-servlets.xml, and so on).

---

1. You don't have to call this file testng.xml; the only requirement is that it meets the DOCTYPE. However, for convenient purposes, we've used the term testng.xml throughout the book to describe this file.

Overview

A `testng.xml` file contains a TestNG suite, which is, as we discussed in Chapter 1, the largest unit of work in TestNG (a suite contains tests, which contain test classes, which contain test methods). Every time you run TestNG, you can run one or more such suites. Here is a simple example of invoking TestNG with several suite files:

```
java org.testng.TestNG database-tests.xml functional-tests.xml
```

This appendix is exclusively focused on the XML aspect of `testng.xml`, but you can refer to Chapter 6 to find out how this file can be manipulated programmatically.

This file respects the hierarchy described previously.

- The root tag of this file is `<suite>`.
- A `<suite>` tag can contain one or more `<test>` tags.
- A `<test>` tag can contain one or more `<classes>` tags.
- A `<classes>` tag can contain one or more `<method>` tags.

In our experience, most `testng.xml` files stop at the `<classes>` tag, but being able to specify `<methods>` tags is particularly useful for suite files that are automatically generated (such as the ones created by the Eclipse plug-in, or the `testng-failed.xml` file, which is explained in Chapter 2).

To make things more concrete before we dive into the structure of this file, here is a simple `testng.xml` example file.

```
<!DOCTYPE suite SYSTEM "http://testng.org/testng-1.0.dtd" >

<suite name="TestNG JDK 1.5" verbose="1" parallel="false"
    thread-count="2">
  <test name="Regression1" >
    <classes>
      <class name="test.parameters.ParameterSample" />
      <class name="test.parameters.ParameterTest" />
    </classes>
  </test>
</suite>
```

Don't forget to specify a DOCTYPE in suite files, which will help TestNG validate your XML file and make sure the syntax is correct. Also, don't be intimidated by the reference to the DTD located at http://testng.org/testng-1.0.dtd. Even though this URL is valid and does point to the current DTD (we can view it in a browser), the TestNG distribution is configured to look up this DTD locally, and since this DTD is included in the distribution, TestNG should never have to go over the network to validate files.

Scopes

Even though the structure of `testng.xml` respects the test hierarchy described in the previous section, it is possible to add extra tags, as we will discuss soon. Some of these tags can sometimes be found at either the `<suite>` or the `<test>` level. If a tag is present in both these tags, the value defined at the lowest level will always override the one defined at the `<suite>` level, which allows you to use a simple inheritance mechanism.

In the following sections, we'll examine all the tags accepted inside a `testng.xml` file, and the beginning of each section will start by listing all the valid attributes and children of each tag. In case you are not familiar with XML terminology, here is a quick explanation.

In the following example, `<suite>` and `<test>` are tags, and `name` and `thread-count` are attributes. Additionally, `<test>` is a child tag of `<suite>` (it can appear only inside a `<suite>` tag).

```
<suite name="A suite" thread-count="2">
  <test name="Test1" />
</suite>
```

XML Tags

This section gives a list of all the tags that are allowed in the `testng.xml` file.

`<suite>`

This is the root tag of your `testng.xml`. It describes a test suite, which in turn is made of several `<test>` sections. Table C–1 gives a list of all the legal attributes it accepts.

The only mandatory attribute is `name`, which will be displayed in the reports that TestNG generates.

Table C–1 Attributes for the `<suite>` tag

Attribute	Description	Type	Default value	Allowed values	Mandatory?
`name`	The name of this suite.	`String`	—	—	Yes
`verbose`	The level or verbosity for this run.	`Integer`	1	0–10, 10 being the most verbose	No
`parallel`	Whether TestNG should run different threads to run this suite.	`String`	none	`tests`, `methods`, or `none`	No
`thread-count`	The number of threads to use, if parallel mode is enabled (ignored otherwise).	`Integer`	5 if parallel is enabled	1–n	No
`annotations`	The type of annotations you are using in your tests.	`String`	JDK	`javadoc` or `JDK5`	No
`time-out`	The default timeout that will be used on all the test methods found in this test.	`Integer` (milliseconds)	0 (no timeout)	0–n	No

The `verbose` attribute is mostly used when reporting a bug or when trying to diagnose the execution of a test run that didn't go the way you expected. It will display traces on the console that will help you find out how TestNG interprets the various bits of information supplied, such as what groups were included or excluded, what methods were run and why, and so on.

The `parallel` and `thread-count` attributes are usually used together, and two of the values for `parallel` deserve further discussion.

1. `tests`: All the test methods found in the same `<test>` tag will be run in the same thread, but methods that belong to different `<test>` tags might be run in different threads.
2. `methods`: All the test methods found in this definition file might be run in a different thread, regardless of whether they are located in the same `<test>` or not.

First of all, notice the use of "might" in these two descriptions. This comes from the fact that the thread pool size you are using might not be big enough to run all these test methods in different threads, and it is therefore possible that two methods in two different `<test>` tags might reuse the same thread even though parallel was set to `tests`. The important thing to remember here is the guarantee that whenever you use `parallel="tests"`, the test methods inside a given `<test>` (and by extension, the business code they exercise) do not have to be thread safe.

`parallel="tests"` is very convenient when you want to leverage TestNG's multithread running capacity but the code being tested is not 100% multithread safe. In such cases, make sure that all tests that exercise this code are placed in the same `<test>` tag in order to guarantee that all the methods will be run sequentially.

Let's illustrate this with an example. Consider the following class.

```java
public class Thread1Test {
  @Test
  public void t11() {
    System.out.println("Thread11, thread:" +
      Thread.currentThread().getId());
  }

  @Test
  public void t12() {
    System.out.println("Thread12, thread:" +
      Thread.currentThread().getId());
  }
}
public class Thread2Test {
  @Test
  public void t21() {
    System.out.println("Thread21, thread:" +
      Thread.currentThread().getId());
  }
```

```
@Test
public void t22() {
  System.out.println("Thread22, thread:" +
    Thread.currentThread().getId());
  }
}
```

Table C–2 shows the outputs we will see for different settings for the `parallel` attribute (with a `thread-count` of 5).

Table C–2 Output of the example class with different `parallel` settings

Attribute value	Output	Remarks
parallel="none"	Thread11, thread:1 Thread12, thread:1 Thread22, thread:1 Thread21, thread:1	All the methods are running in the same thread.
parallel="tests"	Thread22, thread:8 Thread11, thread:7 Thread21, thread:8 Thread12, thread:7	Only the methods in the same <test> tag are running in the same thread.
parallel="methods"	Thread11, thread:7 Thread12, thread:8 Thread22, thread:9 Thread21, thread:10	All the methods are running in a different thread (the thread pool is big enough to contain them all, but otherwise, we would see a few threads being reused).

The `time-out` attribute is a convenient way to declare a `time-out` that will be applied to all the test methods in this suite. We can still override it locally with the `timeOut` attribute of the `@Test` annotation.

<packages> **and** <package>

These tags can be specified inside a `<suite>` element. They define a set of Java packages to include or exclude from the suite. Table C–3 lists the legal attributes for the `<package>` tag.

Table C–3 Attributes for the `<package>` tag

Attribute	Description	Type	Default value	Allowed values	Mandatory?
include	The list of packages to include in this test.	A Java package name or regular expression.[a]	—	—	No
exclude	The list of packages to exclude from this suite. If a method belongs to a group that's both included and excluded, it will be excluded (similarly to ant).	A Java package name or regular expression.	—	—	No

a. This is a real regular expression (".” to stand for any character, "*” for 0 or more times, and so on).

Note that you can specify one or more `<package>` tags under `<packages>`, which will result in all the classes in these packages being automatically considered as potential test classes by TestNG. Here's an example.

```
<suite name="Packages">
  <packages>
    <package>
      <include name="test.nested.*"/>
      <include name="test.gui"/>
      <exclude name="test.db.*"/>
    </package>
  </packages>
</suite>
```

`<parameter>`

A `<parameter>` tag defines the name and value of a parameter that will later be bound to an `@Parameters` annotation. You can define any number of `<parameter>` tags in `testng.xml`. Table C–4 lists the legal attributes for `<parameter>`.

Please see Chapter 2 for a full discussion of this tag.

Table C–4   Attributes for the `<parameter>` tag

Attribute	Description	Type	Default value	Allowed values	Mandatory?
`name`	The name of this parameter, which needs to be matched by an `@Parameters` annotation in your source.	`String`	—	—	Yes
`value`	The value to be given to the Java parameter.	`String`	—	Any string that can be converted to the Java type of the element this parameter will be bound to	Yes

`<suite-files>` and `<suite-file>`

These tags allow you to reference additional `testng.xml` files that should be run on top of the current one. This is convenient when the test code base contains many XML files that all need to be run from one place. A `<suite-files>` tag can contain any number of `<suite-file>` tags. Table C–5 lists the legal attribute for `<suite-file>`.

Table C–5   Attribute for the `<suite-file>` tag

Attribute	Description	Type	Default value	Allowed values	Mandatory?
`path`	The path name to a valid `testng.xml` file (absolute or relative to the current directory).	A valid path name	—	—	Yes

Here's an example of using these two tags.

```
<suite name="Single" >
  <suite-files>
    <suite-file path="./testng.xml" />
    <suite-file path="../test-14/testng.xml" />
  </suite-files>
</suite>
```

Note that the `testng.xml` that uses the `<suite-file>` tag can contain `<test>` tags as well.

`<method-selectors>`, `<method-selector>`, `<selector-class>`, and `<script>`

A method selector is Java or BeanShell code that TestNG will invoke in order to determine whether a test method should be included or not in a test run. You can specify this code in two different forms:

1. By giving the name of a Java class file, which needs to implement `IMethodSelector`
2. By embedding BeanShell script directly inside the `testng.xml` file

Table C–6 lists the attributes for `<selector-class>`.

Table C–6 Attributes for the `<selector-class>` tag

Attribute	Description	Type	Default value	Allowed values	Mandatory?
name	The name of the Java class.	A Java class that can be found on the class path	—	A valid Java class that implements `IMethodSelector`	Yes
priority	The priority of this method selector. Lower priorities are always run before higher ones.	Integer	—	—	Yes

Table C–7 Attribute for the `<script>` tag

Attribute	Description	Type	Default value	Allowed values	Mandatory?
language	The name of the language.	String	—	Only beanshell is supported at the time of writing.	Yes

Table C–7 lists the attribute for the `<script>` tag.

If you use the `<script>` tag, make sure you surround your code in a CDATA section, so that XML characters such as < and > do not get interpreted by the XML parser.

```
<suite name="BSH">
  <method-selectors>
    <method-selector>
      <script language="beanshell"><![CDATA[
        groups.containsKey("test1")
      ]]></script>
    </method-selector>
  </method-selectors>
</suite>
```

`<test>`

A `<suite>` tag can contain one or more `<test>` tags, each of them describing which classes should be part of this run and other information. `<test>` can also be the parent of tags that can be declared on `<suite>` (e.g., `<parameter>`), in which case the values defined inside `<test>` will override those defined at the `<suite>` level.

Table C–8 lists the attributes for the `<test>` tag.

Table C–8 Attributes for the `<test>` tag

Attribute	Description	Type	Default value	Allowed values	Mandatory?
name	The name of this test.	String	—	—	Yes
annotations	The type of annotations that TestNG should look for in the classes.	String	JDK5	JDK5 or javadoc	No
junit	Whether TestNG should run these tests as JUnit tests.	Boolean	false	true or false	No
parallel	Whether TestNG should run the methods found inside this tag in different threads.	String	none	none or methods	No
thread-count	The number of threads to use if you are running in parallel mode (ignored otherwise).	Integer	5	—	No
time-out	The default timeout that will be used on all the test methods found in this suite.	Integer (milliseconds)	0 (no timeout)	0–n	No
verbose	The level of verbosity for this run.	Integer	1	0–10, 10 being the most verbose	No

`<groups>`, `<define>`, **and** `<run>`

The `<groups>` tag allows you to specify two pieces of information related to test groups:

1. The list of groups that should be included and excluded from the run with `<run>`, followed by one or more `<include>` tags
2. The ability to define new groups made of already-existing ones with `<define>`, followed by one or more `<include>` tags

The following example defines a group call `all` made of the methods from `front-end` and `database` but excluding all the methods in `broken`.

```
<suite name="Test">
  <test name="Regression1" >
    <groups>
      <define name="all">
        <include name="front-end" />
        <include name="database" />
        <exclude name="broken" />
      </define>
      <run>
        <include name="all" />
      </run>
    </groups>
  ...
```

`<classes>` **and** `<class>`

`<classes>` is a child of `<test>`, and it enables you to define Java classes that should be considered for inclusion in the test run. Note that the test methods found on these classes are not guaranteed to be run since other factors such as group inclusion or exclusion can eventually lead to these methods being skipped. Table C–9 lists the attribute for the `<class>` tag.

Table C–9 Attribute for the `<class>` tag

Attribute	Description	Type	Default value	Allowed values	Mandatory?
name	The fully quali-fied name of the Java class.	String	—	A Java class name that can be found in the class path.	Yes

`<methods>`

`<methods>` is an optional child of `<classes>` that allows you to specify exactly which methods of the given class should be considered for inclusion in the current test run. `<methods>` can contain any number of `<include>` and `<exclude>` tags that further specify the names of these methods.

Here is an example using both `<classes>` and `<methods>`.

```
<suite name="TESTNG-59 Suite" >
  <test name="TESTNG-59">
    <classes>
      <class name="test.testng59.Test1">
        <methods>
          <include name="test1"/>
          <exclude name="test3"/>
        </methods>
      </class>
    </classes>
  </test>
</suite>
```

Migrating from JUnit

In this appendix, we explain how existing JUnit 3 tests can be migrated to TestNG. Whether you choose to use the command line or an IDE, the migration tools will typically perform the following operations on existing tests:

- Adding the relevant TestNG imports
- Adding `@BeforeTest` to `setUp()` methods and `@AfterTest` to `tearDown()` methods
- Adding `@Test` to all public methods whose names start with `test`

The tool modifies your source files, but none of these changes alter the code inside test methods in any way, which makes this process fairly nonintrusive. You still have the choice of not overwriting your sources if you want to verify the results yourself (this is described below).

JUnitConverter

`JUnitConverter` is a tool included in the TestNG distribution that lets you convert existing JUnit classes to TestNG. It can be invoked in different ways.

From the Command Line

The main class for `JUnitConverter` is `org.testng.JUnitConverter`. It understands the following options:

```
Usage: java -cp (classpath) org.testng.JUnitConverter ↵
(-annotation | -javadoc) -srcdir <source_dir> (-d <output_dir> ↵
-restore | -overwrite) [-source <release>]
```

Table D–1 gives a list of all the options you can pass to `JUnitConverter` from the command line.

Table D–1 Options understood by `JUnitConverter`

Option name	Type	Description
-annotation	Boolean	If present, the generated sources will use JDK5 annotations. This option is mutually exclusive with −javadoc.
-javadoc	Boolean	If present, the generated sources will use Javadocs annotations. This option is mutually exclusive with −annotation.
-srcdir	An existing directory	This directory is the root of the sources of your JUnit tests. Java files under this directory must be placed in locations that match their package declarations.
-d	A directory (which will be created if it doesn't exist)	The location where the converted files will be placed. This option is mutually exclusive with −overwrite.
-overwrite	Boolean	If present, the converted files will overwrite the JUnit files. This option is mutually exclusive with −d.
-quiet	Boolean	Don't show any output during the execution.
-groups	String	The list of groups that all the generated methods will belong to.

For example, assume that `junit/src/test/JUnitTest.java` contains the following JUnit test.

```
package test;

import junit.framework.TestCase;

public class JUnitTest extends TestCase {
    public void setUp() {}
    public void tearDown() {}
    public void test1() {}
    public void test2() {}
}
```

You can invoke JUnitConverter as follows (assuming the TestNG jar is already on the classpath).

```
java org.testng.JUnitConverter -d output -annotation -srcdir ↵
junit/src
```

The following file will be generated in output/test/JUnitTest.java.

```
package test;

import org.testng.annotations.AfterMethod;
import org.testng.annotations.BeforeMethod;
import org.testng.annotations.Test;
import junit.framework.TestCase;

public class JUnitTest extends TestCase {

  @BeforeMethod
  public void setUp() {}

  @AfterMethod
  public void tearDown() {}

  @Test
  public void test1() {}

  @Test
  public void test2() {}
}
```

Let's invoke the converter with –javadoc this time.

```
java org.testng.JUnitConverter -d output -javadoc -srcdir ↵
junit/src
```

The result is now the following.

```
package test;

import junit.framework.TestCase;

public class JUnitTest extends TestCase {
  /**
   * @testng.before-method
```

```
  */
  public void setUp() {}

  /**
   * @testng.after-method
   */
  public void tearDown() {}

  /**
   * @testng.test
   */
  public void test1() {}

  /**
   * @testng.test
   */
  public void test2() {}
}
```

From `ant`

`JUnitConverter` can also be invoked from an `ant` build file. Table D–2 lists the `ant` attributes equivalent to some of the command line flags shown in Table D–1.

Table D–2 Correspondence between the command line and `ant` options of `JUnitConverter`

Command line	Type	ant attribute
`-annotation` / `-javadoc`	Boolean	annotations
`-srcdir`	An existing file path	sourceDir
`-d`	A file path	outputDir
`-groups`	String	groups

Here is an example of a `build.xml` file that defines and then uses the `JUnitConverter` ant task.

```
<taskdef name="junit-converter"
         classname="org.testng.JUnitConverterTask"
         classpath="${build.jdk15.dir}"/>

<target name="convert">
  <junit-converter
      outputDir="output" annotations="true" sourceDir="junit/src"
      groups="junit"
      />
</target>
```

Integrated Development Environments

This section explains how to use TestNG with the major Java IDEs.

Eclipse

In Eclipse, migrating a JUnit class to TestNG is achieved with the Quick Fix action (Ctrl-1 on Windows and Linux, Option-1 on Mac OS X). Simply place the text cursor on the class to convert and invoke the Quick Fix action, which will display as shown in Figure D–1.

Note the two new Quick Fixes added by the TestNG plug-in: One will convert the class using TestNG JDK5 annotations, while the other will use Javadocs annotations. Just like all Quick Fixes, each of them is presented with a preview that provides an idea of what the source code will look like if you apply this fix. And of course, you can always revert it with a simple undo.

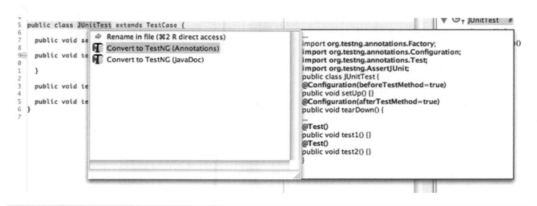

Figure D–1 Quick Fixes for TestNG available in Eclipse

IDEA

IntelliJ IDEA's TestNG plug-in also provides intentions[1] to automatically migrate JUnit-based classes. This can be done either on a number of classes or within a specific class.

If the plug-in is installed and the migration intention enabled, opening a JUnit-based test case in the editor will show the intention icon. Clicking on this icon (or via the keyboard, Alt-Enter or Apple-Enter on Mac OS X) will bring up the migration option, as shown in Figure D–2.

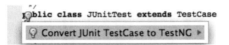

Figure D–2 Converting a JUnit class to TestNG in IDEA

Selecting this intention will modify the class to use TestNG annotations. Note that this will handle both tests based on JUnit 3 and tests based on JUnit 4 annotations. The default conversion is to JDK 5-style tests; once that is done, there are further intentions to allow you to easily switch the annotation style to a JDK 1.4–compatible Javadocs comment style.

The converter will automatically handle a variety of situations that cannot be dealt with via simple text replacement; these include a deeply nested `TestCase` hierarchy, import handling, and placement of annotations on the correct methods. It will also modify some of the JUnit-specific assertions to Java native asserts, wherever possible.

If the intention is not shown, it has likely been disabled in the current highlighting scope. To fix this, go to Preferences → Errors, and edit the IDE highlighting profile. TestNG will have an entry in that list, and you can verify that it is enabled, as shown in Figure D–3.

---

1. Intention is the IDEA equivalent of Eclipse's Quick Fix feature.

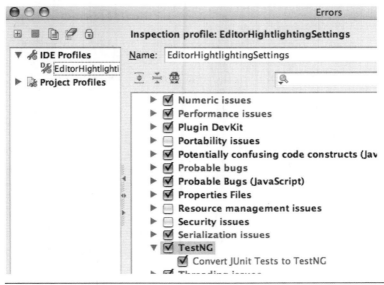

Figure D–3 Enabling TestNG intentions in IDEA

Incremental Migration and JUnit Mode

Running a tool that modifies an entire code base can be intimidating, so TestNG makes it possible to perform the migration at your own pace.

The first step is to create a `testng.xml` that will run all the existing test classes with TestNG in JUnit mode. For example, let's assume you are trying to migrate the two JUnit classes `com.example.Test1` and `com.example.Test2`. You would start by creating the following `testng.xml` file.

```
<suite name="Converted JUnit suite" >
  <test name="JUnitTests" junit="true">
    <classes>
      <class name="com.example.Test1" />
      <class name="com.example.Test2" />
    </classes>
  </test>
</suite>
```

Notice that the `<test>` tag sets the `junit` attribute to `true`, which instructs TestNG to use the JUnit runner for all the classes specified inside this tag. If you run TestNG on this `testng.xml` file, you should obtain the exact same result as if you ran it with JUnit.

Once you have verified this, it's time to start converting tests. Pick a class, say, `Test1`, convert it to TestNG with either of the approaches explained earlier, and then move it to its own `<test>` stanza.

```
<suite name="Converted JUnit suite" >

  <test name="JUnitTests" junit="true">
    <classes>
      <class name="com.example.Test2" />
    </classes>
  </test>

  <test name="Converted">
    <classes>
      <class name="com.example.Test1" />
    </classes>
  </test>

</suite>
```

Notice that the converted class has been moved inside a `<test>` tag that no longer runs in JUnit mode. After you've verified that the tests are still running as expected, repeat this process until you've completely eliminated the classes inside the `<test junit="true">` stanza.

Because of the differences between TestNG and JUnit, it is not possible to run the same class with two different modes, so be aware of a common mistake: As you start converting classes, it's possible to forget to move a class in the proper tag (from a `<test junit="true">` tag into a simple `<test>` one, which will run in TestNG mode). This results in the tests inside this class being completely ignored.

Converting JUnit Code

Migrating tests from JUnit to TestNG is not just about converting annotations. Since the programming models of the two frameworks differ significantly and TestNG was designed to address some aspects of JUnit perceived as deficiencies, there are several ways in which you can simplify existing JUnit code as you convert it to TestNG. Because of the complex nature of these conversions, you will have to perform them manually, although one might hope that at some point in the future, some of them will eventually be automated by the IDE as refactorings. Note that for some of the simpler cases (such as some assertions), the IDEA plug-in already handles the conversion automatically.

The following sections cover some of these conversions.

Assertions

JUnit contains a class called `junit.framework.Assert` that offers various `assert` functions. The methods are basically overloaded versions of the following functions.

- `assertTrue`: Verify that an expression is true.
- `assertEquals`, `assertSame`: Verify that two objects are equal.
- `assertNotSame`: Verify that two objects are not equal—the opposite of `assertEquals` (this avoids the use of the `!` operator, therefore making the code easier to read).
- `assertFalse`: Verify that a certain expression is false (same reason).
- `assertNotNull`: Verify that an object is non-null (same reason).

All these methods usually have the same signature: The first parameter is a `String`, which will be shown if the assertion failed, and the remaining parameters are the object(s) on which the test will be performed.

TestNG includes this same class in its distribution as `org.testng.` ↵ `AssertJUnit`, thereby guaranteeing that all assertions will continue working when you migrate tests.

TestNG also includes another `Assert` class in `org.testng.Assert`, and the only difference with JUnit's class is that the `String` parameter is always the last parameter[2] and that the expected and actual values are reversed.

```
// JUnit
assertEquals("The two accounts should be equals", a1, a2);
// TestNG
assertEquals(a1, a2, "The two accounts should be equals");
```

---

2. This code uses static imports to make the code more readable.

The reasoning behind TestNG's method is that when you read assert methods in code, the first thing you want to know is which objects the assertion is being performed on, and the string that will be displayed in case this assertion fails is of little interest.

The TestNG converter tools will generally leave existing assert methods untouched, but as you start writing new tests with TestNG, you might prefer TestNG's signature over JUnit's. At any rate, you are free to use both, stick to only one type of asserts, or simply rely on the JDK's `assert` keyword.[3]

Running a Single Test

It has always been surprising to us how often we need to run a single test. Tests are often perceived as being useful as a whole and valuable only when an entire suite is run, but the reality is that running a single test is very common, especially in the following scenarios.

- The suite we just ran showed that several test methods failed, so we need to investigate them one by one. (Keep in mind that whenever a test method fails, it can indicate either that the business logic it exercises is broken or that the test method itself has a bug in it.)
- We are currently writing a test method, and we need to run it in isolation from all others to verify that it works as expected.

JUnit provides only one way to run a single test method: by creating a `TestCase` object and passing as a `String` the name of the test method we want to run.

Here is an example of a JUnit test suite that runs only one test method on the `JUnitTest` class.

```
public static TestSuite suite() {
  TestSuite result = new TestSuite();
  result.addTest(new JUnitTest("test2"));
  return result;
}
```

The problem with this approach is that we need to modify this code whenever the test method that we want to run changes (e.g., because we

---

3. Keep in mind that older versions of the JDK don't enable asserts by default, so running tests without the `-ea` flag on these versions will result in your asserts being simply ignored. Because this has tripped us so many times, we tend to avoid JDK asserts as a general rule.

renamed it or moved it to a different class), so over the years, programmers have developed specialized test runners based on this functionality to make it easier to rerun single tests (e.g., such a test runner could pick the name of the method to run from a text file, thereby avoiding the need to recompile code to run the test case).

IDEs also leverage this functionality to make it trivial to rerun a single test method: We can usually right-click on the test method and simply ask the IDE to run this method and no other.

The various TestNG IDE plug-ins offer similar functionality, but they also give more options whenever we want to run one test method. The three possible approaches are these:

1. Including a test method
2. Including a test group
3. Using `testng-failed.xml`

These three approaches are described in the following sections.

Including a Test Method

This is the most direct way to proceed: We pinpoint exactly the test method we want to run in a specialized `testng.xml` that runs only this method (we like to call this special file `testng-single.xml`).

```
<suite name="Single">
  <test name="Run one method">
    <classes>
      <class name="test.backend.Encryption">
        <methods>
          <include name="encryptDigits" />
        </methods>
      </class>
    </classes>
  </test>
</suite>
```

This will instruct TestNG to run the test method `test.backend.`⏎
`Encryption#encryptDigits`.

This approach has a couple of downsides.

■ This XML file needs to be updated whenever we want to run a different test method from last time.

- It will most likely break if we ever decide to rename the class or the method.

For these reasons, we usually prefer to use the next approach.

Including a Test Group

This time, we include a group instead of a method.

```
<suite name="Single">
  <test name="Run one method">

    <groups>
      <run>
        <include name="single"/>
      </run>
    </groups>

    <classes>
      <class name="test.backend.Encryption" />
    </classes>
  </test>
</suite>
```

There is an old saying in computer science lore: "Any problem in software can be solved by adding one level of indirection." This is exactly what we did here. Instead of referencing a method name, which is fragile, we included a group, and then we have the option of changing what methods belong to this group without having to modify this XML file. Whenever we want to investigate a specific method, we simply make it part of the `single` group (and we remember to remove the method we investigated previously from that group).

Using `testng-failed.xml`

While the previous two approaches work, they still seem a bit tedious to use, especially since very often, the reason why we want to run a single test method is because a test run just showed that this particular test method is failing.

This is why whenever a test fails, TestNG creates a file called `testng-failed.xml` that contains all the information needed to rerun only these failed tests. We can pass this file directly to TestNG as soon as the failed run finishes.

See Chapter 2 for an in-depth description of this feature.

Maintaining State between Invocations

JUnit reinstantiates your test class before each test invocation in order to guarantee isolation, which makes it difficult to maintain state throughout a test class. A common JUnit design pattern has therefore emerged to work around this problem: using static fields.

Consider the following example, which needs to test an instance of the class Account. This object is being read from the database, which can potentially be an expensive operation. Since the object is read-only throughout the entire test case, there is little point in reading it from the database over and over again.

Here is a slow version of this implementation.

```
public class JUnitTest extends TestCase {
  private Account account;

  public void setUp() {
    // Bad:  will be invoked before every test method
    account = Account.readFromDataBase();
  }

  public void test1() {
    // use account
  }

  public void test2() {
    // use account
  }
}
```

The problem with this code is that every time a new test method is added, the test class will incur a significant slowdown because the database is being queried once for each method.

The following variation will therefore perform better.

```
public class JUnitTest extends TestCase {
  private static Account account;
```

```
public void setUp() {
  if (account == null) {
    account = Account.readFromDataBase();
  }
}
}
```

In this code, we introduce a static field, which guarantees that its value will be preserved even if the class is reinstantiated every time, and we make sure in our setUp() method that the call to the database is performed only once.

However, the introduction of a static field in the class can cause a few subtle bugs.

- We can't easily run the same class to test different instances of the account object. Once this object is initialized, it never gets overwritten.
- We can't use this test class several times in the same JVM. If we do, the same value will be kept inside the static field, regardless of whether the database value has changed between the two invocations.
- The class is more fragile in the face of invocations from multiple threads, and we will therefore need to add some synchronization to make it thread safe.

By design, TestNG does not reinstantiate test classes before each invocation, thereby leaving us in complete control of instance fields. TestNG also offers the annotation @BeforeClass to indicate a test method that will be invoked once before the first test method on that class is invoked.

The TestNG version of this same class is therefore trivial.

```
public class TestNGTest {
  private Account account;

  @BeforeClass
  public void setUp() {
    account = Account.readFromDataBase();
  }

  @Test
  public void test1() {
    // use account
  }
}
```

Suite-wide Initialization

Whenever we need system or functional testing, tests typically need a certain environment to be set up before they can even run. For example, testing a Web site will require the Web server and/or HTTP daemon to be running. Testing a Java EE application will require that the application server is started (which itself might need to create connection pool and other resources). This initialization is typically performed once at the very beginning of the entire test suite, and it is torn down after all tests have run.

The traditional way to achieve this result with JUnit is to use the class `TestSetup`, a decorator used in JUnit whenever we need to implement custom initialization logic.

The code usually looks like this.

```
public static Test suite() {
  TestSuite ts = new TestSuite(MyTest.class);
  TestSetup result = new TestSuite(ts) {
    public void setUp() {
      // define one-time setup
    }
  };

  return result;
}
```

Porting such code to TestNG can be easily achieved by using the `@BeforeSuite` and `@AfterSuite` annotations on initialization logic.

Class-wide Initialization

There is actually no easy way to perform this with JUnit, but the approaches generally used include specifying a static test method that will execute its logic only once and then wrapping the runner by calls to these static methods. We will not get into details on how this can be achieved, but we'll note that TestNG supports that class-wide initialization natively with the `@BeforeClass` and `@AfterClass` annotations.

The AllTests Pattern

JUnit allows us to assemble tests in many different ways. The default mechanism is to create a `TestCase` and just let JUnit invoke all the methods that start with `test`, but it is also possible to customize which tests get run with the `suite()` method.

With JUnit, we can create a special method called `suite()` that returns a collection of tests. In turn, we can either add these tests as entire test classes or pick a subset of test methods by naming them explicitly.

Here is an example of this pattern.

```
public static Test suite() {
  TestSuite suite = new TestSuite("Front-end tests");
  suite.addTestSuite(HtmlTest.class);  // (1)
  suite.addTest(XmlTest.suite());  // (2)
  suite.addTest(new WsdlTest("wellFormed"));  // (3)
  suite.addTest(new WsdlTest("endPoint"));  // (3)
  return suite;
}
```

In this example, we show three ways to build a dynamic test suite with JUnit.

1. Cause all the tests of the `HtmlTest` class to be included in the test suite.

2. Cause only the tests specified in `XmlTest#suite` to be included in the test suite. This is referred to as a custom suite. Note that since the top-level `suite()` can include further `suite()` methods, we can reuse this pattern recursively.

3. Cause only the methods `wellFormed` and `endPoint` of the class `WsdlTest` to be included in this suite.

This is a very flexible design pattern: Since we define these suites, classes, and test methods in Java, there is no limit to the kind of test suites we can create.

Because this design pattern is so prevalent, it has been named the All-Tests pattern and by convention, suite methods that create such test suites are usually placed in a class called `AllTests`. To make things easier to keep track of, it is also very common to have an `AllTests` class in each package of the test hierarchy so we can easily identify which main test class we should invoke whenever trying to run a subset of the entire test code base.

Nevertheless, this design pattern suffers from several flaws.

a. It will break in the face of refactoring. Consider what happens when we rename `WsdlTest#wellFormed` to `WsdlTest#isWellFormed` (or if we decide to move this method in a different class). Since the method is referenced as a string in the example, chances are that refactoring IDEs will not rename that string, thereby breaking the entire suite, which can result either in a runtime error (which would be a good outcome, since we'd be able to fix this problem, albeit manually) or, worse, with no error at all and the tests running one less test method than expected.

b. It's not clear when adding a JUnit test class to the suite whether we should invoke its `suite()` method or add it as a whole (`addTestSuite` does not check whether the suite we're adding contains a `suite()` method).

c. Whenever we want to create a different combination of tests or run a combination of tests that does not already exist, we need to modify Java code, thereby requiring a new compilation.

d. Assume that we have five custom suites as shown above, each of them exercising a different part of the code. We create a new test method, and now we have to check these five custom suites and decide whether the new test method should be included in it or not. Of course, the test method will automatically be run if it is added to `HtmlTest` (since this suite includes the entire `HtmlTest` class), but it might not be included if we added this method to `XmlTest` (we'd have to read the `XmlTest#suite` source to make sure), and it will definitely not be included in this suite if the new method was added to `WsdlTest` (since this suite includes only two very specific test methods of that class).

For these reasons, it is recommended to modify such code in your JUnit tests when you are migrating to TestNG, and you can easily do this with test groups.

Let's turn our attention to how we should convert the tests with groups and why it's a good idea to do so.

The first point is easy to address: Instead of creating a custom suite, the responsibility of defining which test methods should be run now falls on the methods themselves. Whenever we create a new test method that should be included in the `front-end` tests, we just put this method in that group. If the method should also be included in other overlapping groups, we add these as well (they could be `fast`, `functional`, `unit`, `xml`, `html`, `servlet`, `jsp`, and so on).

Here is a possible way we could address the three scenarios with groups.

```
@Test(groups = "front-end")
public class HtmlTest { ... }
```

```
public class XmlTest {
  @Test(groups = "front-end")
  public void f1() {}

  @Test
  public void f2() {}
}

public class WsdlTest {
  @Test(groups = "front-end")
  public void wellFormed() {}

  @Test(groups = "front-end")
  public void endPoint() {}

  @Test
  public void validConnection() {}
}
```

This example shows that all the test methods of `HtmlTest` will automatically be added to the `front-end` group, while the classes `XmlTest` and `WsdlTest` define only a subset of their test methods as belonging to this group. Once we've defined our groups, running the correct methods is just a matter of including the right groups, and this is done via the many ways we can invoke TestNG (command line, ant, IDE, and so on).

Let's review the limitations of the AllTests pattern and see how test groups address them.

a. *It will break in the face of refactoring.*

Since groups are defined in annotations, refactoring test methods will not break anything: No matter what methods are named, the groups they belong to will not be affected.

b. *It's not clear when adding a JUnit test class to the suite whether we should invoke its `suite()` method or add it as a whole.*

This point is tied to a JUnit design flaw, so it's not relevant for this analysis.

c. *We need to modify Java code.*

Running a different set of methods simply boils down to including or excluding a different set of groups, which doesn't require any new recompilation. We can also define new groups in `testng.xml`, which further reduces the need to recompile Java code whenever we want to modify or expand the group organization.[4]

d. *We're not sure where new methods should be added.*

Because the responsibility of defining what functionality a test method exercises is now up to the group, the suite runner no longer has the burden of hardcoding the test methods it should run. TestNG is now in charge of this logic, and it will automatically run the correct methods based on what groups they belong to. If we decide to create a new test class (which is therefore not referenced in any customized suite yet), the only action we need to do once we have put all the test methods in the relevant groups is to declare this class to TestNG (we need to do this only once). Then the test methods inside this new class will automatically become part of the correct test run based on what groups get included and excluded at runtime.

As tests are converted from JUnit to TestNG, the `AllTests` classes can safely be removed since the decision of which tests to run is now entirely performed at runtime.

Testing Exceptions

Since there is no support for testing exceptions with JUnit 3, the following pattern has traditionally been used.

```
try {
  functionThatShouldThrow();
  fail("An exception should have been thrown");
}
catch(SQLException ex) {
  // passed:  this is the exception we are expecting
}
catch(IOException ex) {
  fail("Expected SQLException, got IOException");
}
```

The pros and cons of this approach are described Chapter 2.

---

4. To be fair, it's possible that, as we build our test hierarchy, we may realize that we should have created more groups to capture more fine-grained scenarios. In this case, we obviously have to go back to the test sources and add the relevant groups to the methods, which will require a recompilation, but this scenario will become less and less likely as we eventually settle on a good set of group names.

Occasionally, we have also seen the following variation.

```
assertThrows(SQLException.class, new Runnable() {
  public void run() {
    functionThatShouldThrow();
  }
}

public static void assertThrows(
    Class<? extends Exception> expected,
    Runnable r)
{
  try {
    r.run();
  }
  catch(Exception ex) {
    if (! expected.isAssignableFrom(ex.getClass())) {
      fail("Expected exception " + expected + " but got " + ex);
    }
  }
  fail(r + " should have thrown an exception " + expected);
}
```

This second approach leverages the `Runnable` class to simulate a closure and capture the logic that is expected to throw a method. For this reason, some people might find it preferable to the first approach, which forces us to remember to organize the `try` and `catch` blocks in a certain (fairly unintuitive!) way.

Either way, these two constructs are made obsolete with TestNG's support for exception testing, which is achieved as follows.

```
@Test(expectedExceptions = SQLException.class)
public void shouldThrow() throws SQLException {
  functionThatShouldThrow();
}
```

As you can see by comparing the code snippets, the code that uses `@Test` to specify which exceptions are expected is much more concise and easier to read than its counterparts.

The Parameterized Test Case Pattern

This design pattern allows us to simulate parameter passing to JUnit test methods. The idea is to pass these parameters to the constructor of the test class, store them into fields, and then use these fields in the test methods where they are needed. Since we discuss this pattern at length in Chapter 2, we will not repeat this discussion here.

As explained in the section about parameters above, TestNG supports passing parameters to methods natively with the `@DataProvider` annotation, so any occurrence of the parameterized test case pattern can be replaced with an `@DataProvider` annotation with the following benefits.

- Each test method is now passed the exact parameters it needs.
- The parameters are no longer shared by all the test methods.
- We do not need to instantiate our own test classes (and therefore, use our own suite): TestNG will automatically pass the correct parameters to the test methods that use a Data Provider.

Index

471